W9-AGX-743

WINGATE JUNIOR COLLEGE

A GENERATION ON TRIAL

A

GENERATION

ON TRIAL

U.S.A. v. Alger Hiss

BY

ALISTAIR COOKE

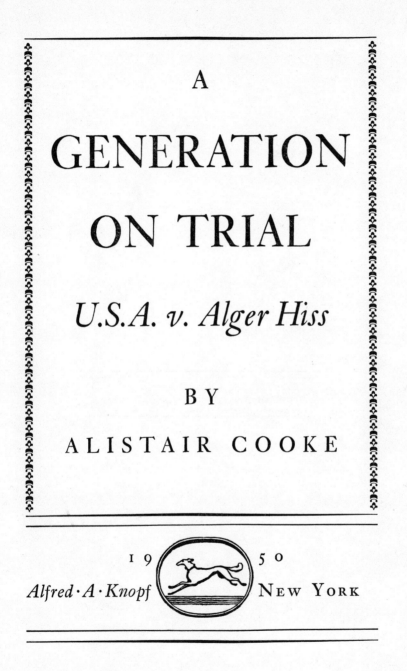

1 9 5 0

Alfred · A · Knopf   NEW YORK

WINGATE JUNIOR COLLEGE

2989

THIS IS A BORZOI BOOK,
PUBLISHED BY ALFRED A. KNOPF, INC.

Copyright 1950 by Alistair Cooke. All rights reserved. No part of this book may be reproduced in any form without permission in writing from the publisher, except by a reviewer who may quote brief passages in a review to be printed in a magazine or newspaper. Manufactured in the United States of America. Published simultaneously in Canada by Mc-Clelland & Stewart Limited.

PUBLISHED SEPTEMBER 19, 1950
SECOND PRINTING, NOVEMBER 1950

PREFACE

❀

SINCE all writing is an exercise in drawing up an armistice between a man's private fancies and the real world outside, an author explaining what his book is about is usually as helpless as a man pulling himself up by his bootstraps. It is easier, however, to be a censor than a creator. And there is a better chance of the author's knowing what his book is not than what it is. It seems to me worth saying at once what this book is not, because it was written during something very like a seventeenth-century religious war, when the outside pressure to swallow whole the Hiss story or the Chambers story, and to join one or other of the entailed crusades, was almost irresistible. I sincerely hope that, whatever pain or pleasure may be got from this book, it will profoundly disappoint people looking for a revivalist tract or for ammunition for a side already chosen. No matter what its outcome through the higher courts may be, this case will, I suspect, offer for some time to come, and perhaps forever, as many puzzles as the celebrated Wallace case (the Liverpool chess-player, not the Iowa politician). The sophisticated will jump from these sentences into the assumption that I am already staking out an "objective" seat on the fence. That is not possible either. Although fence-sitting is the occupational hazard of foreign correspondents, even a journalist is a man and presumably conducts his life on certain assumptions of what is just, tolerable, obscene, and so forth. Certain principles, which are irrespective of the innocence or guilt of Alger Hiss, and which I take to be fundamental to our survival as a free society that is also a decent one, were flouted long before this affair came to trial. It was these excesses that disturbed me most and that especially, I thought, ought to be editorialized about in the proper place. About these things—the gallivantings of a drunken press, and the interference in personal liberty of Congressional committees undoubtedly sweating in the

v

17Fs1 Pub 2.63 (3.50)

cause of virtue—I find it hard to be temperate. But even here there were serious popular misunderstandings about what the House Committee on Un-American Activities had a right to do and what it had not; and I soon saw that a report which started with the trials themselves would be unfair both to the defendant and to the House Committee. Accordingly what I am putting down is a record of the trials of Alger Hiss, from the first accusation to his conviction, to which I hope puzzled and fair-minded people will turn in order to make up their own minds about the proper verdict.

This is not, then, a "dope" book. There is nothing here for anyone who wants to learn the inner life of Hiss and Chambers or anything at all about them that was not available in the proceedings of both Trials. I am not qualified to write such a book, since I knew and know none of the principals in the case. It struck me early on, in fact, that this disqualification—which so far as I can gather is unique among the populations of Washington and New York City—might be turned to good account if it could be guarded. I made a point, therefore, of not talking to the Hisses or the Chamberses and of limiting my contacts with the lawyers on either side to checking points of law and at one stage borrowing Trial transcript when the courthouse copy was unavailable.

The problems of reporting an American criminal trial are very formidable. Friendly people, hearing you are writing a book about one, say they are eager to "get to the bottom of the whole thing" or will agree to settle for "the gist" of it. This reminds me of Roosevelt, confronted by his writers with two drafts of a speech that roughly represented two fundamentally opposed philosophies, saying: "Weave them together." There were times in the writing of this chronicle, of the Trials especially, when it would have been a pleasure to abandon the job in hand and turn to some altogether more bracing and straightforward chore—inventing a religion, say, that would embody what is characteristic of Christianity, Fascism, Communism, atheism, and technocracy.

To ask for the gist of a human conflict is a downright Anglo-Saxon approach rooted in the assumption that what is elemental is also elementary. It might be very much easier to do with an English trial, which, when it is competently managed, runs to two or three days; when the issues are complex or the counsel prolix, to six or seven days. In the United States the constitutional guarantee of "the right to a speedy and public trial" overlooks the natives' love of rhetoric, and passion for documentary detail, and tends more and more to mean the right to go bankrupt to pay for interminable litigation. I am aware that criminal trials were bound to take longer, once courts of appeal were invented, and once it became practically an obligation for a defendant to take the stand; for the first of these developments made judges more cautious and the prosecution more thorough and deliberate, and the second encouraged the practice of the lengthiest form of cross-examination. But the American inclination to substitute technique for honest argument, and a wealth of exhibits for incisive pleading, has also played its part in making trials run on for weeks and months. The judge in the First Trial warned the jury it might last a couple of weeks. It ran into six weeks. The Second Trial lasted over nine weeks. The trial of Harry Bridges ran twenty weeks, the trial of the eleven Communists just under nine months. Twenty-odd years ago Lord Birkenhead, a former Lord Chief Justice, deplored the tendency even in Britain (once she had thrown off the palsy which condemned such trials as that of Warren Hastings to run on for years) for trials to get longer (he meant they were lasting five days instead of one) and pointed out that a fair trial within a man's means was an elementary promise that nations bred in the common law were bound to honor. It is possibly the American view (though I have not heard it) that British trials are superficial and the rules too restrictive. The British could fairly retort that in America the rules of evidence are so lax that it is more than a lawyer's reputation is worth not to bring in the kitchen sink.

However this may be, the fact is that whereas in English trials the judges hold the counsel to a much stricter rule of relevancy, and the defendant is privileged to know the whole prosecution case in advance, the federal courts by contrast proceed in a luxury of leisure and discursiveness and surprise evidence that shocks everybody but Americans. In reporting them, a stranger expects to summarize the prosecution on Topic A, and the defendant's countering argument, and then go on to Topic B. But what happens is that the prosecution begins by reviewing Topics A, B, C, D, E, F, G, and H; in cross-examination the defendant challenges F, H, and A in that order; in redirect, H and B come up again; on re-cross, we have C, F, and a long, puzzling digression on B. With the chief witnesses, counsel leap from note to note like vaudevillians on a trick xylophone.

The newspaper reporter, watching his front page and his city editor, simply glorifies in one plunging "lead" the most obviously dramatic topic of the day and makes it up to his conscience by corralling the unreported hours of testimony into a pen of final paragraphs in which "earlier in the day" rubs shoulders with "under questioning in the morning" and "the defense also touched on." Consequently, most newspaper reports of a trial are, inevitably, inadequate. To write a bare, faithful sequence of the testimony of the average court day would require a piece of about five thousand words, which would then constitute a little less than one sixth of the testimony taken. Very few papers allowed their men covering these Trials more than fifteen hundred or two thousand words at best. In consequence, most of the reporting I saw was meager or atrociously slanted in one direction or another.

There is also the painful practical question of accurate hearing and transcribing. I doubt that one American newspaperman in a hundred is even moderately proficient in a reliable system of shorthand. My own is a mixture of the relics of Pitman learned at a tender age, a dash of Gregg, a flourish of Speedwriting, and frantic personal abbreviations. While the Trials were on, I thought my own dispatches compared favorably with the work of the American dailies I saw, with the exception of the excellent summaries done by Murray Marder, of the *Washington Post* in the First Trial, and the incomparable reports by Thomas O'Neill of the *Baltimore Sun* in both Trials. But even when I was convinced I had got what was essential, and correctly transcribed what was decisive or moving, a later study of the court transcript destroyed even this lingering professional pride. It is appalling to discover what mishearings a man is capable of unless he has fortified his ears with the ability to transcribe a steady two hundred words a minute.

For this book, then—which is, of course, newly written from scratch—all the reported dialogue is taken directly from the court reporters' transcript, which is now a matter of public record. I have fallen back on my daily dispatches only for what turned out to be invaluable reminders of the oscillations of mood and tactic, the conflict of personalities—in a word, the human spectacle of the courtroom. Once I had decided on this system, the main problem began to loom: how to organize an analysis of the evidence taken a topic at a time. This method ought to be ideal and sounds very neat. But in practice, I soon found, it destroys the possibility of a true report, anticipates crucial moves and confessions, obliterates the human conditions of the lawyer's practice, and compresses everything into conclusions that might be damaging to one side or the other. I decided therefore that the only legitimate opportunity of letting the reader render his own verdict would be to have the raw material come at him in very much the way it came at the jury. The jury did not have the privilege of lawyers' briefs or partisan analyses. And I hope that nobody likely to read this book would want to be enticed into a verdict by more simplified means than the jury had at their disposal. I have occasionally pulled together testimony on a single theme, when it was given at the same stage of the Trial (for example, cross-examination of the same witness). And it seemed fair enough to put together in a single list most of the character witnesses who appeared in the First Trial. For the rest, this is a chronicle, hour by merciless hour, of a trial by jury.

The Second Trial presented a different problem. No citizen in his right mind would want to sit through two trials of the same case. And no reader however conscientious would care, I imagine, to go over the same ground for another two hundred pages. For weeks on end the Second Trial often felt and sounded like a repeat performance of the First. What was different about it was the approach of the two counsel, the theory of evidence on which the judge appeared to be proceeding, and of course the new testimony. What I have tried to do is to indicate the demonstrable change of tactics; the sharp main difference in the judges' view of what was evidence on a collateral matter; and to add to the exhaustive testimony of the First Trial a brief report of such new evidence, or testimony, on each main topic as each side seemed to think would affect the outcome. There is the danger, in thus isolating some testimony in a separate chapter, of making the new witnesses have far more weight than they did in fact carry in the surrounding avalanche of the old. The reader will simply have to remember that most of the new witnesses were shuffled inconspicuously in with the rest. Only the psychiatrists, and Mrs. Massing, and Mrs. Murray (the colored maid) stood out in the courtroom as new, lonely, and important figures.

THIS approach to a political trial that aroused some of the hottest evangelism in decades was not calculated to attract willing helpers. If I had needed help, it would have been from drones anxious to read and check seven thousand-odd pages of court testimony and about fifteen hundred pages of House Committee testimony. But this is the only chore that must be done by the author and nobody else. So it was a one-man job throughout. Once people discovered that my interest in the Trials was a human one—and my only polemical anxiety was about such odd things as a citizen's right of privacy, the mischief of bills of attainder, and the debatable function of grand juries—the bushbeaters fell away like autograph hounds before a movie star's stand-in. But I should like to pay my thanks to a handful of friends, most of whom will be surprised to know they helped at all. I hasten to say, in this sadistic age, that they are not to be blamed for anything that appears in this book, and that if they are guilty of any unfashionable sin, it is not from association with me.

First, I owe my warm gratitude, in this as in many other assignments, to Alfred Wadsworth, editor of the *Manchester Guardian*, who allowed me to sink the frail ten-page bark of an English paper with a daily load of two thousand words, more or less, to write about something that no other English newspaper was wasting a line on. My debt to Professor L. B. Namier, for going over the documents in the case and saving us all much fruitless speculation, is far bigger than his short quoted opinion might seem to warrant. Sir Hartley Shawcross was generous enough to look over the first part of this preface and save me from a couple of blunders in it. I should be heartless indeed if I did not say here how thankful I am to several members of the working press who—when for various personal and professional reasons I might have missed half-hours, and in the Second Trial some days, of important testimony—gave me fill-ins of what had been happening and made it possible for me to pick up a sensible thread of the day's hearing. For these brotherly devotions I pay my respects to John Chabot Smith, of the *New York Herald Tribune*, James Bell of *Time*, Malcolm Logan of the *New York Post*, and the aforementioned aficionados Thomas O'Neill and Murray Marder. The encouragement of Blanche Knopf, Bill Koshland, and Harold Strauss, and the labor of Gerald Gottlieb on the Index, is something that is commonly assumed to be the badge of the publishing trade, but it ought not to go unmentioned nevertheless. I can only marvel and remain dumbly grateful at the patience of Heleyne Pauling, who was willing to type this manuscript usually at the most uncomfortable hours of the night and day. Finally, it is almost shamefaced to acknowledge the help of my wife. For the months of the brooding and the writing, she

cushioned this labor with a sympathetic stoicism that no naturally
gay soul ought to have to assume. My debt to her is as great as such
things can be.

One other thing should be said. There is room for many sorts of
book about this case. It would be interesting to see a legal study of the
trial tactics, done by some competent practitioner from another country: an English advocate, say, or one practicing under the Napoleonic
Code. I should like myself to see a psychological literary analysis of
the dialogue of the confrontation scene in the hotel, which I have
thought worth reproducing here at some length (it would have, I fear,
to be done by somebody not much below the level of William Empson, the English critic—which is a very tall order). A useful dialectic
job could be done by substituting the word "Nazi" wherever the
word "Communist" appears in this affair; it would probably teach us a
good deal about what was interchangeable, and what was not, in the
attitudes of the Left to Fascism in the late 1930's, and the attitudes of
the Right to Communism in the late 1940's. I suspect they are much
closer than we know, for anybody's comfort; one's willingness to
credit somebody else's brutality has a lot to do with who you think is
being mistreated.

I have tried not to have fun with the four principal witnesses:
Mr. and Mrs. Hiss, and Mr. and Mrs. Chambers. This restraint apart,
I cannot apologize for the random ironies, spontaneous reflections,
and jokes that come in elsewhere. To delete these would expose the
author to the grave charge of having edited his total apprehension of
the Trial scenes out of a misguided sense of good taste. My dispatches
to my paper have been, as I have noted, a great help here. They contain observations on the spot which at this distance of time, and in
view of the verdict, might cause a twinge in some sensitive spectators.
But I think it would be a mistake to suppress now what honestly
struck one spectator as odd or depressing or humorous or charming at
the time. A tragedy is disturbing, and too strong meat for many
people, to the extent that it involves all the human elements. One
way of making it tolerable, and therefore untrue to the human situation, is to reduce it to the limited conflict of cops and robbers and so
join the cheering squad of one side or the other.

A. C.

New York City
May 1950

CONTENTS

❊

A GENERATION ON TRIAL

REMEMBRANCE OF THINGS PAST

THE 1930'S

❀

"*It was quite a different atmosphere in Washington then than today.*" —ALGER HISS

"*I am going to ask you to sort of throw yourselves back to those years 1937, '36, '35, '34, because unless you do that you don't quite grasp what the thinking was in those times.*"
—THOMAS F. MURPHY

WE are about to look at the trials of a man who was judged in one decade for what he was said to have done in another.

Ten years is a long time in the memory of any man. And when this accuser and his accused were first asked to tell their story before a Congressional committee, each of them was called on to make an effort that is bound, in the nature of memory, to start a quarrel. If a husband and wife were asked on their tenth anniversary to tell how they fell in love, even a desire to be gallant in each other's behalf would produce strangely different versions of the truth. It is doubtful indeed whether "the truth" of the most amiable relationship can ever be recalled correctly. For we all want to justify our present feeling about life; and we therefore try to give to the past a consistency we can be proud of, or an inconsistency we can now appear man enough to disown. We remember what we must, either for our self-respect or our interest, or even for our discomfort; for if conscience makes cowards of us all, it also keeps the sense of cowardice flourishing

3

in us as the price of refusing to admit that some things we have done are shameful.

To know whether a man is telling the truth, even in the most limited sense, about something he did a long time ago, we need to know what he has to gain or lose today from the story he tells. It is natural that an accuser should have a more lively memory than his victim, since one man accuses another before the law for a purpose: to get back something he has been robbed of, to redress a wrong that has festered through the years, or—as the accuser maintained in this case —to expose a conspiracy against the safety of his country. Also, the man who feels himself wronged has better cause to remember his humiliations than the man who professes he never was the cause of them.

We are at the start confronted with a problem that is a constant of the human situation: of how memory relates to guilt. It is a problem that cannot be solved by a legal definition of "fact." The English and American courts have had the sense to side-step this most human dilemma by making a rule that preserves the dignity of the court and at the same time flatters the ordinary citizen. They simply pass the problem on to the jury. The judge explains in all criminal trials that "the law" is something highly specialized they cannot be expected to know about; and that if any problems of "the law" arise, he will explain them. But it is up to the jury to decide matters of "fact." They alone, with their corporate knowledge of human nature, must judge what is true and what is not. It is the beguiling theory of the jury which G. K. Chesterton expounded with more romance than historical truth: "When it [our civilization] wants a library catalogued, or the solar system discovered, or any trifle of that kind, it uses up its specialists. But when it wishes anything done which is really serious, it collects twelve of the ordinary men standing round. The same thing was done, if I remember right, by the Founder of Christianity."

This handsome admission that the facts of the case are beyond them does not make either the judge or the opposing lawyers excuse themselves from seeking the facts or doing their damnedest to imply that there is only one tolerable version of them. On the contrary, the whole art of direct examination is to coax from a witness a recital that sounds honest and plausible; and the art of cross-examination is to throw the most sinister aspersions on the most humdrum facts of birth, life, love, and work. In this way the lawyers make melodramatic amends for their magnanimous concession to the jury. If they are to yield the judgment of the facts, they make sure thereafter that the privileged twelve shall be able to get at them only through the most dramatically prejudiced presentation of them.

To put on this extraordinary performance, the law and the lawyers have assumed for centuries that a man is more or less the master of his memory. And the interminable job of the prosecutor and the defense attorney is to discover discrepancies of memory on the understanding that the man who cannot match his memory of big and little things is a liar. This is an immense assumption. And up to the end of the nineteenth century nothing that we knew about the working of the mind had come along to make it absurd. It has been badly and permanently damaged, however, by the lifework of Freud and his followers. And as we learn more about the workings of conscience, and unconscious memory, no doubt our courts of law will, at a cautious distance of time, come to amend their views of what is material, what is relevant, what is discrepant, what is a fact, and what is evidence.

Within the limits of this essential absurdity the courts do a noble job. And probably there are just as many innocent men set free as go to jail, even after jury trials. It may be said that in the following case, the jury was faced with no such nicety as deciding when a man is telling a lie that he honestly believes to be the truth. They were faced with a contradiction so gross that they had simply to decide whether Chambers's story was a wholesale fabrication or whether Hiss was making a blanket denial of an experience it would have been fatal to admit in part. By any definition of the truth, however naïve, one or the other was on a lying spree.

But this at once asks the question: Why? And to expect the jury to answer it we have to assume they know how far a man will go to deny his conscious memory (if Hiss was the liar), or how far lying can be a sincere pathological occupation (if Chambers was the one). Since memory has been observed as one function of fantasy—that is, of wishing—and its operations have become a specialized study, there may come a time when we can have no more confidence in a jury's verdict in a perjury trial than patent lawyers have in the run of judges assigned to patent suits. The "ordinary man looking on" has a limited experience of systematic political lying and a robust medieval view of mental sickness and expects a deranged person to foam at the mouth or babble like Ophelia. He is skeptical of the information that a man able to add figures, to feed and clothe himself neatly, to make jokes and talk with attentive intelligence may be dedicated beyond all scruple or mad beyond all cure. But he does know, as another axiom of our simple, melodramatic folklore, that "one may smile and smile and be a villain." And thus a tissue of lies is generally assumed to be a mark of villainy. Which is the villain, was the question the jury was asked to decide, and—in the First Trial at any rate—they were assisted in this simple view of perjury by the rhetoric of both counsel.

The issue was very simple. Chambers, an ex-Communist, had accused Hiss, formerly in the State Department during the New Deal, of having at that time pilfered confidential State documents and passed them on to him in the service of Communism. Chambers said that Hiss had been a Communist then and was his best friend in the party. Hiss denied all of it. He said that he had never known the man as Chambers, that the man was never more than a deadbeat acquaintance. Hiss denied he had ever been a Communist or anything like one. Chambers later produced a wad of documents that he said were the stolen papers. These documents were shown by the State Department's experts to be typed copies or photostats of authentic State papers. They were said by the F.B.I.'s typewriter experts to have been done on an old typewriter that once belonged to Hiss. Hiss admitted both these facts.

To begin with, the dice were loaded against Hiss. He would have somehow to discover the missing typist or so impress the jury with his reputation and apparent integrity that they would take his word and consign the typewriter and Chambers's possession of the documents to oblivion.

Ultimately the jury was forced back, as we all were, on the documents and the typewriter, as also on their hunches, on their instinctive or considered preference for the behavior of one man over the other. There must be many other things that influenced them which it would be idle to guess at: the physical and social types of the two men, the comparative appeal of their wives, the kinks and prejudices and personal chemistry of attraction and repulsion that are involved in liking or disliking another human being. But there is one element in this choice that overwhelmed everyone who came near the case, that indeed caused it to come up in a court of law, and that turned it into a newspaper circus.

This was the element of politics.

In the summer of 1948, when the names of Hiss and Chambers were bannered across the front pages, the United States was convulsed, as at no time since the 1920's, with fear and hatred of the Soviet Union. A Congressional committee, the House Committee on Un-American Activities, had been warning the country for years about the treacherous intentions of Communists when to do so seemed to show a perverse obsession with the lesser of two evils. To most Americans in the 1930's the Communists were moonstruck intellectuals. To the New Dealers, they were useful minute-men who would alert the countryside to the menace of Fascism. To Catholics, they were anti-Christ. Since this House Committee, once Representative Martin Dies became its chairman, showed a marked allergy for the un-American activity of Communism, and a dogged indifference to the epidemic possibilities of Fascism,[1] its investigations were thought mildly absurd during the late thirties and downright egregious in the four years when—however distasteful it may now be to recall—the Soviet Union was embraced as a full fighting ally; an embrace, it is worth saying, that was offered not out of magnanimity but out of a keen preference for survival.

The House Committee, however, persisted in its obsession through the lean years of the New Deal into the fat years of what was called the Cold War, when popular feeling about Russia cooled and soured. In 1948 the Committee was riding a current spy scare with an investigation into espionage. It had been saying for years that the Communists got a sure foothold in the administrations of Franklin Roosevelt. It had never proved it. But in the summer it looked up among others an ex-Communist, one Whittaker Chambers, now a respectable magazine editor, who reminded the Committee of a list of alleged spies and participating fellow travelers he had given nine years before to Mr. Adolf Berle, then an Assistant Secretary of State. It was a list of once young New Dealers who, he said, were expertly organized through the mid-thirties as the official secret underground of the Communist Party in Washington. Some of them had since become fairly prominent in labor circles and two or three of them in Henry Wallace's Progressive Party. One of them had been an adviser to President Roosevelt at the Yalta Conference, which just then the Republicans

---

[1] Up to the beginning of the Second World War, the Committee's reports show a preferential concern for Communism over Fascism in the proportion of about 8 to 1.

were making out to be the occasion of a wholesale sell-out to the Russians.

This looked like vindication beyond the dreams of the long-suffering House Committee. It confirmed the worst anxieties of a greatly changed America. It froze the condescension of people who had smiled sympathetically at President Truman's opinion that the House Committee was dragging "a red herring" across the campaign trail of a Presidential election year. The Committee was rewarded with resounding publicity and the grudging admission, from unlikely people, that it was after all perhaps made up of vigilant and patriotic men. The room where it held its hearings was a Roman circus panting for the entrance of dazed Christians. Into this arena walked, of his own volition, one man—the only man on Chambers's astonishing list who wished immediately to deny his accuser. He was Alger Hiss.

Hiss was almost unknown to the public eye, though the subsequent craving for a full-blooded New Dealer transmuted him in no time into the protector of great statesmen, and President Roosevelt's high-policy adviser at Yalta, a fiction that the defense counsel in the following trials curiously abetted. Hiss was not a policy-maker or ever much more than a devoted and able State Department officer just below the first rank. But he had organized the United Nations Conference on International Organization at San Francisco. He had flown back to Washington, as somebody had to, with the signed Charter. He had gone, in a humble capacity, to the Yalta Conference. His prestige in the Roosevelt Government and the United Nations, or rather the prestige that could be thrust upon him in restrospect, made him a very precious commodity to the House Committee. He became a point of honor and an object of rare suspicion when, of all the underground men named by Chambers, he asked to deny the charge before the Committee, challenged Chambers to repeat it outside the privilege of a Congressional hearing, and, when Chambers obliged, brought suit for defamation of character. Chambers then produced his old State papers.

The Department of Justice took an interest and reopened a grand-jury investigation into espionage that had been sitting on and off for fourteen months in New York. The grand jury called Hiss and Chambers many times and on the last day of its sitting indicted Hiss for perjury, implying that it believed Hiss had passed the State papers to Chambers in 1938. The statute of limitations protected Hiss from an indictment for espionage. But though the count was perjury, the implied charge was espionage. There was a strong desire, in both those who believed Hiss guilty and those who believed him innocent, to make him out to be a more representative Rooseveltian figure than he was. Among the House Committee, which had a Republican majority when the inquiry and the subsequent indictment came about, there was the eager wish to nail the curse of Communism on the coffin of the New Deal and so exorcize the legion of "liberal" and "bureaucratic" spirits that had been loosed on Washington fifteen years before to gibber down two decades and supposedly terrify the country. Among Hiss's supporters there was a defensive reaction to the Republican inference that while Russia was now the cause of all our ills, it was so only because we had been betrayed by the New Deal into diplomatic recognition of the Soviet Union and Heaven knows what exchanges of policy. I have said it is a natural thing to want to make the past consistent with the rationale of our present self-respect, or to want to confess an inconsistency when we have confidently outgrown it. This impulse is very strong in America, where people want the best of everything, believe Time is the Siamese twin of Progress, and refuse to let even experience shake them from their belief that happiness is manageable. If we are now baited in every direction by the Russians, it does not satisfy Americans to say that this is the turn of history. It must mean that somebody entrusted with our welfare betrayed us or blundered. A nation with a religious trust in Progress simply cannot admit that even when the best is done, hard times may follow.

In such a nation no man's honor is above suspicion. For where all the people feel it is their right to know all "the truth" all the time, the laws that discourage snooping into a man's past—the libel laws, especially—are made purposely lax. A public man has to watch his step, for he may be confronted at any time with inconsistencies from his past that are not the permissible inconsistencies of the time. Politicians know this better than most men and are always on guard to qualify a bold political stand and see that their ground is well tunneled with avenues of escape. It is what gives to American political promises their evasive legalism and to American campaign rhetoric its depressing devotion to all virtues that are abstract. If Sir Stafford Cripps were an American politician, he would be made to defend in 1950 the plea for a common front with the Communists which in 1939

had him expelled from the British Labour Party.[1] And Mr. Harold
Nicolson would very likely have been debarred from any responsible
job in the Second World War because in 1931 he had edited a magazine run by Sir Oswald Mosley. (What vulnerable character witnesses
these honorable men would have made if the accident of citizenship
had put them on call in either of the Hiss trials!). This compulsion to
judge the 1930's by the hindsight of the 1940's was not restricted to
the House Committee on Un-American Activities, or to Republicans
sniffing for a campaign scent in the year of a Presidential election. At
its most foolish, the House Committee wanted to prove that the New
Deal was a calculated flirtation with Communism, and that the follies
and treacheries it claimed to have on file were the first act of a drama
that ended in Pearl Harbor, the Russian domination of eastern
Europe, and the loss to American influence of the whole of China.
But short of this forgivable partisan lunacy, most Americans who took
an interest in the trials of Alger Hiss were affected in much the same
way.

Those who were for Hiss or against him felt their own pride and
past political judgment to be at stake. Many Democrats and old New
Dealers felt that Hiss was a gallant protagonist of the younger liberal
crowd that went to Washington in the New Deal's first crusade. They
feared, as the others hoped, that a verdict against Hiss would be a
verdict against the New Deal. Whatever Hiss or his lawyers might
say later, the House Committee thus succeeded, before he ever came
to trial, in making a large and very mixed public identify Hiss with
what was characteristic of the New Deal.

There were other and fascinating motives that impelled people to
take one side or the other, or even to take no side at all. The common
man, in the century that is supposedly his, might sense with a certain
awe that Hiss was an uncommon man. It is doubtful whether many
members of the juries would easily place in their experience the social
type either of Hiss or of Chambers. Mr. Thomas Murphy, the Government prosecutor, was ready for this insight and was quick to re-
assure both juries that they could forget it. "It doesn't make any
difference whether they went to Harvard or P.S. 36," he remarked

---

[1] By 1950 there was some anxiety on both sides of the Atlantic over the appointment in the Labour Cabinet as Secretary of War of Mr. John Strachey, admittedly a
Communist sympathizer during the 1930's.

without any regrets, "this is a great leveler, this courtroom—a great leveler."

There were many conservative Easterners, Democrats and Republicans, of gentle upbringing or social pretension who felt as a threat from below what the common man might sense as an imposition from above. To these, Hiss was easily forgivable: he represented the breeding, the graceful probity, the plain living and high thinking, of a waning New England tradition. And the attack on him from the reputedly "untidy" and vagabond Chambers, a brooding intellectual and an admitted former Communist, was the old threat of the great unwashed against the genteel tradition.

There were many young and middle-aged onlookers, lawyers and newspapermen especially, who resisted just this recognition or self-consciously scorned it. They belonged to the fast-ripening American breed of the unfooled, the chronically unconvinced, the man who before the appeal of conflicting certainties keeps up a hardboiled neutrality. This mode of feeling, developed as a mask by the generation that hurt its ideals in the First World War, has already passed into American literature and journalism as a narrative style in novels and news magazines. In the movies it has thrown up one favorite contemporary type—the "private eye" as played by Humphrey Bogart. In life it provides a useful refuge in skepticism for people who don't propose to sacrifice comfort to principle; for it is surely a disguised form of playing safe and the easiest parody of serenity available to the bewildered and the thoroughly scared. I mention it here because its hard-bitten asides were always on hand in the corridor outside the courtroom. It gave the correct cynical touch to the "objective" reports of some newspapers. It debased the political trial and the personal tragedy of Hiss and Chambers by writing about the one without misgiving and the other without compassion.

There were many other attitudes and strange carriers of human curiosity that paraded around the courtroom corridor the raw material for a shelf of unwritten novels by Proust, Dickens, Henry James, Kafka, Conrad, and Koestler. But the impulse that united everybody looking on was the impulse to see the New Deal on trial, and by association to expose or deny an old, steady conspiracy with the Soviet Union. There is a root injustice in this. And I am not pretending that anyone who has lived through this time can be free of it. But because the events of 1938 were throughout this melancholy tale felt

and judged in the political climate of 1949, it seems to me essential
to recall a few forgotten obvious things about that time in order to
make plain what is meant by saying that these events aroused "an
America that was greatly changed."

The brief account I have given of the House Committee's investigation, and the fuller account that is to come, are not meant as the
background to the Trials. They are the first act of a drama that began
on that August day in 1948 when Chambers accused Hiss, and ended
with the verdict of the second jury. To hope to understand that
drama, if only as dimly as it may be understood in our day, I believe
we must recognize its true background and attempt, however im-
perfectly, a comparative reading of the political climate of the 1930's
and the political climate of the late 1940's.

*"Mr. President we have come here to tell you that unless something is
done to provide employment and relieve distress among the families of the
unemployed . . . we will refuse to take the responsibility for the disorder
which is sure to arise if conditions continue. . . . The unemployed
citizens whom we represent will not accept starvation while the two major
political parties struggle for control of government. . . . There is a growing demand that the entire business and social structure be changed because
of the general dissatisfaction with the present system. We cannot longer
ignore this situation."*

IT would be an interesting experiment in prejudice to give this letter
today to a handful of American political leaders and news editors and
ask them who wrote it; so far have we come from the conditions that
prompted it. It is a plea made to President Hoover in May 1932 by
the most conservative of American labor unions, the Railway Brother-
hoods. Five months later the Governor of Nevada closed the banks
for twelve days, and three months after that, in February 1933, the
Governor of Michigan declared a moratorium on the banks of his
state. Banks were failing every hour. Prices and wages tumbled after
each other without pause. It was anybody's weary academic guess
whether there were by then ten or eleven or twelve million unemployed. In two weeks gold and currency were being withdrawn at the
catastrophic rate of fifteen million dollars a day. Gold and capital
were being shipped so recklessly that the dollar sign became a question

mark on the foreign exchanges. The Reconstruction Finance Corporation, which in less than a year had tried to rescue over five thousand
banks with loans totaling $850,000,000, started to lend heavily to the
railroads. On the famous 4th of March, the day of Franklin Roosevelt's first inauguration, nearly all the banks in forty-seven states had
closed their doors in response to a presidential proclamation based on
emergency powers [1] that neither the new President nor the old, their
Attorneys General or Secretaries of the Treasury, or the governor of
the Federal Reserve Board, were sure they could legally invoke. It
seemed as if "the entire business and social structure" was indeed
about to founder.

Only a month before, Adolf Hitler had become Chancellor of
Germany.

These two paragraphs sum up the two great political events that
were to absorb the energies and feed the anxieties of the American
people through the decade of the 1930's. At their back was the tramp
of Fascism. In front and all around them was the long struggle with
the Depression.

It may seem testy at this late date to identify again the two mon-
sters of the New Deal years. It is possible that Daniel in his later years
could be nonchalant, or honestly numb, about his ordeal in the lions'
den. But it was in one or other of these moods that the testimony of
the Hiss case was heard. And to have any clue to the ideals and acts
of the protagonists, we must try to do seriously what Mr. Murphy,
the Government prosecutor, casually advised a couple of times in the
Second Trial: "to sort of transport yourselves back to those days in
order to grasp what the alleged intellectuals were thinking of. . . .
There were people who felt that the advance of Nazism and Fascism
. . . was being stemmed or stopped by nobody but the Russians.
. . . So you can see how a person of Chambers's intellect and Hiss's
intellect could become . . . involved with that type of thinking of
these foreign philosophies."

Allowing for the pardonable simplification of a prosecuting counsel, we can safely say that a great many people other than "alleged
intellectuals" getting "involved with . . . foreign philosophies" had
the same feelings. During the very months when Hiss was supposedly
passing documents to Chambers, Mr. Winston Churchill, who rarely

---

[1] Under the "Trading with the Enemy Act."

alleges what he does not think and who tends to set fashions in ideas rather than get involved in them, was earnestly seeking an alliance with the Soviet Union and bemoaning a foreign policy whereby Britain was "disengaging" herself from Russia and the United States, "the two mighty nations whose extreme efforts" would be "needed to save our lives and their own."

While the parliamentary governments of Europe were to spend the next six and a half years first in doubting the continental ambition of Nazi Germany and then in buying it off, the United States was exercised most of the time in trying to put a prostrate economy back on its feet. Time is a gentleman, someone has remarked, and it is mercifully impossible for many Americans to recall now the shabby despair and the ranging violence of the period in which Roosevelt took office. Like the surrendered Russian armies of the First World War who were said to be too tired to sin, the legions at the soup kitchens in every American city, and the vagrants in tar-paper shacks down by the riverbanks, were too exhausted in spirit to hold any theory or look for a place to put the blame. Like mountain goats they drifted dumbly in search of stubble. But America was still the land of the middle class, the largest middle class in the world. And it was left to them, to the wage-earners with their savings gone, the fore-closed farmers, not least the businessmen and small broken bankers, to all who had prospered in the twenties and still had the energy to feel the outrage of betrayal; it was left to them to berate "the system," the bankers, and capitalism itself; it was they who spawned demagogues who proposed radical surgery on an America which, they said, had been poisoned by "the bankers, the brokers, the politicians." Huey Long in Louisiana, Father Coughlin in Michigan, Dr. Townsend and Upton Sinclair in California offered between them everything from a poor man's dictator and a capital levy to an old-age pension. For a short dreadful time these men were the real possible alternatives to a social-security act. There was abroad for at least three more years what Raymond Daniell called "a national yearning for an easy way out, a general desire to reap the benefits of collective action without swallowing the prescription of Dr. Marx."

This sentence fairly suggests the only alternative system that most people knew about in those days. To the middle-class American of 1933, Communism might be a bogeyman haunting the American economy, but the Soviet Union was nothing remotely like the physical threat to the continent of America that it has since become. Communism was the invention of a dead German, half-mystic and half-devil, a prophet who had hypnotized the Western World into believing that nineteenth-century capitalism could grow no more and was bound to be succeeded by Communism and some sort of world state in which no man would own property or earn profits. The fear of this world state, considered as something plotted by international spies which would emerge the day after a violent revolution of working people against their employers, was at its height in America in the years after the success of the Russian Revolution and in the early 1920's. As the prosperity of the twenties ripened, the fear was suppressed. As we can now see, it was never overcome. That is to say, as long as the facts of life seemed to show that capitalism was healthy, we could laugh off the prospect that Communism would succeed it. This is not the same thing as denying the premise that if capitalism fails, Communism will succeed it. Possibly it has been the major triumph of Marx that in his grave he has bewitched the capitalist world into unconsciously accepting that premise. This is true, especially true, of extreme conservatives, who are in this sense the most unregenerate Marxists. Any change in the status quo, they feel, even when the status quo seems bankrupt, must be a change in the direction of Communism. The result was that the bankers, the industrial employers, the shippers, and the chambers of commerce fretted themselves into epilepsy through the middle years of the New Deal imagining that national labor unions, social security, and public works were the first sure symptoms of Communism. It should be said in 1950 that very few of them meant by this that there was a workers' arrangement with the Soviet Union.

But in the first years this reaction was dulled by the native flavor of the recipes offered by such as Dr. Townsend and Father Coughlin; by the willingness of President Roosevelt to begin with a national solution dear in its first form to the United States Chamber of Commerce; and by the national hunger for a personal leader. Mr. Roosevelt had said in his inaugural address that it might be necessary to disturb "the normal balance" of Congressional and Presidential powers. But there was none to blame him, much less to call him dictator or, as they did when the bent of the New Deal was obvious, Roosevelt II. Very few people were worried about other totalitarian alternatives. The word "totalitarian" was not yet in our vocabulary.

Communism was something remote and barbaric, but in so far as it was known to be a system, it was thought of as self-enclosed, as the prescribed punishment for not making capitalism work, not as one of various forces at work to replace parliamentary institutions and civil liberties. And almost nobody knew or cared about the typical economic policies of Nazism and Fascism. What was called for was strong and resolute action, with few stipulations about method or doctrine. And Mr. Roosevelt and his advisers acted with a resolution that for many months was the wonder of the nation. They introduced a farm relief act, which was to offer the farmer a subsidy against the curtailment of his crops and set a "fair" price for what he grew, at a stable level somewhere between the best and the worst years of modern agriculture. For industry and business, there was to be the National Industrial Recovery Act.

The NRA, as it was called, is a remarkable example of how far Americans are likely, in a profound depression, to abandon their traditions in the noisy pretense of affirming them. For what was obscure at the time, but is now quite clear, is that the first official act of the New Deal was an economic solution of the extreme Right. Read against the later background of the New Deal—the fight for national industrial labor unions, the permanent extension of social security—and the rise in Europe of Socialist states, the National Recovery Act is a puzzling document. I doubt that a man from Mars, briefed about the general principles of what at the time was thought to be the liberal "left of center," and told that Roosevelt's later contribution to American government was to be of that kind, would credit that the NRA could possibly have come out of it. For it relied by dictate on a method of keeping the economy going that was second nature to big businessmen when they grow bigger and also irresponsible. It was a method so masterfully and widely resorted to by the earliest American fortunes in oil and railroads that it provoked the earliest effective federal law in a democratic society to deal with it: the Sherman Act.

This was the method of protective monopoly, through its various stages of trade associations, price fixing, combinations in restraint of trade, and holding companies. This method was now made the law of the United States. It was this that President Roosevelt came to fall back on in the crisis of the Depression. (It is noteworthy that in the second great crisis of his rule, that of heavy and rapid production for war, he again forsook the battle against monopoly he had waged through the late thirties and—advising the oil companies, for instance, in 1941 that the anti-trust laws had better be forgotten—approved a lusty return to the only system by which America always feels able to deliver the goods.)

The National Recovery Administration appropriated the law-making power of Congress, suspended the anti-trust laws, and sanctioned government by trade association by requiring the employers to draw up a binding code for about seven hundred industries and businesses. It did appreciate the dangerous mood of labor in the crisis, and the minimum dignity labor had won in the Norris-La Guardia Act of 1932, by repeating the guarantee in that act of "the right to organize and bargain collectively" without restraint. Without this clause, which ironically seeded the growth of a labor movement that in its later power would have paralyzed the nation's work rather than submit to a tittle of this monstrous law, the NRA would have been seen for what it was: America's first fling at National Socialism, done to the happy tumult of parades in all the big cities and the distribution of emblems—of a blue eagle—to "loyal" factories, companies, stores, and citizens. It was done, however, by sincere men in the belief that they were radical liberals. And it was abolished later not because it was seen by Mr. Roosevelt or the people to be a central seizure of economic power on the Nazi or Fascist model but because its grand strategy of totally restricting competition was too much for the stomachs of the traditional old men on the Supreme Court. It is a warning example of confusing the doer with the thing done. Enough millions of Americans rallied to the personal courage of Franklin Roosevelt to do in that desperate time almost anything he wanted to have done. If Roosevelt thought himself to be a liberal and said so far and wide, then what he did must surely be liberal. People were willing to believe in him for the mischievous reason that millions of people do believe in saviors; not because they examined his ideas and found them liberal, but because, like terrified and starving populations everywhere, their individuality is a dog's life, and all principles are meaningless except the one they are ripe for: the leader principle.

The United States was saved from this extraordinary betrayal of its past in the short run by the Supreme Court and in the long run by the benevolent character of Mr. Roosevelt. It was not saved by an awakened popular sense of liberty. This offered to an alien who had come from a libertarian country the first surprising hint that liberty is not in our time a markedly American passion. Equality is the watch-word: equality of privilege in prosperity, and equality of care in hard times.

It may seem superior to accuse the New Deal at this distance of having got off to a Rightist start, and some readers may say that I am doing, in a rather perverse way, what I have deplored in the 1949 presentation of a 1938 conspiracy. But the NRA is the most telling example I can find of the ideological innocence of the early New Deal, and a proof that in a bankrupt moment the American people, who have always thought their political history was somehow quite different in kind from that of old, cantankerous Europe (Andrew Jackson thought America could never have slums), were faced with much the same alternatives as the Germans. The Americans had reserves of democratic discipline in the courts to fall back on which the Germans didn't. And President Roosevelt had an almost tactile sense of history which prompted him to see that the next big constitutional guarantee must be to the workers, who in Germany had their impotence flat-tered by being told they belonged to a virile master race, and their fear of Communism played on to the point of hysteria, so that they surrendered overnight the most advanced labor movement in the world.

The surest sign that America would not be allowed to renovate capitalism again without the privileged co-operation of labor came from the West Coast. The longshoremen, who had done without safe-guards against depression for eighteen years after their union was sup-pressed, began a strike in 1933 for the minimum wages and working conditions that were to be made law by the New Deal. Within four years, their ringleader, Harry Bridges, who was at first automatically damned as a Communist,[1] became the chief Pacific Coast organizer of the Committee for Industrial Organization, the national industrial union that John L. Lewis hewed out of the American Federation of Labor and through which, by 1938, he had made the masters of Amer-

---

[1] For eleven years, from 1939 on, the federal Government tried and failed to prove that Bridges was a Communist. He was cleared in Immigration hearings in 1939, ruled "a deportable subversive" in 1941 (in 1945 the Supreme Court reversed this ruling by 5 to 3, when Justice Frank Murphy wrote: "The Bridges case will stand forever as a monument of man's intolerance to man"). In April 1950 he was convicted of perjury in denying he had ever been a Communist, and sentenced to five years in prison.

ican steel and coal and automobiles yield to the permanent unioniza-
tion of their labor.

The consent of the workingman in making capitalism over was
secured by the labor and social-security legislation that Roosevelt,
never much interested in labor problems, soon saw as the essential
compromise that had to be made if America was to avoid the economics of Communism and the slave society of Fascism. Roosevelt
was a country-squire Democrat with a mania for trees, which was at
first a convenient solace to the industrialists and bankers who saw
him as an inoffensive Jeffersonian who would probably take expert
advice. But he saw, about three years before they did, that America
might take the lead with a third alternative: an industrial democracy. Again it is hard to remember now how home-grown this alternative appeared to Americans and how rousing to the harassed parliamentary democracies of Europe. Englishmen abruptly changed their
itinerary, which used to be Concord, Philadelphia, New York, and
Niagara Falls, to take in Negro housing projects in Atlanta, a glimpse
of John L. Lewis before a Senate committee, and later the Tennessee
Valley Authority. At a discouraging time for representative democracy, Europeans saw a strong free labor movement, planted across the
American continent, making and riding in Mr. Ford's *folk-wagons*,
which the German workers had been promised in the far future as the
unique reward of their enslavement.

I have reported this bargain with the workingman as a political
achievement and perhaps implied, very wrongly, that its astuteness
was generally welcomed. There was a necessary third party to the
bargain—the employer. And in the act of wooing a supporter, Mr.
Roosevelt had the well-known romantic distaste for third parties.
Few of his most unflagging idolaters will now deny that if the idea
of an industrial democracy was to be realized for long, it would require
a confident partnership, and a willingness to share economic power,
between the Government, business, and labor. Mr. Roosevelt ex-
asperated this partnership, and made it very difficult for his successor
to maintain, by anticipating the worst from industry and business and
therefore usually getting it. In the years 1936 and '37, time and again
when businessmen were in a corner licking their wounds, the President
would rise, especially at press conferences, and scatter salty sentences
about the continuing fight for the common man against his enemy the
"economic royalists." It was Mr. Roosevelt's way of resolving a

grudge, which everybody was busy doing through the thirties: a way of finding the scapegoat of the Depression, of identifying what had been wrong with "the system" and swearing that it should not happen again. This universal hobby made it something of a crime in the 1930's to confess to the profession of banker. In self-defense the businessmen looked around for contemptible analogies. They decided Roosevelt was "a traitor to his class"; later, when Hitler became the most execrated threat to the democracies, Roosevelt was called a dictator hell-bent for Fascism.

What is remarkable today is that there should have been, throughout the great organizing campaign of the labor unions, not so much but so little serious talk of a Communist plot to take over American labor. It was always a handy insult and in California, at the first rising of the longshoremen, the state started a committee to investigate "subversive" acts. But this was the reflex of the twenties. And in fact the battle for a native labor movement was won at that time. Seasoned labor leaders like David Dubinsky, Philip Murray, and even one so young as Walter Reuther tended to get annoyed in the late forties with people who came to warn them about the tactics of Communists boring from within. It must be irritating to give an interview to a man who wants to cry wolf when some of your best friends were eaten by them twenty years ago. For the most formidable hold that the Communists ever had over an American labor union was held over the garment industry in 1926. In the needleworkers' strike called in that year, Hillman and Dubinsky literally had to shoot it out with the Communists who had almost superseded their leadership. Both sides called on the arsenals of various racketeers and Broadway gamblers. A ruthless habit was acquired, of enlisting the summary persuasions of gangsters, which both sides fell back on in the do-or-die battles of the 1930's. But this time, for all the impetuous cross-fire of Communist slogans, the sides were the employers and the labor unions. (It may be worth an aside to foreign readers who wonder about this emergency resort to the sawed-off machine gun to remark that in a nation of a hundred and fifty millions of mixed blood, where often it appears that sheer energy is the only specific for survival, violence is never far below the surface. In good times it explodes in its surface form of sentimentality. For sentimentality is a kind of violence— the lush response to the small provocation, the pseudo-heroism of a quick and emotionally satisfying partisanship. In bad times it finds its true level, and brutality is accepted as the one sure path to power. This is worth remembering at all critical times in American politics.)

The struggle for the garment industry ended with the rout of the Communists and the moderate liberal leadership of Dubinsky restored. The next tussle with the Communists came in the forties, and the final break in the second, the realistic, period of "the Red Menace." To encourage the support of his second term by labor as a solid body, Mr. Roosevelt made the risky, and as it turned out premature, suggestion that the labor leaders should renounce the strong tradition of American labor politics and form their own political party. The American Labor Party was accordingly set up by the men who had the best personal reasons for hating the Communist Party they had had to defeat. But after 1941, when the Communists presumed on their new-found loyalty to the war effort, there was another ideological battle for control of the American Labor Party and Dubinsky marched his union out of it and set up the Liberal Party. By 1948 the Communists were strong enough to pledge the A.L.P.'s support to Henry Wallace for President. And the group that had forced Dubinsky out of the party quit in turn. By 1949 Mr. Roosevelt's brainchild, the American Labor Party, was for all practical purposes the labor division of the Communist Party. This is the kind of permutation that old Roosevelt enemies in 1949 liked to ascribe to malevolent intent on his part, if not to a stealthy arrangement with the Soviet Union, far back in the thirties; when in fact the nature of Communism and the true power of the Soviet Union were so little understood that, among many of the younger New Deal faithful, Communists were thought of as enthusiastic archetypes of an established New Deal. As we know from the testimony of more people than Chambers, the Communists were very happy to be taken at that valuation and their secret agents were able to penetrate into the New Deal and pick up a good deal of its foreign intelligence, to an extent that most of us had never guessed and that will probably always remain in dispute. But I am anticipating what was to become a preoccupation of 1949: the question of "how deep" Communist agents got into the New Deal, how much Communist content was there in the ideas fashionable among New Deal leaders.

The labor movement of the thirties was a domestic movement. And if there were a good many Communist ideas in the "liberal" movement that went along with it, they were thought of as being useful fertilizers of an American renaissance. They were not generally thought of as a virus that, like the Dutch elm beetle, blights the whole tree. It is very hard to "throw ourselves back" into a sensible appreciation of this mood. Today Americans are encouraged to think of Communism as they think of Negro blood: no matter if you are ninety-nine per cent white, the revelation in your family of one per cent of Negro blood makes you one hundred per cent colored. By 1949 a clause of the Immigration Act was being interpreted so strictly in this vein that it became difficult for anyone to get into the country who truthfully admitted ever having been a Communist, or a fellow traveler. An English poet who thought he had been a Communist for a couple of months in 1938 had to use a lot of influence in 1949 to get permission to lecture on Goethe at Harvard. Since a Communist coming here for a set and sinister purpose would be the last person to admit ever having been a Communist, he would probably get in. Whereas the way was barred to a good many disillusioned people from Europe with special knowledge of Communist tactics—anti-Communist resistance men, for instance, who had courage as well as skill to offer.

In the 1930's, it is necessary to insist, Americans (with the exception of the Dies Committee) were not disposed to go "screening" ideas for their chemical Communist content. If it had been pointed out then that the Communists thought poverty or Fascism was a bad thing, a hundred-per-cent American could agree with alacrity and not feel his patriotism was being impugned. The wasteful habit of fighting the Communists when they were right did not become popular until, in the late forties, we ran into the rigid climate of the Cold War.

The 1938 collection of President Roosevelt's public papers was called "The Continuing Struggle for Liberalism." And among the liberals who were the general staff of the New Deal, the proselytizing word was "socially conscious." In the optimistic and rather muddled idealism of the period, this word was never defined. It did not mean, as I have suggested it might usefully mean, a consciousness of the responsibilities of the whole of American society—a working partnership between the state, business, and labor. It meant rather that one ought to be conscious of the neglected rights of the underdog, of the poor farmer, the industrial worker, "the forgotten man." This was a natural prejudice of the time, since the New Dealers like everybody else felt guilty at having just discovered the poor; but unlike some other people they meant to do something about it. Indeed, the rediscovery of the American poor was in the 1930's one of the great impulses to popular entertainment, drama, and literature. And it went far beyond the legislative preferences of the New Deal.

The catchwords and slogans that flourished under the New Deal are vivid expressions of this idealism. The American Government was to devote itself to the resurrection of "the forgotten man," known also in Government reports that delved into American misery as "the under-privileged." These were to be helped at the Government expense to "prime the pump" of the nation's dried-up productive resources. Thus emancipated from "the horse and buggy days" and the depradations of "economic royalists," all Americans at last would come to share "the more abundant life." Later, as Fascism superseded the anxieties of the Depression, the American people were urged to reject the faint-hearted chauvinism of "isolationists," boldly "quarantine aggressor nations," and receive all others like "good neighbors," as "men of goodwill" ought to do. There could be no going back. For "this generation" had "a rendezvous with destiny."

Looking back at it now, one gets the impression that America was atoning for its extraordinary indifference to working-class life through the prosperous 1920's; and was letting off a pæan of gratitude that the lower classes had not revolted. Hollywood had a stream of movies about the heroic misery of miners and poor farmers, culminating in a version of John Steinbeck's best-seller about Dust Bowl refugees, *The Grapes of Wrath.* (By 1949, incidentally, this had become the only American movie that the Russians were willing to show in all their satellite countries. But it was not made with this in mind.) The Library of Congress sponsored a project that unearthed a wealth of American folk-songs and work-songs altogether different from the politer Negro spirituals, the Stephen Foster ballads, and the genteelized mountain songs that had always passed for folk-song. Whitman became a favorite source for calendar texts and captions for photographs and documentary films showing what the New Deal was doing to build dams and reclaim the overworked topsoil of American farms. The workingman was the ideological hero of the time. Carl Sandburg could give to a poem the title *The People, Yes,* with no obscurity intended or inferred. In rounding up a tribute to the workers of the whole country, the New Deal made the discovery, and passed it on to a surprised populace, that the landscape of America was vast and varied and pretty much unknown. It sponsored—as a relief project—the writing of a series of state guidebooks. By the time these had written up special regional subjects, architectural oddities and folkways, the series ran to several hundred volumes. The United States, which had had no guidebooks worth the name, now had the best. This amounted to a very vigorous propaganda movement, a belated celebration of "the people," meaning vaguely the working classes, and in the late thirties it achieved its object of strengthening the badly shaken faith in the material resources and the human buoyancy of America and of purging away some of the guilt of the Depression.

But what I have called the universal hobby of looking for the Depression scapegoat (with a prejudice in favor of blaming "the bankers") did not exhaust itself until Nazi Germany began to suggest more pressing doubts about the future, especially about the chances of the United States staying out of the war that was ahead. The two anxieties coincided in a national concern about armaments and profits which seemed while, it was on, very shrewd and timely. In 1933 Hollywood made a movie about a President kidnapped by villains vaguely recognizable as financiers wanting to start a war. In March 1934 the magazine *Fortune* ran a long and rueful article called "Arms and the Man." It was read and talked about everywhere, it was written into the *Congressional Record*. In April the Senate adopted a resolution directing an investigation into the arms industry. It was set up under the chairmanship of Senator Nye and spent three years collecting a mass of information about how armament firms were organized and operated, their connections with banking houses and Foreign Offices. (Alger Hiss, by the way, was chief assistant legal counsel for the committee.) The investigation succeeded, as Senate investigations very often do, in amassing such mountains of contradictory evidence that people could make the most of their favorite testimony and keep their preconceptions intact. Among other things that had never been publicly confessed by bankers and soldiers and sailors, it came out that munitions-makers did make alarming profits, that they were an international cartel sharing technical secrets, that they financed deprecatory lobbies at international peace conferences, that they were indifferent to American interests when a bargain was afoot, that they habitually soaked the Government, manipulated profits as rents, ducked war taxes, and in general behaved much as the *New Masses* had always said they did, and as the newly popular

Diego Rivera painted them in the vigorous murals that were much in vogue then among the intelligentsia. The Navy, it seemed, was not averse to putting on fleet movements as a sort of floating industrial exhibition of the newest gadgets. And the big banking houses, J. P. Morgan most of all, were given a thorough and embarrassing public audit.

President Wilson came out very badly, as a President whom the bankers did not need to kidnap since he was made out to be so pitifully their creature, forced to extend credits when they called the day, and browbeaten into foreign loans that put him in the business of war-making long before he was to declare a war for democracy. "The popular idea of Wilson as the pure idealist who went to war for the sole purpose of saving democracy," wrote Charles Beard, underestimating the indestructibility of pure idealism, "was shattered beyond repair." What was at least shaken for a time was the traditional assumption that the handling of foreign policy ought to be the prerogative of the President and his Secretary of State. For another scandalous item that was given the sort of apocalyptic treatment only the American press can keep up for weeks was the report that President Wilson and Secretary Lansing had "falsified" when they denied having any knowledge of Allied secret treaties before the United States was in the war. The suspicion, which the Nye Committee managed to sow, that the President and his Cabinet were not the most reliable guardians of the national interest produced the astonishing proposal that hereafter the whole nation should take a vote to decide whether to go into a war. The so-called Ludlow referendum hung around, as a typical talisman of the time, until the rude certainty that Hitler meant business buried it in a House Committee in January 1938, on the assurance of the President that it was a brave impracticality "that would cripple any President in his conduct of our foreign affairs."

What the Nye investigation did, when most of the evidence was forgotten, was to leave a bad taste in the head, a popular conviction that once you started laying down principles of conduct, they would only play into the hands of bankers and munitions-makers, who knew how to make a war with them. In a nation therefore which, more than most, trusts to lawyers to solve the problems of human conduct, it was put up to the lawmakers to work out some foolproof formula for keeping out of war. The Congress evolved what came to be known as "the new Neutrality" and between the summer of 1935 and the spring of 1937 passed three Neutrality Acts which were written on the theory that the best way to stay neutral was to abandon what had been in international practice known as neutral rights; that is to say, to clear the high seas of American ships, to prohibit loans to a belligerent or the sale of his bonds, and to forbid the export of arms. To this extent the Nye investigation did take away much of the President's discretion in foreign policy, though in the third Neutrality Act he managed to get the famous "cash and carry" provision, which gave him the power to let belligerents come and get what they wanted and ship it away themselves. The mood of the country was to approve what came to be called a policy of "isolation." A few older men who had been active in the war or the peacemaking protested that the American people had fallen into a shallow and dangerous fashion; namely, as Newton Baker put it, of believing that "our entry into the war was . . . either the result of pressure and special interests of one sort or another . . . or we were beguiled by propaganda from overseas." Walter Lippmann wrote up a favorite theme that looked academic enough until the first two years of the Second World War proved it: "the invisible, the unexamined, and unrecognized premise of American isolation has always been an international system in which naval power in British hands is predominant over all other military power."

These were unpopular voices, conservatives (worse, Anglophiles, probably) who were all for leaving intact the President's historic right to run foreign policy with the help of the State Department. But most people—Republicans, most Democrats, the onlooking middle class, the young New Dealers—shared in the mid-thirties a feeling that in 1949 they would have wanted to investigate as subversive, even Communist, propaganda. It was the belief that nations spoiling for a fight could be ignored, that armaments were a racket, that decent men by concentrating hard on loathing war could exorcize it. (A Yale professor, one Edwin Borchard, went so far as to maintain that neutrality could be adopted by the United States as a permanent policy, a rewarding philosophy on the Swiss model.) In 1936 the playwright Robert Sherwood (who has a value apart from his talent of being a reliable barometer of popular sentiment and indignation) wrote a play, *Idiot's Delight*, which won a Pulitzer Prize. It would be unlikely to do so today. The villain of the piece is a munitions tycoon, and all the forceful arguments are given to a Communist who is led away and shot, which causes even a "neutral" American vaudeville manager to feel bad. It is full of a throbbing sympathy for "simple" people (what was soon to be known as "the little man")—for an engaged couple, for Frenchmen walking the fields, for the helpless innocence of nature. It abounds with apostrophes like: "Is it nothing to you that millions . . . ?" and "Who is it did this dirty trick on a lot of decent people?" and bitter asides about the tycoon ("He can give you all the war news. Because he *made* it"). It ends with the vaudeville manager and his old girl dashing off champagne and singing *Onward, Christian Soldiers* as the bombs fall.

If this now seems offensively naïve and shows a pretentious superiority to recorded history, we should remember that few people live by the lessons of history and Americans have always claimed the privilege of making it up as they go along. To say the least, they had made a nation on a new continent out of an eighteenth-century document. They had kept it intact for a hundred and fifty years. And, since the long-range bomber and the submarine had not yet discounted the providential geography of the United States, they did what any other nation three thousand miles from a threatening gun would do. They decided their own invulnerability was due to special virtue. They thought the best way to avoid getting tricked by foreign policy was to have none. And when Fascism loomed more and more obviously as the thing that would have to be fought, they included it in the antiwar cult as one of the interchangeable elements of war and sin. The slogan "against war and Fascism" was endowed with something of the mystical force of the refrain of a Negro spiritual. To point out its logical contradiction was to bring sophistry to bear on an act of faith. It was also, bewilderingly, to invite being called a Fascist.

Now that there has been another war, it is doubtful if a popular crusade could be whipped up just yet against Henry Kaiser and Andrew Higgins, the Chase National Bank, the inventor of radar or the Norden bomb sight. Nobody was more grateful for their heinous services in 1941–5 than the majority of the American people, who had backed the Neutrality Acts, damned the bankers, and were for peace at any price. It would be more fashionable today to rewrite that last sentence to read: "Nobody was more grateful for their heinous services in 1941–5 than the prewar liberals and fellow travelers who were for peace at any price, until the price was the invasion of Holy

Russia." But not to make a bad-tempered exception, let us say that all of us have been sobered into a very old admission that we all abhor war until it comes into our own back yard. For most Americans, the back yard was Pearl Harbor. For the Communists and some fellow travelers, it was the Niemen River.

We were very far from this admission in the late 1930's—so far from any agreement about America's position in the world that even with more than six million unemployed, the debate over domestic policies was overtaken by the debate on foreign policy. And into the frenzy of it was drained most of the evangelical fervor of the New Deal. By 1938 the tramp of Fascism was an earthquake. And the heroic "common man," the New Deal's symbolic worker with a firm jaw and the will to pour molten steel or take up contour plowing late in life, turned into "the little man," an object of concern to all who thought Mr. Roosevelt, his former champion, was going to send him off to war. (Samuel Grafton, as late as 1940, when Mr. Roosevelt sent Sumner Welles for consultations with the belligerents, could write: "Let the little man keep a weather eye on the smoothies who love to make big and heroic decisions for him.") The panic of the isolationists was due not only to the nagging knowledge that there are some decisions in American government which can be taken by the President and nobody else, and that when the time came he could probably, and constitutionally, do very much what he wanted; but to miserably mixed feelings about their own foolproof Neutrality Act. They might take public pride in this latest improvement on Mr. Monroe's chastity belt, but it was tempered by the glum suspicion that these things never work.

Meanwhile, Mr. Roosevelt went on with maddening serenity insisting that even a Neutrality Act should allow for a distinction between "good" nations and "bad," between "aggressor" nations and their victims. Most people wanted to deny this distinction, the more so when they felt in their bones it was true. They did what Americans do when they are uncertain how they ought to behave in the modern world: they constructed from the writings of the Founding Fathers a chrestomathy of wise sayings meant to show that the twentieth century is no different from the eighteenth. The phrase "the American way" came in and was used to justify the hope of going into quarantine against the infection of Europe's coming war. There was a new distrust of foreigners. This was very strong, from about 1938 right through the phony war, because of a new and irritating change in the allegiances that were open to Americans. In the First World War each side had its strong supporters in the United States. Professor Münsterberg could make a moving appeal at Harvard for the Germans, which was applauded by very respectable people. Allied and German propaganda in the United States was an open battle of wits. But this time Americans were overwhelmingly against Hitler. At Munich they were to jeer at Britain and France for not being a man. There was no chance at all of American help for Germany. The only change in the American status would be a change away from neutrality. And the only people who could make that possible were the democracies of Britain and France. So Allied propaganda was what you had to fear. It is, I think, reasonable to say that through the years of their neutrality Americans were more afraid of their sympathies than of a military threat to the continental United States if the Nazis won. They had to keep up a separate annoyance at the British and French as at potential seducers who have the run of the house.

During this time a European new to the United States must have marveled at the tireless ransacking in Congress and the newspapers of the works of Jefferson, Washington, Franklin, John Adams, Hamilton, and others. It is true that the best American traditions have sprung from these colonial scriptures. Unfortunately, this is not to say that Americans pondered the universal issues of their Constitution or learned again the hard-won wisdom of *The Federalist*. Indeed, according to several surveys done just before and during the Second World War, only a pathetic fraction of high-school graduates went into life having a fair acquaintance with the events that shaped their country or the principles that made it into a nation. The new affirmation of "the American way" and "Americanism" was not a delighted rediscovery of the best of American law and habit. It was a tribal chant, uttered most fearsomely by the fearful, in the hope of warding off such evil spirits as Hitler—used most often by men whose instinct when faced by the ancient enemy (I mean a tyrant) that has always threatened, and will always threaten, free men, was the instinct of retreat. There was in this regression a willful assertion of "difference," of being God's chosen, which was disturbingly similar in many ways to the Nazi doctrine of the master race. And, by one

of those human distortions which make men assert a special virtue
and become like its opposite, America, too, found itself riding waves
of anti-Semitism.

IT is now time to tighten this little narrative into a brief account of
what was happening in Europe and America in the first three months
of 1938, which is the period when Chambers got the State papers, and
when therefore the weight of Hiss's alleged treason has to be assessed.

Towards the end of 1937 the political issue that more than any
other divided people in the United States, France, and Britain was
the civil war in Spain. To the American liberal, the issue was plain:
a Fascist military dictatorship, shamelessly aided by the Catholic
Church, was conquering its democratic homeland. To the true American Catholic, the issue was even plainer: a soldier in Christ had taken
the first stand against what Catholics had complained all through the
New Deal was the ignored enemy—the godless enemy of Communism.
The liberals pointed to the cynical intervention of the Germans and
the Italians on Franco's side; the Catholics, and some Republicans,
pointed to the Russian intervention on the Loyalist side. There were
many young men not Communists or fellow travelers, there were
Catholics even, who felt that the Spanish war was a rehearsal of the
coming showdown with Nazism and Fascism and that it was time to
take a stand, as many reluctant millions would have to do within two
years.

The British Government, wishing a plague on both Spanish
houses, was at the time more concerned with the meddlesome intervention of Mussolini. The British hoped that if a war with Germany
was coming, they might with the help of the French limit it to north-
ern Europe and keep Mussolini isolated, doing no harm to the historic
British passage of the Mediterranean. The Russians, too, thought this
might be done. In the following March, Foreign Minister Litvinov
told the American Ambassador that "Italy is by no means safely
anchored to the Hitler Axis."

The British Conservative Government then in power could not
bear to believe that Hitler had set an unchangeable course. And the
Labour opposition, with all the Leftist faith in creating an object by
believing in it, had preached pacifism and disarmament down this
frustrate decade. Lord Halifax went on a "sports visit" to Göring

and came back with the assurance, which Prime Minister Chamberlain accepted with relief, that the only thing in the way of German-British friendship was the colonial question. This was too much for the one Conservative Minister with an active conscience. Anthony Eden visited Chamberlain to nag him about the slow pace of British rearmament and was told to go home and take an aspirin. Eden responded eagerly when, in January 1938, Sumner Welles told the British Ambassador in Washington that President Roosevelt was so distressed over the international situation that he was ready to call a conference in Washington of the British, French, German, Italian, and American governments. Mr. Chamberlain politely declined because he feared it would upset British negotiations with Italy that foresaw recognizing the Italian occupation of Abyssinia. Roosevelt was appalled and Secretary Hull told the British Ambassador quite correctly that the American people would be shocked by a concession that would "be represented as a corrupt bargain."

That was the end of a possible showdown by conference, at which at least Hitler might have learned something about the prestige and intentions of the Roosevelt Government. Mr. Eden now went reluctantly to Paris to arrange the settlement with Italy. While the three powers were at it, the Chancellor of Austria gave in to Hitler's demand that the chief Austrian Nazi—Seyss-Inquart—should be put in the Cabinet. In Paris the Italians refused to talk about Austria, and a broken Eden resigned, merely hinting at the Roosevelt offer in his resignation speech in the House by mentioning "one most important decision of foreign policy" on which he fundamentally disagreed with Chamberlain. Churchill wrote the epitaph on the incident: "The other day Lord Halifax said that Europe was confused. The part of Europe which is confused is that part ruled by parliamentary governments."

Now Hitler summoned the Austrian Chancellor, Schuschnigg, and bullied him into incorporating the Austrian Nazis in the Nazi front the Germans ran in that country. Nevertheless, Schuschnigg hoped against hope for help from Italy and dared to call a plebiscite. Hitler told him to call it off and resign and put Seyss-Inquart in his place. Schuschnigg had the awful courage to refuse. And on the 13th of March, Hitler entered Vienna.

The American newspapers began to report Europe in black banner headlines, which were only rarely to be rested until the autumn of

1945. The Congress, arguing over a naval appropriations bill, felt that war was near enough to get alarmed by a rumor that there was a secret understanding with the British about the combined use of Anglo-American sea power. Secretary Hull scotched this suspicion with a trenchant "No."

There were still seven million unemployed in America, which had had the setback of a new, and very serious, recession at the end of 1937. This was the first depression in an America supposedly fortified against depressions by the economic control legislation of the early New Deal. If there was a time in the thirties when wobbling Marxists were strengthened in their fatalist doctrine that depression is the wages of boomtime sin, and that salvation lay only in Communism, this was it. Old Mother Bloor came back from Moscow with the happy news that in Russia there was "no worry . . . no fear." Earl Browder and William Foster, the two leading American Communists, sailed home from Russia and preached nothing more godless than the word received from Stalin himself, which was that Communists everywhere must recognize the practical menace of Fascism and co-operate with the "capitalist democracies." If there was a time when idealistic Americans of the Left—bred in depression, embittered by the physical violence used to break industrial strikes, made cynical by the arms investigation and the now seeming failure of the boasted new fiscal controls—could feel no compromise of their patriotism in "co-operating" in turn with the Soviet Union, this was it. This was just the time when Julian Wadleigh, doing as he believed what was right for America, passed out of the State Department to Chambers for transmission to the Soviet Union four-hundred-odd documents: the voluntary subscription of an American fellow traveler to the fight against Fascism.

At this most anxious juncture in the affairs of Europe and America, the fellow traveler was never more acceptable to the administration or less suspect to the American public. Because Wadleigh admits to having been one (whereas Hiss does not) and risked his life and career for a principle, he is a perfect example of the type, and I am not sure that his refusal at the Second Trial to revamp his 1938 beliefs, or to be discreet about the House Committee, does not make him the one sure tragic figure of the Hiss case. Probably it is tasteless to tease at this point the distinction between pathos and tragedy, and for my rather cold-blooded purpose I will say only that Wadleigh is the

proper point of departure into the endpiece of this discussion—the
sweeping change between 1938 and 1948 in the American attitude
to Russia. For Wadleigh, among others, was broken by it.

In the Second Trial Wadleigh was pressed by the defense counsel
to admit a conflict of loyalties, back in 1938, to the Soviet Union and
to his own country. Whatever his motives, his response to this line
of attack was historically correct. Most fellow travelers in the late
thirties were not badgered by a conflict; they were excited by a fusion
of loyalties, which, in fact, most Americans felt or at least acquiesced
in during the wartime alliance with the Soviet Union. The defense
counsel asked Wadleigh if he was aware of no "treachery" in "stealing" State papers to give to the Russians. His reply was to refuse to
allow the notion of stealth and to say to the imputation of treachery
that the papers "were to be used against Germany and Japan." Did
he believe, then, in "the American way of life"? Wadleigh thought
for a while and replied: "Substantially I did." We have now to look
into the change of mood towards the Russians which made such replies convincing as a recollection of an old crusade.

THE mood that most young people picked up during the 1920's, or
were taught to feel, was that the First World War was the death-
rattle of nationalism. Dr. Johnson's remark about patriotism ("the
last refuge of a scoundrel") was suitably misunderstood by the most
respectable people because they wanted to believe that the League of
Nations had recognized a new reality, and the one that alone could
promise world peace. The airplane carrying bombs had demonstrated
in war, as the Wall Street crash eventually did in peace, that the nations of the modern world were fatally dependent on each other and
that we should all henceforth sink or swim together. I remember as a
boy being very impressed by the originality of a threat in one of
J. L. Garvin's editorials in the London *Observer*. It was to the effect
that "we shall not go to the next war; it will come to us." The visible
collapse of the League of Nations in the 1930's did not discredit its
principles; it only showed that we were somehow too wicked to live
by them. Humanitarian people, and liberals especially, looked around
in the decline of the League for the next best thing. They thought
they had found it in "collective security" against any warlike nation.
"Collective security," like Christianity, was never seriously tried.

And when it was clear that the threat to the peace was coming from Fascist Italy and Nazi Germany, then the thing was to get as many non-fascists on your side as possible. Nazism might appear to the British Foreign Office as the resurgence in a new uniform of Britain's oldest enemy, which she had been on the watch for ever since the Armada—any Continental power out to dominate the continent of Europe. But to the liberals, which in the 1930's meant to the Left, Fascism was nationalism at its most diseased, far gone in Germany, weaker but virulent in Italy, already a Japanese plague over China. What more logical, then, than that the resistance to it should be international?

The one big nation that did not merely assist this view but had a whole philosophy about it was the Soviet Union. It was easy to forget in the 1930's the Russian dogma of "world revolution," and the Russians assisted this forgetfulness by proclaiming the crusade of the "Popular Front" against Fascism, at a time when they could get from the European powers no better guarantee of help against a militant Germany than a treaty with France, which they suspected all along. Declared Communists could keep up the classic talk of a new order of society, of social justice and equality of economic opportunity; and—when you had no intimate acquaintance with how this paradise was being imposed on the people of Russia—it sounded just like the New Deal. Consequently it didn't seem to matter much in the 1930's where a liberal left off and a fellow traveler began. For if you were properly conditioned by the great work of the Webbs, and by the travelers' tales of the enchanted generation of John Reed, you could accept the Soviet Union without misgiving on both counts of its "international" policy: the promise of an improved lot to the poor everywhere; and the brave invitation to form a common front against the Fascists and Nazis. The young foreigners who fought on the Loyalist side in Spain called themselves the "International Brigade." When the national governments of the democracies were helping Hitler to believe that there was no place they would put up a stand, no issue they would fight him on, the Soviet Union looked to many people like a tower of courage and good sense with its straightforward appeal to all anti-Fascists, all progressive movements, socialists, and liberals, to join together and draw a line beyond which Hitler could be dared to go. It was unpleasant to be reminded in 1950 that, as the record of the abortive French and British negotiations with Moscow in 1939 showed, it was the Soviet Union that had been ready to draw the line at Czechoslovakia.

It was not strange, then, in a world harried by the rages of Adolf Hitler, and the brutality of his purges and pogroms, that many people should honestly admire the uncompromising foreign policy of the Soviet Union and see in its domestic policies only what could be made out to be similarly inspiring. Somebody has surely said that if the Soviet Union had not existed in the thirties, in the image in which liberals wanted to see her, it would have been necessary to invent her. That is what was done. To most Americans, Russian propaganda was tiresome but unfrightening because the forms it took (the Russian movies) and the objects it idolized (a trans-Siberian railroad and Mongol peasants flexing their biceps over mowing machines) were remote from American interests or the sort of political issue Americans could get excited about. To the liberals, Russia was a vast progressive school on the steppes. Rumors of "purges" could not be reconciled with any of the disciplines known to American politics. "Forced labor" sounded odd and, in view of the people who objected to it, was probably a "reactionary" tall tale. The bitterness today of people like Eugene Lyons and William Henry Chamberlin and Malcolm Muggeridge is surely forgivable. They were always out of step with the movements they sponsored, addicts too early, cured too soon.

This was the climate of liberal opinion in the thirties. By the late 1940's all but the most tenacious fellow travelers had decamped in genuine horror at the revealed suppression of personal liberty and, as Malcolm Cowley was to put it in the First Trial, "jumped off the Moscow Express." And the positive fear and hatred of Nazism which most Americans had felt in the thirties was now turned against Russia.

There is no need to distinguish between the events that caused the liberals and fellow travelers such painful and reluctant disillusion and those that caused practically all Americans to be aware, in the moment of their own unwilling rise to world power, of an enemy as powerful as Hitler and just as menacing to their democratic traditions. One could say that the first tiff among the liberals came over the Russian state trials of the thirties. And that the first omen to the rest of the country came in the Russian violation at the San Francisco Conference of the Roosevelt agreement about forming a postwar Polish government on "a broad democratic base." Everybody's disillusion will be covered by naming what seem to me to be the three events that turned American opinion from mild suspicion, to alarm, then to implacable and feverish distrust.

The first was the Russian state trials of the thirties, which confronted the fellow traveler for the first time with evidence of the wide terror spread by secret police and challenged him to give some decent explanation of the institution of forced confession, or even of open confession that looked to most Westerners pathological. This put up to the fellow traveler a direct moral challenge, something he had not expected to have to face from a nation that boasted of its solicitude for the individual man and for the equal rights of the rich and poor.

The second was the Nazi-Soviet Pact of August 1939. This horrified everybody by showing the Russians to be just as alert to national self-interest as the democratic powers had always been. But because the Russians had set the ideological tone and almost persuaded their enemies that they were "holier than thou," the revulsion against their awareness of the real world was all the more violent and outraged. (It came out in the Nuremberg documents that Stalin had balked at Ribbentrop's overtures towards a declaration of German-Russian friendship, anticipating the obvious bewilderment of his own people, who would have to learn to love a nation that had poured over Russia what Stalin called "pails of manure." This actual phrase had to be deleted from the preamble to the Nazi-Soviet Pact.)

The third, and I think deciding, stage of American revulsion towards Russia was the suicide of Jan Masaryk, on the 10th of March 1948. This event shocked American opinion, across the whole spectrum of political belief, as nothing since the Nazi-Soviet Pact. It exemplified—in the coup by pretended "free" election—a consequence of Russian "protection" which up to that time, even with Poland and Rumania absorbed in what could only be called the new Russian Empire, had been a theoretical squabble among liberals and nervous fellow travelers. It ended once for all in our time the hope that the "Popular front" could salvage from an alliance with the Communists any decent independence for non-Communists. Czechoslovakia was a favorite republic of the United States, who had been indeed godfather at its christening. Thomas Masaryk was sentimentally thought to have been the only true son and heir of Woodrow Wilson. His son Jan Masaryk had in the United Nations gamely solaced the fears of the Western powers about Russian pressure. "There *is* no Iron Curtain," he would say with a charmingly fatigued sort of tolerance. He had been full of reassurances, from San Francisco to Lake Success, that it was the prudent and regular thing for a little country to turn to the nearest big power for protection and that it was feasible to maintain in the little country all the democratic usages and freedoms as the West defined them. These reassurances grew increasingly hectoring, then circumspect, flickered into a bitter hope, and were extinguished in the last days. When he knew them to be hollow, Masaryk ended his life.

This incident confirmed the general fear that Russia was building an empire of her own by a ruthless combination of the techniques of the old British trader and the new Nazi storm-trooper and the Gestapo. It put an end to second thoughts about Russia, stimulated the Truman administration policy of investigating the "loyalty" of all Government employees, and in the act gave to the F.B.I. an unparalleled investigating authority in American life. It roused American Senators who had been calling the impending European Recovery Program "Operation Rathole" to demand night sittings until the bill was passed. It assured the passage of the bill. The next month the House appropriated another $50,000 for the House Committee to stay on the trail of un-American, which by now meant exclusively Communist, activities. This license financed, as we shall shortly see, a ferocious hunt for remaining traces of fellow travelers and liberals whose connection with the Roosevelt administrations might explain the sudden nightmare of Russian power not as a fact of life but as a waking plot initiated long ago in the reign of the New Deal.

The plight of the fellow traveler was, after one decade, quite pitiable. He had now to explain away what for most Americans were already monotonous horrors: the unflagging bombast and intransigence of Mr. Gromyko and Mr. Vyshinsky in the United Nations; their refusal to define atomic inspection according to Webster or the Western understanding; the Russian consolidation of eastern Europe in an imperial adventure depressingly old-fashioned. There was not even any longer the doctrinal comfort of the "Popular Front," for the Kremlin had thrown it out as an arch-heresy and had appropriated of all things the old Nazi master-race dogma. They had done this subtly through the Lysenko theory, popularly through edicts proclaiming to the humblest native of the Union of Soviet Socialist Republics that he was one of the chosen people (*Civis Sovieticus Sum*) and that for the protection of his pride of race the old laws had been restored forbidding him to travel outside his community, to leave the country, or to talk with "capitalistic" foreigners. For the preservation of his pristine Soviet sensibility, a code of virtue was elaborated, with all the fanatic solemnity we had always thought of as a German vice: it laid down what was Russian and good, as against what was "capitalistic" and "cosmopolitan" and bad, in biology, literature, medicine, textile manufacture and the shade of a lipstick, in economics and the effect of brush strokes on canvas, in the treatment of children and the care of plants, in astronomy, lyric poetry, and the striking of a musical chord.

The repentance of the old American Left rose from an apologetic wail to the commanding confession of Whittaker Chambers that he felt it "necessary" to "destroy" himself in order that America might continue to live by her traditions. Edmund Wilson would not again write a book of travel through "two democracies" and leave the off-hand implication that the other one was the Soviet Union. Max Eastman wept freely at meetings where he could be persuaded to recall the brutalities of the M.V.D. Samuel Putnam paused in his translating of *Don Quixote* to confess that his period as a fellow traveler and Communist had been one of "misguided humility." The break with Moscow had been for most of these the resolution of some unexplained personal torment or an ultimate admission that their stomachs were just as queasy as the next man's over the apparent reversal of Soviet policy. In the late thirties an American religious weekly once wrote an editorial entitled "On to Moscow or Back to Sin." By 1950 the text had been changed, in a confessional book by several former Communist sympathizers, to read *The God That Failed*. Few of the fellow travelers in their published writings before the end of the Second World War gave notice of rejecting the Soviet Union on the solid grounds that, weighing the good with the bad, it had been found grievously wanting as a democracy or that it represented a regression —familiar to history but not to us—to a society under the dictate of a combination élite corps, priesthood, and prison guard; or that while it achieved an abject kind of equality, it repulsed at every turn that libertarianism which is the familiar central tradition of the Western World.

This was nothing new to a few forgotten old fogies who had enough knowledge of history to temper their idealism. The Politburo protects itself as summarily, and by the same device, as Richelieu's

Chambre de l'Arsenal. And although it was part of the popular cant in 1949 to say that you could not be too suspicious of your neighbor because the Russians, and their agents abroad, had adopted a wholly new technique of terrorizing people into conformity; on the contrary, the Russian idealogical zeal, and the methods used to exact loyalty to it, can be easily understood by Westerners if they look, say, at the Jesuit proselytizing of Bohemia, Poland, and Italy in the seventeenth century by men dedicated in theory to political democracy and in practice to the most ruthless enforcement of the true faith. Most of the disciplinary code used by the Soviet Union to secure the internal safety of the country and to justify the "protection" of the satellites could have come from the rules of the Jesuits or even from the maxims of the canon law. Consider Bellarmine: *"libertas credendi perniciosa est . . . nam nihil aliud est quam libertas errandi"* (freedom of belief is pernicious, it is nothing but the freedom to be wrong); and, from *Liber Sext.: "In malis promissis fidem non expedit observari"* (there is no obligation to keep faith with heretics). Our inability to recognize the enemy we were soon to have to deal with derives I think from the grand error of the Left in the 1930's: which was to attribute to the Soviet Union aims that were nineteenth-century, humanitarian, and Protestant—only much more thoroughly and efficiently so. The fact we have just wakened up to (which the military alliance of the Second World War made it essential to overlook at the time) is that nothing has ever been further from the Russian purpose, their history, or their temperament than Protestantism, humanitarianism, liberalism, or the golden rule. George Orwell put it another way in an essay written in 1940: it was the sin of the Left in the 1930's, he said, to "have wanted to be anti-fascist without being anti-totalitarian." Very true, but this also was hindsight, the enviable hindsight of an old-style radical intelligence, for which young American and British Leftists had lost their taste.

To hear, much before 1945, the arguments that everybody was using in 1950, one had to go to older Europeans, to the French social historians and *passé* English Liberals (as distinct from liberals) who had never been so absorbed with the American passion for equality but had been for a century and a half always on guard against invasions of their liberty; to Halévy, whose last work before the Nazis got him bore the uncompromising title of *L'Ère des tyrannies*, in the plural; most of all to Bertrand Russell, who wrote in 1920 a regretful prophecy,[1] of what was entailed in Soviet Communism, in calm and noble terms that the reluctant liberals of our day would give their eye-teeth to have written twenty years later. There was the interesting exception of Arthur Koestler, who however had the painful advantage over his British and American colleagues of having known the restraints of Communism in the flesh as well as in the mind. For whereas to the British and American intelligentsia words like deportee, displaced person, commissar, forced labor, secret police, purge, and sabotage were part of their debating vocabulary, Koestler and his Continental kind knew them for the known passwords to humiliation, torture, and death. And from 1949 on, the great danger to the liberty of the individual in the United States lay in the likelihood that popular opinion would no longer recognize the difference between the people who had used this debating vocabulary sympathetically in the past, and the people who had used it in their daily trade of espionage. A man who could be shown to have been a doctrinaire Communist or a fellow traveler in the thirties would have a harder and harder time proving, in the fifties, that he had not been a member of the Communist underground. After the Hiss Trials, and because of the Second verdict, this was, in fact, exactly what happened. And in the Senate especially there was an alarmed minority ready to make political hay by blurring this distinction between an old sympathizer and an old spy.

I HOPE that this little history has, without bullying the reader into accepting all the things in it, sharpened the point that 1938, when the plot of these trials was being acted out, and 1948, when the plot was unraveled and judged in public, were far enough apart to constitute almost two periods of history. It is true that there is no such thing in literature or history as a "period." But this fact, which everyone knows, does not invalidate the divisions that historians and literary critics make, nor does it save the necks of villains who some other time might have been made heroes or martyrs. The Fall of Constantinople is an awesome date to schoolboys, and bad teaching can leave them with the assumption that in 1453 people went around agreeing that that was the end of the Middle Ages and it was time to have some

---

[1] *The Practice and Theory of Bolshevism.*

modern history. It is an arbitrary date coolly chosen later to mark the peak of a watershed separating wholly different modes of life. A literary student who is any good can distinguish at sight a piece of English prose written, say, in 1730 from another written in 1830. The main point is that these changes in the climate of ideas, of what is thought socially tolerable, vary greatly in their speed and intensity. There are long stable times, like the Victorian Age in England, and short unstable periods, as that between about 1780 and 1810, when a way of thinking and feeling crystallizes quickly and powerfully and then just as quickly goes to pieces. An acute student might mistake a prose passage in E. V. Lucas for one in Charles Lamb, for Lucas was writing at the end of a century whose fundamental views of leisure, human character, eccentricity, and the like were stated at the beginning by Lamb. But he would be a bad student who confused a paragraph in Hemingway with one from Bernard Shaw, even though the books they were chosen from were written only twenty years apart.

In the same way it appears likely that a man accused of anything from adultery to espionage in the early Victorian Age in England, and another man accused of the same things sixty years later, would run into much the same sympathies and prejudices. It has been shown, I believe, that the severe change in the political weather between 1938 and 1948 would bring no such charity, or the indulgence of settled convictions, to bear on the confession of Julian Wadleigh or the denials of Alger Hiss; whose tale must now be told.

PART TWO

AN INTERNATIONAL EPISODE

SUMMER, 1948

❧

THE month of August 1948 came in with seasonably sticky weather to aggravate the tempers of a Congress unseasonably recalled by President Truman for a midsummer session. The President had put up eleven measures for emergency passage which, he broadly implied, could alone save the Eightieth Congress from going down in history, or at least in the Democrats' coming Presidential campaign, as the "Do Nothing" Congress. The Congress took an indifferent revenge by defeating eight of these bills and passing two others that did little more than register a protest on principle against inflation and inadequate housing. A workmanlike filibuster by Southern Democrats against the perennial poll tax quickly killed off the session. Back to the steaming grass roots went the Democrats to blame the Republicans for inflation. And back went the Republicans trumpeting some alarming testimony before two Congressional committees which seemed to show, or could be made to show, that the administration was criminally "soft" towards Communists, if it was not actually riddled with them. The Democrats were probably closer to the popular mood, because the nagging obsession of everybody just then was high prices; they had been going up and up until it seemed that they would never settle along that "high-level plateau" that the Government economists had confidently predicted. The automobile companies announced their third price rise in a year. Hogs at Chicago were tagged at $31.50 the hundredweight, an untouchable record. First in Dallas, and then across the country, disgusted housewives paraded in front of butcher shops and asserted the embattled matron's right to demand, without effect, that "something must be done."

Overseas, the former Western Allies and the Russians were glaring at each other across a morass of Continental problems frozen by the Cold War. The Americans, the British, and the French were conferring with the Russians in Moscow to try to break the Soviet blockade of the Western sectors of Berlin. From three thousand miles away, and to a nation that expects a surcease of politics and history in the summertime, the Berlin blockade was a great bore, a disheartening reminder—repeated in the unceasing recriminations at Lake Success—that the Russians worked and plotted day in and day out twelve months of the year and, like the poor, would be always with us. Yet there was some cause for pride in the exploit of the American and British forces engaged in Operation Vittles, the air-lift that flew food and coal and medicine into the besieged sectors we had jointly agreed to govern and to hold.

More congenial summer news came from London, where the Americans were running and swimming and jumping to beat the band, in the fourteenth Olympiad. In London, too, the British Government announced it would assure a permanent national opera by taking over the Royal Covent Garden Opera, while in New York the Metropolitan Opera Association, a confessed victim of free enterprise, socialite charity, and stiff union contracts, canceled the next opera season. Along Broadway, the phonograph stores blared out through the warm midnights a record of a song Al Jolson had made for the Israelis. A sentimental movie biography of Babe Ruth opened three weeks before its hero was to die of cancer. The Communist Party of America was holding its annual convention. It had come a long way in ten years and its once beloved Earl Browder had been expelled for advocating co-operation with capitalist countries; for although this had been the only true faith in 1938, it was now an unforgivable heresy. The platform of the late thirties was revamped to read, in 1948: "for peace and against Fascism and inflation."

Harold Stassen, the forgotten man of the recent Republican convention, retired for the time being into the presidency of the University of Pennsylvania. The two winning candidates, Governor Dewey of New York and President Truman, were catching their breath before taking off on their cross-country campaigns, which could only end, as everybody knew, in depositing Mr. Dewey in the

White House and Mr. Truman in limbo. There were the usual statistical floods in China and the usual rise in polio cases in the United States. A flock of B-29's were almost at the end of the first such flight around the world.

On the 2nd of August a French flying boat with fifty-two aboard vanished somewhere in the Atlantic. A thunderstorm broke over New York.

That same afternoon all this news and much more had passed over the desk of a plump man in his late forties sitting in his office high up over Rockefeller Plaza. He was the editor of a news magazine, and these chronicles of politics, plagues, and sudden death were the daily grist of his trade. By the late afternoon he must have had the somber satisfaction, as well as the disquiet, of knowing that within twenty-four hours he alone would brush most of these great and trivial events off the front pages of the newspapers. He had just been visited by a certain Mr. Stephen W. Birmingham, who will need no other claim to fame among his friends than that on the 2nd of August 1948 he served on one David Whittaker Chambers, senior editor of *Time* magazine, at 9 Rockefeller Plaza, New York City, a subpoena to appear the next morning in the New House Office Building in Washington. Mr. Chambers would be asked to tell the House Committee on Un-American Activities what he knew "regarding Communist espionage in the United States Government." Nine years ago he had tried to tell his story to the White House and been sidetracked to an Assistant Secretary of State. At intervals through the war years he had told some of it to the agents of the Federal Bureau of Investigation, the investigating arm of the Department of Justice. Now he would be able to tell it for the first time in public.

It has been said that the House Un-American Activities Committee (which we shall henceforward call the House Committee) had embarrassing need of Chambers at such a time: that he had a scandalous accusation to make of the Roosevelt administrations just when the Committee was floundering in failure and public ridicule; and that one of the Committee's investigators luckily recalled enough of the Chambers story to persuade the Committee to stake its survival on this man's testimony. For another Congress was passing away and the House Committee was due to expire at the end of December.

This is shrewd hindsight, but it is not true. There is no need to disprove it, either, by taking the Committee's own glowing conviction that in 1948 it had come through "the most active and productive period" in its history. But it is as well to review what it had done, and failed to do, in the months before Chambers started the sequence of events that within four months was to bring the Committee its first indictment by a grand jury, rather than by "presentment."

THE committee had started the New Year in the satisfaction of see-ing a federal district court bring to trial ten [1] Hollywood screen writers. They had refused to say if they were Communists, in a series of hearings that the witnesses, just as much as the Committee, were responsible for turning into a squalid and rowdy parody of a court of law. (It was the Committee's misfortune that its flamboyant pro-cedure misled people unused to Congressional hearings to think that what they were seeing was in fact a court hearing riding roughshod over the rules of evidence and in other ways getting alarmingly out of hand.) The Committee had then hounded the identity and associa-tions of Gerhart Eisler to the point where the Department of Justice stepped in to arrest him, to have him sentenced to prison (for passport fraud) and finally deported. From the evidence of the names it had dredged up in making this catch, the Committee tried to prove the existence of a big passport ring, a thesis that did not seem to interest many people outside the readers of the Hearst newspapers and the big-city hives of the Communist penitents. But the Committee did get one Leon Josephson cited and eventually sentenced for contempt of Congress. Others were to follow including the general secretary of the Communist Party. And in March the United States Court of Ap-peals made the interesting ruling that the House Committee was constitutional and was within its rights in asking a witness whether he was a Communist. This may hardly seem like much of a triumph. The Committee is a committee of Congress like any other. It has the power to subpoena witnesses, and their records, and put them under oath, and bring them in contempt of Congress if they resist its powers.

---

[1] Only two of them were brought to trial, on an understanding with the other eight that all ten would stand or fall by the result. The two were convicted and their final appeal turned down by the Supreme Court in April 1950, on the implied ruling that if a witness did not claim his constitutional privilege to refuse to answer for fear of incriminating himself, the Committee had a right to know whether or not he was a Communist.

But the Committee was goaded by the press to become its own worst enemy. And these fundamental parliamentary privileges came to be overlooked by many nauseated and well-meaning people because of the Committee's passion for the public hearing, its flair for melo-dramatic publicity, its quick umbrage at passing insults from the President or the Department of Justice, and its habit of fixing frivolous and tricky witnesses, honest men and scoundrels, with the same steady baleful eye.

In March the Committee turned to consider the security of the nation in the necessarily secret field of atomic energy. And here the Committee touched its nadir of bad judgment. It accused a Dr. Ed-ward Condon, the director of the National Bureau of Standards, and a scientist who had had something to do with the atomic bomb, of being "one of the weakest links in our atomic security." The docu-mentary source of this very serious charge was an F.B.I. letter that actually cleared Dr. Condon from suspicion of knowing or dealing with Soviet agents. Dr. Condon was never brought before the Com-mittee. He asked the Department of Commerce to investigate him, and its loyalty board cleared him. This was not enough for the House Committee, which subpoenaed the records of this investigation. When the Secretary of Commerce, Mr. Averell Harriman, refused to re-lease them, the Committee talked belligerently about impeaching him, but simmered into a preoccupation with its own "evidence." Dr. Condon, who by now was Dr. Condon's most ardent investigator, asked the Atomic Energy Commission to review his record. After a long investigation the Commission cleared him absolutely on the 15th of July. The serious American press again chanted its regrets over the Committee's ineradicable habit of presuming guilt and defying the ac-cused to salvage his innocence. The *New York Times* commented: "The Thomas Committee may now proceed, as it threatens to do, after more than a year of baseless rumor-mongering . . . if good and faithful servants, so judged by those who best know them and their work, are to be persecuted in this fashion our governmental research is likely to fall into the hands of drudges and time-servers."

But if to the outsider this was the low ebb of the Committee's fortunes, the Committee lustily refused to recognize it. There were several good public arguments it could use to defend itself. If the House of Representatives had felt itself at all embarrassed by the Committee, it could after all have withheld any more money to keep it going. What the House did, in March—when Czechoslovakia was falling to the Communists—was to vote the Committee a record appropriation of $200,000 by the forceful majority of 337 to 37; and then go on to reinforce this vote of confidence by passing a "Communist-control bill" sponsored by two members of the Committee. (It was shelved by the Senate.) And if Communism in the United States was an impotent strain of the Russian breed, why had the President set up the previous year a permanent loyalty record of the Government's employees? And why had a federal grand jury been sitting in New York since April 1947 to determine how real was the threat of Communism to the American Government? The second question was answered resoundingly a few days after Dr. Condon was cleared, when the grand jury indicted the twelve members of the board of the American Communist Party on charges of teaching and advocating the overthrow of the Government of the United States by force and violence. This indictment made inevitable a court test of the legality of the Alien Registration Act of 1940 and would confront the American judicial system with the historic responsibility of deciding once for all whether a Communist was by that definition alone a man sworn to overthrow by force the American system of government. If the Supreme Court should say he was, then the Communist Party would be automatically a criminal conspiracy and all Communists would be liable to imprisonment. In that day the House Committee would receive the keys of the kingdom.

But the Committee had a very good private reason for thinking that although many of its forays into the Robbers' Roost country had returned empty-handed, it was now on the heels of a whole gang of sinners. The Committee's investigators were diligent scouts, some of them former F.B.I. men. And they had collected—the Committee says no later than February 1948—a bulging file of their own (from police records, Communist Party membership lists, surrendered letters, and other unidentified sources) which convinced them that there had been in prewar Washington an amount of organized espionage that would shock the country to know about, and maybe give pause even to hot liberals, whose proper contempt for the Committee's public methods was usually built on the assumption that there was pitifully small and ineffectual proof of any plot, treason, or indictable indiscretion among the New Dealers the Committee seemed so morbidly anxious to resurrect and crucify. The Committee thought it knew better. It had heard about one witness who had gone before the New York grand jury; it had checked her story and recognized pay-dirt. She was an obscure former Communist named Elizabeth Bentley. The Committee resolved to subpoena her, once she was free from her oath of secrecy to the grand jury. The twelve Communist leaders were indicted. And the lady was free. She promptly recounted her story in a lurid newspaper series and excited the curiosity of a Senate subcommittee looking for Communists in what in more care-free days would have been thought the very unlikely field of "Expenditures in the Executive Department." The House Committee got her next. It was all the more disposed to press her testimony because the Committee was then feeling slighted and more than normally peeved at the Department of Justice, which had let a secret blue-ribbon grand jury in New York, called to study espionage, recess without returning any indictments.

Before she was heard, on the last day of July, the Committee members agreed vigorously with themselves that, in view of the evidence given to the New York grand jury, the "findings" of the Senate subcommittee, and "the information we are going to get this morning," the United States attorney in the District of Columbia ought to be asked to convene "a special blue-ribbon grand jury" in Washington to look into espionage. Then the chairman, the Honorable J. Parnell Thomas, turned to Miss Bentley and she began her story.

I do not propose to parrot the names of the thirty men and women whom she readily identified as "attached" or "unattached" members of two Communist spy rings she said had worked in and around the Government. Some asked to come before the Committee and denied every charge. Some were subpoenaed and, of these, ten refused to affirm or deny their alleged friendships or their membership in the Communist Party, on the constitutional grounds that they might "incriminate or degrade" themselves. This is their undeniable privilege under the Bill of Rights; but the people who were quick to claim it were just the people Miss Bentley had confidently named as the ringleaders. Certainly there was something suspect about the almost ritual consistency with which they refused to admit the friendships or associations that, according to Miss Bentley, had made up the espionage rings. And it seems to me difficult to avoid the conclusion

WINGATE JUNIOR COLLEGE

of Representative Mundt, the Committee's acting chairman at many
hearings, that this extreme recourse to the Fifth Amendment [1] by
the particular people who seized it put them in "a very bad light."
But even the most suspect of them have the broader right not to be
judged by their behavior on privileged occasions outside a court of
law. And I know no way of compromising this principle, which is
what most of the newspapers did. There are some things that cannot
be done to the joint satisfaction of your conscience and your city
editor, and while the conscience is a hard taskmaster, the city editor
is the paymaster. But in this chronicle, at any rate, there is no pressing
reason to reprint the names of the alleged members of Miss Bentley's
two spy rings. There would be no excuse for mentioning them at all if
several of the people she named did not overlap the Hiss case and bear
on the Communist "apparatus" in which Chambers was to include
Hiss.

Miss Bentley, a well-educated and impressionable woman, had on
a European trip been upset by the conditions of Fascism in Italy.
When she came home she got into the American League against War
and Fascism and from there, in March 1935, joined the Communists.
She became what she called a "medium active" member, and her first
job was as an undercover agent working in the Italian Library of Information in New York. By the time the German armies had gone
into Russia, she was acting as a liaison between the Communist Party
and "individuals and groups who were employed in the United States
Government and in positions to furnish information . . . political,
military, whatever they could lay their hands on." She carried away
information given her, she said, by people in the Farm Security Administration, the Treasury, the War Production Board, the Pentagon
Building, the Board of Economic Warfare, and the Office of Strategic
Services. The leaders of one of these spy rings, she said, was a Nathan
Silvermaster, who turned over to her many documents from his
group, some of which were typed and others photographed in the
basement of Silvermaster's house. She showed most of the material to

---

[1] "No person shall be held to answer for a capital, or otherwise infamous crime
unless on a presentment or indictment of a Grand Jury, except in cases arising in the
land or naval forces, or in the militia, when in actual service, in time of war or public danger; nor shall any person be subject for the same offense to be twice put in
jeopardy of life or limb; nor shall be compelled in any criminal case to be a witness
against himself, nor be deprived of life, liberty, or property, without due process of
law; nor shall private property be taken for public use without just compensation."

Earl Browder at Communist headquarters in New York. She was
sure that Silvermaster was a Communist and "probably an agent of
the NKVD," the Russian secret police. He had testified before the
Committee in May and refused to say whether he was a Communist or
not. He was to do so again. He had also testified before the New York
grand jury.

At the end of the day's hearing, there was an interesting argument
about the status of the Committee and its right to confront a new
witness with the testimony of an old one outside his presence. Representative Hébert of Louisiana thought the man ought to be present.
The incorrigible Representative Rankin of Mississippi protested that
"we are not supposed to bring all these men who are charged with
treason or conspiring to overthrow this Government before this committee. This is a form of grand jury by a committee of the House of
Representatives. No grand jury ever calls a defendant." It would be
hard to assert so many confusions of law and liberty in three sentences.
Mr. Rankin is a lawyer and Mr. Hébert is not (and was subsequently
dropped from the Committee on that ground). But it was Mr.
Hébert who came in to say a few home truths. "I disagree with my
colleague from Mississippi," he said, "that this is a grand-jury investigation. If anybody puts in jeopardy an individual who is charged
with being a Communist, I think in fairness that this individual should
be allowed his day in court here in public hearing as well." The Committee had no obligation to people named in executive session, "but
the minute we allow a witness on the stand to mention any individual,
that individual has a right to come before this committee." Mr.
Rankin was unconvinced. He grumbled that "it certainly is putting
the cart before the horse when you have the witness before you who
has the testimony." In this flip way did some members of the Committee ignore the old and necessary distinctions between hearsay and
evidence, between what is alleged and what is true.

When her chief contact [1] in New York died in 1944, Miss Bentley
said she was thrown for the first time "into direct contact with Rus-

---

[1] Miss Bentley gave this man's name as Jacob Golos. He came into the news in
May 1950 when the Department of Justice announced the arrest of one Harry Gold
on espionage charges. He was said to have confessed to charges made in London by
Dr. Klaus Fuchs, a confessed atomic spy then in an English prison. Gold was charged
with being the link between Fuchs and Russian agents and was said to have admitted being recruited into espionage work by this same Golos.

sians who had just come over from Russia." They "made no bones of
the fact that they had contempt for American Communists with their
vague idealism" and "that they were using the American Communist
Party as a recruitment for espionage." She went for protection to
Earl Browder, but after he "hemmed and hawed . . . Moscow pulled
the strings, and he just fell out from underneath me and told me that
there was nothing that he could do." She immediately stopped paying
her party dues, wondered for a while how she could get out of the
Party, and about a year later got her courage up and went to see the
F.B.I. The Department of Justice had known her story for about two
years and partly because of it had decided in the spring of 1947 to convene the New York grand jury.

On the general question of how a Government worker might come
to believe that his ideals transcended his loyalty to his country, there
were two pertinent passages. Mr. Hébert asked her what could persuade a native-born, well-educated American to join up with the
Communists. She replied that she had in time come to accept the
argument "that they put to almost any liberal who is dissatisfied with
various conditions in this country which, of course, exist, and there is
no denying them." The argument was: "If you feel like a liberal, and
if you feel that these conditions are bad, then you should ally yourself with the group that will be strong and disciplined and intelligent
and that could really do something about these conditions." As for
"whether it was American or not, they represented themselves to be
an American party."

But, asked Mr. Hébert, how did they mean "to impose their
system on the American people, without the overthrow of the American form of government"?

"That was not mentioned at all in those days, possibly because
that was during Earl Browder's regime, at which point you will remember they did not come out in the open with any revolutionary
program. We were told that the only solution was education, that
people must be taught, so that we would finally get a majority of
American people to vote that particular regime into power."

But did it never occur to her that she was doing wrong when she
met people and handed them secret information during the war? No,
she said, it did not.

And "it never did come to you . . . that you were performing a
disservice to your Government?"

"No; I was thoroughly sold on the conviction that no matter what happened in my lifetime I was building a decent world in the future."

Did it not occur to her that "Russia was supposedly our ally in this war, and they did not have to resort to these means to get secret information"?

"It never occurred to me that way because I think the mistake you make when you look at Communism is that you take it as an intellectual process. It is not. It is almost a religion and it gets you so strongly that you take orders blindly."

She conceded towards the end that not all the people she took information from knew where it was going, and she explained that most of them were Communists who wanted to see a Communist government in this country. They therefore believed they were giving help to Communism, not to Russia as a foreign power. But she agreed with Representative Nixon that even so they had signed affidavits or taken oaths to the United States of America and were thus inescapably "placing the interests of the Soviet Government above that of their own Government."

Miss Bentley stepped down, soon after Representative McDowell had thanked her for having the courage "to walk through the valley of the shadow of publicity."

It need hardly be said that Mr. McDowell had coined a euphemism. The ensuing publicity was dazzling. Her story entailed a bizarre fate for a Vassar girl. It suggested that the murky sort of plotting that had overturned Czechoslovakia was already going on in our own basement; and she named names in the Roosevelt administrations with an abandon that made useful material for the imminent Republican campaign. At his press conference the President called the whole investigation "a red herring" dragged by the Republicans across the campaign trail. The Communist convention in New York seconded him by passing a resolution condemning the Congress for ignoring "the bread-and-butter issues" in its frivolous wish to put on "a three-ring Communist spy circus." What was overlooked then, in the barrage of campaign rhetoric being laid down by three parties (Henry Wallace and his Progressive Party had just finished their first convention in Philadelphia), and in the sweating impatience of the Congress to go home, was the interesting fact that Miss Bentley's story was so specific that if it were corroborated, the House Committee would very soon take on the glory of the minute-men; and if it were disproved, the Committee would go down as a discredited band of vigilantes. However, it was the pleasant sensual summertime of baseball, beachcombing, and back-porch lounging, and the newspapers had great fun with Miss Bentley, joked about her as a "blonde spy" who had somehow turned into a brunette; and hardly anybody bothered to see an omen, two days later, when Louis Budenz, another relapsed heretic, a former editor of the *Daily Worker*, independently corroborated much of her story before the Senate subcommittee, thought she had truly described the process of Communist espionage, and estimated there must have been "several hundred" Communists in "relatively important places" in the Government. This man was to come before the House Committee later in the month and implicate Hiss. In the midsummer of 1948 few Americans had the sense, which the House Committee had already taken, that a new period of American history was opening, in which decent people would shed their view of espionage as a convention of melodrama in central Europe and begin to wonder if it might not have been a day-to-day occupation in their own Government; in which the graveyard sleuthing for the fat of the New Deal would turn up an appalling rattle of skeletons; in which the word "spy" would come to lose its alien attributes and be allowed as a possible role even for a Yale or Harvard man in a Brooks Brothers suit.

FROM AN ACCUSATION TO AN INDICTMENT

❧

My vouch against you, and my place i' th' state
Will so your accusation overweigh,
That you shall stifle in your own report,
And smell of calumnie. —MEASURE FOR MEASURE

ON the 3rd of August 1948 the House Committee on Un-American Activities, continuing its "Hearings Regarding Communist Espionage in the United States Government," came to order in public session shortly after eleven o'clock: Republicans Karl Mundt, chairman, of South Dakota, John McDowell of Pennsylvania, Richard M. Nixon of California; Democrats John E. Rankin of Mississippi, J. Hardin Peterson of Florida, and F. Edward Hébert of Louisiana; investigators Robert E. Stripling, Louis Russell, William Wheeler, and Donald T. Appell; and Mrs. A. S. Poore, editor for the Committee.

The portly little man stood, raised his right hand and took the oath, and gave his full name as David Whittaker Chambers.

He had no sooner identified himself and his job, and admitted to having been a paid functionary of the Communist Party from 1924 to 1937, than he asked if he might read a statement, which would make clear why he had broken with the Party and why he was there that morning.

Almost exactly 9 years ago—that is, 2 days after Hitler and Stalin signed their pact—I went to Washington and reported to the authorities

55

what I knew about the infiltration of the United States Government by Communists. For years international communism, of which the United States Communist Party is an integral part, had been in a state of unde-clared war with this Republic. With the Hitler-Stalin pact, that war reached a new stage. I regarded my action in going to the Government as a simple act of war, like the shooting of an armed enemy in combat.

At that moment in history, I was one of the few men on this side of the battle who could perform this service.

I had joined the Communist Party in 1924. No one recruited me. I had become convinced that the society in which we live, Western civili-zation, had reached a crisis, of which the First World War was the military expression, and that it was doomed to collapse or revert to barbarism. I did not understand the causes of the crisis or know what to do about it. But I felt that, as an intelligent man, I must do something. In the writings of Karl Marx I thought that I had found the explanation of the historical and economic causes. In the writings of Lenin I thought I had found the answer to the question, What to do?

In 1937 I repudiated Marx' doctrines and Lenin's tactics. Experi-ence and the record had convinced me that communism is a form of totali-tarianism, that its triumph means slavery to men wherever they fall under its sway, and spiritual night to the human mind and soul. I resolved to break with the Communist Party at whatever risk to my life or other tragedy to myself or my family. Yet, so strong is the hold which the insidious evil of communism secures on its disciples, that I could still say to someone at the time: "I know that I am leaving the winning side for the losing side, but it is better to die on the losing side than to live under communism."

For a year I lived in hiding, sleeping by day and watching through the night with gun or revolver within easy reach. That was what under-ground communism could do to one man in the peaceful United States in the year 1938.

I had sound reason for supposing that the Communists might try to kill me. For a number of years I had myself served in the underground, chiefly in Washington, D.C. The heart of my report to the United States Government consisted of a description of the apparatus to which I was attached. It was an underground organization of the United States Com-munist Party developed, to the best of my knowledge, by Harold Ware, one of the sons of the Communist leader known as "Mother Bloor." I knew it at its top level, a group of seven or so men, from among whom in later years certain members of Miss Bentley's organization were apparently recruited. The head of the underground group at the time I knew it was Nathan Witt, an attorney for the National Labor Relations Board. Later, John Abt became the leader. Lee Pressman was also a member of this group, as was Alger Hiss, who, as a member of the State Department, later organized the conferences at Dumbarton Oaks, San Francisco, and the United States side of the Yalta Conference.

The purpose of this group at that time was not primarily espionage. Its original purpose was the Communist infiltration of the American Government. But espionage was certainly one of its eventual objectives. Let no one be surprised at this statement. Disloyalty is a matter of principle with every member of the Communist Party. The Communist Party exists for the specific purpose of overthrowing the Government, at the opportune time, by any and all means; and each of its members, by the fact that he is a member, is dedicated to this purpose.

It is 10 years since I broke away from the Communist Party. During that decade I have sought to live an industrious and God-fearing life. At the same time I have fought communism constantly by act and written word. I am proud to appear before this committee. The publicity inseparable from such testimony has darkened, and will no doubt continue to darken, my effort to integrate myself in the community of free men. But that is a small price to pay if my testimony helps to make Americans recognize at last that they are at grips with a secret, sinister, and enormously powerful force whose tireless purpose is their enslavement.

At the same time, I should like, thus publicly, to call upon all ex-Communists who have not yet declared themselves, and all men within the Communist Party whose better instincts have not yet been corrupted and crushed by it, to aid in this struggle while there is still time to do so.

This was enough to send the wire-service correspondents dashing out to file a startling lead for the evening papers. Chambers went on to say that the apparatus he was talking about was organized with "a leading group of seven men, each of whom was a leader of a cell." (The printed record says "the" cell, which is evidently a mishearing.) He named Nathan Witt as its first head and the following as its members: Lee Pressman, Alger Hiss, Donald Hiss, Victor Perlo, Charles Kramer (alias Krevitsky), John Abt, and Henry Collins. The organizer was Harold Ware, son of Mother Bloor. (The Committee henceforth was to identify this apparatus as "the Ware-Abt-Witt group," to distinguish it from Miss Bentley's Silvermaster and Perlo groups.) The employment records of some of these were read into the record, a proceeding which evidently shows that before this hearing the Committee investigators knew the names of the people to be accused. (Chambers was to testify in the First Trial that two investigators came to see him in New York early in June 1948.)

Chambers told what he knew about the Government careers of these nine men, whose Party dues he said he had regularly collected. When he left the Party, the only man he tried to persuade to break with him was Alger Hiss, who "absolutely refused to break."

"He cried?" asked Mr. Stripling, anticipating nothing but the truth.

"Yes, he did," said Chambers, "I was very fond of Mr. Hiss." He mentioned that Mrs. Hiss was present and that she also "is" a Communist.

He then recalled that he had also approached with the same intention one Harry Dexter White, former Assistant Secretary of the Treasury, and co-author of the Bretton Woods monetary plan. Chambers was not positive White was a registered member of the Party, but "he was certainly a fellow-traveler so far within the fold that his not being a Communist would be a mistake on both sides." (White was heard at his own request on the 13th of August and denied that he had ever been a fellow traveler. He put in a reminder to the Committee that the Bill of Rights had been included in the American Constitution as a protection against "star chamber proceedings." To which Mr. Nixon retorted that star chambers recognized no right of the accused to defend himself and reached a judgment on the spot. Mr. White elaborated eloquently on the constitutional guarantees of witnesses, cross-examination, and the other regulated protections of a court of law. He was given a long and courteous hearing; and he asked to rest during his testimony because he was recovering from a severe heart attack. He died three days later.)

At some stage the leadership of the group was in dispute. Nathan Witt resigned and John Abt was elected in his place. Chambers added the reminder that "the head of the whole business," meaning the Communist underground in the United States, was a man called J. Peters. He it was who decided (about 1936, Chambers thought) that one or two members of the group "were going places in the government," were within reach of positions of "power and influence," and it would be a good idea to release them, as a tactical precaution, from any further intercourse with the apparatus. Their only connection with J. Peters would be through Chambers. One of these promising men "clearly was Alger Hiss."

There was much desultory questioning about many other people the Committee seemed to have reason to suspect. Chambers was also encouraged to explain Communist tactics and was invited to distinguish between Fascism and Communism, an invitation he discreetly declined as raising philosophical questions that would "require almost a book to develop." Then Mr. Mundt, the chairman, said: "Mr. Chambers, I am very much interested in trying to check the career of Alger Hiss. I know nothing about Donald Hiss; but as a member of the Foreign Affairs Committee, the personnel committee, I have had some occasion to check the activities of Alger Hiss while he was in the State Department. There is reason to believe that he organized within the Department one of the Communist cells which endeavored to influence our Chinese policy and bring about the condemnation of Chiang Kai-shek, which put Marzini in an important position there, and I think that it is important to know what happened to these people after they leave the Government. Do you know where Alger Hiss is employed now?" Chambers replied correctly that he was the head of the Carnegie Foundation [1] for World Peace. (It ought to be noted that Mr. Mundt's passing reference to "one of the Communist cells which endeavored to influence our Chinese policy" is a highly tendentious bit of grammar. It was neither common knowledge, nor verifiable knowledge, so far as I know, that United States policy on China was influenced by a Communist cell. And General Marshall himself was quite capable, when the time came, of condemning Chiang Kai-shek.) Chambers was fairly sure he had reported all the names of the group to Mr. Adolf Berle, Assistant Secretary of State, whom he had been directed to nine years before, two days after the signing of the Nazi-Soviet Pact. Mr. Berle showed "considerable excitement," but seemingly the Government did nothing about this knowledge.

That was all. The chairman thanked Mr. Chambers for his testimony and for his "courage and good patriotism." For the Democratic minority, Mr. Rankin added a tribute to "a splendid witness."

NO sooner was Chambers off the stand than a Baltimore newspaperman telephoned the Carnegie Fund in New York and told Hiss what had happened. That evening Hiss sent a telegram to the Committee asking to be heard in denial. The next morning the Committee met in

---

[1] i.e., Endowment.

open session to question Silvermaster, on Miss Bentley's accusation; and Mr. Mundt, again in the chair, announced that of the twenty-five or thirty people named as members of the three spy rings, only three people had come forward to ask to appear. He produced two telegrams. One was from a doctor and his wife in Pittsburgh, both "assumed" by Miss Bentley to belong to the Silvermaster cell. The other was from Alger Hiss. Mr. Mundt read it out:

My attention has been called by representatives of the press to statements made about me before your committee this morning by one Whittaker Chambers. I do not know Mr. Chambers and insofar as I am aware have never laid eyes on him. There is no basis for the statements made about me to your committee. I would appreciate it if you would make this telegram a part of your committee's record, and I would further appreciate the opportunity to appear before your committee to make these statements formally and under oath. I shall be in Washington on Thursday and hope that that will be a convenient time from the committee's point of view for me to appear.

His request was promptly allowed and he appeared in open session the next morning, the 5th of August. He too had a statement, which he began at once to read:

I was born in Baltimore, Md., on November 11, 1904. I am here at my own request to deny unqualifiedly various statements about me which were made before this committee by one Whittaker Chambers the day before yesterday. I appreciate the committee's having promptly granted my request. I welcome the opportunity to answer to the best of my ability any inquiries the members of this committee may wish to ask me.

I am not and never have been a member of the Communist Party. I do not and never have adhered to the tenets of the Communist Party. I am not and never have been a member of any Communist-front organization. I have never followed the Communist Party line, directly or indirectly. To the best of my knowledge, none of my friends is a Communist.

As a State Department official, I have had contacts with representatives of foreign governments, some of whom have undoubtedly been members of the Communist Party, as, for example, representatives of the Soviet Government. My contacts with any foreign representative who could possibly have been a Communist have been strictly official.

To the best of my knowledge, I never heard of Whittaker Chambers until in 1947, when two representatives of the Federal Bureau of Investigation asked me if I knew him and various other people, some of whom I knew and some of whom I did not know. I said I did not know

Chambers. So far as I know, I have never laid eyes on him, and I should like
to have the opportunity to do so.

I have known Henry Collins since we were boys in camp together.
I knew him again while he was at the Harvard Business School while I was
at the Harvard Law School, and I have seen him from time to time since
I came to Washington in 1933.

Lee Pressman was in my class at the Harvard Law School and we
were both on the Harvard Law Review at the same time. We were also both
assistants to Judge Jerome Frank on the legal staff of the Agricultural Adjustment Administration. Since I left the Department of Agriculture I have
seen him only occasionally and infrequently. I left the Department, according to my recollection, in 1935.

Witt and Abt were both members of the legal staff of the AAA. I
knew them both in that capacity. I believe I met Witt in New York a year
or so before I came to Washington. I came to Washington in 1933. We were
both practicing law in New York at the time I think I met Witt.

Kramer was in another office of the AAA, and I met him in that
connection.

I have seen none of these last three men I have mentioned except
most infrequently since I left the Department of Agriculture.

I don't believe I ever knew Victor Perlo.

Except as I have indicated, the statements made about me by Mr.
Chambers are complete fabrications. I think my record in the Government
service speaks for itself.

He was asked to summarize his education, and when he came to
mention that Judge Jerome Frank had invited him to Washington to
work for the Agricultural Adjustment Administration, he had a brush
with Mr. Nixon, a dark, intense man, younger than Hiss, whose
tenacity in pursuing this whole affair brought it in the end into the
courts. Mr. Nixon asked Hiss to name any other Government officials
who had urged him to come to Washington. Hiss replied he would
rather not—"so many witnesses . . . use names rather loosely before
your committee." Mr. Nixon thought it would make Hiss's case
stronger if he named the others. Hiss maintained that "regardless of
whether it strengthens my case or not," he would prefer to mention
no more names unless Mr. Nixon insisted on a direct answer. Mr.
Nixon insisted. Hiss later admitted that John Foster Dulles had first
approached him about becoming the president of the Carnegie Endowment. He said that at that time he had no notion Chambers had
told Mr. Berle he was a Communist. This led the chairman, Mr.

Mundt, to say something that was obviously very much on his mind. He wondered aloud what possible motive "a man who edits *Time* magazine" would have for mentioning the names of the brothers Hiss in a conspiracy involving six other men about whose "subversive connections" Mr. Mundt at least had little doubt. Hiss warmly shared the chairman's bewilderment. "You can appreciate the position of this committee," Mr. Mundt said rather tactlessly. "I hope the committee can appreciate my position, too," was Hiss's inevitable rejoinder. Mr. Mundt said the Committee surely could and he was only wanting to find out the facts. Hiss wished he might have seen Chambers before he made his accusation; to which Mr. Rankin contributed a typically facetious irrelevance by saying that after all the "smear attacks" against the Committee made by *Time*, he wasn't surprised "at anything that comes out of anybody connected with it."

Hiss was thereupon shown an Associated Press photograph of Chambers, which the chief investigator remarked was probably of a heavier man than the Chambers his friends knew fourteen years before. He looked intently at it and said that for all he knew it might be a picture of the Committee chairman. He would not want to swear that he had never seen the man the picture represented. Again he said he would like very much to see the original in the flesh.

He was asked about a call from the F.B.I. and frankly admitted that in 1947 two agents came to see him, asked him if he was a Communist, and put other questions "not unlike the points Mr. Chambers testified to in the course of their investigation." Also, the previous year, when he came back from the United Nations General Assembly meeting in London, Mr. James Byrnes, then Secretary of State, had warned him that he was in danger of being called a Communist on the floor of Congress. Mr. Byrnes thought it was a very serious matter and advised him to go directly to the F.B.I., preferably to its director, J. Edgar Hoover. Hiss at once called Mr. Hoover, who was out of town, and arranged to see his second in command. He was "courteously received" and obliged with a recital of the organizations he could recollect ever having joined.

Mr. Stripling, the chief investigator, read to Hiss the part of Chambers's testimony about his breaking with the Party and the scene at which Hiss was said to have wept. Did he not ever recall anyone, under the name of Chambers or any other, coming to his home in Georgetown, "and such a conversation as this"? Hiss replied that he certainly did not. Mr. Stripling was strangely impressed by this denial and turned to the chairman: "Mr. Chairman, there is a very sharp contradiction here in the testimony. I certainly suggest Mr. Chambers be brought back before the Committee and clear this up." Mr. Mundt agreed that the Committee was either badly confused or else Chambers must have mistaken Hiss for his brother. Hiss was quick to give his "absolute" opinion that his brother was just as unlikely a conspirator as himself. Mr. Nixon too, and apparently the whole Committee, suddenly and genuinely saw the possibility of a mistaken identity on the part of Chambers. In these and all the subsequent proceedings this was a moment of rare innocence. And for the first—and last—time the cloud over Hiss lifted. Mr. Nixon thought the Committee might avoid a "useless appearance" of Chambers if it could arrange to confront the two men in private and test the possibility of a mistake.

Now the investigator questioned Hiss about the place where he was supposed to have met the other underground agents. No, Hiss could not recall having been there. Such of them as he did know were all casual professional acquaintances in the Government. Lee Pressman he had known well, at Harvard and in Washington, and liked and admired him in both places. But he was never aware that any of them were Communists, and so far as he knew he did not now know any Communists at all. He told freely about a quarrel in the Agricultural Adjustment Administration that led to the resignation of several of the staff. He modestly admitted his part in drafting the Yalta agreement and surprised Mr. Mundt by saying that he had opposed the agreement promising American support for three Russian votes in the Assembly. Mr. Mundt was glad to hear it. He had had no knowledge of the Manchurian railway concession to the Soviet Union, and he had had nothing to do with the China policy proclaimed by the State Department just before General Marshall started out on his mission to China. He had "lent his influence" to support the Security Council's right of veto. It was, he said, "practically the unanimous position of the American government."

After these matters of high policy, Mr. McDowell seemed ready to relax into the farewell courtesies. "Mr. Hiss," he inquired, "do you feel you have had a free and fair and proper hearing this morning?" Hiss gave the quick sweeping nod and smile that a puzzled audience, in one place and another, was to learn to know well in the following eighteen months. "Mr. McDowell," was the gallant response, "I think I have been treated with great consideration by this committee." He wished again, however, he might have met the Committee in private "before there was such a great public press display . . . of completely unfounded charges against me." Denials, he added, do not always catch up with charges. Mr. McDowell was confident that "in your case" they would.

Mr. Nixon just wanted to know if Hiss thought the Government should make every effort to look into the alleged subversive acts of Communists in the United States. Hiss looked up brightly. Did he hear "every effort"? Then he would reply, every effort "compatible with the protection of the reputations of innocent persons." But Mr. Mundt wanted to be quite sure that Hiss believed there should be no positions in the Government open to Communists. It was all very civilized and genial now. And again Hiss evidently felt blithe enough to make nice distinctions, lightly sauced with irony, which then and always afterwards appeared to sit sourly on Mr. Nixon's stomach. Through the following dialogue Mr. Mundt had a sporting eyebrow up. But Mr. Nixon never smiled and never took his eyes off Hiss's face.

MR. HISS: As I say, I am not an expert on that question. Whether someone who is sweeping the halls, or a charwoman—I really don't know.

MR. MUNDT: If you were in charge?

MR. HISS: I wouldn't make the same kind of investigation, I would say that.

MR. MUNDT: If you were in charge of an executive agency would you employ a Communist as a charwoman if you knew it?

MR. HISS: That is what President Roosevelt used to call an "iffy" question.

MR. MUNDT: Do you want to give me an "iffy" answer?

MR. HISS: I don't think I shall ever have that decision to face. I think, trying to answer your question very responsibly, I would not.

Mr. Mundt expressed the chair's appreciation for the witness's "very cooperative attitude" and "forthright statements" and for his being the first among all the accused to ask to deny the charges. And again Mr. Rankin, for the Democratic entail, congratulated him on not refusing to answer questions on the grounds of possible incrimination. Hiss bowed his thanks, and the hearing was at an end.

HERE, then, was the accuser and his accusation answered.

To tell the story of the sequence of events between the accusation and the indictment, and the subsequent testimony before the House Committee, may arouse misgivings in some readers on the score that some of the testimony was secret, that it mentions incidents and people not allowed into the proceedings of the First Trial, and that it might prejudice the proper assessment of the charge in the Trials. Anyone brought up to pay something more than lip service to the fundamental decencies of the English and American common law, which more than anything else in our culture give point to our claim to respect human dignity, is bound to pause before serving up as a mass of "evidence" the exhaustive record of the House Committee. I have made such a pause. The testimony the Committee hears cannot help seeming ruthless and assertive because the Committee is, after all, looking for culprits; and innocent witnesses give the appearance therefore of baiting it. But it is only fair, I think, to the Committee to recognize, as a full reading of its printed record shows, that in spite of its evangelical attack and the jingoism and scurrility of some of its members, the crimes of putting people into discreditable associations, and presuming guilt before innocence can be proved, were committed far more by the press than by the Committee. Very often innocent people were harmed by the mere act of reinterpreting the Committee's testimony in the newspapers. But the worst indignities were done by the headline-writers, whose slap-happy professional immunity is something that can be cured not by lamentation but by law. It was the feature writers who did a serious disservice to the motives and even to the legitimate procedures of the Committee, and such irreparable damage to Hiss that by the time he came to court an acquittal could be only a first step towards a distant prospect of vindication.

The reader, however, can hardly be left with the plot stated and totally denied. It is reasonable to want to know how the Committee came to take one man's word against another's, how Hiss became obliged to force the hand that ruined him, and how the Government was compelled to move into a mystery it was loath to recognize as

anything but an electioneering trick. Since Hiss insisted, in a later
House hearing, that he wanted to have the Committee publish the
record of all its sessions, public and private, no harm can be done at
this date, I think, by explaining these points and briefly chronicling
the sequence of events that explain themselves. I shall try to keep
within these limits, maintaining that all the relevant detail of the
House hearings and the complex charges that Chambers elaborated
there ought fairly to be spread out in the Trials.

ON the 7th of August, then, Chambers was called back before the
Committee in private session, to see first if he had mistaken Hiss's
identity. Mr. Nixon, who had suggested that the two men be confronted in private, was in the chair. He asked immediately if Chambers had seen the newspaper photographs of Hiss and if they showed
the man he accused. Chambers said he had and they did. It does not
take much imagination to read in the rapid and searching dialogue
that followed Mr. Nixon's early doubts about the Chambers story.
How did Chambers know that Hiss was a Communist? "I was told by
J. Peters." He was told by J. Peters? What "facts" had J. Peters given
him? "Mr. Peters was head of the entire underground" in the United
States. But did he have "any other evidence, any factual evidence,
to bear out" his claim that Hiss was a Communist? "Nothing beyond
the fact" that Chambers knew him as "a dedicated and disciplined
Communist," who handed in his Party dues, and presumably Mrs.
Hiss's, once a month for two years. Was there a Party membership
card for Hiss? Underground agents of the Party, Chambers replied,
never carried them.

Mr. Nixon pressed Chambers hard for intimate knowledge of the
Hiss family—their children, nicknames, servants, pets, their various
addresses and furniture (Chambers said he had stayed several times
overnight with the Hisses); Hiss's taste in books, food, hobbies. (Hiss
was a bird-watcher and Chambers mentioned he'd once been excited
at seeing "a prothonotary warbler.") Chambers replied evenly to all
this, unburdening a wealth of detail about the Hisses that could come
only from the closest and most observant friendship or from a tireless
detective job. The Committee's workmanlike curiosity can be seen
from the mere layout of the printed record: it is nearly all single-line
dialogue.

On the 16th, Hiss was brought into a private session. The regular chairman, Mr. J. Parnell Thomas, presided for the first time.

Mr. Nixon again did most of the questioning. He began by explaining the Committee's open-minded bewilderment and asked Hiss "to bear with me" if some of his questions seemed to go over old ground. When did he first hear the name Whittaker Chambers? He heard it from the F.B.I. in 1947 along with a lot of other names they asked him about. Did he ever know, between 1934 and '37, anybody by the name of Carl (Chambers had said that according to underground custom he was known to Hiss by a pseudonym, not by his real name)? Hiss replied he knew a Carl, but not this one. He never knew anyone by the name of J. Peters. He had made only social visits to any apartment Henry Collins might have lived in (Chambers said this was where Party dues were turned over). He wouldn't want to testify for sure who was there at those times. He had never paid any money to Collins or any of the other alleged conspirators in any sort of transaction. He was shown two different pictures of Chambers and said they didn't recall anyone, but the likeness was "not completely unfamiliar." He again repeated his wish to see the man face to face. And Mr. Nixon promised him it would be arranged. He couldn't possibly believe he wouldn't remember someone who had stayed overnight several times.

Mr. Nixon started to check on Chambers's astonishing knowledge of the Hisses and their ways of life. He asked if Mrs. Hiss could come to testify. She was then summering in Vermont and Mr. Nixon was sorry if it meant she would have to come all the way to Washington with her small son. Perhaps it would be better if a subcommittee went up to New York to see her there.

Up to now the record reveals no sign of distrust or resentment between Hiss and the Committee. He asked, however, to mention a point that had "angered and hurt" him, and Mr. Nixon allowed he was free to say anything he liked. Hiss was clearly worried at not having been acquainted with what Chambers had said to the Committee the last time in private. He feared that what he might say now would somehow leak to Chambers and help him build up a "very persuasive" *ex post facto* case. Mr. Nixon took this, a little testily, to imply that "the Committee's purpose in questioning you today is to get information with which we can coach Mr. Chambers so that he can more or less build a web around you." Hiss did not mean to imply any such thing, he said. He just felt he had the right to protect himself and his reputation against possible leaks from the processed record. Mr. Stripling came in with the assurance that the Committee members at this stage had "a very open mind"; that the testimony so far had been turned over to the United States Attorney; that without any "pre-arrangement" with Chambers the Committee had asked him to talk about the Hisses, and he had "rattled off details" for hours.

Hiss suddenly said he had written down on a pad in front of him the name of a man he had known in 1933 and 1934 who "not only spent some time in my house but sublet my apartment." Maybe, said Hiss, he was "overanxious about the possibility of unauthorized disclosure of testimony," but he thought it was unfair to ask him to put down a record of personal facts which might help someone who wanted to injure him.

Hiss had touched the crucial anxiety that many people have felt about Congressional hearings that run in an interrupted series: how independent are independent Committee investigators? Is there, when a grand jury is sitting, an informal working arrangement with the F.B.I.? Has an accuser the right of private access to a committee between hearings? In short, how is a suspect witness to ensure that his confidential testimony shall not leak to his accuser?

At this stage in the inquiry Hiss's fears might seem excessive, even suspicious, to an outsider; for, as Mr. Nixon told him, everything the Committee knew so far could be corroborated by third parties. But Hiss was not an outsider. He was the victim (he had implied as much in mentioning "my present frame of mind") and it is not hard to imagine the feelings of a man once the idea had occurred to him that he might be damning himself out of his own mouth. In a jury trial this danger is anticipated by the rule that a defendant need not testify against himself. What Hiss was begging was some corresponding protection in a Congressional hearing. It was a plea that the Committee could respect in several ways. It could recess and work out its own code of fair practices—an unlikely magnanimity at this stage of the pursuit. It could remind the witness that Congressional committees have a practically unlimited right of questioning, and this is indeed how Congress does its spadework. (Hiss might have reflected, and so might the Committee, that he himself had given some unhappy moments, as the prosecutor in the Senate arms investigation, to such vulnerable public reputations as J. P. Morgan, the du Ponts, and

Bernard Baruch.) Or the Committee could have agreed it would henceforth call off all private hearings, which was what Hiss in effect wanted it to do. "I would like him [Chambers]," he said, "to say all he knows about me now . . . let him tell you all he knows, let that be made public, and then let my record be checked against the facts." Mr. Thomas, the Committee chairman, settled it quite briskly by saying: "Questions will be asked and the Committee will expect to get very detailed answers."

They started to check old Hiss addresses, and Hiss again put forward his plea. "If this Committee feels—" he began. Mr. Thomas broke in with "Never mind feelings. You let Mr. Nixon ask the questions and you go ahead and answer it." At least two members of the Committee were losing their patience. Mr. Stripling said: "Let the record show, Mr. Hiss, you brought up this *ex post facto* business. Your testimony comes as *ex post facto* testimony to the testimony of Mr. Chambers. He is already on record." Mr. Stripling didn't want to infer, though, that Hiss knew what Chambers had said. Mr. Nixon made the counter-plea to Hiss to accept the good faith of the Committee. They were there only to "test the credibility of Mr. Chambers, and you are the man who can do it." Frankly, he said, he must insist. Hiss said if they insisted he would "of course" answer. But then he told what was troubling him. Had not the Committee heard secret testimony from Chambers before his first appearance in public? No, sir, said Mr. Stripling. But, said Hiss, there was a press report to that effect; "didn't he meet with you in executive session?" Mr. McDowell put in that on the morning of Chambers's accusation they had had about two minutes with him to get his name and job. Still incredulous, Hiss asked: "Didn't you know his testimony—that he was going to testify about me?" No, said Mr. Stripling.

Even now Hiss would not let the doubt lie. He feared that "through no fault of any official of this committee" what he was going to say that day might leak out. Mr. Hébert made a third to the couple of Committeemen who were wearying of this hypersensitiveness. He said he had come to no conclusion—"we did not know anything Mr. Chambers was going to say. I didn't hear your name mentioned until it was mentioned in open hearing."

"I didn't know that," said Hiss.

Well, Mr. Hébert would "put it on the line . . . up to a few moments ago you have been very open, very cooperative. Now you have hedged . . . whichever one of you is lying is the greatest actor that America has ever produced." Hiss went right on, matching the Committee's rising anger: he found it difficult, he said, to sit there and control himself while Mr. Hébert implied that Chambers's record, his having been a former Communist "and traitor to his country," suggested no choice of the more credible witness.

"Mr. Hiss," Mr. Hébert said, ". . . you show me a good police force and I will show you the stool-pigeon who turned them in. Show me a police force with a poor record, and I will show you a police force without a stool-pigeon. We have to have people like Chambers or Miss Bentley to come in and tell us . . . I don't care who gives the facts to me, whether a confessed liar, thief, or murderer, if it is facts."

They understood each other at last, if on rather rugged ground. And to smooth it down, Mr. Nixon came in again. If the Committee could prove that Chambers never knew Hiss, then perjury would be established, and there would be no need to go into the rest of it. They had asked Hiss about any servants he might have employed in the thirties as a test of Chambers's credibility. And if Hiss could give them the names, they would appreciate it.

Mr. Nixon had managed to restore the mood they met in. Hiss did his best to recall forgotten servants and remembered one. From a rough memorandum he had made on the way down to Washington he began to list the houses he had lived in. Mr. Nixon suggested a recess to let Hiss telephone his wife in Vermont. The Committee held a short discussion off the record away from Hiss. When they resumed, an odd and touching thing happened. Mr. Nixon said the Committee thought it would be an imposition on Mrs. Hiss to ask her to meet them at such short notice. It would do if Hiss and his wife set the time at their own convenience. Hiss responded to this unexpected gallantry by saying, first: "That is kind of you," and then at once throwing them a plum they had not asked for: "The name of the man I brought in—and he may have no relation to this whole nightmare— is a man named George Crosley. I met him when I was working for the Nye Committee. He was a writer. He hoped to sell articles to magazines about the munitions industry." They took him up immediately on the man's appearance: "blondish hair," very bad teeth, married to a "rather strikingly dark person," with one child, a baby. Hiss went smoothly along recalling the summer he had rented an apartment to this trio. They had stayed for a night or two with the Hisses in their new house before their furniture arrived and then moved into the apartment. He didn't know the man very long, for he turned out to be "a deadbeat," made no effort to pay the rent, and Hiss concluded: "I had been a sucker and . . . he was just using me for a soft touch."

The Committee went on drawing more and more detail out of Hiss about the personal things that Chambers had testified to. And more and more of Chambers's memories tallied with Hiss's story of himself, an omen that the Committee kept to itself in what must have been an amiable, dead-pan scene. For when Hiss said he was an amateur ornithologist, Mr. McDowell (who by an ironic coincidence was one too) casually asked him if he had ever seen a prothonotary warbler. Hiss said: "I have right here on the Potomac. Do you know that place?"

"Have *you* ever seen one?" Mr. Nixon asked, obviously of Mr. McDowell.

"Did you see it in the same place?" Hiss asked.

"I saw one in Arlington," said Mr. McDowell.

Hiss seemed far from a conspiracy in this shared, lyrical moment. "They come back and nest in those swamps," he said. "Beautiful yellow head, a gorgeous bird. Mr. Collins is an ornithologist, Henry Collins. He's a really good ornithologist, calling them by their Latin names."

Mr. Nixon snuffed out the little flare of good-fellowship. "What schools do you recall your son attended in 1934 to 1937?" Hiss gave them readily and went on to tell of his boyhood, of an automobile drive he probably took with this man, of various loans that had never been paid back.

There are two or three points that ought to be put in here; they are a firm guide to the Committee's line of thinking that the burden of proof was beginning to fall on Hiss. Chambers had mentioned in secret session that Hiss was deaf in one ear. Mr. Stripling, the Committee investigator, now mentioned that Hiss had his hand up to his ear. "Are you hard of hearing in your left ear?" Not to his knowledge, said Hiss. "You did that before the committee in open session and did then. If you are having difficulty, we can all move this way." There is no notation in the record that they did. It was just a small point.

Shortly before Mr. Nixon finished his questions, he made a present to Hiss of the thought that it was natural for him to feel that his word should carry greater weight than Chambers's. Unfortunately, Mr.

Nixon added, Chambers felt the same way because he had volunteered
the story. A little later Mr. Nixon suddenly wondered if "under the
circumstances, for the assistance of the committee in this matter, you
would be willing to take a lie-detector test. . . . Mr. Chambers
. . . said he would." Hiss had expected it and said so. He had heard a
report that Chambers was willing to submit to one (nobody asked
about the source of this "leak"). He had talked to lawyers who had
very little confidence in these "so-called" tests. Not even the F.B.I.
regarded it as scientific. Mr. Nixon replied they had the best man in
the country on hand for it. Hiss obviously wanted no part of it. He
would have to know, he said, who was conducting it and what kind of
test it was. He had heard it "registers more emotion than anything
else." He certainly didn't want "to duck anything that has scientific
or sound basis." He would have to "consult further." Mr. Nixon
granted that "emotion" did enter into it, and Mr. Chambers was
"also" a very emotional man. But Mr. Nixon had confidence in it.
(This was the last we were to hear of the lie-detector.)

There was more about Hiss's family. But Mr. Nixon thought the
time had come to bring the two men face to face. And he wanted to
arrange it. Hiss didn't care whether it was done in public or private.
For once, all the misgivings about publicity came from the Committee. "If you have a public session, it will be a show," said Mr.
Nixon. "It will be ballyhooed into a circus," Mr. Stripling thought.
And he urged a private meeting. Hiss listened to this without comment, until he remarked that if they were considering him, "after
what has been done to my feelings and my reputation, I think it would
be like sinking the Swiss Navy." On the whole, though, he thought he
preferred to get it over with in public.

At last it was agreed that Chambers should be asked his preference.
Mr. Nixon thought Hiss ought to be given a copy of the day's testimony for his own use. And it was arranged that Mrs. Hiss should
testify in New York, with "absolutely no publicity," some time before
the confrontation, which they agreed to hold on the 25th. Everything
ended in a better spirit than it had begun. Hiss was reassured about
"leaks"; Mr. Nixon had shown something more than a legal vigilance;
and the last line of the testimony recorded Mr. Stripling's promise
that "Mrs. Hiss be heard in absolutely executive session." The Committee thanked Hiss. Hiss thanked the Committee for their "courtesies."

WITHIN twenty-four hours all this good feeling had shriveled and Hiss was parting from yet another meeting in a blaze of despairing anger. The Committee must have decided that night, of the 16th, to confront the accuser and accused without delay. Hiss and Chambers were telegraphed to appear early the next evening in room 1400 of the Hotel Commodore in New York City. Hiss appeared at 5.35 with a friend, in the presence of Mr. McDowell, as chairman, Mr. Nixon, a research man for the Committee, and its four investigators, including Mr. Stripling. It was a two-room suite. Chambers was apparently kept in the bedroom. In the sitting-room Hiss took the oath, was told he might smoke and make himself comfortable. Mr. McDowell explained that this meeting had been called to confront the two men and it probably wouldn't take more than ten or fifteen minutes. Hiss asked to make a statement, and into it he poured a pent-up bitterness that steams up from the printed page. He wanted the record to show that on the way down he had heard of the death of Harry Dexter White (the former Treasury man who had complained of a heart condition as he testified to the Committee four days before). Hiss was not sure he was in the best mood for testimony. He had other things to say. The day before, he had been told that everyone in the room, in Washington, was going to take an oath of secrecy. He would like to record that the first thing he had seen in the *New York Herald Tribune* that morning was a statement to the effect that the Committee had asked him to take a lie-detector test. He would also want the record to show that he had read in the papers that the Committee had asked him to have Mrs. Hiss testify in private. There were other bits of his testimony in the papers. They could have come only from the Committee. That is why he had brought a personal friend with him this time.

Nixon was pretty sure that the *Tribune* story had used "sources outside the committee and outside the committee staff." McDowell, as the chairman, was "greatly disturbed." He too had seen the papers. He could only say he joined Hiss in "feeling rather rotten about the whole thing" and promised that if the word was found to have come from an employee of the Committee, "he will no longer be an employee of the committee."

It was a bad start and an unanswerable complaint. There was nothing to do but get on with the grisly business ahead. An investigator left the room and came back with Chambers, who was motioned to a chair opposite and, no doubt, away from Hiss. No fantasy of this scene could convey with a more distressing tension than the printed record the sense of a personal encounter that began circumspectly enough and ended in a naked and desperate scramble for reputation.

MR. NIXON: Sit over here, Mr. Chambers. Mr. Chambers, will you please stand? And will you please stand, Mr. Hiss? Mr. Hiss, the man standing here is Mr. Whittaker Chambers. I ask you now if you have ever known that man before.

MR. HISS: May I ask him to speak? Will you ask him to say something?

MR. NIXON: Yes. Mr. Chambers, will you tell us your name and your business?

MR. CHAMBERS: My name is Whittaker Chambers.

(At this point, Mr. Hiss walked in the direction of Mr. Chambers.)

MR. HISS: Would you mind opening your mouth wider?

MR. CHAMBERS: My name is Whittaker Chambers.

MR. HISS: I said, would you open your mouth? You know what I am referring to, Mr. Nixon. Will you go on talking?

MR. CHAMBERS: I am senior editor of *Time* magazine.

MR. HISS: May I ask whether his voice, when he testified before, was comparable to this?

MR. NIXON: His voice?

MR. HISS: Or did he talk a little more in a lower key?

MR. MCDOWELL: I would say it is about the same now as we have heard.

MR. HISS: Would you ask him to talk a little more?

MR. NIXON: Read something, Mr. Chambers. I will let you read from—

MR. HISS: I think he is George Crosley, but I would like to hear him talk a little longer.

MR. MCDOWELL: Mr. Chambers, if you would be more comfortable, you may sit down.

MR. HISS: Are you George Crosley?

MR. CHAMBERS: Not to my knowledge. You are Alger Hiss, I believe.

MR. HISS: I certainly am.

MR. CHAMBERS: That was my recollection. (Reading:) "Since June"—

MR. NIXON (interposing): Just one moment. Since some repartee goes on between these two people, I think Mr. Chambers should be sworn.

MR. HISS: That is a good idea.

MR. MCDOWELL: You do solemnly swear, sir, that the testimony you shall give this committee will be the truth, the whole truth, and nothing but the truth, so help you God?

MR. CHAMBERS: I do.

MR. NIXON: Mr. Hiss, may I say something? I suggested that he be sworn, and when I say something like that I want no interruptions from you.

MR. HISS: Mr. Nixon, in view of what happened yesterday, I think there is no occasion for you to use that tone of voice in speaking to me, and I hope the record will show what I have just said.

MR. NIXON: The record shows everything that is being said here today.

MR. STRIPLING: You were going to read.

MR. CHAMBERS (reading from *Newsweek* magazine): "Tobin for Labor. Since June, Harry S. Truman had been peddling the labor secretaryship left vacant by Lewis B. Schwellenbach's death in hope of gaining the maximum political advantage from the appointment."

MR. HISS: May I interrupt?

MR. MCDOWELL: Yes.

MR. HISS: The voice sounds a little less resonant than the voice that I recall of the man I knew as George Crosley. The teeth look to me as though either they have been improved upon or that there has been considerable dental work done since I knew George Crosley, which was some years ago. I believe I am not prepared without further checking to take an absolute oath that he must be George Crosley.

MR. NIXON: May I ask a question of Mr. Chambers?

MR. HISS: I would like to ask Mr. Chambers, if I may.

MR. NIXON: I will ask the questions at this time. Mr. Chambers, have you had any dental work since 1934 of a substantial nature?

MR. CHAMBERS: Yes; I have.

MR. NIXON: What type of dental work?

MR. CHAMBERS: I have had some extractions and a plate.

MR. NIXON: Have you had any dental work in the front of your mouth?

MR. CHAMBERS: Yes.

MR. NIXON: What is the nature of that work?

MR. CHAMBERS: That is a plate in place of some of the upper dentures.

MR. NIXON: I see.

MR. HISS: Could you ask him the name of the dentist that performed these things? Is that appropriate?

MR. NIXON: Yes. What is the name?

MR. CHAMBERS: Dr. Hitchcock, Westminster, Md.

MR. HISS: That testimony of Mr. Chambers, if it can be believed, would tend to substantiate my feeling that he represented himself to me in 1934 or 1935 or thereabout as George Crosley, a free lance writer of articles for magazines. I would like to find out from Dr. Hitchcock if what he has just said is true, because I am relying partly, one of my main recollections of Crosley, was the poor condition of his teeth.

MR. NIXON: Can you describe the condition of your teeth in 1934?

MR. CHAMBERS: Yes. They were in very bad shape.

MR. NIXON: The front teeth were?

MR. CHAMBERS: Yes; I think so.

MR. HISS: Mr. Chairman.

MR. NIXON: Excuse me. Before we leave the teeth. Mr. Hiss, do you feel that you would have to have the dentist tell you just what he did to the teeth before you could tell anything about this man?

MR. HISS: I would like a few more questions asked. I didn't intend to say anything about this, because I feel very strongly that he is Crosley, but he looks very different in girth and in other appearances—hair, forehead, and so on, particularly the jowls.

Hiss was now asked to repeat his testimony about subrenting his apartment to the Crosleys (which would have been in the spring of 1935) until the lease ran out. He thought perhaps seventy-five dollars a month was the rent they'd agreed on. With Hiss's version fairly well established, Mr. Nixon went on: "And then there was some conversation about a car. What was that?" Hiss had testified earlier in the hearings that he had "sold" a car to Chambers, "thrown it in" with the apartment, since it had only a "sentimental value" and he had another car at the time anyway. In pursuing this topic the Committee stumbled on its first solid doubt about Hiss's word; moreover, it was the sort of doubt that could be resolved by documentary evidence, as in the end it was resolved to the Committee's satisfaction. Now Hiss said Crosley was looking for a car to use in Washington and get away at week-ends. "You came to just the right place," Hiss recalled saying to him. He had a 1929 Ford, one of the first model-A Fords, and Hiss threw it in "as part of the total contract" covering the apartment.

Other episodes of the relationship started to come back to him. He remembered Chambers coming once with a rug, which he said he'd had from a wealthy patron and which he then offered in part payment. Hiss still had it.

Hiss's going on in this way, confidently amplifying a rather close relationship with a figure who had been an unnamed shadow the day before, struck Mr. Stripling as not so much a digression from the confrontation as a spurning of it. "I certainly gathered the impression," he said, "when Mr. Chambers walked in this room and you walked over and examined him and asked him to open his mouth, that you were basing your identification purely on what his upper teeth might have looked like. Now here is a person that you knew for several months at least," a man he had had in his home, to whom he had given a car and leased an apartment. Hiss countered that he was not given on important occasions to snap judgments. He saw hundreds of people in Washington at that time. This man denied the name of Crosley. He would like to ask questions of him but Mr. Nixon had forbidden them. The Committee hastily lifted this ban and agreed they should each question the other. Hiss turned again to confront Chambers.

MR. HISS: Did you ever go under the name of George Crosley?

MR. CHAMBERS: Not to my knowledge.

MR. HISS: Did you ever sublet an apartment on Twenty-ninth Street from me?

MR. CHAMBERS: No; I did not.

MR. HISS: You did not?

MR. CHAMBERS: No.

MR. HISS: Did you ever spend any time with your wife and child in an apartment on Twenty-ninth Street in Washington when I was not there because I and my family were living on P Street?

MR. CHAMBERS: I most certainly did.

MR. HISS: You did or did not?

MR. CHAMBERS: I did.

MR. HISS: Would you tell me how you reconcile your negative answers with this affirmative answer?

MR. CHAMBERS: Very easily, Alger. I was a Communist and you were a Communist.

MR. HISS: Would you be responsive and continue with your answer?

MR. CHAMBERS: I do not think it is needed.

MR. HISS: That is the answer.

MR. NIXON: I will help you with the answer, Mr. Hiss. The question, Mr. Chambers, is, as I understand it, that Mr. Hiss cannot understand how you would deny that you were George Crosley and yet admit that you spent time in his apartment. Now would you explain the circumstances? I don't want to put that until Mr. Hiss agrees that is one of his questions.

MR. HISS: You have the privilege of asking any questions you want. I think that is an accurate phrasing.

MR. NIXON: Go ahead.

MR. CHAMBERS: As I have testified before, I came to Washington as a Communist functionary, a functionary of the American Communist Party. I was connected with the underground group of which Mr. Hiss was a member. Mr. Hiss and I became friends. To the best of my knowledge, Mr. Hiss himself suggested that I go there, and I accepted gratefully.

MR. HISS: Mr. Chairman.

MR. NIXON: Just a moment. How long did you stay there?

MR. CHAMBERS: My recollection was about 3 weeks. It may have been longer. I brought no furniture, I might add.

MR. HISS: Mr. Chairman, I don't need to ask Mr. Whittaker Chambers any more questions. I am now perfectly prepared to identify this man as George Crosley.

MR. NIXON: Would you spell that name.

MR. HISS: C-r-o-s-l-e-y.

MR. NIXON: You are sure of one "s"?

MR. HISS: That is my recollection. I have a rather good visual memory, and my recollection of his spelling of his name is C-r-o-s-l-e-y. I don't think that would change as much as his appearance.

MR. STRIPLING: You will identify him positively now?

MR. HISS: I will on the basis of what he has just said positively identify him without further questioning as George Crosley.

MR. STRIPLING: Will you produce for the committee three people who will testify that they knew him as George Crosley?

MR. HISS: I will if it is possible. Why is that a question to ask me? I will see what is possible. This occurred in 1935. The only people that I can think of who would have known him as George Crosley with certainty would have been the people who were associated with me in the Nye committee.

MR. STRIPLING: Can you name three people whom we can subpena who can identify him as George Crosley?

MR. HISS: I am afraid I will have to confer with the individual members. The people, as I recall them, who were on that staff—and they were in and out of Washington constantly—were Mr. Raushenbush. I would like to consult Steve Raushenbush. I don't know whether Crosley ever called on him.

MR. NIXON: Where is he now, Mr. Hiss?

MR. HISS: I don't know.

MR. STRIPLING: He is in Washington.

MR. HISS: Robert Wohlford was one of the investigators.

MR. NIXON: Do you know where he is?

MR. STRIPLING: Department of Justice.

MR. HISS: I don't remember the name of the very efficient secretary to Mr. Raushenbush. Miss Elsie Gullender, I think her name was. Do you know the whereabouts of Miss Elsie Gullender? If his first call was at the central office and he was referred to me, Miss Gullender might remember him. She saw many, many people. If his first call was directly to me, as the press had a perfect right to come to any of us, directly and individually, and as the legal assistant, as the counsel, I shared seeing the press with Mr. Raushenbush; and on the particular matters where I was the investigator and counsel presenting the case, I saw practically all the press. In the cases he was handling, he saw practically all the press.

MR. NIXON: Mr. Hiss, another point that I want to be clear on, Mr. Chambers said he was a Communist and that you were a Communist.

MR. HISS: I heard him.

MR. NIXON: Will you tell the committee whether or not during this period of time that you knew him, which included periods of 3 nights, or 2 or 3 nights, in which he stayed overnight and one trip to New York, from any conversation you ever had any idea that he might be a Communist?

MR. HISS: I certainly didn't.

MR. NIXON: You never discussed politics?

MR. HISS: Oh, as far as I recall his conversations—and I may be confusing them with a lot of other conversations that went on in 1934
and 1935—politics were discussed quite frequently.

May I just state for the record that it was not the habit in
Washington in those days, when particularly if a member of the
press called on you to ask him before you had further conversation
whether or not he was a Communist. It was a quite different atmosphere in Washington then than today. I had no reason to suspect George Crosley of being a Communist. It never occurred to
me that he might be or whether that was of any significance to me
if he was. He was a press representative and it was my duty to give
him information, as I did any other member of the press.

It was to the interest of the Committee investigating the
munitions industry, as its members and we of its staff saw it, to
furnish guidance and information to people who were popularizing
and writing about its work.

I would like to say that to come here and discover that the ass
under the lion's skin is Crosley, I don't know why your committee
didn't pursue this careful method of interrogation at an earlier
date before all the publicity. You told me yesterday you didn't
know he was going to mention my name, although a lot of people
now tell me that the press did know it in advance. They were apparently more effective in getting information than the committee
itself. That is all I have to say now.

MR. MCDOWELL: Well, now, Mr. Hiss, you positively identify—

MR. HISS: Positively on the basis of his own statement that he was
in my apartment at the time when I say he was there. I have no
further question at all. If he had lost both eyes and taken his nose
off, I would be sure.

MR. MCDOWELL: Then, your identification of George Crosley is
complete?

MR. HISS: Yes, as far as I am concerned, on his own testimony.

MR. MCDOWELL: Mr. Chambers, is this the man, Alger Hiss, who was
also a member of the Communist Party at whose home you stayed?

MR. NIXON: According to your testimony.

MR. MCDOWELL: You make the identification positive?

MR. CHAMBERS: Positive identification.

(At this point, Mr. Hiss arose and walked in the direction of Mr.
Chambers.)

MR. HISS: May I say for the record at this point, that I would like to invite Mr. Whittaker Chambers to make those same statements out of the presence of this committee without their being privileged for suit for libel. I challenge you to do it, and I hope you will do it damned quickly.

I am not going to touch him [addressing Mr. Russell]. You are touching me.

MR. RUSSELL: Please sit down, Mr. Hiss.

MR. HISS: I will sit down when the chairman asks me, Mr. Russell, when the chairman asks me to sit down—

MR. RUSSELL: I want no disturbance.

MR. HISS: I don't—

MR. MCDOWELL: Sit down, please.

MR. HISS: You know who started this.

MR. MCDOWELL: We will suspend testimony here for a minute or two, until I return.

Hiss wondered if the Committee could ask Chambers to repeat his charges in public—that is, outside his immunity as a Congressional witness. The Committee thought this was none of their business. The doubts about Hiss were gathering fast in Mr. Stripling's mind. He asked Hiss if he were fully aware "that the public was led to believe that you had never seen, heard or laid eyes upon an individual who is this individual . . . and now you do know him?" Hiss replied he said he had never laid eyes on Whittaker Chambers. "Mr. Stripling," he scolded, "you are stating your impression of public impression." Absolutely, said Mr. Stripling. Mr. Nixon clinched the identity in a running fire of questions to which Hiss repeated all his denials about Communism but said this was the man to whom he had given a car, may have talked about politics, a man who would "cap any story with a story of his own," a man who was "a sort of combination Jim Tully-Jack London writer."

Other members of the Committee were fretting by this time. When Hiss protested against the Committee's advancing the date of this confrontation, Mr. Parnell Thomas, the regular chairman, who had walked in a little earlier, asked if Hiss didn't believe he would be called much earlier than the 25th when (in Mr. Thomas's portentous phrase) "you built up this Mr. Crosley." Hiss said he certainly did not. Again Mr. Stripling invoked the catechism about Communism

and the association of Chambers, Hiss, and the other alleged conspirators. Again Hiss replied with a rattle of "I did not's." And he
again turned the challenge onto the Committee by asking what were
their intentions about publicizing this session. Mr. McDowell could
only speak for himself and moan: "I don't know, I don't know."

The Committee retired, presumably into the bedroom, for an
off-the-record discussion; the record by omission leaves the appalling
implication that Hiss and Chambers were left alone at the bidding of
Mr. McDowell to "make yourselves comfortable"! They came back
to take formal note that Hiss had "definitely recognized Whittaker
Chambers as the person whom he knew as George Crosley" from the
fall of 1934 to the fall of 1935. As a result the full Committee would
meet in public session in Washington on the 25th, and both Hiss and
Chambers would be subpoenaed to appear. Hiss must have been
stewing in impatience while the Committee was out, for the final
passage shows him with all his defenses down:

MR. HISS: May I make a statement at this point for the record?
THE CHAIRMAN: Just a minute.
MR. HISS: Oh, yes.
    (There was a short pause.)
MR. HISS: Has the minute passed yet, Mr. Chairman?
THE CHAIRMAN: Make it 2 minutes, then. Wait until we get through,
    please.
MR. HISS: I have been waiting some time. I was told this would take
    15 minutes. You now want me to take 2 minutes.
THE CHAIRMAN: Do you have anything further?
MR. STRIPLING: I just want to make the subpena out.
MR. CHAIRMAN: Go ahead.
MR. HISS: I would like to say that the service of a subpena is quite
    unnecessary on me. I would be very happy to appear and I told
    the committee yesterday if they asked me to appear without talk-
    ing about subpenas, I, of course, would be there. I was asked
    yesterday also by the committee—and since the committee seems
    to change its mind so quickly and frequently, I would like to get
    it clear—I was asked yesterday to make arrangements for Mrs.
    Hiss to come down from Vermont to meet in executive session
    with a subcommittee.

    As I mentioned earlier, I was told it would be without publicity. That was volunteered by the committee, although I read about it in the papers this morning. Does the committee still desire to hear Mrs. Hiss in executive session or have you changed your mind?

THE CHAIRMAN: There is no decision on that.

MR. HISS: Yes; there was a decision. I have asked her to start down from Vermont.

THE CHAIRMAN: Well, you asked her to start down from Vermont.

MR. HISS: At your request.

THE CHAIRMAN: Believing that she would appear on what date?

MR. HISS: As early as possible was the request you made of me, considering her own convenience and whether she could get somebody to stay with our child.

MR. CHAIRMAN: Is she on the way from Vermont?

MR. HISS: I hope she is on her way by now.

THE CHAIRMAN: If she is on her way now, I think the subcommittee would be glad to hear her.

They agreed to see her in New York, in the same hotel room.

MR. HISS: What would be the most convenient hour for you?

MR. NIXON: Ten o'clock in the morning.

MR. MCDOWELL: If she is on her way.

MR. HISS: I cannot be sure she is on her way.

MR. NIXON: If you could tell us she is going to be here, we would be willing to stay over.

MR. HISS: I cannot guarantee it.

THE CHAIRMAN: Can she be in Washington on Monday morning?

MR. HISS: God, she just made arrangements, if she succeeded at all, to get somebody to stay with the kid 2 or 3 nights.

THE CHAIRMAN: You don't know whether she has made arrangements or not?

MR. HISS: I believe so.

THE CHAIRMAN: You don't know; you just believe so.

MR. NIXON: I will stay over tonight. There is no objection to this. Just let us know. I don't want to stay a week.

MR. HISS: I don't want her to stay a week. Where can I reach you tonight?

MR. NIXON: You can reach me at this hotel; and if you will simply let me know if she will be here any time tomorrow, I am perfectly willing to be here.

MR. HISS: Vermont trains are unpredictable. May I ask if she is privileged to have anybody with her?

MR. NIXON: Absolutely.

MR. HISS: May I come with her?

MR. MCDOWELL: Yes.

MR. HISS: Thank you. Am I dismissed? Is the proceeding over?

THE CHAIRMAN: Any more questions to ask of Mr. Hiss?

MR. NIXON: I have nothing.

THE CHAIRMAN: That is all. Thank you very much.

MR. HISS: *I don't reciprocate.*

THE CHAIRMAN: Italicize that in the record.

MR. HISS: I wish you would.

(Whereupon, at 7:15 p.m., the subcommittee adjourned.)

A subcommittee of one, Mr. Nixon, was on hand next morning in the same room; and presumably there was a stenographer. Mrs. Hiss appeared with her husband and with the friend who had accompanied him the day before. Mrs. Hiss preferred to "affirm" rather than "swear" to the oath. Did she at any time, Mr. Nixon asked, between the years 1934 and 1937 know a man going under the name of George Crosley? She did. How did she first become acquainted with him? Well, it had been a business relationship with her husband; she didn't think she could pretend to an acquaintance with him. She didn't have the "vaguest" recollection where and when she met him. She faintly remembered "this man and his wife looking at the apartment which we sublet to them" and distinctly remembered their spending two or three days in the Hiss house before taking over the apartment lease. And what sort of a man was this Crosley? She had "a very dim impression of a small person, very smiling person—a little too smiley, perhaps." She didn't recall ever taking a trip with him or when she last saw him. Her only impression was of having been "a little put out." Put out about what, Mr. Nixon asked. "Well, I think the polite word for it is probably I think he was a sponger."

That was all Mr. Nixon wanted. Hiss thanked him for his courtesy. Mrs. Hiss, at any rate, had had an easy time; no rankling, no badgering of her past. "It all," she remarked, "seems very long ago and vague."

WHETHER or not the Committee still held the balance of credibility in doubt, there were other events happening in the meantime to tip it against Hiss. Between the 3rd of August, when Chambers first told his story, and the public confrontation of the 25th, the seven alleged members of the Chambers apparatus (the so-called Ware-Abt-Witt group) had been called before the Committee. All of them, except Donald Hiss, refused, under the protection of the Fifth Amendment, to answer whether or not they were Communists or had ever known most or all of the other members of the "spy ring." Donald Hiss freely admitted knowing most of the seven in an innocent, professional way, and he said he had never seen Whittaker Chambers in his brother's apartment. This left Alger Hiss as the one accused man who had asked to deny all knowledge of a conspiracy; who knew all of the others except one; who denied ever having been a Communist or knowing any of the others as such; who yet identified Chambers under a name he disavowed; and who now was obliged to bring witnesses to corroborate the existence of George Crosley.

THE public session in Washington on the 25th was everything Mr. Nixon and Mr. Stripling feared it might be. The caucus room of the Old House Office Building was packed to the doors long before the session began. It was a day of infernal heat. And for the most of ten hours the Committee and the witnesses sweltered in the atomic glare of television lights. The cameras buzzed and roamed like speculative flies over the dripping audience; catching open-mouthed citizens in moments of unsuspected prurience or vanity; demonstrating to countless households, up and down the Eastern seaboard, television's peculiar and terrifying gift for casting an intensely private eye on scenes of the utmost publicity; elbowing along the Committee table and taking long, revealing glances at the darkly handsome Mr. Nixon, the unmoving bald head of Mr. Parnell Thomas, and the skeptical shruggings, ash-flickings, and nose-rubbings of Mr. Karl Mundt, who came to the point of saying out loud that at first he had been charmed by Hiss but was now inclined to share his wife's view that he had been taken in by the man's "suavity."

The Committee's uneasy neutrality was running out. Hiss had brought along his lawyer. And since he seemed to respond now either like a guilty man refusing to be drawn into any declarative statement or like an innocent man using every legal aid to protect him against the day of a court hearing, the Committee broke through its imposed restraints and put the burden of proof unmistakably on Hiss. He antagonized them at the start by his maddeningly gentle refusals to say yes or no to questions that must have seemed to a stranger to entail no more than an ordinary memory for dates. He was here, was he not, in response to a subpoena? He had received the subpoena, yes. But he was here in response to it, wasn't that correct? "To the extent that my coming here quite voluntarily after having received the subpoena is in response to it,—I would accept that statement."

Hiss and Chambers were told to stand up.

Did Hiss know this man? "I identify him" as George Crosley. When did he so know him? "According to my best recollection"—and he would repeat that he had not had the opportunity to consult records—he first knew him some time in the winter of 1934 or 1935. When did he last see him? "Prefacing my answer with the same remarks," he would think some time in 1935.

They turned to Chambers. And then, as always through this harrowing day, he replied colloquially, casually, without a hint that he was implying legal ambiguities or expecting others to infer them. Did he know this man? He did. Who was he? Alger Hiss. When did he first meet him? He thought about 1934. When did he last see him? About 1938.

"Have a seat, Mr. Chambers," said Mr. Stripling.

There were two items that formed the core of the Committee's new suspicion. And for that reason, they are all we need to go into here. One was Hiss's urgent obligation to find somebody else who knew George Crosley. The other was his account of the 1929 Ford he had "thrown in" with the sublease of the apartment—a topic on which the Committee had already procured disturbing documentary evidence.

Of the three people formerly on the Nye Committee whom Hiss had suggested as being likely to recall George Crosley, a new York newspaper had been in touch with one, who reported he had no recollection that would help. The Committee confirmed that the second was dead, and announced that the third could not be traced. The Committee's investigators had also asked the Library of Congress to check their files for any articles written by George Crosley. The Library conscientiously replied that it had found nothing written and published by "George Crosley or Crossley" between 1929 and 1941. The Copyright Division had nothing. But in the Public Catalogue there were two references: a G. Crosley had written a book of poems in 1905, a G. E. Crosley, M.D., a pamphlet on ultra-violet light in 1936. (This was also the last authoritative trace of George Crosley, writer or onetime acquaintance of Alger Hiss.)

Hiss was asked to review his testimony about the car. His best recollection was that he had told Crosley he had an old car which had "practically no financial value"; that since his best recollection was that he had "at some time" both a Plymouth and the old Ford, there was no point in letting the Ford deteriorate on the street, as it had been doing for a year or two. What Crosley did with the car he frankly didn't know. His recollection was that he had a Plymouth "during part of the same time" that he had the Ford.

Mr. Stripling whipped out a certificate of title from the files of the local Motor Vehicles and Traffic Bureau. It showed that Hiss bought the Plymouth on the 7th of September 1935. Hiss protested that he had had no access to records and had always testified according to his best recollection. Mr. Nixon came in to remind him that he had been given a copy of all his testimony before the Committee. Hiss demurred. He had had it after "a long, hard pull." But he had received it forty-eight hours after the testimony was complete, had he not? "If it is 48 hours," said Hiss, "it is 48 hours." The record would show. Had he not had the testimony for the last five days? That was correct.

Mr. Nixon, the most watchful of all the Committeemen, was straining at the leash. He had only another minute to go before he was free of it forever. He would try again to get Hiss to say whether he gave the car or sold it, or threw it in, or transferred the title.

"Now, returning to the automobile, did you give Crosley a car?"

"I gave Crosley, according to my best recollection—"

"Well, now, just a moment on that point, I don't want to interrupt you on that 'to the best of my recollection,' but you certainly can testify 'Yes' or 'No' as to whether you gave Crosley a car. How many cars have you given away in your life, Mr. Hiss?"

An unfriendly laugh went round the room. Couldn't he recall whether he did or did not give Crosley that car? Hiss would say only that according to his best recollection "I definitely gave Crosley the use of the car, as I was able to give him the use of my apartment." Mr. Mundt reminded Hiss that on the 16th he had said: "sold him an automobile." Hiss acknowledged that if that was in the record, that was what he said. Mr. Mundt looked hard at him. "You certainly know, and we know that you know, whether you got that car back. . . ."

"You know a great deal, Mr. Mundt," was Hiss's comment.

Very well, then, Mr. Nixon would read every reference to the car there had been, in all the House testimony. He read pages of dialogue, and it led only to Hiss's objecting to the Committee's privileged access to records he hadn't seen. But he finally said that he "gave Crosley the use of the car" and that whether "I gave him the car outright, whether the car came back, I don't know." He would add that this transaction "coincided with the sublease," but it might have been later. Mr. Nixon wondered if it was likely he'd have given the car to Crosley after he failed to pay the rent. It might very well have happened, Hiss contended.

Mr. Nixon would not drop this issue, for a reason we were soon to see. The Committee was trying to persuade Hiss into a direct statement unprotected by the shield of "my best recollection," because it needed only a positive answer to be able to face Hiss with a positive refutation in the shape of a transfer of title (to the car) which bore the signature "Alger Hiss." The Committee had got a photostatic copy of this from the records of a motor company that Chambers had said was used by the Communist underground as an unobtrusive channel for passing on cars to needy organizers. A Committee investigator was put on the stand. He had been to a certain Cherner Motor Company, subpoenaed their records, and found that on July 23, 1936 (a year after the car was supposedly made available to Chambers) Alger Hiss had signed over the title of the car to the company, and that the same day the car was sold or transferred to one William Rosen, giving an address that the Committee had found to be false. There was no proof of a sale, no money was mentioned on the transfer to Rosen, but what was certain was that Hiss had assigned the car to the company and they had delivered it the same day to Rosen.

Hiss was put back on the stand. This was a gun barrel of explosive evidence, and Mr. Nixon's finger was on the trigger for an hour. But Hiss peered legally into the barrel and declined to see that the bullet bore his name. He did not like the idea of swearing to a signature on a photostat. He would prefer the original. The original, Mr. Stripling said, could not be removed from the Department of Motor Vehicles.

Hiss asked if they had it in their possession now, and Mr. Stripling assumed so. "Well," said the chairman, "if that were the original, would it look any more like your signature?" Another gust of laughter from the audience showed the way the wind was blowing.

The Committee had subpoenaed a man in the State Department who had notarized Hiss's signature. He knew Hiss, and Hiss knew him. Would he be likely to notarize a forged signature? Definitely not, said Hiss, and conceded it was his own hand. The Committee relaxed. Mr. Hébert spoke for it in asking if, now that his memory had been refreshed, Hiss could finally recall the transaction with the Ford. "No," he replied, "I have no present recollection of the disposition of the Ford."

Mr. Hébert pressed his lips together. "You are a remarkable and agile young man, Mr. Hiss," he said, and slumped back to fume.

In the afternoon any further disposition of the Committee to give equal weight to Hiss's credibility was almost visibly abandoned. Mr. Hébert enlarged on his observation about Hiss's "agility": "I repeat you are a very agile young man and a very clever young man and your conduct on all appearances before this committee has shown that you are very self-possessed and you know what you are doing and you know yourself why you are answering and how you are answering. Now, that is the reason why I am trying to find out exactly where the truth lies. I can't understand and I can't reconcile and resolve the situation that an individual of your intellect and your ability who gives to casual people his apartment, who tosses in an automobile, who doesn't know the laws of liability, who lends money to an individual just casually, is so cautious another time."

Of course, the Committee's documentary evidence had been damning. But more damning still to Hiss's reputation, or the hope of retrieving the respect he had in earlier sessions, was the persuasive psychological force of a hearing that had taken on the sound and appearance of a cross-examination in court. Hiss assisted this powerful deception by abruptly adopting the vocabulary of a trial session, evidently determined at last to fortify a legal case against any possible thrust of a perjury charge. One hundred and ninety-eight times, by the Committee's count, Hiss had qualified his replies with some such phrase as "According to my best recollection." The spectator had to shake himself from time to time out of this trance to appreciate that he was not in a court of law, that Hiss was not a defendant, that there was no right of rebuttal, no cross-examination of the accuser; that, in a word, it was the heyday of the public prosecutor (and in the wrong place). They went over everything, dredging up most of the previous testimony and putting it up to Hiss to certify the haul. At the end Hiss could only plead that the Committee would ask Chambers on his behalf where he now lived, where he had lived from 1930 on, and how long at each place; what was his given name and what names he had used since; what was his complete employment record with the Communist Party. Ask him, he said, for a bibliography of all his writings, ask him if he had been convicted for any crime. Ask him if he had ever been treated for any mental illness. Ask him about his marriage and how many children he had and where his wife lived now. Ask him "the circumstances under which he came in contact with this Committee and to make public all written memoranda which he may have handed to any representative of the committee. I would like to know whether he is willing . . . to make the statements so that I may test his veracity in a suit for slander or libel."

They asked Chambers all this, and much more, all except the last two questions, which by a curious irony had rounded off the last set speech Hiss was to make to this Committee in this investigation. These were to be answered soon enough and in another place, and not at the Committee's entreaty either.

Chambers was a very different witness. Placidly, directly, he ran through names and places, nodded assent, recited the whole charge with the air of a man sportingly reiterating a list of vital statistics before an insurance company that was sorry it had misplaced them. Only once did the inventory turn into confession, when his voice faltered and through tears he said he was testifying against his former friend "with remorse and pity, but in a moment of history in which this Nation now stands, so help me God, I could not do otherwise."

THREE days later the House Committee issued an interim report on its espionage hearings. It recorded its opinion that Hiss had "changed his position on the car and testified in a manner which to the Committee seemed vague and evasive"; that this "evasive testimony . . . raises a doubt as to other portions of his testimony . . . while Chambers, on the other hand, was for the most part forthright and emphatic in his answers"; that "the confrontation of the two men and the attendant testimony from both witnesses has definitely shifted the burden of proof from Chambers to Hiss, in the opinion of this Committee. Up to now, the verifiable portions of Chambers's testimony have stood up strongly; the verifiable portions of the Hiss' testimony have been badly shaken and are primarily refuted by the testimony of Hiss versus Hiss.''

TWO nights after this last hearing, Chambers appeared on a national radio program and said that Alger Hiss "was a Communist and may be now." Within the month, on the 27th of September, Hiss brought suit for defamation in Baltimore. Through the fall the public could assume that the affair would take the usual course of the law, which in America is leisurely to the extent of plunging the litigants into a busy obscurity from which frequent notices of postponement, trials, sentences, appeals, petitions, more appeals, periodically pluck them back to the attention of a surprised public. The best information from the tipsters in Washington was that the House Committee would let the case lapse. And after the Presidential election, which through the awful night of the 2nd of November shook the Republicans' grasp of the real world, it appeared that the House Committee itself might simply fade away. For the House of Representatives had gone over to the Democrats, which was one infallible reason why the Hon. Mr. Parnell Thomas would be unseated from his chairmanship.[1] Two other Republican members of the Committee, Mr. McDowell and Mr. Vail, were defeated for re-election.

But something happened during a pre-trial hearing in the Baltimore defamation suit that was to snatch the affair out of the hands of the Committee, throw it at the head of the Department of Justice and from there into the lap of a grand jury. Neither the public nor the House Committee heard at the time what took place in Baltimore on the 17th of November, and the public had no inkling of it until the 4th of December, when the newspapers were thrown into a tumult again by the report that Chambers had surrendered to the Committee what he swore were films of secret State documents passed to him by

---

[1] There was another. Later in the month he was indicted by a federal grand jury on four counts of having systematically "padded" his Congressional payroll. He was sentenced and sent to jail in December 1949, while Hiss was still in the middle of his Second Trial.

the spy ring. With two House investigators standing by, he had taken them on a dark December night out of a pumpkin on his farm. This circumstance seemed to add the final bathos to the Committee's gift for melodrama. To the administration faithful, warming to Mr. Truman again after his astounding re-election, the House Committee was as much of a butt as the dogged old Nevada prospectors who tried to mine silver in a hayfield. Mr. Nixon, it appeared, had signaled this wildcat strike by remote control from the Caribbean after he heard that Chambers and his lawyers had gone strangely mum on inquisitive reporters. Mr. Mundt flew in from South Dakota. The House Committee announced it had posted a twenty-four-hour guard on these historic "pumpkin papers." A week later some of these documents, all dated in 1938, were released to the press. Much good liberal and Democratic fun was had over such pearls as the news that the Germans and Italians had exchanged staff officers, that the Japanese had tried to buy a manganese mine on a Costa Rican island where no manganese was known to exist, that the American Consul General in Vienna had flashed the secret opinion (at a time when Europe was cowering before the impending Austrian démarche) that "it seems possible Hitler is seeking a foreign political triumph at the expense of Austria."

The playfulness over these documents was just as partisan as the Republicans' hunt for Communists had been. It was short-lived.

On the night that the Committee announced its strike (the 4th), Alger Hiss made a statement that looked too prosy to steal any headlines from the gorgeous scene in the pumpkin patch. He said that while Chambers was being examined by the Hiss lawyers in Baltimore, "Mr. Chambers produced certain documents which I consider of such importance that I directed my attorneys to place them at once before the Department of Justice." What did not become known for a week or more was that these documents were a wad of typewritten copies of State Department secret documents, and written memoranda that Chambers asserted were in Hiss's handwriting. This was the event of the 17th of November. Hiss's lawyers had challenged Chambers to show proof of his relationship with Hiss, and he produced these papers. By yielding them at once to the Department of Justice, what was in the papers became a Government secret, and Chambers would be under oath to say nothing about them.

The Department of Justice dared no longer fall in with the administration view that the "pumpkin papers" were an entertainment.

On the 4th it called back the New York grand jury, which had been comatose since October, and on the 6th showed them enlargements of the pumpkin microfilm. On the Sunday, the 5th, the House Committee went over the pumpkin microfilm enlargements with Mr. Sumner Welles, who had been Under Secretary of State at the time when they were assumed to have been stolen. He said to the House Committee two days later that these papers were in the most secret code and their transmission to a foreign power in 1938 would have been most perilous to the interests of the United States. The House Committee and the Department of Justice were now racing each other to see which could get there first with the most incriminating evidence. The grand jury subpoenaed Hiss and Chambers, and the Committee in chagrin called off an announced public hearing. All through the following week Hiss and Chambers were before the grand jury, and Mrs. Hiss appeared once. The House Committee, foiled of its star witnesses, called others and began to release the story of the typewritten documents and handwritten papers Chambers had forfeited in Baltimore. The Department of Justice glowered and thundered at the Committee for its "premature and ill-advised disclosures." President Truman, at a press conference, kept stubbornly to his line that the spy investigation had been a campaign red herring. With remarkable pointlessness at this stage, he announced that the House Committee was a dead agency.

On the 10th, Whittaker Chambers resigned from his job with *Time*. Mr. Nixon had been terrified for days that Chambers would be the one the grand jury would indict and "thereby probably destroy the only opportunity to indict other individuals, because the star witness will be an indicted and convicted person."

Three days later Hiss offered to resign from the presidency of the Carnegie Endowment. His offer was tabled and he was given three months' leave of absence with pay. On the 14th Mr. Adolf Berle was called before the grand jury.

Between the Baltimore documents now in the hands of the grand jury and any conclusion the jury might draw from them there was a missing link, which the public could not then know about. Since the 17th of November the F.B.I. had been chasing after the typewriter on which the Baltimore documents must have been copied. They did not find it, but they ascertained its make and the peculiarities of its typeface. What they did find in their ransacking of many old relationships of the Hisses were two letters typed long ago by Mrs. Hiss. These, too, were shown to the grand jury. And on Wednesday, the 15th of December, the last day of its statutory life,[1] the grand jury handed in an indictment. It read as follows:

The Grand Jury charges:

1. That, on the 15th day of December, 1948, at the Southern District of New York and within the jurisdiction of this Court, Alger Hiss, the defendant herein, having duly taken an oath before a competent tribunal, to wit, the Grand Jurors of the United States of America, duly impanelled and sworn in the United States District Court for the Southern District of New York, and inquiring for that district in a case then and there pending before said Grand Jurors in which a law of the United States authorizes an oath to be administered, that he would testify truly, did unlawfully, knowingly and wilfully, and contrary to said oath, state material matter which he did not believe to be true, that is to say:

2. That, at the time and place aforesaid, the said Grand Jurors, inquiring as aforesaid, were conducting an investigation, entitled *United States v. John Doe*, pertaining to possible violations of espionage laws of the United States and any other Federal criminal statutes.

3. That it was material to this investigation to ascertain whether the espionage or other statutes of the United States had been violated by the unlawful abstraction or removal of secret, confidential or restricted documents, writings, sketches, notes or other papers by persons employed by the United States Government, or by the furnishing, delivery, or transmittal of any such documents, writings, sketches, notes or other papers to any unauthorized persons, and whether the defendant Alger Hiss had any knowledge of any such violation.

4. That, at the time and place aforesaid, the defendant Alger Hiss, duly appearing as a witness before the said Grand Jurors, and then and there being under oath as aforesaid, and having been duly advised of the nature of the investigation then and there being conducted, testified falsely before said Grand Jurors with respect to the aforesaid material matter, as follows:

Q. Mr. Hiss, you have probably been asked this question before, but I should like to ask the question again. At any time did you, or Mrs. Hiss in your presence, turn any documents of the State Department or any other Government organization, or copies of any other Government organization, over to Whittaker Chambers?

---

[1] Another hundred talesmen were ready to form a new grand jury if the old one felt its investigation was unfinished.

A. Never. Excepting, I assume, the title certificate to the Ford.

Q. In order to clarify it, would that be the only exception?

A. The only exception.

JUROR: To nobody else did you turn over any documents, to any other person?

THE WITNESS: And to no other unauthorized person. I certainly could have to other officials.

That the aforesaid testimony of the defendant, as he then and there well knew and believed, was untrue in that the defendant, being then and there employed in the Department of State, in or about the months of February and March, 1938, furnished, delivered and transmitted to one Jay David Whittaker Chambers, who was not then and there a person authorized to receive the same, copies of numerous secret, confidential and restricted documents, writings, notes and other papers, the originals of which had theretofore been removed and abstracted from the possession and custody of the Department of State, in violation of Title 18, U.S. Code, Section 1621.

COUNT TWO

1. The Grand Jury realleges all of the allegations of paragraphs 1, 2 and 3 of the First Count of the Indictment.

2. That, at the time and place aforesaid, the defendant Alger Hiss, duly appearing as a witness before said Grand Jurors, and there and then being under oath as aforesaid, and having been duly advised of the nature of the investigation then and there being conducted, testified falsely before said Grand Jurors with respect to the aforesaid material matter, as follows:

Q. Now, Mr. Hiss, Mr. Chambers says that he obtained typewritten copies of official State documents from you.

A. I know he has.

Q. Did you ever see Mr. Chambers after you entered into the State Department?

A. I do not believe I did. I cannot swear that I did not see him some time, say, in the fall of '36. And I entered the State Department September 1, 1936.

Q. Now, you say possibly in the fall of '36?

A. That would be possible.

Q. Can you say definitely with reference to the winter of '36, I mean, say, December '36?

A. Yes, I think I can say definitely I did not see him.

Q. Can you say definitely that you did not see him after January 1, 1937?

A. Yes, I think I can definitely say that.

MR. WHEARTY: Understanding, of course, exclusive of the House hearings and exclusive of the Grand Jury.

THE WITNESS: Oh, yes.

That the aforesaid testimony of the defendant, as he then and there well knew and believed, was untrue in that the defendant did, in fact, see and converse with the said Mr. Chambers in or about the months of February and March, 1938, in violation of Title 18, U.S. Code, Section 1621.

THE grand jury's indictment confirmed the House Committee's judgment but did not excuse its procedures, especially its inability or disinclination to do anything about the leakage of private testimony to the newspapers. Before Hiss was indicted by the grand jury, before indeed most people knew there was one sitting, his name was a by-word and his reputation already very seriously damaged. It is fair to say that some of this damage had been done by Hiss himself, but it was the kind of self-inflicted harm that any witness at bay might do to himself. The point is that in a country which holds to the grand-jury system no man, however suspect, ought to have to perform a preliminary rescue of his innocence before a public tribunal. This was pitifully clear at the time and there was some brave indignation about it; but the good that might have come out of it was recruited into the rival crusades that were then forming to martyrize Hiss or Chambers. The guilt or innocence of Alger Hiss was not the test of the House Committee's conduct. What ought to have come from the editorial anger, and the lamentations in Congress, was a new law to ensure that a thoroughly innocent man would not lose his job and his good name before a grand jury had the chance to indict or exonerate him. That the Congress, in a nation where legislation is initiated by Congress, has a right and duty to hold wide investigations is beyond dispute; and that the press is free to be as informative as it chooses is theoretically undeniable. How is it, then, that in practice these two excellent freedoms can together compound the personal ruin of innocent men?

The question is all too easily answered. The more unjust a Committee happens to be in its procedures, and the more "dramatic" the conflicts between witnesses and Committeemen over issues that are publicly exciting, the more easily and unconsciously will the Committee room be accepted by the people as a court of law. In a Senate investigation into "loyalty" in the State Department, which the conviction of Alger Hiss and a subsequent kind word about him from the Secretary of State brought into being in 1950, the chairman one day made an interesting slip: "at this very serious trial—er, hearing." The *New York Times* the next morning reported that the chairman had vindicated the suspected man "from the bench." The reader will recall, too, Representative Rankin's profound misconception that the House Committee was a grand jury. He was unfortunately righter in fact than he knew. For the real mischief of a Congressional committee irresponsibly run amounts to this: that when it is investigating matters beyond the reach of the statute of limitations, it levels at suspect witnesses (by indirectly impugning their security and their good name) an oblique threat of attainder; and when it is investigating matters within the reach of the statute of limitations, it is directly usurping the function of the grand jury. So far the citizen's only protection against these risks is the tact or magnanimity of the chairman in deciding when to retire into private session. It is clearly too frail a protection for the witness in the waiting-room. Even the most sympathetic and informed of foreign observers have paused to shudder at the fate of an American's liberties that lie outside the protection of the courts. "Whatever else may be said for the American system," writes Denis Brogan, "it has signally failed to tame the American people's passion for interference, with or without due process of law, with the rights of others . . . such rights as the courts do not protect are held on very poor security indeed, whether they be of property or of liberty." [1]

There is only one fair solution of this dilemma: the enactment of new laws. Between the indictment and the First Trial, Senator Scott Lucas tried without success, in a resolution brought before the Senate in January 1949, to set a binding code of fair practices for all Congressional committees. He suggested that anyone should have the legal right to appear before a committee that had heard him accused; the right to compel the committee to subpoena up to four persons in his defense; and the right of a stenographic transcript of the testimony. I wonder if this approach would not tend to help irresponsible Committees even further along in their imposture of a court of law.

---

[1] *Government of the People*, page 31.

It would be better, I think, to limit public hearings, ban all forms of news photography,[1] and forbid public hearings altogether for some defined sorts of testimony (that, for instance, attacking the character of absent persons). It seems fair enough to forbid a committee to accuse anyone in its printed reports who has not been acquainted with the charge and had the chance to defend himself. The reader will already sense that once committees were restored to a prescribed dignity in their conduct, the fundamental problem would remain of restricting the press reports of them. As long as there are public hearings, there is bound to be good and bad, responsible and malevolent, newspaper accounts. A revision of the libel and slander laws, as they apply to the press, has been long overdue. And I can see no good argument against forbidding the publication of anything "alleged" to have gone on at a private hearing, or against holding newspapers responsible for airing such leaks.

The popular ferment over these issues was diverted, over the winter of 1949, into drumming up campaigns for and against Congressional investigations, and lining people up in immovable positions on the side of Hiss or Chambers. From these passionate irrelevancies we were rescued, after several legal delays, on the last day of May 1949, when the Trial of Alger Hiss began.

---

[1] Representative John S. Wood, Democrat, of Georgia, the new chairman of the House Committee in the 81st Congress, announced at the end of January 1949 that henceforth radio recorders, newsreels, television and news photographers would be barred from the Committee's hearings.

PART FOUR

THE FIRST TRIAL

❋

The trial of all crimes, except in cases of impeachment, shall be by jury, and such trial shall be held in the State where the said crimes shall have been committed. . . .

—The Constitution of the United States of America,
Article III, Section 2

In all criminal prosecutions, the accused shall enjoy the right to a speedy and public trial, by an impartial jury of the State and district wherein the crime shall have been committed . . . and to be informed of the nature and cause of the accusation; to be confronted with the witnesses against him; to have compulsory process for obtaining witnesses in his favor, and to have the assistance of counsel for his defense.

—The Bill of Rights, Article VI

AT

The United States District Court, Southern District of New York

UNITED STATES OF AMERICA
v.
ALGER HISS, Defendant

Judge:—

Hon. Samuel H. Kaufman, District Judge
and a Jury

New York City, Tuesday, May 31, 1949
at 11.30 o'clock a.m.

Appearances:—

For the Government—

John F. X. McGohey, Esq., United States Attorney
By Thomas F. Murphy, Esq., Assistant United States Attorney
Thomas J. Donegan, Esq., Special Assistant to the Attorney
General

For the Defendant—

Debevoise, Plimpton & McLean, Esqs., Attorneys for the Defendant

Lloyd Paul Stryker, Esq.
Edward C. McLean, Esq.
Harold Rosenwald, Esq.
Harold Shapero, Esq., of Counsel

THE JURY

❋

A barrier to the tyranny of popular magistrates in a popular govern-
ment. . . . —ALEXANDER HAMILTON

The glory of the English law. . . . —BLACKSTONE

The jury makes the orderly administration of justice virtually im-
possible. . . . —JUDGE JEROME FRANK

NOW at last this affair had come to the place where the popular
suspicion of innocence or guilt should start, not end: to a court of law.
Nothing by this time could undo the mischief already done to Hiss's
reputation. But here he would have what he had craved, what was no
more than his due: his own counsel and witnesses. He would have
order, and the protections of the common law, and a presumption in
favor of his innocence. And here at any rate the restless mob could
come, a little shamefacedly, to be put back into the old-fashioned
shafts of the judicial system.

A press photographer was turned away at the door of the courtroom by a scowling marshal. The courtroom itself was a handsomely
paneled chamber with green leather chairs, with pilasters and pedi-
ments recalling the democratic beast to the eighteenth century and
the graceful Virginians who helped devise this government of laws.
It was designed to seat no more than about a hundred and fifty
meditative folk who could sit upright, forgo tobacco, and restrain
themselves from their normal attitudes of rest and amusement. This
puts quite a strain on the American male, and by the time the bailiff

came through the judge's door, the assembled talesmen and cramped reporters were sitting forward with the obedient, bulgy-eyed look of a baseball crowd marooned in a Sunday school. The judge came in, a pink, genial rabbit of a man, who almost vanished behind the high bench. A melancholy clerk looked to see that everybody was standing and read: "Hear ye, hear ye! All persons having business with the United States District Court, Southern District of New York, draw near, give your attention, and you shall be heard." We sat down. The clerk spun the drum and started calling names.

All morning the judge rocked in his big chair, and the counsel passed the board of names back and forth. Altogether some forty-odd talesmen were called and most of them were found wanting. Twenty-nine of them confessed to being mortal on the grounds of prejudice towards Communists or former Communists. One big-browed man of obvious intelligence came through to the last hurdle. But a lifted eyebrow from the judge made him think again. He admitted he was afraid after all he did have certain preconceptions about Communism, and especially about Mr. Chambers, which might blur his judgment. He was excused and strode blushing from the courtroom.

There was an unreal moment when one troubled candidate, not quite sure whether to dump his coat and lean back with the chosen ones, asked and was given time out to consult his conscience. In the context of l'affaire Hiss this indulgence had the originality of an invocation to prayer in the middle of a bullfight. Judge Kaufman put his fingertips together and breathed tactfully down at his papers. The counsel consulted their watches and fingernails. The spectators stared at the talesman. The clerk of the court scrutinized the flag drooping beside the bench. All that could be heard, far off like the sigh of angels, was the whir of the air-conditioning. The talesman looked up and whispered that his conscience was clear. The Government waived its challenge. And another juryman was seated.

After about two and a quarter hours the inviolate dozen had been hand-picked, ten men and two women. They swore they had no connections with or opinions about the counsel, the Government, the Luce publishing empire (publishers of *Time*). They found themselves to be without prejudice, bias, or possible preconceptions about the House Un-American Activities Committee, any other branch of the Government or agency of the law, any of the public figures who had appeared or might appear in this case, any sympathy or antipathy to the principals. They were sure they could weigh the testimony of a sworn Communist as impartially as that of any other man. They positively had emerged unconvinced and unseduced either way, by any newspaper report or radio comment or neighborly talk.

These twelve incorruptibles included:

A General Motors manager,
A marine accountant,
An office manager,
A gasoline delivery superintendent,
A credit analyst,
A (lady) real-estate broker,
A clerk,
A dressmaker,
A production manager,
An unemployed hotel manager,
A secretary,
A mail-advertising man.

No wily capitalists or Communist-hunters these; just twelve of the ordinary saints looking on. The list was closed, the disqualified candidates who were left made for the door, and the newspapermen spread out. The judge told the jury they would not talk about the case, or let other people discuss it with them; that they would "so far as humanly possible do justice as between the parties in the light of the evidence and the instructions that are going to be given you by the Court." Two alternates were chosen. And since Mr. Lloyd Stryker, for the defendant, was impatient to take up one or two "purely law matters" (including the dismissal of the indictment, no less), the judge bobbed to the jury to leave for the day. A woman alternate nervously wanted to know if during the time of her service (it might be two or three weeks, the judge thought) she would be free to go home and meet her ever-loving spouse. Indeed she would, said the judge, and the jury retired.

A PLEA FOR DISMISSAL

❄

THE well of the court was formed by two wooden palisades that started at the walls and curved in two regular arcs to a central aisle. Behind the well were six rows of benches. The well was lined on one side with a jury box of two rising tiers, on the other by two rows of green leather chairs for privileged guests. Filling the middle of the well were two long rectangular tables, placed parallel to the judge's high bench. At the front one sat the counsel for the prosecution; at the rear table, the counsel for the defense. Behind them again, and immediately inside the palisade, sat the defendant. On one side of the bench, nearest the jury, was the witness stand. On the other side, the American flag, surmounted by a gilt eagle. This was the uniform pattern in all the handsome courtrooms of this thirty-story Federal Court House.

Once the jury had left, the Government lawyers, at the front table, slumped comfortably in their chairs, while a bustle at the rear table and some whispered shuffling of papers ended in a small, burly man rising and shooting his cuffs as he moved towards the jury box and faced the bench. From now on, whenever he was on his feet, he was to dominate the courtroom, and that indeed had been his career. Eleven years before, Lloyd Paul Stryker, defense attorney for Hiss, had been the gallant and, in the end, the weeping defender of the late Jimmy Hines, a famous Democratic district leader. It was a classic case meant to prove that the then profitable rackets, which levied tribute on every New Yorker who bought food or sent his linen to a laundry, could never stay in business if they were not able to rely on the protection of political leaders and perhaps even of the courts.

Hines was convicted, the thesis proved, and Tammany was dealt, as it is every ten years, a mortal blow. This was all accomplished by the cunning prosecuting talent of one Thomas Edmund Dewey. Indeed, the day of the verdict, when Mr. Stryker had exhausted his famous vox humana appeal and stood tearfully over the ruined Hines, and when Mr. Dewey stood in a corner beaming at reporters, was the day when this dark young man with the toothbrush mustache began to get those ideas about the White House that enticed him down a tantalizing decade.

Mr. Stryker, however, was wonderfully well recovered from this and similar humiliations. His bristly white hair grew in front to a single strand of rope, combed down like Caesar's; and he began to move easily around the courtroom with the proprietary air of an elder Roman senator managing to convey to the spectators, if not to the bench, that he had been called upon to share the dispensation of justice with the presiding judge. Judge Kaufman was quietly amenable to this treatment and leaned attentively as Mr. Stryker moved to dismiss the indictment on the following grounds:

1. That the testimony on which Mr. Hiss was indicted had come on the last day of the grand jury's life and so could not possibly obstruct justice, whereas it was written into the perjury statute, "and in the federal laws by a long series of enactments . . . that the testimony alleged to be false must in some wise obstruct justice."

2. That the testimony was not material, because the grand jury was looking into espionage, any evidence of which had long since been barred by the three-year limit of the statute of limitations; and because the supposed espionage was done in Baltimore, "in a district over which the Grand Jurors of the Southern District of New York have no jurisdiction whatever."

The judge thought that "it may be" the grand jury was looking into espionage "not necessarily for the purpose of finding the indictment but for the purpose of finding facts." Mr. Stryker ducked his head in appraisal of the judge's point. But he also had a point. A man is indicted for burglary, say. He says he "didn't have six jimmies and . . . climb the second-story window." And he is acquitted. "The Government may not then wreak its vengeance by . . . turning around and indicting him for perjury in that he falsely said he did not commit burglary." Similarly, "if the Government fails in one of its quests in convicting somebody, it can't turn around and have some more fun and indict the man for perjury." The analogy, he maintained, was "complete and perfect" and he had, if the judge cared to see them, "several very excellent memoranda of law" which an assistant was preparing. He frankly expected the judge might take these motions under advisement rather than rush into a dismissal right away. Judge Kaufman nodded to Mr. Stryker for his considerateness and conveyed that he rather thought he might prefer to wait and ponder. In great good spirits, everybody bowed and tiptoed out of the courtroom.

THE OPENINGS

❀

THE newspaper reports and pictures of the first day's proceedings had reminded people that the trial of our times was about to begin. And on the day of the openings, there was a gaping crowd on the steps of the courthouse and a long queue lined up inside the lobby. Long before half past eleven, the court was packed and the only moving figures were the ushers and the marshal, scrutinizing the green passes of the newsmen, challenging gate-crashers, keeping a disciplinary eye roving over the fanning women, the Daumier neck-craners, and those listless morons with open shirts and granular eyelids who manage to shuffle into the back benches of every courtroom in the world. The counsel and their assistants strolled in wheeling files and carrying briefcases. And then Mr. Stryker. And then a slim, handsome man and a small woman seated themselves in the well of the court and smiled and chatted with the defense counsel. The man sat back and looked around and folded his arms. And there was a rustle of sibilants as people put their heads together or half rose and pronounced his name.

It was not hard to see, after watching him for a while, why those who whispered knowingly about his positive guilt seemed oafish. He had what anyone must envy who has come to know that youth is a bloom that sags and vanishes if there is no good bone to let it rest on. He had a fine articulation of chin and mouth and brow and nose that would defy softening tissue and leave him handsome at eighty. Only the eyes failed to match the serenity of his bone structure. They were deep-set and agile. But the rest of him was all in style. There was nothing gangling or boorish about him. He had one of those bodies that without being at all imposing or foppish seem to illustrate the finesse

of the human mechanism. He moved instinctively towards the eco-
nomical gesture, and whatever he did had a rather charming gravity
and grace: when he deferred with a dark smile to some lady tapping
across the well of the court; when he unfolded his handkerchief and
wiped his nose; when he uncrossed his legs, and his head tilted over to
the left, as a lever effortlessly helping his left ankle onto his right knee.
In any society, a very striking member. In this, surely he was of that
species which exists in the teeth of the American democratic theory
and is yet another human proof of the superiority of matter over
mind: an American gentleman, one of the incomparable human
products, all the rarer for the heavy parodies that crowd it out, the
glossy tailored caricatures of metropolitan society, and for its non-
appearance ever in the movies, except by accident and unwittingly
as a cowboy, a farmer, a "character" part. Here was a subject for
Henry James: a product of New World courtesy, with a gentle certi-
tude of behavior, a ready warmth, a brighter and naïver grace than the
more trenchant, fatigued, confident, or worldlier English prototypes.

All this was deducible from watching him, provided the watcher
presumed his innocence. I sat next, at the Second Trial, a well-known
American journalist who exercised his privilege to think otherwise.
He never said so, but he spent most of his time in court laboring over
what he took to be pencil portraits. He was, I imagine, probably the
worst cartoonist, amateur or professional, in America. What in a
promising but untrained hand might have been a primitive power
was in this man gross incompetence. He showed me with preening
pride a drawing of what he saw as Hiss. He had, without of course
having the skill to do it deliberately, foreshortened the forehead and
slanted it at an apish angle. The eyes were slits emerging from the
ears. The ears were a squirrel's, flat against the head. The mouth was
an acromegalic pout. It was a roughhand sketch of Neanderthal man,
or Frankenstein's monster drawn with the toes. Between this conception of Hiss and the man I saw was the range of prejudice, from the
eye to the brain, that the spectators spanned once they had got a good
look at him.

We rose for the judge, the clerk again did his old English chant—
"Hear ye, hear ye!" We drew near and gave our attention. And after a
whispered discussion at the bench between the judge and counsel,
Judge Kaufman stroked his bow tie and smiled. "Will you proceed,
Mr. Murphy?"

MR. Thomas Murphy, the Government prosecutor, was a towering hulk of a man in a double-breasted suit, and at first glance a baffling sight in an American court of law. The big face with small round features, the hair line symmetrical as a wig, the walrus mustache that slept peacefully between his nostrils and where his lower lip must be; and above all, the mild blue eyes: all this balanced on a vast straight back and sprawling limbs composed the regulation type of a conscientious British guards officer watching for any tactics not in keeping with the dignity of a court-martial. But when he came to his feet and opened his mouth, the likeness collapsed. If he recalled anything English at all, it was the solid guardian of the law whose midnight shadow ambles down every village lane quieting the fears of all good men and true. A big, odd-looking, unpretentious man with a sun-tan, a golf-club playing captain probably, whom Mr. Stryker, squared back in his chair, could look on with the pleasant condescension of a star performer in the wings for the promising youngster who opens the show.

Very simply Mr. Murphy recited what all the best handbooks lay down as the ritual differences in function between the judge, the counsel, and the jury. Fortunately, he said, "our respective jobs . . . are pretty well defined, so one does not overlap the other."

What was this case about? The Government charged that the defendant had lied twice: once when he said he never gave documents to Whittaker Chambers, and again when he said he never "saw or conversed" with the man after the 1st of January 1937.

"How are we going to prove that?" They would prove it just as you would prove a child of yours lied. "Lying, as we know, is a sort of mental process. It goes on underneath the bone and hair . . . it is not like taking a photograph. We are not going to give you photographs of the man lying. We are going to prove it." If a child of yours came home and said he was in school on Tuesday, and you found the child was marked absent, "that would make you begin to doubt, at least, that the child was telling the truth. But then if you pressed it a little further and you found your brother saw the child in a movie on that day, I daresay you would come to the conclusion, rather rightly, that the child was lying."

That was what they would do here. Mr. Chambers would appear and say "in the most explicit fashion that . . . over a period of time from 1937 and part of 1938, this defendant, violating his sworn duty, handed over secret and confidential documents to him, Chambers, a Communist, when obviously he did not have any right to them at all. He handed them over in wholesale fashion." It was not "just a little thing that happened one afternoon or two afternoons." The jury would be shown 65 typewritten sheets, either copies or paraphrases of original State Department documents, 47 in number, dated in the first three months of 1938. They were all secret, one of them so secret that the Government could not let them see it.

And how would the Government show Chambers was telling the truth? Because they had the documents and would have the State Department men confirm that they were identical with highly confidential documents on file in the Department. These documents were typewritten. "You can see immediately that the question of a typewriter, ownership of the typewriter, became important." Chambers would say that Mrs. Hiss typed them by arrangement between the three of them. Hiss brought them home, Mrs. Hiss typed them, Hiss took them back the next morning. F.B.I. agents had asked Mr. Hiss if he had a typewriter. Yes, he said he had. He couldn't remember the make, but he thought it might be an Underwood that his wife got from her father, a retired insurance agent. Hiss thought he had it in the different houses they lived in, and he had put "the end of 1938 as about the last time he saw it." His wife, he thought, had given it away then or sold it to a second-hand-typewriter dealer in Washington. That was his recollection on the 4th of December 1948.

The F.B.I. scoured the city but couldn't find it; "they shook down the City of Washington to a fare-thee-well," between twenty-five and thirty agents. But no typewriter. But they were able to find papers and letters from the Hisses "that were obviously written on that typewriter at or about" the time the documents were typed. One was a letter to a school where their little boy was going. Another was a letter to an insurance company. The third was a speech Mrs. Hiss prepared for her college alumnae association.

Mr. Hiss came forward and offered a specimen "he thinks comes from that same typewriter." Armed with these, the F.B.I. experts found out, and would so testify, that 64 out of the 65 sheets "were undoubtedly typed on a Woodstock typewriter, pica type, 10 letters to the inch." One paper [1] had been done on another typewriter.

---

[1] Henceforth to be known throughout the Trials as Baltimore Exhibit No. 10.

"Now," said Mr. Murphy, and where some lawyers would bend forward for the catch he reared back and looked down, dropping his voice: "if we prove to you, as Mr. Chambers will, that he got the documents from Hiss, and we prove that they were typed on a typewriter in his possession or control, and that the documents themselves came from the State Department, and some of them right from his office, I daresay you will be convinced that Hiss lied in the grand jury."

There were also four handwritten documents, on small bits of paper, which Chambers said he had from Hiss. They were notations on documents Hiss hadn't an opportunity "of extracting."

Chambers would explain the procedure that was agreed on in New York City between him and Hiss and a man by the name of Colonel Bykov. Hiss would take from the State Department documents "relating generally to Germany" and give them to Chambers, who in turn was to photograph them or have them photographed and turn over the developed microfilm to Colonel Bykov. This went on "for many, many weeks," but not enough material was coming to them that way because "Chambers would only come to Hiss's home perhaps every ten days or two weeks, and he would take that night only the documents that Hiss had brought home that night." The documents had to be returned each morning, "so you can see that in the whole period of ten days or two weeks quite a few documents were not going back to Bykov." So they decided to have Mrs. Hiss "copy or paraphrase" the daily batch and deliver these to Chambers along with the originals available on the days that he called. Thus there were three types of documents: typewritten copies, photographs of originals, and handwritten notes. Hiss would admit that three of these last "look like his," but the Government would prove "conclusively that all four are in his handwriting," from comparison with a questionnaire they had which Hiss had filled out when he became a lawyer.

There would be other witnesses than Mr. Chambers who would corroborate his story in detail. But, said Mr. Murphy, stroking his walrus, he was going to ask them to be extremely patient when he put Chambers on the stand. He would want them to hear his complete story, "as I have done." Otherwise they would be in no position to test his credibility. "Bear in mind," Mr. Murphy admonished, his bushy eyebrows up, "that Chambers has testified for almost—not testified, but cross-examined for—1300 and some odd pages." [1] He had testified before the House Committee. His testimony before the House Committee was published and available to the defendant to prepare his case.

"Now when you've heard all of this testimony I want you then to go back . . . and see on which side the truth lies. I want you to examine Chambers. I want you to listen attentively; watch his conduct on the stand; watch the color of his face; watch the way his features move, because"—and here Mr. Murphy, raising his voice, handed Mr. Stryker the sort of admission a defense attorney prays for—"if you *don't believe Chambers* then we have *no case* under the Federal perjury rule."

That was no more than the judge would tell them: "you need one witness plus corroboration, and if one of the props goes, out goes the case."

The Government would welcome, "actually welcomes, a searching cross-examination" of Chambers. The Government asked them to "examine what motive he would have for lying, and I daresay you will be convinced as I am that he is telling the truth and that what Mr. Hiss told the grand jury were lies."

FIVE minutes later the court was reassembled, the jury came back, and after Mr. Murphy's modest effort the knowing ones licked their lips at the vintage prospect of a Stryker opening.

Mr. Stryker paced over to the jury box, buttoned his coat, and dramatically welcomed the absence of dramatics. "The days of the Klieg lights, the television, and all the paraphernalia, the propaganda which surrounded the beginning of this story are over." Here they were in a "dignified, calm and quiet and fair court of justice."

He turned and strolled thoughtfully beside the rail. He agreed with a great many statements made by his learned friend Mr. Murphy. He would point out, however, that the indictment carried a bill of particulars, which the Court had asked for, which "made it perfectly plain" that the times when it was alleged, in the second count, that Hiss saw Chambers were the times when the documents

---

[1] Before the Hiss lawyers in the Baltimore pre-trial hearing.

were supposed to have been passed. "So that really then, although stated in two counts, the charge is a simple one. . . . Did Hiss testify truthfully that he did not give or hand restricted documents to Chambers?" That was all there was to it.

Mr. Stryker was quick to receive with open arms Mr. Murphy's closing admission: "if you don't believe Chambers the Government has no case." The whole issue was thus reduced, by the Government's own confession, to a determination of "whether or not you believe Chambers."

He agreed with Mr. Murphy on another point, about the child being in a movie when he said he was not. He agreed with Mr. Murphy's "commonsense way" of solving that problem. "That is just what I think, if I may say so, you should do."

This was all suspiciously amiable, but Mr. Stryker coughed and turned on his heel and added his own touch. "Now, suppose a dearly beloved child was charged with some delinquency or other, what would be the first line of approach? . . . you would want to know, wouldn't you, who was the person that made this charge against your child? What kind of a person is he? Is he an honest man? Had he been a God-fearing, truth-loving and truth-telling man? How did he live? What had he done?" They would surely want to know this, to consider the accuser and the accused.

So, said Mr. Stryker, scanning the twelve faces with visible admiration, they would hear from a man by the name of Chambers who —"I gather from the prosecution's opening and from the charge in the indictment"—would say he received these documents. Well, Mr. Stryker would lay before them "in the most straightforward way" all the evidence in his possession to help them judge between the accused and his accuser. Mr. Stryker would like the jury to consider him their servant.

By the way, they had better know that an indictment "itself imports nothing, proves nothing . . . every man and woman in this country is presumed to be innocent until the contrary is shown beyond a reasonable doubt." Not like "some Continental countries, Russia for example." We are, he declaimed, turning fervently towards the bench and the drooping flag, "in the United States of America living under the blessed stars and stripes with all the blessed heritage of liberty and justice that has come down to us."

Mr. Stryker was overcome for a moment. Then he knitted his brows. "Now, I was about to say, who is the accused?" What was his life, what had he done? He would tell them.

Alger Hiss was born in Maryland in 1904. If he was not mistaken, it was on the 11th of November, long before "that date has the significance that it has to some of us old timers." He was educated in the public schools, went on to Johns Hopkins University "with honor, with credit, with distinction, with high honors, winning the approval, the trust, the confidence, and the favorable opinion of all who knew him." So it had been ever afterwards, at Harvard Law School—"his conduct was such and scholarship was such that" he was put on the board of the *Harvard Law Review*. And then, out of some five or six hundred, he was chosen for a post "given only to a young man not only of signal scholarship but of character: the post of secretary to the great Justice Oliver Wendell Holmes." Up to this point, said Mr. Stryker, everyone had believed in this young man and trusted him. And now he was to be "trusted with secrets, the revelation of which might bring infinite disaster to various people or to the Court itself."

Mr. Stryker marched proudly to the end of the box. He wheeled and pointed a short straight arm at Hiss, listening intently. Mr. Stryker reddened and threw his eyes up to heaven and cried: "Well, Alger Hiss was good enough for Oliver Wendell Holmes, and of the many character witnesses I shall call, if the case gets that far, I shall summon with all due reverence the shade of that great member of the Supreme Court."

Mr. Stryker resumed his pacing and went on numbering the laurels of the Hiss career. Member of a distinguished law firm in New York. Then to Washington to join the A.A.A., the "Agricultural Adjustment something, whatever it is." Then counsel for a Senate investigating committee. Again trusted, again found to be "a man of honor, a man of high integrity." Then to the Solicitor General's office of the United States. Then to the State Department. And again trusted, "as he matured and grew older, trusted more and more." Trusted so much that he came under the eye of the President of the United States. And so as an adviser at the Yalta Conference.

Mr. Stryker raised his small, fine hands, bringing an offering of an honorable man. "As people live," he said gently, "so they are. I mean, a person could get by maybe a year or six months, but here the years roll on." Now Hiss was chosen secretary of the Dumbarton Oaks

Conference, which began to work out the Charter of the United Nations. "He was weighed in that crucible and not found wanting." He did so well that he was sent out to organize the great conference at San Francisco. "There in his hands were countless secret documents of the most important character belonging to his country. Again he was weighed in the balance and not found wanting." And who was chosen to take the original charter back to the President of the United States?—"Why, it was Alger Hiss."

And then what happened? Many years ago a great philanthropist, Andrew Carnegie, set up an endowment for international peace and for its first president was chosen "one of the greatest statesmen we have had in a century, Elihu Root." When he died, "a great gentleman of this city [Nicholas Murray Butler], president of a great university," was chosen as the second president. And when *he* died, the trustees (who are "not stupid men") looked around "to get the best man they could in America, the most trustworthy man." They selected Alger Hiss.

Mr. Stryker lifted his right arm as if to swear a terrible oath. "I will take Alger Hiss," he cried, "by the hand, and I will lead him before you from the date of his birth down to this hour even, though I would go through the valley of the shadow of death I will fear no evil, because there is no blot or blemish on him."

Mr. Stryker broke his devotional stance and walked up the court looking warily over the spectators.

"Now who," he asked, "is the accuser?" And he turned again.

He was a man "who now styles himself J. Whittaker Chambers," who "began changing names early," before he was a Communist. When he became one, he made "a considered choice." He chose to join a conspiracy to overthrow the United States "by any means," especially by lying. For twelve long years this man Chambers, "alias Adams, alias Crosley, alias Cantwell, alias a great many other things . . . was a member of this low-down, nefarious, filthy conspiracy . . . against the land that I love and you love." He cheated his Government on income taxes and "filed no returns for the money he was being paid for the prostitution of his soul." He wrote a "filthy despicable play" in college, about Jesus Christ, and was dismissed. And how did he get back? By lying.

This was the man who out of the blue in 1948, "in the summer time, the first man in the world," accused Alger Hiss.

What else? Quite a lot. This man said he got the documents in
1938, yet Mr. Stryker would prove this man had said under oath more
than once that he left the Communist Party in 1937. When the
House Committee asked him how he knew Hiss was a Communist
(Mr. Stryker lifted a bound volume of testimony and held it at arm's
length, like an infidel's Bible, and read from it):

"Question: How do you know?"

"Answer: Because somebody told me."

Mr. Stryker bounced the volume contemptuously on the table.

And now Chambers was asked if he had any other factual evidence.
And what did he say? He said: "Nothing excepting that he accepted
party discipline." Long after the Committee hearings, he "concocted . . . this phantasmagoria about Bykov and these documents." That was on the 17th of November. He had a strong duty to
tell that story to the Committee. But what did he offer in evidence?
"Nothing, nothing, nothing, and he is under oath." Also under oath,
and with "unction," he had told the Committee he was now "a God-
fearing man."

And what did Hiss do? Did he skulk? Did he hope nothing would
be done about it? (Mr. Stryker glared for a moment at the jury to see
if anyone dared suppose Hiss was that kind of animal.) No, he telegraphed the Committee and went and testified and denied the charge
—"the spontaneous reaction of an honest man." Then they showed
him a picture of this fellow, whom he couldn't identify. He said he
would like to see the man, and he did so, and he said: "That's the
man Crosley, whom I knew in 1934."

It was one o'clock and the judge wondered how much longer Mr.
Stryker was going to take.

Mr. Stryker wished to "abide by your Honor's and the jury's
wishes," but the jury looked benign. So he coughed and promised to
be brief.

Well, said Mr. Stryker, what's said before a Congressional Committee is said on privilege. So Alger Hiss dared Chambers to say the
same things in public. And he did say them—"of course, nothing
about espionage"—and then Alger Hiss sued, "the good old-fashioned
thing for an American to do to sustain his honor." Chambers was then
called to Baltimore by Hiss's lawyers and repeated, under oath, substantially the same story.

"Now," said Mr. Stryker, watching the clock and everybody's lunch cooling, "follow me; now follow me. His wife is called as a witness. She and Chambers had concocted and drawn up a perjurious written statement to aid her in her recollection. And when she was asked to see how she could do without her husband's memorandum, well, she went to pieces. She cried. The libel suit was going on the rocks. That was on the 16th of November of last year, and then on the following day, for the first time in the history of the world . . . he (Chambers) then says, 'Well, I have been in turmoil the last week, and . . . I could not even depose at this time.' " But now finally he had decided to tell it. Sixteen times he had had a chance to tell about espionage, to Mr. Berle in 1939, to the F.B.I., to the State Department's security officer, to the Committee, to the grand jury; and now, when a libel suit is "tumbling around his head," for the first time he tells about the documents. And what did Alger Hiss do? He slapped a libel suit on Chambers, and it was he, Hiss—not Chambers—who insisted the "authorities" should know about them. "Is that the conduct of a guilty man?"

And when Hiss was asked about a typewriter, "he bent heaven and earth through my good friend here, Ed McLean, a stalwart lawyer," and told him to get the typewriter if he could find it. Hiss would suppress nothing. "And here are these F.B.I. fellows, and let us see, what did Mr. Murphy say they did . . . turned Washington upside down?—something like that wasn't it, Mr. Murphy?"

"Pretty close," Mr. Murphy murmured at his table.

"Shook it down?" the judge suggested.

Mr. Stryker gave a short nod. "Well," he said, "we haven't the opportunities for shaking anything down that Mr. Chambers had, but we happened to have a stalwart, honest man . . . just a lawyer; and he went down to Washington time and again. He inspected garrets and he poked around in cellars . . . and at last"—Mr. Stryker took in the whole court with a look of pleasant scorn—"he found it and produced it from the then owner, a truckman who had gotten it through a long series of colored servants that they (the Hisses) had."

Mr. Stryker put his thumbs in his vest and announced that he had the typewriter in his possession and he would "consent under such reasonable provisions as his Honor may prescribe to let these F.B.I. eyes who couldn't find it come down and look at it all they want."

Was *that* the conduct of a guilty man?

"Mr. Stryker," said the little judge, popping up over the bench, "I think we'll have to adjourn now."

On Mr. Stryker's promise to be through in two minutes, the judge went out of sight again.

Well, there was much more, but he was going to let these ladies and gentlemen get their lunch. Suffice it to say that Mr. Hiss found Chambers to be "a glib and interesting talker. Mr. Chambers is all that. You will hear him. He is a very able man. He is a writer, a dramatic writer. Alger Hiss was interested in what he thought was another Jack London." There was no one to warn Alger Hiss, "as I now am alerting you." Mr. Stryker paused at the corner of the jury box. He roared into his peroration:

"In the warm southern countries, you know, where they have leprosy, sometimes you will hear on the streets among the lepers a man crying down the street."

Mr. Stryker lifted his eyebrows and his voice into a plaintive wail.

" 'Unclean, unclean,' at the approach of a leper. I say the same to you at the approach of this moral leper.

"Thank you."

THE WASHINGTON HOMES

OF ALGER AND PRISCILLA HISS

1934 through 1938—
[from the telephone company's records of
connections and disconnections]

3411 O Street, N.W. up to June 9, 1934

2831 Twenty-eighth Street, N.W. . . . . from June 9, 1934
to July 2, 1935

2905 P Street, N.W. . . . . from April 19, 1935
to June 15, 1936

(duplicate connection between April 19 to July 2)

1245 30th Street, N.W. from July 1, 1936
to December 29, 1936

3415 Volta Place, N.W. . . . . from November 29, 1937
to November 1, 1943

THE CASE FOR THE GOVERNMENT

❧

IT was agreed at the start to exclude all witnesses from the court-room, except Mrs. Hiss, who so far had sat inside the well next to the defendant. Mr. Murphy began by taking the precaution of seeing that the text of the indictment, and some relevant statistics, could go into the record undisputed. He called the secretary of the grand jury, and two of the court stenographers who had taken the record on the 15th of December. He called employees of Washington telephone, electricity and gas light companies, who produced documents from their files to fix the dates of Hiss's various residences.[1] Mr. Stryker made a masterly show through all this of being tolerantly bored and baffled. If the jury could take it, his lolling pose seemed to say, so could he. At one point he was shown a document, found it inexplicable, and gestured to the painstaking Mr. Murphy: "Go ahead, go ahead."

While everybody else was tapping pencils and watching the clerk of the court stamp these exhibits, the judge asked for the next witness, and to the astonishment of the yawning spectators a fat, sad-looking man in a baggy blue suit walked in from a door behind the bench and took the stand. It was Whittaker Chambers. The agency reporters came to with a bound. And Hiss folded his arms and lifted his chin. Some of the previous testimony had been strangely inaudible, an irritation it was possible to ascribe to the weird acoustics that are often the price of high ceilings and elegant paneling. But suddenly, as a stopping clock makes you aware for the first time of its ticking,

---

[1] See opposite.

121

the air-conditioning went off and the voices swam suddenly into focus in a pool of dead silence.

"Mr. Chambers," Mr. Murphy began in a low, casual voice, "when were you born?"

He was born on the 1st of April 1901, in Philadelphia. His parents moved to New York when he was still a small child, and he spent most of his boyhood years at a village on Long Island called Lynbrook. After high school at a neighboring village, he went to Columbia University. He'd meant to go to Williams and went up there to take an examination in German, but after only one day he decided it was an expensive place and he came back and entered Columbia, to take a liberal-arts course. That would be 1920, he thought. He edited a literary magazine and left college at the beginning of his junior year. He drifted for a while and, in the summer of 1923, he believed, went to Europe with two other students. He went to Germany, to Belgium, to France, and then back home.

Mr. Murphy leaned forward very slightly.

"As a result of that trip and what you saw, did it leave any impression with you?"

Mr. Stryker jumped to his feet.

"I object to that. Suppose it did?"

"Sustained," said the judge.

Chambers quietly replied: "It left a profound impression."

Mr. Stryker was on his feet again striding towards the witness. He thrust a red face at Chambers. "Just a moment, you heard the Judge rule."

"Just a moment, Mr. Stryker," the judge protested.

Mr. Murphy was not to be left out. "Wait a minute," he shouted, "I object to Mr. Stryker arguing with the witness."

"Mr. Stryker," the judge admonished, looking hard at him, "please address your remarks to the Court."

"I am sorry," said Mr. Stryker with his head up.

Mr. Murphy stretched himself.

"And you too, Mr. Murphy," said the judge.

Mr. Murphy was sorry too. This was only the first of countless such flurries, which at first served the purpose of demonstrating Mr. Stryker's bouncing alertness to the rules. Later they undoubtedly fetched some sympathy for Mr. Murphy, if not for the witness.

Mr. Stryker slumped again in his chair and Mr. Murphy went on quietly coaxing from Chambers the details of his political education. He started on an impressively casual recital of his reading, and of his study of Fabian Socialism.

"Of what?" snapped Mr. Stryker.

"Fabian Socialism," drawled Chambers.

Mr. Stryker sniffed. "Oh, that," he seemed to say.

Mr. Murphy got from Chambers that he had written a play at Columbia under the pseudonym of John Kelly and that after it appeared in a college magazine he had "had difficulties" with his dean and subsequently left the college. He re-entered it again when he returned from Europe and got an evening job at the public library to help him meet his fees. He had had no religious upbringing and there came a time when he thought of joining the Communist Party. He did join it and got the humble job of collecting from news-stands unsold copies of the *Daily Worker*, for which he subsequently went to work as a writer, taking stories from the daily papers and giving them "a Communist slant." In time he became the foreign-news editor.

It seemed he would go on unhindered with his life as a Communist, but Mr. Stryker abruptly came to his feet and protested on what turned out to be a crucial point of law. The jury was dismissed. And Mr. Murphy, sensing the drift of Mr. Stryker's coming objection, prepared to fight it. Mr. Stryker thought that by this time Chambers had been sufficiently identified as a Communist and that what he did with his party friends in the years before he met Alger Hiss had no bearing on the charge. Mr. Murphy admitted he meant to tell the story of Chambers's Communist life all the way from his conversion, through the Hiss episode, to his defection. He thought it would be an injustice to the Government if he was required to stop "in 1925 or 1926 . . . and jump right to 1938." The judge assumed, correctly, that Chambers would charge Hiss with being a Communist and say he had met him through his party activities. The judge doubted whether such a line was admissible, because "the Court of Appeals in this State has held that the calling of one a Communist is a libel *per se*." But what worried him most was the prospect of getting away from the issue of the indictment, and the propriety of letting the Government supply a motive "for a charge with which we are not concerned in this case." Mr. Murphy thought it all came down to a simple rule of law, which Judge Learned Hand had once commented on: that if in proving the ultimate crime other crimes are proved, "it is just unfortunate." Mr. Stryker came in at last to say that Mr. Murphy was confused, whereas his Honor's conception of the law was completely correct. The rule was that if other crimes are "sufficiently closely connected in point of time and place" so as to be an integral part of the crime *sub judice*, then such evidence as Mr. Murphy's ought to be allowed. But the Court could not allow "merely prejudicial testimony just because the Government thinks it's fun to put it in."

Mr. Murphy, standing at the bench, was mildly outraged. He said in a loud voice he was not having half as much fun as Mr. Stryker. Judge Kaufman leaned over the bench and chided Mr. Stryker for an "ill-advised" comment. Mr. Stryker shook his white head and thought so too. It would be much more help, the judge said, "if we did not indulge in personalities." Mr. Stryker groaned out his regrets. He was sorry for it, he was tired. "I am sure I do not mean," he said, stalking off round the room and snapping invisible suspenders, "that he is having fun at all."

Mr. Murphy inhaled a breath of patience through the ensuing laughter and thought better of it.

Judge Kaufman took Mr. Stryker's last point, but thought this was a different situation. Mr. Murphy went on to say that he had no intention of proving a crime merely by proving an association with Communists: "as far as we know to date it is not a crime to be a Communist." But Mr. Stryker said he was not willing by holding his tongue to appear to acquiesce in testimony that might be something the witness knew or that might be hearsay.

The judge was unhappy about the whole thing and said he would willingly receive instruction, which Mr. Stryker was delighted to offer in the form of a legal memorandum he would submit the next morning. The judge agreed, and Mr. Stryker and his legal beavers hurried off to sweat it out through the night over what the judge called "one of the most important points in the case."

THE next morning Mr. Stryker delivered his memorandum and the day began with a long argument in chambers. Mr. Murphy felt that credibility was so important that it was essential for the jury to hear the whole of Chambers's Communist story. The judge felt that since the jury had no means of checking it, it might be "self-serving." If it was so for the direct examination, Mr. Murphy warned, so it would be for the cross-examination. But the judge thought that what was sauce for the goose was not always sauce for the gander, a worldly proposition that Mr. Murphy applied as a proof of his growing belief that in the federal courts "the rules of evidence apply against the Government and not the defendant." Judge Kaufman repented enough to decide that he would let Mr. Murphy "sketch" the rest of Chambers's career up to his meeting with Hiss, but not in the detail of the previous day. "Fine," said Mr. Murphy, and the judge and counsel came into court.

Mr. Murphy stationed himself again at the far end of the jury box, the imperturbable Chambers locked his fingers across his lap, and Mr. Murphy settled down to several hours of questioning, which, except for the scornful challenges of Mr. Stryker (who kept up a guerrilla cry of "immaterial" or "a conclusion" or "irrelevant" or "speculative") brought from Chambers an unbroken tale of Communist plotting. Before the day was done we had heard in well-remembered detail the steps—Tawney, the Webbs, G. D. H. Cole—by which he had been led to read the *Communist Manifesto* and a pamphlet (*The Soviet at Work*) that brought him into the Communist Party; his work as a free-lance translator; his marriage to one Esther Shemitz, a Communist sympathizer; his discharge from the public library on the false charge of having stolen books; his entry into the Communist "underground" early in 1934; his first meeting with Hiss that spring or summer; the long friendship with the Hisses; the assignation in New York with Colonel Bykov to arrange the theft of State papers; the method of photographing them, the copying of them on Mrs. Hiss's typewriter; the subsequent disillusion of Chambers with the party, his attempts to woo the Hisses away with him, and the scene when Hiss had wept and refused. He said all he had said before the House Committee and much more. He sat there, heavy-lidded, cool, and capacious, answering—and, until he got the trick of yes or no, opining—in an easy conversational tone. He threw off names and dates so generously that Judge Kaufman had some of them struck out as prejudicial.

He met the Hisses when they were living in the Twenty-eighth Street apartment, saw Hiss about once a fortnight thereafter, always at his home. He never went to his Government office, either when he was with the Agricultural Adjustment Administration or when he moved to the munitions investigation. When the Hisses moved to the P Street house, they suggested that Chambers should live in the Twenty-eighth Street apartment until the lease expired. There was no talk of rent. He and his wife and three-year-old daughter took them up on it. They brought down with them from Baltimore the baby's collapsible bathtub, a high chair, and other baby things. Mrs. Hiss once came for lunch. They lived there till June maybe, and moved up to New York to stay in the apartment of one of Chambers's old student friends, Meyer Schapiro. After that they went to a community called Smithtown [1] on the Pennsylvania side of the Delaware River.

While Hiss was working for the Nye Committee (the Senate munitions investigation), Chambers said he had a conversation with him to arrange for Hiss to procure documents from the State Department in the name of the Nye Committee. Soon afterwards Hiss gave him documents so obtained. He photographed them and returned them and turned the developed films over to a man called J. Peters. Chambers had said this man was present at his first meeting with Hiss.

Mr. Stryker was watching like a cat for the dreaded identification of Peters, and when Mr. Murphy wondered if he might ask "when he first met J. Peters," Mr. Stryker sprang to his feet crying: "Pardon me. If your Honor please, I made an objection in what I thought was a timely fashion, anticipating exactly what happened. All of this testimony had no relevancy or materiality whatever to the charge in the indictment and I move to strike it all out."

The judge denied the motion, and Mr. Stryker plumped down again very much unrelieved. The judge intervened a little later to wonder if the witness was testifying that in a period of over a year's acquaintance with Hiss he could remember only two conversations with him. This was a false inference and Mr. Murphy hotly protested it. He asked Chambers if he could recall any others. At that moment he didn't think he could. But he was going on to say: "I think it is natural—" Mr. Stryker objected "to what he thinks is natural," and the phrase was struck out. It was plain that even under his golfer's tan Mr. Murphy was beginning to bridle. The judge was

---

[1] In the Second Trial, it was spelled in the record *Smithton*.

calling the strike-outs on him as doggedly as a Yankee umpire on a Dodger hero.

At last Mr. Murphy was able to get from Chambers that some time early in the spring of 1935 he came up on the train from Washington to New York with Hiss, to meet a Colonel Lamb. Another time he met Hiss in New York, and they went to a movie house in Brooklyn, there by prearrangement to meet Colonel Bykov. They walked along by Prospect Park to the Grand Army Plaza and presently reached Chinatown and went to a restaurant.

"Who is Colonel Bykov?" Mr. Murphy asked. And again Judge Kaufman would not allow an identification. The judge himself took on the delicate job of getting Chambers to describe this conspiracy without leaving any implications or "conclusions" about the leading role of Colonel Bykov. Chambers had barely mentioned that the meeting in the movie house was "to make the original connections," when Mr. Stryker leaped on the word, and "connections" was struck out. The judge wondered if anything was said about who Colonel Bykov was. And Mr. Stryker came roaring in again on Chambers's reply: "There was no reason for such a conversation." It was struck out.

Mr. Murphy, heaving with impatience by now, reluctantly went back to an earlier conversation, in the recounting of which Chambers was at last able to get in that Colonel Bykov was "the head of the underground apparatus with which I was then connected and with which Alger Hiss would also be connected." Had he known Bykov before this meeting? Yes, he had. The Colonel had told him, some time around Christmas 1936, to buy some rugs. He got his friend Meyer Schapiro to buy four Oriental rugs from an Armenian in New York and have them dispatched to a George Silverman in Washington. One of them—a bright rug with a small pattern—had gone to Alger Hiss. Chambers swore he had seen it in a closet of the Hiss home at Thirtieth Street. He added, in his matter-of-fact way, that "the rug was a present from the Soviet people in gratitude for the work of the American Communists."

Thereafter, at the Chinatown meeting in New York, Colonel Bykov told Hiss that the Soviet Union was "threatened greatly by the rise of Fascism" and that if Hiss could get documents out of the State Department files he would be helping greatly in the defense of the Soviet Union. Hiss was asked "point blank" if he could get them.

He said he could and he did. There was a suggestion from the Colonel that Donald Hiss might also be able to get some, but Alger Hiss replied that " 'he was not sure his brother was yet sufficiently developed for that.' "

So from about February 1937 on, Hiss began to pass documents, cablegrams, reports, and dispatches. Chambers photographed the early batches, which he picked up about every ten days, and later got somebody else to photograph them. This was done in Baltimore, most of it by a Felix Inslerman. The originals went back to Hiss, and the photographs went to Bykov. Some time in the summer of 1937, at Bykov's suggestion, the procedure was changed, in order to get more material. The new system was what Mr. Murphy had mentioned in his opening: Hiss brought home documents every day, his wife typed them, and these made a mounting pile to add to the originals Hiss brought home on the days of Chambers's visits. Chambers said both the originals and the typewritten copies were photographed, and he then returned the originals and destroyed the typewritten copies of the others. This system went on until "shortly before I broke with the Communist Party in April, 1938." (He had first said before the House Committee that he broke in 1937. He had given the same date, and denied being an espionage agent, twice to the F.B.I.—once in 1942 and again in 1945. Judge Kaufman thought this discrepancy was very material to the case; and later on in the trial he acquainted the jury with these inconsistencies made in F.B.I. reports.) Chambers was not allowed to say what caused him to break. But he did say that he left the place he'd been living and went into hiding in another place in Baltimore, on "the old Court Road." He kept some of the Hiss documents—both typed and filmed—put them in an envelope, and sent them to his wife's nephew, Nathan Levine, a New York attorney. He told him to put them away in a safe place. Shortly afterwards Chambers and his family drove to Florida, "thinking that that was a good miscellaneous place to disappear." He drove down there in a car he'd bought on a trade-in in the fall of 1937.

"Was it a new or used car?" Mr. Murphy asked.

"It was a new car."

"Do you remember how much you paid for it?"

"Something like $800 or $900, I believe."

"And did you trade in another car with it?"

"I did."

"Where did you get the money to pay for that car?"

"Part of the money was given to me by Alger Hiss."

"How much?"

"$400."

In Florida he translated from the German a book about the founder of the Red Cross. The following spring he got a job on *Time* magazine as a book reviewer, through the offices of an old friend, Robert Cantwell (whose real name, Lloyd Cantwell, Chambers himself at one time used). He came to be a senior editor of *Time*, and that is what he was when he resigned in December 1948, by which time he was earning about thirty thousand dollars a year. He bought a farm in Westminster, Maryland, about 1940, and he had gone down there at one time for a long spell when he had a breakdown, diagnosed as a heart condition. When he broke with the Communists, he became an Episcopalian, and later joined the Quakers.

Mr. Murphy suddenly turned to the early days of the friendship with the Hisses and asked if "Mr. Hiss at any time *gave* you an automobile." No, said Chambers, he did not. But Hiss gave him the use of his Ford roadster while they were in Washington in 1935.

"Did you ever have any conversation with Mr. Hiss about the disposition of that car?" asked Mr. Murphy. Mr. Stryker was up in an instant and the counsel went up to the bench out of the jury's hearing. When Mr. Murphy walked back to his post, he was visibly disgruntled at the judge's decision to exclude any mention of what Hiss was supposed to have done with the car.

Chambers was now asked if he had ever taken any extended trips with Hiss. He said he had and told of a trip with Mr. and Mrs. Hiss up to Peterboro in New Hampshire, to see Harry Dexter White. He recalled this trip particularly, because they had seen a summer stock company perform *She Stoops to Conquer*. They stayed overnight.

Mr. Murphy's lieutenants at the front table put their heads together, nodded, and held a small package ready for Mr. Murphy's final topic. Mr. Murphy put the back of his hand on his waist and nonchalantly asked Chambers to say if the envelope he had sent for safekeeping to Nathan Levine contained typed documents and some developed films.—That was right.—And did he receive them from Mr. Hiss at his Volta Place residence?—Yes, he did. Mr. Murphy walked over to his table and took the package from an assistant. Very distinctly Mr. Murphy told Chambers he was going to show him a number of documents and he was to say whether or not these were the documents they were talking about.

Chambers leaned forward, the audience stirred, and Mr. Murphy walked to the witness stand and handed Chambers a big dirty brown envelope. For many minutes Chambers bent over the documents, coolly turned the pages, read on and on, shuffled them, stacked them, and handed them back to Mr. Murphy.

"And what," asked Mr. Murphy, "is your answer?"

"Yes, these are the documents."

In the same way Mr. Murphy took two little rolls of film and asked Chambers to examine them. He cocked his large head and squinted at them. He thought he'd need a magnifying glass to identify them. All right, said Mr. Murphy, "subject to correction let them be marked."

Mr. Murphy walked back again and smoothed out the rumpled folds of coat that rippled like contour plowing across the enormous acreage of his back.

"Mr. Chambers," he said brightly, "when was the last time prior to 1948 that you saw the defendant, Alger Hiss?"

"I saw Alger Hiss around Christmas, 1938."

"And where did you see him?"

"I saw him at his home on Volta Place."

"And did you have a conversation with him at that time?"

"I did."

"Did I ask you if anyone was present? If I didn't, I meant to."

"Mrs. Hiss was present."

After an objection, Chambers was allowed to give the substance of the conversation: which was to the effect that he urged the Hisses to break with the party, that they refused, that Hiss thought it a great pity Chambers should break, because he understood "a new and more important post was to be given to me." They also told Chambers that they knew who he was (he had been, so far as he knew, known to them only as Carl, but it was "possible" he had used the name of Crosley). They said no more about that, but Hiss asked Chambers what kind of a Christmas he expected to have. He had replied: "Rather a bleak one." Whereupon Hiss went away and came back with a little wooden rolling-pin as a present for Chambers's daughter.

Mr. Murphy was maneuvering now to spring the final, damning sentence. He got Chambers to tell again how he had produced the documents; how—when Mr. Marbury, Hiss's Baltimore lawyer—had requested any correspondence with Hiss he might have kept, he went up to Brooklyn, got the envelope from Levine, saw that it contained other things than correspondence and handwritten notes, couldn't decide whether or not to introduce the documents in evidence, and finally at his lawyer's persuasion did so. He readily admitted he had never testified anywhere about them before his Baltimore pre-trial hearing; and to a question from Judge Kaufman, he said that if he had been asked up to then either by the grand jury or the House Committee if he had any documents, he would have said no.

Mr. Murphy rested on his elbow and took his final tack. Did he know Mr. Adolf Berle?—Yes, he did, when Mr. Berle was an Assistant Secretary of State.

"Did you have a conversation with him in Washington?"

"I did."

"And in that conversation did you name the defendant Alger Hiss?"

"I did."

"Did you name him as a member of any political organization?"

"I named him as a member of the Communist Party."

"And did you name others?"

"Yes, I did."

Mr. Murphy dropped his huge frame into his chair with the muttered admission: "You may examine."

MR. STRYKER came out of his chair like a rocket that starts the firework show. The spectators responded with such a buzz at the thought of the marvels to come that Judge Kaufman had to quiet them down. Mr. Stryker ran a cupped hand down his stubbly forelock, tweaked his nose, flexed his knees, and shot out in a high tenor:

"Mr. Chambers, do you know what an oath is?"

He supposed he did. Well, what was his definition?—It was a declaration that a man makes when he promises to tell the truth.

"And in our courts," said Mr. Stryker, "it is an affirmation made by a man who calls on Almighty God to witness the truth of what he says, is that right?" Chambers agreed it was.

Mr. Stryker looked menacingly at a paper he was holding. "In the months through the month of October, 1937, you were an under-handed enemy of your country, doing what you could against its interests in favor of a foreign country, is that right?" Mr. Stryker jerked his ear around to catch the inevitable affirmative. Mr. Murphy rose to object, but the judge stoically remarked that this was cross-examination. Nobody knew it better than Mr. Stryker.

Yes, said Chambers. Mr. Stryker showed him a photostat of an oath of office he had taken when he got a job in Government, in the Works Progress Administration. Mr. Stryker put the paper to his nose, made a remark about the age of his eyes, and then held it off at arm's length against the light and read in a clarion voice: "I, Jay David Chambers, solemnly swear or affirm that I will support and defend the Constitution of the United States against all enemies, foreign and domestic, and that I will bear true faith and allegiance to the same; that I take this obligation freely, without any mental reservation or purpose of evasion, and that I will well and faithfully discharge the duties of the office of which I am to enter"—Mr. Stryker brought the paper down and held it at his side like a sword—"so help me God."

"That," said Mr. Stryker, tossing the hypocrisy onto Mr. Murphy's table, "was false from the beginning to the end, was it not, Mr. Chambers?"

"Of course," said Chambers.

"What?" spat Mr. Stryker.

"Of course."

"And it was perjury, wasn't it?"

"If you like."

"And you did it in order to deceive and cheat the United States Government . . . is that not true?"

"That is correct."

"Yes or no?"

"Perfectly true," said Chambers.

From an application form accompanying the oath, Mr. Stryker noted various omissions in the record of Chambers's education. He had, for instance, put in "summer courses in the University of Brussels," but had left out Columbia. Why was that, Mr. Stryker wanted to know.

"I think," said Chambers quite blithely, "probably I didn't want to be traced."

"You-didn't-want-to-be-traced? !" Mr. Stryker's voice hit the ceiling and he threw an incredulous stare at the jury. Mr. Murphy unwound his long legs and asked to talk to the bench. The counsel went to the bench, and when they came back, Mr. Stryker made a point for a while of not turning to the jury.

Still maintaining his air of outraged propriety, as if he had never heard such scandal in a courtroom, Mr. Stryker asked if Chambers had not written a play at Columbia that involved an offensive treatment of Christ. "Highly offensive," Chambers acknowledged. And had he not had to leave Columbia on account of it? He had. And then didn't he get back to Columbia by lying to the dean? He didn't remember that. He didn't eh? Mr. Stryker picked up a student letter written by Chambers, squinted and grunted over it, complained he couldn't read the writing, and so put upon Chambers the odium of reading aloud the sentence: "I lied to him quite simply and told him I wanted to teach history."

This was only an item in a dreary inventory of derelict experiences, which Mr. Stryker spent the next morning scavenging from the last thirty years of Chambers's apparently troubled life. Chambers admitted being charged with stealing books from the public library, whereas he had taken twenty or thirty from Columbia. He admitted living as a boy of seventeen in a noisome "dive" in New Orleans where a drunk and a prostitute also lived. He admitted living with a woman not his wife and bringing her to live with him in his mother's house on Long Island. He agreed he had once said that the reason his mother let him do this was "because she had lost one son and did not want to lose another." In a series of low monosyllables he admitted how he had refused to join a suicide pact with his brother Dick, who had killed himself by illuminating gas.

For the rest, he concurred with monotonous aplomb with most of Mr. Stryker's ringing propositions—that he had adopted many names; that he had been dedicated to the "wiping out of all religion"; that he was at all times, as an active Communist, an enemy of his country pledged to obey the party, if need be "to lie, to steal, to rob, or to go out into the streets and fight." He invariably replied in a level voice: "correct" or "that is right" and sometimes "of course" and "why, certainly." By noon it was thoroughly insinuated by Mr.

Stryker, and boredly conceded by Chambers, that so long as he was a Communist there was no honor in him, as the word is understood by Mr. Stryker's "ordinary God-fearing American citizen."

Now it appeared that Mr. Stryker would have to face the less rewarding job of meeting Chambers on the common ground of their Christian orthodoxy, for since about 1942 Chambers had been a Quaker. Slowing the pace to a comfortable, ironic strut, Mr. Stryker asked sweetly: "Then there came a time, did there, Mr. Chambers, when you repented and reformed and became a God-fearing citizen, is that right?" Yes, he had tried to.

"Just when did you reform and repent? What month?"

Chambers ruminated over his spiritual turmoil through the autumn and winter of 1937 and said that his repentance "took its final form" when he broke with the Communists in April 1938.

Mr. Stryker looked up at the high windows. "Your repentance and your regeneration was slow, right?"

"Perhaps it was comparatively fast."

"Has it been completed now, do you think?"

"Well, it never stopped. It never is in any man's life, is it?"

All right, said Mr. Stryker turning away, so "from that point on you had the same, decent attitude toward the oath an honest man would have, is that right?" That was true.

"And you did away with lying and stealing and all that, right?"

"Yes, I thought so."

Mr. Stryker tried to make something of Chambers's admitted practice, on the *Daily Worker*, of getting news out of the *New York Times* and rewriting it. Chambers implied it was the universal practice; he did the same thing on *Time*. He would not concede that rewriting with a new interpretation amounted to "falsifying and lying." The implication was so rich for the blood of the newspapermen in court that they crooned and chortled to the point where Judge Kaufman came up over the bench frowning for the first time.

Mr. Stryker went into a quiet passage in which he reminded Chambers of his introduction to a certain Isaac Don Levine, through whom—after the Nazi-Soviet Pact of 1939—he came to tell his story to Mr. Adolf Berle.

"Tell me," asked Mr. Stryker, circling around his prey, "in that talk with Mr. Berle did you say anything about knowing or seeing a Colonel Byk—Bayk—Beck-ov and taking Mr. Hiss around through the wilds of Brooklyn . . . ?" He did not. And did he tell Mr. Berle that he had "confederated and conspired with Mr. Hiss" to get papers from the State Department? He did not, no. So that when he swore before the House Committee that he had told Berle all he knew, that was a false statement?—Yes.

Mr. Stryker triumphantly abandoned his pincer movement and, seeing Chambers's new-found respectability centrally exposed, started a head-on attack.

"Did you have a high, God-fearing man's regard for an oath in August of 1948?"

"Yes."

Did he say anything to the State Department security officer, in 1944 and '45, about Bykov or the receipt of documents? No. Did he tell the F.B.I. on the several occasions he saw them? He did not.

"Well," snorted Mr. Stryker, a simple favorite exclamation he used as if it were the German *"also."* He turned his back on Chambers and said over the heads of the spectators: "Did you in October, 1948, testify before the grand jury in this building?" Yes, he did. And when he was asked there whether or not there had been any espionage, did he say there was not?

"I answered I had no knowledge of it."

Mr. Stryker read a section of the Baltimore deposition to prove that when the grand jury in New York had asked him, in October 1948, about espionage, he had replied he had "no direct knowledge of it." Mr. Stryker strutted grandly away from the uncomplaining form of Chambers.

"Then the fact is, is it not, that you were asked directly by the grand jury under oath whether there was any espionage, and you said you had no recollection?"

"That is right."

"Was that answer true or false?"

"That answer was false."

Mr. Stryker glanced at the clock. It pointed at two minutes to one. He took a great sniff and declaimed to a staggered courtroom: "Then you admit that you testified falsely and committed perjury before the grand jury in this building, is that right?"

"That is right," said Chambers, as easily as he had answered everything else.

Mr. Stryker buttoned his coat and looked again at the clock. "Your Honor," he said, "I would like to stop right there."

MR. STRYKER had the week-end to enjoy his triumph and was evidently full of it when he came back on a scorching Monday. For he began by playing another cadenza on a theme the audience was humming when it came in. We knew by now to the point of nausea about the long unhappy life of a brooding adolescent and a Communist unbound by a Christian oath. More than anything else, we knew that before the 17th of November 1948 he had told nobody about Bykov or about any espionage with Hiss. Yet Mr. Stryker kept turning over this melancholy story for any bad odors previously undetected.

All morning he commuted between the end of the jury box and the fat volumes of evidence from the House hearings and the Baltimore deposition. He got from Chambers the admission that before the House Committee he had "intended to suppress the fact of espionage," and of course said nothing to the House Committee about Bykov and State Department documents; that, by the same token, he had not told the House Committee the real purpose of his visits to the Hisses or given the proof he had to support his claim that Hiss was a Communist. Mr. Stryker was well pleased with these probings and began to chalk up the number of entailed perjuries. Other than those, there were innumerable discrepancies between dates and places Chambers had mentioned here and in previous testimony. Mr. Stryker sweated to add these to the score on perjury, but Chambers simply said his testimony in the past had been correct as far as it went, that he remembered things now he didn't remember then.

In spite of the clammy and oppressive heat, Chambers was noticeably more comfortable than he'd been on his first day on the stand. He had picked up the knack of answering only what he was asked. And he had gauged the harmless muzzle velocity of Mr. Stryker's professional anger. At one point, when Mr. Stryker asked him if he had not testified before the House Committee that Hiss lived at "Dent Place," Chambers said no he had not. Mr. Stryker showed him the printed record to prove it. The printed record, Chambers blandly remarked, was wrong.

Mr. Stryker went on combing through old testimony and eventually stirred the plot with some interesting new admissions. When Chambers had first unearthed the two strips of microfilm from his pumpkin, he had told the F.B.I. he could not recall the circumstances in which they were handed to him. He now swore that the documents photographed on that film had come to him from Hiss.

Mr. Stryker pressed him to recall again if he had ever "secretly disposed" of a typewriter. And he admitted that he had in 1940 taken a Remington portable onto a streetcar or subway or elevated and deliberately left it there, and that he had a motive for wanting to get rid of it.

Mr. Stryker now wanted to see some "mystical" significance in Chambers's feeling about the Christmas present of a child's rolling-pin, which Hiss had supposedly given him at their last meeting— their last meeting as conspirators. Wasn't the rolling-pin significant? No, it was not. Didn't it have "a curious connotation in your mind?" Chambers saw none and wearily asked Mr. Stryker not to try to read something in his mind. But Mr. Stryker often liked to use graphic language that turned out to be a forgotten coining of the witness himself. He pounced on a piece of testimony in which Chambers had confessed that the gift hurt his feelings and had added: "It was what you would give to a child of a renegade." Mr. Stryker read with an incredulous pathos the part of Chambers's testimony about keeping the knowledge of this present from his wife and child. Mr. Murphy could take only so much of it and protested: "Will Mr. Stryker read this straight, your Honor?"

His Honor so directed. And Mr. Stryker, a martyr in the great tradition of Serjeant Buzfuz, said: "Well, your Honor—I am sorry, but I will try to read it in a plain, boring way." Which he accordingly did, with even greater effect.

But Chambers would see no mysticism anywhere. And Mr. Stryker passed on to another melodrama. This was the incident in Brooklyn when Chambers went to reclaim the envelope he had entrusted to his wife's nephew and in it found—so he said—what had come to be the nub of the Government's case.

Yes, he had gone up there last November and Nathan Levine stood on the bathtub and reached into a window in the dumb-waiter shaft. Out of it he pulled an old envelope, which shed dust on the floor. Chambers took the envelope into the kitchen, and Levine went off to the bathroom with a dustpan and whiskbroom. Alone in the kitchen (a point that took several minutes to establish), Chambers opened the envelope and there found the two strips of microfilm, which he later secreted in the pumpkin. (Of course, he found, according to Chambers, everything else: the typewritten documents, the microfilm, and the handwritten memoranda. But Mr. Stryker had a purpose in concentrating on the microfilm.)

"On the 17th [of November] when you produced these typewritten documents that you say you got from Mr. Hiss, you did not produce the films?"

"That is correct."

"You held them back?"

"If you like to phrase it that way."

"I don't like anything but the truth."

"I kept the films."

"And you suppressed them from your lawyer?"

"I did not tell my lawyer."

Did he get right on the phone to the F.B.I., did he call up the Department of Justice?

"The answer is no."

With no success, Mr. Stryker tried to get him to say that he or somebody else had arranged the pumpkins (as the newspapers had reported) in a V-shape, with "this special pumpkin at the apex of the V." Chambers glumly said that if there was some arrangement or design to the pumpkins, it was made "only by Nature."

From the presumption that Chambers remained a devious character long after he had supposedly "repudiated Marx's doctrine and Lenin's tactics," Mr. Stryker was passing on to try to show that he was also either morbidly melodramatic or a clumsy fabricator. Mr. Stryker put into the record that while he was still supposedly conspiring with Hiss, Chambers had used his real name in the Baltimore telephone directory, on the registration of his wife's automobile, on a letter applying for a scholarship for his little girl, and on the application form for his Government job. That was perfectly right, said Chambers. Then Mr. Stryker recalled the alleged last meeting of Hiss and Chambers, in December 1938, when he got the insulting gift. Had he not said that the night he went out to the Hisses' he feared "an ambush"? Quite right.

And what did an ambush mean to Chambers? It meant "either kidnapping or assassination."

And who would do the assassinating, Mr. Hiss or possibly Mrs. Hiss?

"No, Mr. Alger Hiss and comrades."

But in fact, fearing an ambush, he had stayed to supper with a man he had told the House Committee was "a man of great gentleness and simplicity of character"!

Yes, that was Hiss's character. And yes, he had stayed to supper.

And had he not sworn also that—Mr. Stryker read again with a dramatic huskiness—"for a year I lived in hiding, sleeping by day and watching through the night with a gun or revolver within easy reach"?

He had so sworn, and it was true.

Mr. Stryker had hit his characteristic style again. He paced noiselessly up and down. So, he meditated, Chambers had been in hiding for a year, "not stirring out of doors or anything"?

"I stepped outdoors sometimes."

"Just on to the lawn, but not going anywhere?"

"Of course I went to New York on occasion."

Mr. Stryker could hardly believe his ears. "New York while in hiding?" Yes, he did.

"Did you go up in an armored car?"

Chambers turned disdainfully to the judge. Must he answer that question? The judge thought so.

"No, I did not come up in an armored car." Nor had he carried a shotgun.

Mr. Stryker frowned suspiciously.

"You are smiling."

"The facts that you are presenting are a little absurd."

But Mr. Stryker was going to make the most of them and he made scornful capital out of Chambers's public appearances in his dreaded term of penance: the thought of Chambers's coming to New York by daylight, walking about the streets, unarmed, going to Washington without a shotgun, all "in the light of the sun."

It was all very odd, Mr. Stryker implied. Odd enough perhaps to warrant looking for a hereditary strain. There had so far been no obvious connection between the trend of Mr. Stryker's cross-examination and a genial, big-featured man whose presence down front in the courtroom Mr. Murphy had at one point challenged. This man had not remained anonymous for long. At the end of the third day he was identified as Dr. Carl Binger, an eminent New York psychiatrist. Mr. Stryker now started to exchange occasional confidences with him, as he began to draw from Chambers the medical history of his family—a tactic clearly designed to build up a plausible body of facts that might suggest an emotionally pathological background.

What had happened to his maternal grandmother, with whom he had lived as a boy?—"She went insane."

What had his father died of? Chambers said he had died of a heart attack. Mr. Stryker produced the death certificate and noted that the father had died of chronic hepatitis.[1] Chambers had never heard of it. It is nothing psychiatrically alarming, being a liver condition, a sort of cirrhosis, which could have had no sinister significance in this trial unless it was associated with alcoholism. Mr. Stryker just let it stand in the record. He then went into the forlorn tale of Chambers's brother, who committed suicide after two previous attempts and left the sad, Shakespearian comment: "We were gentle people and incapable of coping with the world." Mr. Stryker saw great significance in Chambers's abnormal reaction to this death. And Chambers showed for once a kind of quiet irritation, a discomfort at having this tenderness probed. He admitted he had been "immobile" for several months after the suicide. Mr. Stryker wanted to pin the most literal definition of immobility on Chambers, but he denied he had lost the use of his arms and legs. What was immobile, he said, was "my will." He had expressed it in a poem he wrote just after his brother's death. The last three lines read:

> You know it is the cessation of motion in me I am waiting:
> And not the lack of love, or love of the sun's generation and the motions
> Of bodies, or their stasis, that keeps me—
> But my perfection for death I am waiting.

Mr. Stryker piled on the aspersions. Had he not also written at one time a poem called "Tandaradei"? He had. Mr. Stryker took it up fastidiously and confessed he would not care to read it aloud to a mixed jury. Chambers was forced to start on it and couldn't be heard. So the court reporter read it. It was undoubtedly an erotic tidbit, a Lawretian pastiche about a sexual embrace. But the court reporter

---

[1] Recognized officially later by the judge as nepatitis, which Dr. Binger subsequently refused to recognize as any known disease.

read it with no more passion that a butcher calling off the day's re-
frigerator inventory.

There was more about the books Chambers chose to translate,
some additional inferences silently drawn from further name-chang-
ing; and the fact was noted that Chambers had bought a car in New
York out of Communist funds and sold it to himself when he moved
to Maryland. Then on to his confessed breakdown while he was working with *Time*. Chambers had collapsed for seven months and stayed
most of the time at his Maryland farm, in bed, unable to shave, the
shades drawn. Although a doctor had diagnosed his condition as
angina pectoris, he proffered his own opinion that is was "merely
bodily fatigue."

If Mr. Stryker was building to some great conclusion in this,
either he was foiled by the clock or overnight he thought better of
it, in view of a ruling the judge announced to the jury the next morning.

Mr. Stryker had previously asked to see the record of the New
York grand jury minutes. The judge had thought this not permissible,
but he had promised to look them over for possible discrepancies.
He had done so and found some inconsistencies between what the
witness had said there in October and here at the Trial. He therefore
had allowed Mr. Stryker, for the defendant, to inspect these passages.
The result was that Mr. Stryker went off again on a detective hunt
through this testimony and got Chambers to concede seven specific
acts of perjury before the grand jury. All of it was meant to amplify
and stress the grand confession that Chambers had deliberately withheld the evidence of espionage from the House Committee and the
grand jury until, for one reason or another, the libel action forced
him to unearth it. Mr. Stryker had hit the peak of his cross-examination and he failed to embarrass Chambers into any admission that
his political characterization of Hiss, in his first statement to the
House Committee, was at all malignly intended to tip the scales of
the coming Presidential election. But he did read aloud a passage
from *Time* in 1945, announcing the appointment of Hiss to the San
Francisco Conference, and made Chambers admit that as an editor
of *Time*, reading that passage when he was supposed to be "a fighter
for your country," he had done nothing to warn the Government
about his old co-conspirator. Chambers weakly explained: "I didn't
think it was possible to interest anybody in the subject."

There was a long argument in chambers about Mr. Stryker's right to see the December minutes of the grand jury hearings, at which presumably Chambers had changed his testimony to tell about espionage. The judge let Mr. Stryker have some of them, and Mr. Stryker came back for a last orgy of attributing perjury. Chambers would confess only to mistakes, or better recollection, and not to any intention to lie.

Mr. Stryker was done. In the late afternoon he suddenly boomed: "That is all," and Mr. Murphy rose for the redirect examination.

Making no pretense to the dramatic agility of Mr. Stryker, the huge Mr. Murphy, impressive enough in his own guardsman's physique, was elaborately unfussed. His public emotions, he was there to imply, were those of any competent professional man with a daily job to do. And he clearly wanted to show that Chambers's perjuries were relatively harmless and honorably intended. He began at once to exhibit, with a sensible, no-nonsense air, Chambers's motive in keeping quiet for so long about the Hiss papers.

"Did you tell the grand jury in the month of December, 1948, why you hadn't told them before about Mr. Hiss and the documents?"

"I did."

"Well, then," Mr. Murphy said, standing back confidently relaxed, "tell this Court and jury."

As nearly as he could remember he had told them:

". . . in testifying from August on I had had two purposes: one was to disclose in part and to paralyze the Communist conspiracy; the other purpose was to preserve from injury in so far as I could all individuals in the past in that conspiracy. Any revelation involved injury, but I told them there are degrees of injury and I sought to keep them from the ultimate consequences of what they had done. I was particularly anxious not to injure Mr. Hiss any more than necessary out of grounds of past friendship and because he is by widespread consent a very able man. Therefore, I chose to jeopardize myself rather than reveal the full extent of his activities and those of others."

After three days we knew at last the answer that Mr. Stryker had failed to get. Chambers went on to recount the origin of the libel suit, his appearance in Baltimore before Hiss's lawyers, and how he came to produce the documents. He was asked by Hiss's lawyers for any handwritten correspondence to support his claim to knowing

Hiss. He found the handwritten memoranda (in Brooklyn) and other documents too. He had not up to that time made any charge that Hiss had given him papers. He produced the documents in response to the request of the Hiss lawyers.

And why had he got a job with the Government while he was still a Communist?—"My purpose . . . was twofold: . . . to to establish an identity for myself so that if ever I had to come out against the Communist Party, I would have established the fact that I was working in Washington at the time. My second and lesser purpose was to obtain extra funds whereby I might finance my break."

And now would he tell the Court and jury what was his view of the Communist Party at the time he joined it? (This was signaled by Mr. Murphy as a proper parry to Mr. Stryker's attempt to make Chambers say he had known it mainly as "a criminal conspiracy.")— "My view of the Communist Party was that it was the general staff of the world revolution. I at that time considered that the world was in such a state of social and political chaos that only a surgical operation could save civilization. It seemed to me that the Communist party had a persuasive analysis of the causes for that condition, and a course of action whereby to change the condition, and it offered to the individual an opportunity to help in the salvation of the world."

Mr. Murphy began to repair bit by bit the shredded character Mr. Stryker had left. He asked many questions about Chambers's personal life, encouraging, in a sporting, matter-of-fact way, the view that in taking on so many pseudonyms Chambers was abiding by normal Communist practice; that much of what was disreputable in Mr. Stryker's recital had been freely offered by Chambers in the long questioning of him at Baltimore by the Hiss lawyers; that to them, too, he had made available his medical and insurance records; that he had never connived with the House Committee investigators and had seen two of them once for only half an hour weeks before he was suddenly subpoenaed to appear in Washington; that he had testified there without having refreshed his recollection by referring to any records; that he certainly was not responsible for the Klieg lights and the hullabaloo; that he had been in a hospital only once, for a streptococcic throat, and had never seen a psychiatrist or been treated for a mental illness; that when he left that typewriter on a streetcar or elevated, it was because he had had it from an underground "apparatus" and he was simply "tired of being reminded of the past."

Whenever these passages required a little speech or recital of credo from Chambers, Mr. Murphy would stand with his head down, looking at his left shoe. It provoked a great calm in the courtroom and suggested that Mr. Murphy was not too proud to bow respectfully before a confession of heresy and a humble account of the steps of a touching regeneration. It unquestionably drew some of the melodramatic piety out of many of Mr. Stryker's "revelations," but also magnified, through the telephoto lens of a newly acquired sympathy, the great and perhaps inevitable misfortune of this trial: the unavoidable deception of reinterpreting in the political climate of 1949 the personal relationships and the political climate of the 1930's.

Mr. Murphy looked up and turned, in a livelier way, to more secular matters. He had Chambers describe the outside and the inside of the Hiss house on Volta Place, thus seeking to brush aside both the doubt that Mr. Stryker had cast on Chambers's memory of it, and the implication that the knowledge was only lately acquired. Chambers obliged with the most exact detail about its location on the street, the layout of the rooms, and such interior baubles as Hitchcock chairs, a gold mirror with an eagle on top, walls papered halfway with a mulberry pattern and the lower half paneled. He did the same for the Thirtieth Street house—"a small house set between two others . . . the entrance up a flight of steps," with a dining-room at the back of the house, a basement below street level. He had identified these houses again in a drive around Georgetown, his first in ten years, after the indictment. He had taken this trip with the F.B.I. and pointed the places out without prompting.

As for his not leaping to warn the Government about Hiss's appointment as Secretary General to the United Nations Conference at San Francisco, he had warned Mr. Berle back in 1939, he had warned Mr. Ray Murphy (the State Department security officer) early in 1945. All, he implied, to no avail.

There was danger ahead for the prosecution in the casual mention Chambers had made to Mr. Stryker of another "source" of documents in the State Department. He had identified the man as one Julian Wadleigh, in the Trade Agreements Section. Mr. Murphy now got Chambers to say as explicitly as possible that he was absolutely certain Wadleigh gave him none of the typewritten documents. The microfilm material was the kind that came from Hiss and he was "as certain as I can be" that none of them, either, came from Wadleigh.

At this point Judge Kaufman, who normally sat up there rocking as benevolently as an Easter bunny, turned sharply to Chambers and did the defense an unwitting service by eliciting the most surprising testimony of the day. He wanted Chambers to go over his recollection about the number of "sources of supply" he had in the whole Government service. Chambers thought for a moment and imperturbably answered five, three others besides Hiss and Wadleigh. "Do you want us to understand" asked the judge, "that when you testified before the House Committee in August of 1948, less than a year ago, when you testified in substance that you had nothing to do with espionage, that you had forgotten *all* of these sources of supply?"

Mr. Murphy moved a little anxiously towards the bench. He thought the judge was "distorting something, without intention I am sure." The judge said he would look at the record and ask again later. When he did, it was well established by Mr. Murphy that Chambers had not "forgotten" about the espionage on which this case was based; he had concealed his well-remembered knowledge. There was nothing sinister, either, Mr. Murphy wanted to show, in Chambers's being left alone for a few minutes in the Brooklyn kitchen when Levine had produced the envelope; no supportable implication that Chambers had "inserted" the typewritten documents into an envelope containing only the microfilm. And as for keeping back the microfilm from Hiss's lawyers in Baltimore, that was simple too: he had three rolls of undeveloped film in the pumpkin (where he hid the two surrendered to the House Committee) and he wanted to develop them and see whether they were all germane and then give them to his lawyer all together.

Just to dissipate any further suspicions of the defense about the pumpkin papers, Mr. Murphy had Chambers tell the sequence of events beginning with his trip to Brooklyn. He went up there on a Sunday, the 14th of November. When he saw what was in the envelope he went back to Baltimore that night, and so back to his farm. He told his wife he had "found something that made a great change in affairs." The next day he saw his lawyers, and two days later, on the 17th, he deposited the typewritten documents and handwritten memoranda before the Hiss lawyers at the pre-trial hearing. Some

days later he was served with a subpoena by the House Committee
to turn over any and all material whatsoever connected with the
case. Since the typewritten documents had by then been turned over
to the Department of Justice, he turned over everything else he had—
namely, the strips of microfilm—to two Committee investigators
who came out to his farm and whom he took into his pumpkin patch.

Finally Mr. Murphy wanted to lay the rumor that Chambers
was working out some old grudge in accusing Hiss of being a Communist now. Mr. Murphy reread to him the relevant and by now
celebrated House testimony, in giving which Chambers had become
almost inaudible and come close to tears: "I don't hate Mr. Hiss.
We were once friends and we are caught in a tragedy of history. Mr.
Hiss represents the concealed enemy against which we are all fighting
and I am fighting. I have testified against him with remorse and pity
but in the moment that we are, in which this nation now stands, so
help me God I could not do otherwise."

Was he asked that question and did he give that answer? He did.
"You may examine," said Mr. Murphy.

MR. STRYKER came back for a frontal attack on Chambers's recollection about the source of the microfilm documents. He had said in
Baltimore he did not recollect "that Alger Hiss gave him one particular original from which a photograph was made in this case."
Mr. Stryker hammered at him to say he had directly contradicted
his assertion at this trial that he was certain who gave him all the
documents. Chambers was so unflurried by this seeming discrepancy
that when Mr. Stryker said: "You do see, of course, an inconsistency
between that sworn statement this morning and the testimony I
have just read to you, do you not?" Chambers replied: "I see a very
one-sided and provocative line of questioning." But all Mr. Stryker
could get out of him, either about this recollection or about the
details of the Hiss houses, or what he told Adolf Berle in 1939, was
that he had made "apparent inconsistencies," that his recollection
had always been truly stated at the time.

Mr. Stryker tried to discredit his given motive for not failing to
tell about the espionage activities: namely, "past friendship" and
"desire not to hurt him any more than possible." Chambers felt, he
reiterated, that he had "a Christian duty" not to tell everything. And

"did you," Mr. Stryker sneered, "feel you had a Christian duty to comply with the oath that you had registered in heaven to tell the truth, the whole truth, and nothing but the truth?"

"I felt one outweighed the other."

Mr. Stryker snorted. So, he felt then he had the privilege of "weighing and deciding whether you would reveal" this or that? He denied he exercised any privilege. Did he not keep the knowledge of the microfilm from his lawyer, whom he presumably trusted, and who was defending him in a seventy-five-thousand-dollar lawsuit? That was correct.

How, Mr. Stryker fairly moaned, how could you call a man one day "a concealed enemy of his country" and another day say you wished him no hurt and thought you had not done much damage?

"I had not done an ultimate damage," Chambers stubbornly replied.

Mr. Stryker made an impatient exclamation and moved towards Chambers. "Don't you recognize," he bellowed, "that your explanation for your silence for these ten years on the ground of friendship is another piece of perjury, is a sham, a fraud, having in mind that three months earlier you denounced him as a concealed enemy?"

"I do not."

Mr. Stryker made an imperial shrug and gave up in disgust.

The next morning Mr. Stryker had a final fling at him. Sifting through the parts of the grand jury testimony that the judge had allowed the defense to see, Mr. Stryker fastened on several discrepancies and defied Chambers to tell the jury that there "is honest argument" as to whether or not his answers in two places had been inconsistent. "Of course there is," said Chambers.

Mr. Stryker plumped down and Mr. Murphy rose again, elaborately calm, but still concerned over the inference the jury might draw, from the judge's reading of the grand jury record, that Chambers had lied in this court. He wanted Chambers to prove he had testified to five, and not four, "sources of supply" in the State Department by having him name them. The five sources, said Chambers coolly, were "Julian Wadleigh, Ward Pigman, Harry Dexter White, Alger Hiss, and Vincent Reno." Mr. Murphy then wanted to leave the jury in no doubt about Chambers's motives for holding back his documentary evidence of espionage. He read a long passage from Chambers's testimony to the grand jury in December, in which he explained that until the Nazi-Soviet alliance of August 1939 he had hoped to forget the whole conspiracy. But then he had to say his piece to Mr. Berle. Since no Government inquiry came out of this confession, his memory of the documents "dimmed in my mind," and again his old feeling returned that he "did not want to involve human beings in such a tragic difficulty." Since that time, wherever he had testified, he had had a consistent purpose, which was if possible "to destroy the conspiracy" while doing "no more damage than necessary" to the human beings involved.

Chambers ambled off the stand. To the end, this bulky, pale man with the expressionless, translucent eyes had told what he knew in the manner of one long resigned to a life of profound error and disillusion and the hope perhaps of a little peace and quiet before the end came. He had sat there for six days, but at the end he appeared no more tired than when he had come in, as if he had passed beyond tiredness years ago and turned abjectness almost into a social attitude. Theoretically this is not a dramatic attitude either in a courtroom or on a stage, but it served only to give rein in the spectators to the emotions it held in check in the witness. His whole story was told. We could sit back now and see it as a circumstantial epic touched with just that fragmentary and repetitive color which gave it the quality of a dream, or of a compelling work of fiction, or the true sound of a dead experience dredged up from a sensitive memory.

MR. MURPHY got down now to the corroboration and the questioning of a variety of witnesses—technical experts, F.B.I. agents, humble and greatly awed citizens—who were just the people you would expect to appear if there was any truth at all in Chambers's stories of a loan from the Hisses to purchase a car, the present of a rug, the summer-theater jaunt, the telltale typeface of Mrs. Hiss's typewriter.

First came the assistant vice-president of a Washington bank to testify that on the 19th of November 1937 Priscilla Hiss withdrew $400 from a joint account, leaving a balance of $40.46. The account had been started in November 1936, and this was the first withdrawal. The bald fact was stated and left, and neither counsel speculated about the likelihood of the Hisses' practically robbing their total savings to buy another man a car.

An automobile salesman came in smartly to read from his ledger the entry of the sale of "one 1937 Deluxe Four-Door Ford Sedan," which after a trade-in adjustment on an old 1934 Ford was settled with a cash payment of $486.75. The car was bought, four days after the Hiss withdrawal, by Esther (Mrs.) Chambers.

The headmaster of a Washington school identified a typewritten letter, and a covering note from Alger Hiss, which he had received in September 1936 in answer to his request for a character sketch of the Hiss stepson before he was entered in the school. A letter from Hiss to an insurance company was also identified and put in evidence. An old college friend of Mrs. Hiss stepped up to identify three typewritten papers as the report of Mrs. Hiss on her year in office as the president of the Washington Alumnae of Bryn Mawr. The date was May 18, 1937.

The witnesses shuttled through the court at a rate that must have taxed the jury's ability to keep the jigsaw puzzle intact. But then came a tired-looking, swarthy man, whose name was Touloukian, and when he said that he was a dealer in Oriental rugs, the plot straightened out again. He had sold on the 29th of December 1936 four Bokhara rugs and shipped them, on instruction from one E. Schoen, to Dr. Meyer Schapiro. Schapiro was Chambers's old student friend, and inevitably he was the next witness. He said he had known Chambers since 1921, that the Chambers family stayed in his apartment in the summer of 1935, that he had bought the rugs at Chambers's behest and with Chambers's money and shipped them to Washington.

An F.B.I. man corroborated Chambers's story that a few months before, he had taken a ride with F.B.I. agents in Georgetown, and that with no prompting from the agents Chambers, who was in the back seat, had told them to stop at various addresses, which the F.B.I. men then checked, from photographs they had, as the Twenty-eighth Street apartment house, and the successive Hiss homes on P Street, Thirtieth Street, and Volta Place. Mr. Stryker came in with school-masterly zeal to be sure the F.B.I. had done "a good, careful F.B.I. job" such as, for instance, noticing a church, a playground, an institute for the deaf and dumb, all in the neighborhood of one of the houses. But the F.B.I. man had no recollection, he was just driving the car, he said. And for all Mr. Stryker's swapping of photographs and diagrams with the witness and the jury, the F.B.I. man went out as innocent of Georgetown geography as he was when he came in.

Judge Kaufman thought Mr. Stryker was wasting time, and Mr. Stryker agreed he "apparently" was.

The next witness was another guileless keeper of records. She was in the dean's office at Columbia University. She had with her a file of grades made by old students. One of them referred to a student named Priscilla Fansler Hobson. (Mrs. Hiss had been married once before.) "Can you tell me," Mr. Murphy quietly asked, "whether or not that student passed a test given by the university in English and typewriting?" Before she had time to answer, Mr. Stryker bounded towards the bench, objecting "to the document and the question." But later Mr. Murphy got an F.B.I. man to testify about a statement Hiss had signed; and as a result of it, Mr. Stryker agreed to let the grade-card be put in evidence. And the judge read to the jury a notation on the back: "Passed test in English, typewriting on January 25th, 1927." The next witness was bigger fry, and the back-bench morons bobbed and whispered, wondering at the sudden concentration of the newspapermen on a man who gave his name as Nathan L. Levine.

Here was Mrs. Chambers's nephew, a living witness to one of the more ghoulish episodes in the Chambers story. He could barely be heard, but his monotone gave a sort of confessional weight to the story of the Brooklyn bathroom. Yes, Chambers had visited him last November. Yes, he had gone with him to his mother's house. And what did they do there? He went up to the second floor, went into the bathroom, stepped on the window ledge, and "took from above the back of the linen closet in the dumbwaiter shaft the envelope." He gave it to Chambers "with the dust" and stepped down. And they both went into the kitchen. Then Levine went back alone to clean up the mess.

How did he know the envelope was there? Because ten years ago he had put it there. Who originally gave it to him? Mr. Chambers. It was sealed then and it was sealed when he handed it back on the 14th of November. When he stepped back into the kitchen, Chambers was holding some papers. Then he drove Chambers into New York and left him at the Pennsylvania Station.

"No further questions," said Mr. Murphy. "I have no questions," said Mr. Stryker. And the witness stepped down.

The end of the day brought an upright, earnest New England lady, a Mrs. Stearns, who leaned forward to be sure to get everything straight. She owned a farm in New Hampshire and she was the director of a summer dramatic group in Peterboro. She put on several productions during August 1937.

"Could you tell us what they were?" Mr. Murphy asked.

"Well, I put on *She Stoops to Conquer* from the 10th of August to the 15th of August. I don't remember the rest."

That was about all Mr. Murphy wanted from her. He had a State Department personnel man testify that was a week Hiss was on vacation that year. Had she ever put on that play any other summer? Mrs. Stearns obviously couldn't conceive why that question was asked. She had a wonderfully puzzled manner, as if she had no idea why she was in a courtroom; but since she was there she would oblige these curious gentlemen in every courteous way she could. No, indeed, that was the only time they ever put on that particular play. She remembered too that they had originally advertised the play to run for five nights, but the audiences were so big that they kept it going an extra night.

Mr. Stryker walked gently to the jury box. When, he asked, did she first receive an inquiry about the putting on of this play? Mrs. Stearns was aghast till it occurred to her he meant "when in connection with this trial?" She thought it was towards the end of February or the beginning of March of the present year. Did someone come to see her? Yes. Mr. Stryker walked back and looked stolidly into the spectators. Was it, he trumpeted, "some member of the F.B.I."? Yes, Mrs. Stearns cried. They had asked her if she had ever produced *She Stoops to Conquer* and she had said: "Yes." All right, said Mr. Stryker, and she was dismissed from this mystery.

THEN there appeared a small severe figure in a gray suit and a round blue-black hat, a very dark, thin-lipped woman in spectacles who sat nervously back in the witness chair. It was Mrs. Chambers. Mr. Murphy got her to tell the story of her childhood, of her student days as a painter, of a young womanhood spent in a series of jobs in the radical pattern—secretary to a garment workers' union, advertising manager on a pacifist magazine. Mr. Murphy began to humanize this purposeful life by bringing out that she was the wife, the "first and only" wife of Whittaker Chambers, the mother of his two children, at present living on a farm.

"Do you," asked Mr. Murphy sweetly, "work on the farm?"

"I milk eighteen cows and take care of some forty head of cattle, dairy cattle, and take care also of some six beef cattle, plus some chickens. I guess that's all."

That might be enough to atone, in the jury's minds, for any stock response they might have had towards a radical bluestocking and a Communist's wife. She well knew that Chambers was a Communist, but had never been one herself, though she was sympathetic to the Party.

"Now, did you ever meet a man by the name of Alger Hiss?"

"Yes, I met Alger Hiss for the first time at St. Paul Street [Baltimore]."

Mr. Stryker, who had been as restless as a lion cub through her life-history, jumped up and angrily demanded "a categorical answer."

"We are lawyers here, Mrs. Chambers," said Mr. Murphy with an apologetic smile, "and we want the answer yes or no temporarily."

"Yes."

So she met Hiss in their home in Baltimore, in the summer of 1934, about two months after they'd moved down there. And who introduced Hiss? Well, her husband told her something— Mr. Stryker leaped up again and Mr. Murphy put it another way. After her husband told her something, did she then meet Mr. Hiss?

"Yes. That is, he forewarned me that he was bringing—"

"One moment," from Mr. Stryker again. "I move to strike it out."

Mr. Murphy puffed through his walrus. "Oh, your Honor, can't we be just a little bit more realistic here about this problem?"

"I," announced Mr. Stryker, "am being very realistic about it."

At the next question, Mr. Stryker begged to sit at the Government table in order to hear her. The judge had already moved over into the clerk's place. All this fussing, combined with Mr. Stryker's ringing objections, began to affect Mrs. Chambers. She was a black-eyed woman got up as severely as a schoolma'am in a Hitchcock movie, but the general effect was belied by a frail body and a small voice and a habit of licking her thin lips. Mr. Murphy stood close and bowed his head down, to accommodate his great height to the indulgent attitude he was trying to adopt. He began again.

"Mrs. Chambers," he inquired very gently, "have you ever testified in court before?"

"Never, sir."

But she had been interrogated had she not, in the office of Hiss's lawyer? Yes. And she was examined for hours, wasn't she? That's right, for a day and a half. For a whole day and a half? That was right.

Having thus blandly conveyed to the jury that this was not Mrs. Chambers's first ordeal with one of Mr. Hiss's lawyers, Mr. Murphy said "all right" and started again.

Could she see Mr. Hiss in the courtroom? She hadn't looked, but she did so and saw him. At Mr. Murphy's suggestion, Hiss stood up. And she recognized him. The next time she could recall seeing Hiss was when he and Mrs. Hiss came to dinner.

Could she see Mrs. Hiss in the courtroom? She could.

She went on listing the times of their meeting. There were the times she used to meet Mrs. Hiss in the park to air the baby, the time she came "to our house at 28th Street one day and our maid, Julia, served us both punch"; jaunts on the Potomac, a visit to the zoo. She went on more fluently now, telling a story that was all the more exciting for being a plausible feminine recollection of any ordinary friendship: gifts of furniture, a joint visit to a Dr. Nicholson, a trip to Mount Vernon, the Hisses driving up in their car to deposit the baby's crib and bathtub when the Chamberses moved to New York; a ten-day holiday together in a cottage at Smithtown on the Delaware, where Mrs. Hiss looked after the baby while Mrs. Chambers painted. A token of this kindness was a landscape painting Mrs. Chambers had given to Mrs. Hiss and which she later saw hanging in the Hisses' home. She had also painted a portrait of Timmy, Mrs. Hiss's son, when they stayed with the Hisses on P Street. Then into memories of the Hisses' houses: a long green painted living-room at P Street, a garden terrace done in Spanish tiles, outside the window a gingko tree. Once when the Chamberses set up house in Baltimore, the Hisses gave them a patched rug, a dining-room table, some toys, and "two bird books." One time they lunched together in a department-store restaurant, while Mrs. Hiss "was trying to take a course, register for a course in nursing at Mercy Hospital. I, on my part, met Mrs. Hiss in the Hutzler fountain shop where we had a soda together—Mrs. Hiss herself does not like ice cream."

When she tried to recall the exact times she had been at the Hisses' houses, she had trouble with the dates and fingered her purse, where she said she had a little list, compiled last November with her husband's help, of parallel addresses where she and her husband lived.

But she thought better of it and was sure she could remember "if you have plenty of time to listen to me and bear with me." Mr. Murphy willingly bore with her while she described little reminiscences that attached to the different places the Hisses had lived in during 1936, 1937, and 1938. Ah yes, at the Thirtieth Street house her baby wet the floor, "and Priscilla gave me a lovely old linen towel to use as a diaper." So she went on, a thin, sallow, birdlike woman tiptoeing carefully through her memories, plucking at many an item that would have been preposterously dull might it not also turn into a noose for the honor of Alger Hiss. This was especially true of her memories of Volta Place, where the Hisses lived from the very end of 1937 to 1943, and where by Hiss's sworn statement the Chamberses could never have visited. Well, Mrs. Chambers mused, the Volta Place house was a walled-in garden house, the dining-room had a wallpaper of a faded plum pattern with plum-colored chintz curtains, and there were Hitchcock chairs stenciled in gilt. Mrs. Hiss had a flowered chintz bedspread, bought at a sale.

She remembered going to a New Year's Eve party at Volta Place on the last evening of 1936; until Mr. Murphy showed her a record establishing that the Hisses didn't move there until December 29, 1937. Well, then, she thought it must have been the last day of 1937.

At an objection of Mr. Stryker's to the gratuitous mention of the phrase "we were friends," Mr. Murphy paused for emphasis and asked: "Were you and Mr. and Mrs. Hiss friends?" "Indeed we were," said Mrs. Chambers. And what name did the Hisses call the Chamberses? "I was called Lisa . . . and my husband Carl."

The judge bent his pink face even closer and asked what was the last name by which they were known. Mrs. Chambers smoothly replied: "We never had a last name to them."

This stunned a lot of spectators, who thought they had missed a vital line, and it was a relief to know the judge had heard the same thing. "I don't quite understand that answer, Mrs. Chambers," he said. But it came out exactly as we heard it first: "They always called us by the names either Carl or Lisa." But, the judge objected, Mr. Chambers testified they were known by the Hisses as Crosley. "Oh, no, your Honor," roared Mr. Murphy. To which Mr. Stryker assured his Honor that his Honor's memory was "practically correct." But the name Crosley meant nothing to Mrs. Chambers. Cantwell would have meant something, or Dwyer, or Breen. But not Crosley.

THERE were only a few minutes left that day for Mr. Stryker to come in for a terrifying cross-examination which he had more or less intimated by his protests earlier. He kept telling Mrs. Chambers to keep her voice up and gleamed expectantly at every hesitancy about dates. He asked her to look at a letter she had written in October 1937. Was her husband at that time an underground Communist, yes or no? She believed so. Mr. Stryker fairly shouted: "Don't you know as his wife whether he was an underground Communist at that time or not?"

"I don't have a very good head for figures or dates. I believe so."

Well, did she have any doubt of it? Mrs. Chambers's glasses glittered as she thought hard at the ceiling. Whereupon Mr. Stryker snapped: "Look at the jury or me. Please don't look up. Won't you answer?" Mr. Murphy came up reddening: "I submit that she can look anywhere she wants." Judge Kaufman came over the bench with his bright face blinking. "Now, Mr. Murphy and Mr. Stryker."

Mrs. Chambers licked her lips again and said at him: ". . . if that is the period in which he was in the underground, that was the period in which he was in the underground. I don't know why you are trying to stump me on dates."

Judge Kaufman came to with a start and sang out in his high treble: "Nobody here is attempting to stump anybody. The court will not permit anybody to be stumped. We are attempting to get the facts in a case that is important for the Government and very important for the defendant . . . and it comes with a very bad grace from you to indicate that anyone is attempting to stump you." Mr. Stryker glowered in the most eloquent and hearty agreement and asked when her husband finally broke with the Party, to which Mrs. Chambers replied with some emotion that "it was not a special hour. It was a long time in coming and thought out very thoroughly and suffered through, and he finally broke."

The next day Mr. Stryker started by recomposing Mr. Murphy's sketch of an intellectual female radical, and by the time he was through, Mrs. Chambers emerged as a willing participant in riots, a wifely conspirator, a masquerader under false names, a callow ward of the Communists, beholden for every "piece of bread" she ate to "conspirators seeking to overthrow the Government of the United States by force and violence." That is right, she invariably replied.

And when her husband "reformed and repented," she too gave up "lying and deceiving?" Yes, she said resignedly, "if you put it that way." Now Mr. Stryker held the letter of October 1937, a time he had established was during the Chambers period of "reform and repentance." The letter was a scholarship application for their daughter and identified the father as a "freelance writer and translator." Did she not thereby, Mr. Stryker thundered, suppress the fact that he was an underground worker and a Communist "in order to deceive the school"? Mrs. Chambers had learned by now that Stryker on Conspiracy cannot be usefully gainsaid. And she admitted it was a deception. But a misrepresentation she would not concede. "If I were asked point blank I probably would have told the truth, if it were permitted, if it were possible."

"In other words," Mr. Stryker ran on, "you didn't think it was very much of a misrepresentation to present your husband to this school as a decent citizen, whereas he was . . ."

Mrs. Chambers tensed into life behind her round black hat and her placid spectacles.

"I resent that. My husband is a decent citizen, a great man."

The judge steadied the whirling pair by telling Mrs. Chambers it was her province to answer questions. Mr. Stryker hardly paused for breath:

"Was he a great, decent citizen in October, 1937?"

"When he was in the underground?"

"I just asked a simple question. Was he a great and decent citizen in October, 1937, yes or no?"

"Yes, and always," she shouted, the only time her voice had ever hardened above a regretful whisper.

Mr. Stryker was to make only one other assault on the good faith of the marriage bond between Esther and Whittaker Chambers. This was when he asked her if she was, in the normal habit of "wifely confidence," privy to her husband's secrets. When, for instance, did she first learn that her husband had had documents passed to him out of the State Department by Julian Wadleigh? "Just recently," she replied, ". . . before the House Committee hearings."

Had she ever met Wadleigh? No, she had not. Ever heard of him? No. What, never had Mr. Wadleigh at her house? No. Never to Mr. Wadleigh's house? No.

"Did you ever go to a movie with Mr. Wadleigh . . . or drive along to see the autumn foliage?"

In an acid whisper Mrs. Chambers said: "I did not know Mr. Wadleigh and do not know him today." The same was true of all the other sources, except Hiss.

"In other words, Mrs. Chambers . . . you are telling this Court and jury that Mr. Chambers kept and secreted from you the names and circumstance of sources of documents that he had in Washington?"

"That is right."

"In other words . . . the silence on the subject, even to his wife, was in the conspiratorial pattern, was it not?"

"Oh, yes."

For the rest, for nearly the whole day, Mr. Stryker harrowed her memory for dates. Remembering the glaring discrepancy she had confessed to Mr. Murphy about the date of a New Year's Eve party, Mr. Stryker commuted menacingly between the record of her pre-trial testimony in Baltimore and her testimony in this court. She had said in Baltimore, and again in this Trial, that she and her husband had gone to a New Year's Eve party at the Hisses' home on Volta Place. She had first said the last of December 1936 and later amended it to the last of December 1937. By rapid and adroit readings of other passages in her Baltimore testimony Mr. Stryker established that she had sworn to three parties with the Hisses: one was a housewarming, one a wedding anniversary, the third a New Year's Eve party. The question, was where was each party held? Two of these, she maintained, were at the Hisses', and the wedding anniversary at the Chamberses' home in Baltimore. Through periods of long silence Mrs. Chambers wrestled with her uncertain memory of these dates. She had said on her own confession she had a poor head for dates and remembered events best by "associating things." But the more she hesitated, the more often her sentences trailed off into rumination, and the more certainly Mr. Stryker seemed to be winning his campaign to show how befuddled she was about any dates whatever, then the less did she appear like a tutored accomplice forgetting her lines. Her replies seemed to spring from a pathetic belief that somewhere deep in her memory, if only she could concentrate her digging in the right place, the truth and the recollection would be found to run in overlapping seams. She appeared really to believe that you have only to pause for honest recollection and the exact transcript of a casual conversation a dozen years ago will come to the surface. But every time she tried it, blinking intently at the ceiling, she discovered to her obvious alarm that the memory is a poor miner and the deep recesses of truth are guarded by Heaven knows what jester. Either that, or she was being dangerously rattled in a painfully memorized story. So she would lick her dry lips again, glare through her glasses, and pallidly reply she was not sure or she was confused or she was probably wrong in that particular.

She weakened on putting the New Year's Eve party at Volta Place. It was probably at Thirtieth Street. She only knew for sure the Hisses' wedding anniversary was at the Chambers home, and Hiss himself brought the champagne. But Mr. Stryker read her Baltimore testimony asserting that the Hisses never visited in the Chamberses' Baltimore home.

"I would not like to give the wrong impression," said Mrs. Chambers.

"No, I would not want you to do that, either," Mr. Stryker added, and cast a suspicious look around the courtroom.

Well, then, the party at Volta Place, since the Hisses had only just moved in two days before, must have been the housewarming. Mr. Stryker sighed patiently in the direction of the judge. "Must have been" may acknowledge error, but, as everybody knows, is not evidence. So Mrs. Chambers bit her lip and drummed her housewife's fingers on the rail, like a woman checking the figures on a grocery bill.

Judge Kaufman leaned gently over. "You were at the 30th Street house on December 31st, 1937? Is that your testimony now, Mrs. Chambers?"

"No, I am trying to recall," she said, and wandered off again into the dark underground of her memory. The judge asked her again if she was sure, and she replied, almost to herself: "I am a little confused right now." Then, said the judge, he would call a five-minute recess to help the witness clear her mind.

When she came back she was less certain than ever. Mr. Stryker, who had pointedly taken his seat during these racking pauses, got up again and with the unwonted gentleness of a huntsman for a prostrate fox said: "So then, whatever else you say you were doing in Volta Place, you were not attending a New Year's Eve party there, is that right, isn't it?" Well, she would think so. Mr. Stryker didn't want to hurry her, wanted her to take plenty of time. At last she decided, whatever her previous testimony had said, that the housewarming was at Volta Place.

Then there was the time, after the Chambers family had moved out of the Hiss apartment on Twenty-eighth Street and gone up to New York, in the summer of 1935. Mrs. Chambers said both Mr. and Mrs. Hiss drove up from Washington to deposit some children's belongings at the new Chambers home. But in Baltimore she had said that only Mrs. Hiss came up. Mr. Stryker was unconvinced by either version.

"When did your memory first get refreshed in such a way that you put Alger Hiss into that trip?" She couldn't recall when she first testified to that. She thought it was when the F.B.I. had first spoken to her. But the F.B.I. hadn't been there in New York in June 1935, had they? No, but "on further mature thought" she remembered Hiss being along.

Mr. Stryker paced towards her and said: "Well, was there any sort of leading question, probably inadvertent, on the part of one of the F.B.I., suggesting that Mr. Hiss might have been there, and that refreshed your recollection about this?"

Mrs. Chambers answered at once, quite quietly and with great dignity: "You are insulting, sir."

As Mr. Murphy came snorting to his feet, the judge's head bobbed over the bench, and his amiable pink face spluttered: ". . . it is not in the province of this witness to make any outbursts and not engage in any name-calling around here. This is too important a case, from the standpoint of the Government and from the standpoint of the defendant. . . . I tell you again not to indulge in suggestions or statements of that kind."

By the end, before he dismissed her, Mr. Stryker had damaged her testimony by echoing the astonishment of the court when she had first said the Hisses never knew her or her husband by a last name. Had she not inherited a maid from the Hisses when she stayed at the Twenty-eighth Street apartment? She had. And what was the maid's name? Julia. And by what name did Julia call Mrs. Chambers? She didn't know. But didn't this maid cook and do housework and have "innumerable occasions each day to speak to you?" That was right. And yet she couldn't tell the court and jury how the maid addressed her? That was right.

She seemed to slip again when Mr. Stryker asked her about a trip the Hisses and Chamberses were supposed to have taken, from the P Street house, off into the country, to Mount Vernon, to see the fall foliage. "Was that the occasion when you told about the magnolias being in bloom . . . what was it?" asked Mr. Stryker idly— "lemon magnolias?"

"Yes."

"Beautiful lemon magnolias?"

"That is right."

"Tell me," said Mr. Stryker, suppressing a yawn, "did you ever see a magnolia bloom in the fall?" "They have occasional blossoms," she replied.

"Well, the bloom," Mr. Stryker cried, lifting his arms out to encompass boundless blossom, "the bloom of the magnolia is in the springtime, is it not, Mrs. Chambers?" She thought it did bloom in the springtime, she wasn't sure.

WHEN Mr. Murphy came in for the redirect examination, his contrasting lack of brilliance was a weapon in itself. "Dark spaces between stars," a modern poet has written, "say what they think common sense has seen." And after Mr. Stryker's formidable smoke barrages, his sudden forays on exposed positions, and the erupting Buzfuz artillery, Mr. Murphy's humdrum approach sounded like the honest tramp of the infantryman.

He had, he said, only a few questions, Mrs. Chambers. He lazily turned a page of the Baltimore testimony. Hadn't she said in Baltimore that the trip to Mount Vernon and the magnolia tree was made some time while they were all in Washington, either at Twenty-eighth Street or at P Street, and that where it fitted in she didn't remember? Yes, she had. And when Mrs. Hiss's maid called or spoke to her, she did give a name to Mrs. Chambers, but Mrs. Chambers couldn't now recall which one it was, was that correct? That was right. And since she had been on the stand had she ever seen the minutes of this trial, or talked to any Government agent, or to him, Mr. Murphy? She had never. And when she testified in Baltimore, the only thing she had in her pocketbook was a piece of paper bearing notes on the chronology of the places where she had lived? That was right. And that again was a piece of paper that Hiss's lawyer had taken from her? That was right.

"No further questions," said Mr. Murphy, and she left the stand.

THE DOCUMENTS

THE next day the Trial went into an anticlimax performed in slow motion. For the Government began to introduce in evidence the documents: the handwritten notes; the typewritten copies, and the photographs, of the State Department documents that Chambers said had been passed to him, in the first three months of 1938, by Alger Hiss. It took a day and a half to do this. The high priest of this tedious ritual was an imperturbable, middle-aged man whose very profession was a challenge to the eyesight and the central nervous system which was now put up to the courtroom audience. He was Mr. Walter Anderson, chief of the State Department's records branch. To his right stood a man-sized easel, flanked by two of Mr. Murphy's assistants, who, like decorators displaying wallpaper samples to a skeptical customer, kept turning over five-foot-high photographed enlargements of the Chambers papers. Mr. Murphy would pick up a paper from a pile on a lectern, have Mr. Anderson identify it as an original document from the State Department's files, then read it aloud to permit the judge and jury to check his reading with the display texts on the easel. Chance plays no part in the laborious professional life of an assistant United States attorney, and sometimes Mr. Murphy would read the original document and then read the Chambers copy, until it was as certain as could be that the two matched.

The original documents were of several kinds. Nearly all the typewritten documents (surrendered at Baltimore) were incoming cables to the Secretary of State from American embassies, consulates, and legations as far apart as Tokyo and Berlin, Paris and Peiping, Vienna and Yokohama, London and Buenos Aires, Rome and Tientsin. They included accounts of diplomatic conversations, especially with the Germans, the Italians, and the Austrians (twelve of them were about Hitler's pressure on Schuschnigg); there were many from the Far East about Japanese troop movements and the landing of military

supplies; from London came a report of the British intention to purchase American aircraft, and reports of intended British policy in
battleship and cruiser construction; there was a long report from
Yokohama on the economic organization of Manchukuo, and an appraisal of this report written inside the State Department.

The microfilm documents (the pumpkin papers surrendered to the
House Committee) were for the most part an internal file from the
Trade Agreements Section of the State Department; memoranda
about these and other matters exchanged between different divisions
inside the Department; a long aide-memoire on German-American
trade policy, written in German and delivered by the German Ambassador to an Assistant Secretary of State; two incoming cables for
the Secretary of State, one from Peiping and one from Hankow; and
the memorandum of a conversation sent by Mr. Francis Sayre to another section in the Department.

The reader will want to know how significant these documents
were to the conduct of the Sino-Japanese War, how plausibly the
European documents in Russian hands might have embarrassed
American policy or imperiled American security, and especially how
they might have led to the Soviet decision to sign a protective alliance with Nazi Germany. This is a natural curiosity whose satisfaction
would require a wealth of diplomatic information and a fineness of
judgment which, it had better be said at once, the reader is not going
to get from me. I have already reported the official opinion of Mr.
Sumner Welles that the breaking of a Government code by a foreign
power always entails a betrayal. (Mr. Francis Sayre, who was Hiss's
boss in the State Department at the time, testified in the Second
Trial to the same effect.) Officials of the State Department told the
Committee there were one or two documents that were too secret to
publish even in 1948 without risking the national security. One whole
section of a document, from Paris, was accordingly kept from the
judge and jury at the First Trial, but it was shown at the Second
Trial.[1]

When Chambers turned the pumpkin papers over to the House
Committee investigators, there was an alarmed and automatic assumption, clamantly encouraged by the Committee, that the most
vital State Secrets of the United States had passed "in the general

---

[1] See page 317.

historical era of the Stalin-Hitler pact" irrevocably into the hands of
the Russians, the Germans, and the Japanese; and that all three
powers knew the State Department's secret codes during and through
the war. (Nothing was said at the time about the universal habit of
foreign offices of changing their codes at the outbreak of war and re-
vising them frequently thereafter; and in the hullabaloo over a proved
conspiracy with the now hated Russians, few people reflected that
officially friendly powers—one of which, assuredly, was the Soviet
Union of 1938—often exchange diplomatic documents in an informal
way.) This explosive assumption encouraged Hiss's defenders to belittle the documents as routine memoranda too technical or politically
innocuous to affect the course of events.

For the Government, Mr. Murphy needed to do no more than accept the State Department's official opinion and pass on to the jury
the conclusion that whatever the diplomatic content of the documents, what was disastrous was the certainty that the Russians at least
had broken the most secret cipher of the United States Government.
It was the defense that later embarked on a political assessment of
some of the documents.

I think a lot of special pleading can be avoided, and a waste of
tendentious speculation saved, by quoting here the expert opinion of
a diplomatic historian whose special field is the European diplomatic
files of the two years before the Second World War, and to whom I
submitted the texts of all the documents. He begins by noting [1] that
the value of these documents is "their possible value to the Soviet
Government . . . [which] clearly depends on what they knew already, and on what they wanted to know—but this it is impossible for
anyone of us to guess or estimate." He remarks that "only about one-
fifth of the printed material falls within the province with which I am
properly acquainted." [These are the ones on Europe.] He disclaims
any special knowledge of "the vast fields of Far Eastern politics, of
American-German relations, or of naval affairs: I cannot therefore
gauge the importance, say, of the technical information contained"
in the two exhibits about British naval policy.

In view of this sensible modesty, it seems fair to assume that
neither Mr. Stryker nor Mr. Murphy, nor Mr. Welles nor Mr. Sayre,
could begin to have a reliable opinion about the political value to the

[1] In a private letter from Professor L. B. Namier, dated April 16, 1950.

Russians of more than a few of these documents. It was left to the newspaperman, the court spectators, and the partisans of Hiss or Chambers to rush confidently in on this untrodden ground. For other amateur historians, who may feel balked by this expert disclaimer of the possibility of expert knowledge, Professor Namier adds the wise warning: "Historical or diplomatic research consists of crossword puzzles, and no outsider can say what particular piece of information may supply the other side with the key to its problem. Hence any leakages have to be jealously guarded against." It is better, he thinks, for the curious "to ask questions rather than venture on any assertions concerning the importance or unimportance of documents of which we anyhow know merely a small fraction."

Nevertheless, the professor agrees that "the essential point is their serving as material for breaking American diplomatic ciphers."

Mr. Stryker had conceded for the defendant that the Chambers documents were indeed true copies of the State Department originals Mr. Murphy was putting in evidence. But Mr. Murphy, his watery blue eyes saying to the jury that this heavy chore hurt him more than it did them, was skilled enough to know that to recite the full texts of these documents, full of great names and mysterious code markings, and display them in all their commanding authenticity on an easel five feet high, might possibly convey to the jury that while experts may make history, it is in the last resort the common man who judges it. So Mr. Murphy propped his great body against the lectern, with one arm akimbo and the other holding the original documents, and rumbled on for hours and hours. The jury slumped and crossed and recrossed its twenty-four legs. The Hisses exchanged a few words, and Alger Hiss, who had kept up an impeccable interest in everything going on, fell a victim to the epidemic yawning. For the first time there were empty benches on the spectators' side, and the newspapermen went out to watch Mr. Stryker pacing the corridor and smoking a cigar; an absence Mr. Murphy was quick to bring to the jury's attention by having the record note that the defendant was represented by "the balance of counsel."

Mr. Murphy hoped this exhausting ceremony would repay him with two conclusions: that the documents were highly secret and that they had gone through Hiss's office.

On the first, Mr. Anderson obliged him by identifying and explaining the markings and code signs and finding that they ranged from a "non-confidential" code to "code D," the most secret of the State Department's ciphers. The second conclusion was harder to establish: it involved the preliminary tedium of educating the jury about the State Department's methods in receiving documents, decoding and marking them, typing and stenciling yellow "action" and white "information" copies, circulating them through the various divisions; the system of noting who had seen them and when they came back, and how many copies went into dead storage in the filing room and were subsequently destroyed. Mr. Murphy got Mr. Anderson to recite from the check list the offices and divisions to which every document had been distributed. Most of them bore the stamp of Assistant Secretary of State Francis Sayre (Hiss was his assistant), showing that he had received them. Some did not. Two of them countersigned the stamp of Mr. Sayre's office with the initials "AH."

When Mr. Murphy at last sat down, a new figure rose at the defendant's table. He was Mr. Edward McLean, a pleasant, tweedy man in his middle forties who had evidently relieved Mr. Stryker of the detective job involved in getting to know the documents. He showed not a trace of indoctrination in the Stryker school and brought to the service of the defendant a reasonable bedside manner meant to calm the jury's fears and show that by a little straightforward analysis the documents could be easily plucked of their sting. How many copies, for instance, were made of an incoming cable? Mr. Anderson thought probably forty to fifty. And each of these documents had gone to about fifteen offices, right? That was a reasonable figure. So that would leave about twenty-five or thirty-five extra copies over? It would. And what happened to them? They were retained in the code room for a week or two and then destroyed. Were they kept in locked files? During the daytime, Mr. Anderson thought the files were unlocked. And about how many people worked in the code room? About eight on each of two day shifts and two or three at night, and a couple of messengers.

"Now," said Mr. McLean, "security regulations were not anywhere near as strict in 1938 as they became during the war, were they Mr. Anderson?" Mr. Anderson thought that was a matter of opinion. Well, they built an iron grille in the hall leading to the code room, and that wasn't there in 1938, was it? No, sir, it was not. About how many people worked in the telegraph room, the decoding room, the revision room, the typists' room, and so on; would he be right in saying about thirty or thirty-five? Mr. Anderson thought that a reasonable assumption.

Mr. McLean took several documents and asked Mr. Anderson to identify the divisions they had gone to. Then he laboriously showed him the State Department's staff register for 1938 and asked him to estimate the total working staff of these divisions. Thus there were 10 people in the Secretary of State's office, 6 in the Under Secretary's office, 4 in the Office of the Counsellor, 21 in the office of Assistant Secretary Messersmith, 30 in the legal adviser's office, 33 in the European Division, 18 in the Far Eastern Division, 28 in the Latin-American Division, 12 in the Division of Current Information, 13 in the Near Eastern Division. Would it not be fair to say that the particular exhibit they were looking at went to offices in which over a hundred people worked? Mr. Anderson couldn't say. Wasn't it "just a matter of arithmetic?" The judge called a recess for arithmetic. After which Mr. McLean did not pursue this assumption, but left it in the air as a mild threat, a prospect, if the prosecution wanted to get awkward, of calling a hundred-odd witnesses to testify about their homework. Instead, Mr. McLean got Mr. Anderson to agree that two of the Government's documents in evidence had never been distributed to the Sayre office. Another was initialed by the offices that saw it but carried no initial from Mr. Sayre (since the distribution list had been mislaid, there was no way of telling whether or not it had been initialed by all the offices that had it). There was a document that had Mr. Sayre's office stamp on the State Department original, but none on the Government's print of the same document. Mr. McLean encouraged Mr. Anderson to conclude that the microfilm was made from a copy that had gone to some other office. But Mr. Murphy objected and the judge thought it was an argument. Finally, there was a memorandum written by Mr. Sayre about a talk with the Czech Minister. He sent it to the Trade Agreements Section on the 19th of February, where a copy was evidently made, and did not get it back until the 2nd of March. Since Julian Wadleigh worked in the Trade Agreements Section, Mr. McLean was prompt to say so and leave it to the jury to draw their own conclusions.

It was then Mr. Murphy's duty to pluck these conclusions from the air and render them innocuous. He got Mr. Anderson to explain, for instance, that there was no obligation to initial a document if you had no suggestions to make about it. The written initials that appeared under printed initials were always the signatures of people who had taken some part in the drafting of a document. Then Mr. Murphy shook down his ace. He took out the Sayre memorandum that had gone on to the Trade Agreements (or Wadleigh) Section on the 19th of February and not been returned until the 2nd of March. Was that right? That was correct.

Mr. Murphy braced his shoulders. "Now, will you tell the jury when the file room got it after Mr. Sayre had it?"

Mr. Anderson bent over his pile of records. He looked up.

"It was received in the files on March 24, 1938."

Next came a prim, meticulous woman of such obviously withering competence, and with her wits so clearly about her, that irony was at once discounted as a possible weapon. Mr. Stryker's shafts of sarcasm would have fallen like dead sparrows at her feet. She was Miss Eunice Lincoln, a veteran of thirty-one devoted years in the State Department. She had been Mr. Sayre's secretary at the time Hiss shared his office. Her desk had been between the rooms occupied by the two men. Mr. Sayre worked with his door closed, Mr. Hiss with his door open. And it would have been hard for anyone to come in unseen. She received and put her stamp on all incoming mail, read it, and sorted it into three piles; trade-agreement documents, in which Mr. Sayre took a primary interest; telegrams to Mr. Sayre, which he was not called upon to answer; and routine Department correspondence, "which he would not in the slightest be interested in." Mr. Hiss usually saw everything in the first two piles and made notes or suggestions on them for Mr. Sayre. When the day was over, and it might sometimes be as late as seven o'clock, she inspected the desks and locked up any "classified" documents she saw lying on them. She had no recollection of Mr. Hiss's making handwritten memoranda of cabled messages. The handwritten memos that Mr. Murphy handed her were, she thought, in Mr. Hiss's hand. They were all on sheets that could have come from official memoranda pads supplied by the Department, but she noted that two of them looked as if they had had the letterhead legend "Department of State, Assistant Secretary," cut or torn off. Yes, she knew Mr. Wadleigh. He came in infrequently and she doubted he had ever taken away any papers.

Mr. McLean stood up for a brief cross-examination. She was not present when Hiss took papers in for a conference with Mr. Sayre? She was not. During the daytime all these cables sat on the desks? That was right. Now, she was not there all the time of every day, was she? No, she lunched and went on vacation. Mr. Hawkins, the head of the Trade Agreements Section, frequently came into the office, didn't he? Yes, he did. Now, if Mr. Hawkins arrived some morning when Mr. Hiss was out and wanted to go into Mr. Hiss's office, would she have stopped him from going in? She would if there was no one in there. "You would?" Mr. McLean repeated with a rising inflection. "Yes," said Miss Lincoln, without batting an eyelid. That was about all the defense wanted to have to do with Miss Lincoln, and she bowed to the judge and was on her way.

Now Mr. Murphy began to bring up his heavy guns and train them on the documents. The first was a vigorous, dark-haired F.B.I. expert, one Ramos Feehan, strictly a laboratory man, who since 1938 had been called in on about ten thousand cases and asked to examine twenty or thirty thousand specimens of questioned handwriting, typewriting, stencils, carbons, ink, obliterated writing, and the like. This was his specialty, and he had been trained for it for three years. "Of course," he added philosophically, "I am learning all the time; there is no end to it." Had he examined the Baltimore exhibits in this case? Yes, sir, he had examined four pages of questioned handwriting and sixty-five pages of typewritten documents. Before Mr. Murphy could get his expert opinion about the handwriting, Mr. Stryker was on his feet explicitly admitting that all four of the notes were in Hiss's hand. Mr. Murphy turned to the typewritten papers. Whereupon Mr. Feehan brightly explained that he had compared the Baltimore documents with four personal specimens of Mrs. Hiss's typing and concluded that all but one (of the documents) had been typed on the same machine. This confession, briskly tossed off in one sentence, was the gravel that stuck in the throats of people anxious to exonerate Hiss on every count of conspiracy and disloyalty. It provoked quick intakes of breath from many casual spectators and a notable respect from the jury; the more so, perhaps, because this witness appeared quite untouched by the emotions of the case. He was a technical expert reporting on his daily round. Evidence is what the laboratory confirms.

"Now, would you want to explain to the Court and jury the basis for coming to that conclusion?"

"Yes, sir," Mr. Feehan consented, and stepped down from the witness stand and into his element. Easels were wheeled towards him, the jury leaned forward. Mr. Stryker asked to sit close by so as "to be out of the way," and Mr. Feehan took a pointer in his hand and began to indicate the telltale characteristics of the Woodstock typewriter with all the basking pride of a travel lecturer much in demand. He pointed smartly to ten characteristic defects or irregularities in the typeface of Mrs. Hiss's admitted specimens which were precisely repeated in all the Baltimore documents but one. This exception he quickly dismissed by indicating a couple of characters that gave a wholly different imprint from the same letter done on the others. This exception too, he remarked, was on a different paper that bore a Government watermark: "this," he said, holding it up to the light and throwing his head on one side as the jury did the same, "is tail feathers." But on the Hiss typewritten specimens and the forty-six other Baltimore documents the jury would kindly notice a small "g," and "e," "i," "o," "u," "d," "a," "r," and "l," and a capital "A." Some of these characters fell below the line of type, others showed a lighter impress on one side than another, one printed what should have been a parallel line as a dropping diagonal. Mr. Feehan explained all this to a blank-faced jury with many a flourish of the special jargon of his trade: this one was "off its footing," he would say, or "notice the light serif."

It being established then, and silently conceded by the defense, that the Baltimore documents and four sample specimens of Mrs. Hiss's typing were all done on the same typewriter, Mr. Feehan turned to two easels on which hung the enlargements of original State Department documents, and the enlargements of the corresponding microfilm or pumpkin papers. His analysis of these fell into four groups: there was a batch photographed from what must have been "a single typing run" done in the State Department; that is to say photographs of one typing operation, whichever carbon copy had been used to make the photograph from. The second batch were undoubtedly photographs of the corresponding State Department documents, but were photographs of different originals from the ones brought here from the State Department file. The third batch, of twenty-six pages, were photographs of twenty-six common typing runs. And the last batch had been photographed from some copy of a single stencil.

Mr. Stryker had been as eager a pupil as the judge and jury. And when all this was explained and Mr. Feehan's lecture was over, the easels were wheeled away, to the great relief of everybody, not least the baffled newspapermen.

THE Government now called Henry Julian Wadleigh, whom most of us had known up to now as a former Government economist, a trade-agreements expert, a non-incriminating witness before the House Committee, and an alleged but never confessed conspirator lurking in the shadows of Chambers's memory. He came stiffly into the courtroom jerking his head around to get his bearings through thick tortoise-shell glasses. He had a shock of dark yellowish hair as rumpled as his clothes, a gaunt, thick-featured face with an open mouth. Here, it came out as the afternoon wore on, was a walking symbol of the shattered gallantry of the idealistic Left, a fugitive from the ruins of the Popular Front and the classless society, an earnest fellow traveler who had now to pay for the pride he felt, a dozen years ago, in trading in the loyalty of his oath of office for the true glory of being in the advance guard of the resistance to Fascism. A man who appeared, as he took the stand, to be no more and no less sinister in 1938 than thousands of other intellectuals in Britain and America who, in the squalid decade before Munich, had held the Soviet Union as a shining thing at the front of their minds. This, however, was 1949.

Mr. Murphy helped him trace his history, and he recounted it in a tense though fluent voice. Son of a Protestant Episcopalian minister, gone abroad as a child, an M.A. of Oxford, a Bachelor of Science of London University, back to America in his mid-twenties to do postgraduate work at the University of Chicago. Then an interest in Fabian Socialism (at this Mr. Stryker threw a weary arm over the back of his chair as if to say "That thing again"). He had worked with the Federal Farm Board, the State Department, the Department of Agriculture, a year with U.N.R.R.A.; and up to the previous year he had been an economic adviser to the Italian Government. Now he was out of a job. He was never a Communist, he said, but there came a time when he decided to "collaborate" with the Party.

"Did there come a time," Mr. Murphy asked, "when you were working for the State Department when you took Government documents out and gave them to people?"

The correspondents of the wire agencies were crouching with poised pencils near the door, ready for another "confession" and another flaming headline.

"Yes."

"—not authorized?"

"Yes."

"When did that begin?"

"As soon as I entered the State Department . . . March, 1936."

He took from his desk whatever he thought would be "of interest" and about once a week put them in a brief case and handed them over on a street corner to one David Carpenter, who would give them back to him next morning. When Carpenter was not around, he gave them to Whittaker Chambers, who was known to him as Carl Carlson.

Mr. Murphy showed him a set of the microfilm documents in evidence. He had no recollection of ever having seen them. There was a possibility he might have handed over one of them, and another would have struck him, if it had come across his desk, as "an unusually interesting one . . . a sufficiently rich find." There came a time, some weeks before he went off on a mission to Turkey about the 9th of March, when Chambers told him not to deliver any more documents for the time being. After the Nazi-Soviet Pact the next year he had misgivings about the noble purposes of the Soviet Union and he was no longer willing to take the risks incurred in what anyway he had always regarded as a "distasteful" operation.

Mr. Murphy moved over from one foot to another and paused. Then he said: "Did you own an Oriental rug?" Yes, said Wadleigh.

Mr. Stryker protested that this was immaterial and Mr. Murphy loudly thought it was very material. The two of them were called to the bench. Judge Kaufman thought it was a prejudicial question and sustained the objection. Mr. Murphy jogged back to his station considerably put out and ended by getting Wadleigh to agree there was no point in showing him the Baltimore documents, since he agreed he had never done any typing. As Mr. Murphy sat down, Wadleigh recrossed his legs and rubbed his knuckles. He was palpably nervous, but his nervousness took the form of a tense and confident jauntiness. He was hand-tailored for Mr. Stryker, who came to with alacrity and started taking his constitutional between the witness and the far corner of the jury box.

During this period he was, was he not, in and about various parts of the State Department, in other people's offices? When official business required it, he was; and at other times for personal calls.

"On some of those occasions when you went on a personal call to other offices, if you found 'a rich find' in there, would it be fair to assume that you availed yourself of it?"

"No, it would not be fair to assume that, and I never did anything so foolish."

Not so foolish? No, the only material he used was what came across his desk.

"Never used any other at all?"

"No."

"Not on grounds of scruple I take it?"—Mr. Stryker was looking out the windows.

"Well, in fact, I did not."

But while he was in sympathy with "the Russian movement" was he not sympathetic to the general tenets of the Party, one of which was lying?

"I would hardly call that a tenet . . . I would call it a procedure."

"I am not going into semantics. I didn't go to Oxford . . . you subscribed to that idea that wherever it was necessary to lie, that was a policy that met with your concurrence?"

"Yes."

Mr. Stryker supposed that he kept his ears open and whenever he heard something that might be useful he eavesdropped? No, he did not.

Mr. Stryker's eyebrows shot up. "Your conscience would have kept you from that?" He just did not eavesdrop on people, Wadleigh replied. Well, if the occasion arose, Mr. Stryker supposed, strutting smartly away from the witness, "you would not have had the slightest conscientious scruple, I take it, Mr. Wadleigh in pilfering documents from other desks, would you?"

"Well," said Wadleigh, holding on to the arms of his chair, "I never did so and the question never arose in my mind." Mr. Stryker turned on his heel and cupped an innocent ear.

"Pardon? I don't like to interrupt, but I was addressing myself to your conscientious scruples."

Wadleigh now became the bright undergraduate, back at his old school, explaining T. S. Eliot to a graying and once respected English master. Conscience wasn't involved, couldn't Mr. Stryker see? Mr. Stryker blew soundlessly through his lips. Wadleigh threw his head back and pondered how to put it without pain. "One gets conscientious scruples," he explained, "when one contemplates doing something, when the question arises, but the question never arose in my mind and therefore I can have no recollection of having had any conscientious scruples against doing it. In other words," he ended, "your question is a hypothetical one."

Mr. Stryker's lower lip fell in awe. His eyes roved waggishly around the room. "I daresay it *is* very faulty," he said, "but you will have to bear with me. I do the best I can."

This might have brought a rebuke from Judge Kaufman if he had not been busy spreading his large hand across a mouth curling from ear to ear. Mr. Stryker looked humbly at his shoes. "I realize you have the benefit of—what was it?—London University and Oxford, too?"

"That's right."

"By the way, you still seem to have some of the Oxford accent, don't you?" Maybe, he thought. Mr. Murphy's trombone protest obliterated this fiddling, and the judge told Mr. Stryker to pass to something else. He therefore picked up a paper and showed it to Wadleigh. It was a top-secret document from his own division. Mr. Stryker read his testimony before the House Committee in which he refused to say if he had ever seen it for fear of incriminating himself. Having checked this, Mr. Stryker snapped: "That's all," and sat down.

MR. MURPHY was almost at the end of his case. He called an F.B.I. laboratory man to say what kind of camera photographed the microfilm documents. He had hardly begun when the judge beckoned counsel to the bench and afterwards announced that without hearing the evidence of two witnesses about to be called he would accept as material and relevant the evidence Mr. Murphy said they were ready to give: namely, that the film came from a Leica camera owned by one Felix Inslerman, whom Chambers had identified as the chief photographer for the spy ring.

Mr. Murphy called his last witness, a meek sedentary type who identified himself as a professional court reporter who had taken down on a stenotype machine the testimony of Whittaker Chambers be-

fore the House Committee at the public session of the 25th of August.
The man began reading over in a professional dirge a wad of Chambers's testimony, and the courtroom stretched and thought that Mr.
Murphy, a comparatively obscure prosecutor, was letting the useful
tension of Wadleigh's confession come unstrung in a trivial defense of
some old discrepancy. But if Mr. Murphy was being inept, he hardly
appeared to know it. He had one ear tilted over, and after getting the
man to explain how stenotype machines transcribed phonetic sounds,
he asked him to look at a certain page and had him read the harmless sentence: "I went to Mr. Hiss, who was then living on"—the
man paused and said: "My stenotype notes phonetically show,
'Balt . . . Balt Place.' " But he had been unsure of his hearing at the
time and made a tear on the paper, which was his custom when he
was in doubt. Afterwards he had checked with somebody and, from
their recollection, amended the symbol.

We suddenly remembered Chambers's denying he had ever put
the Hisses on "Dent Place," when he insisted he had said Volta Place;
and Mr. Stryker's showing him the printed record, and Chambers's
coolly arrogant response: "The printed record is wrong."

"Did you change your notes," asked Mr. Murphy tolerantly,
"after talking with somebody?"

"That is right, sir."

"What did you write in your notes?"

"Dent . . . superimposed over Balt."

Mr. Murphy smoothed out his coat. "The Government rests,
your Honor," he said.

Mr. Stryker was ready with two motions to dismiss the indictment: one, that "the alleged perjury related to immaterial matters,
and the indictment represents an attempt to evade the statute of
limitations"; two, that the Government had "based its case upon the
direct testimony of Chambers, a witness who is so discredited that he
cannot be corroborated." After an argument for two hours in chambers, Judge Kaufman denied both motions; and at the beginning of
the fourth week of the trial Mr. Stryker opened the case for the defendant.

THE CASE FOR THE DEFENDANT

❀

FOR the opening of the defendant's case the court was packed again with strangers, tattling housewives, modish women, and suspiciously idle recruits to the "working press," all come in the hope of seeing Alger Hiss take the stand. But first, it turned out, there was to be a parade of heralds, or character witnesses, and Mr. Stryker with an artist's restraint left these introductions to Mr. McLean. Dr. Harry Hawkins, once the chief of the State Department's Trade Agreements Section, and Wadleigh's boss at the time, was the first. He began by confirming Mr. McLean's understanding that one of the microfilm documents, a photograph of a carbon copy of an aide-memoire, had been sent by him to Mr. Sayre's office, but that the actual document he had sent was an original and not a carbon. He allowed Mr. Murphy's point that once he had signed a document he had no idea whether his secretary would or would not attach carbons to it. He had been in Mr. Hiss's office when it was empty and Miss Lincoln had not stopped him. And what, asked Mr. McLean, was Mr. Hiss's reputation "for integrity, loyalty and veracity?" It was good.

He was one of many to say so: John W. Davis, a former Presidential candidate, and a trustee of the Carnegie Endowment when Hiss was elected president; Dr. Stanley Hornbeck, Hiss's chief at the State Department through the war years; Charles Fahy, formerly Solicitor General of the United States; Admiral Arthur Hepburn, a veteran of the Battle of San Diego, and a naval delegate to the San Francisco Conference; Judge Wyzanski, a district court judge from Massachusetts; and two Associate Justices of the Supreme Court. An assumption was left by a statement Mr. Stryker was allowed to make

that former Secretary of State Edward R. Stettinius would have said
so had he not been too ill even to have a deposition taken. And Mr.
Stryker read solemnly into the record a deposition of Dr. Philip
Jessup, given in Paris and full of the most peremptory legal challenges ("State the reason for your absence from the United States"—
"I am in Paris attending the meeting of the Council of Foreign Min-
isters as Alternate and Adviser to the Secretary of State"). To questions *a*, *b*, and *c*, affecting Mr. Hiss's integrity, loyalty, and veracity,
Mr. Stryker chanted the ringing responses: "a. His reputation for
integrity is good. b. His reputation for loyalty is good. c. His reputation for veracity is good."

Another former officer of the State Department was now called,
a former assistant chief of the Trade Agreements Section called
Darlington. He, too, recognized a microfilm document he had prepared. And he, too, said he had sent on the original and kept the
carbon, which would probably have stayed in his unlocked desk and
then gone into an unlocked file in his office. Yes, he knew Wadleigh
and often had conversations with him about "the work at hand."
There were times when he would go back to his room after lunch and
find Wadleigh reading a paper, a document, on his desk. Wadleigh,
he would say, had "a well-developed curiosity." And yes, he had been
in Hiss's office and Miss Lincoln never tried to stop him. And as for
reputation, integrity, and loyalty, Hiss "had the finest reputation
anyone could have on all those points."

Mr. Darlington was a trenchant diplomatic type more familiar
in Europe than America, and the press was a little rough on his administrative air and accent, calling him a fugitive from a Noel Coward
play and "a cookie-pusher type with manners and accent to match."
When Mr. Murphy asked him if he ever saw Wadleigh take papers, he
replied: "Heavens, no!" as if it were a casual idiom in American. Mr.
Murphy needled him about the exact length of time a carbon would
stay on his desk and he responded with such non-legal reservations as:
"I would be surprised if it stayed in or on my desk for less than, say,
two weeks," or "I think anyone after a lapse of 12 years would have to
reply No. . . . Still I think what I said before gives a better picture." In the end, Mr. Murphy made him squirm into the not very
helpful admission that he had only "a modicum of independent
recollection" of the fate of Government documents and their carbons. A slim, high-domed man from the State Department's com-

munications office confessed under Mr. Murphy's coaxing that
though he knew a good deal about the Department's present procedure in stamping and distributing documents, he was quite unfamiliar with the practice in 1938.

From a Noel Coward play we went into a Frank Capra movie.
A sweet, well-preserved, circumstantial old lady from New Hampshire testified she formerly ran a guest house in Peterboro which had
once been owned by the Society for the Preservation of New England
Antiquities. Smilingly she explained it was now known as Bleak
House. She had started to operate this place in August 1937 and from
the start had every visitor sign the guest book. Did the F.B.I. call
on her in the present spring and take the book away and subsequently
bring it back? Yes, they did. And had she come to New York last
night and been introduced to Mr. and Mrs. Alger Hiss? Yes, she had.
Did she see them sitting in the courtroom? Yes (she gave a fluttery
smile of recognition). And she had never seen either of them before
last night? No, she never had.

This was firm and satisfying; until Mr. Murphy got from her the
fact that a Harvard friend of Hiss had come to borrow the book to
look for the names of Chambers and the Hisses.

Then came a tall, big-boned man with glasses, a nutty all-American type, the farmer with a spry enjoyment of life and no fandangles
about him. He ran a summer camp in Maryland and was called to help
Mr. McLean prove the Hisses had been there, far from Bleak House
and *She Stoops to Conquer*, every day of the Hiss vacation time in
August 1937. Yes, he knew Mr. Hiss very well, about fifteen or sixteen
years. Mr. Hiss's stepson had gone to the camp in 1937, soon after he
broke his leg. He came in on crutches and needed exercises every day,
which Mr. Hiss came to teach him. Were Mr. and Mrs. Hiss near by
in Chestertown, Maryland, that summer? Mr. Hiss was there all the
time, but Mrs. Hiss wasn't because she took "a course in Baltimore."
Did he know when Mrs. Hiss's course was over?

He began to fumble in a pocket and took out a paper. Mr. Murphy
wanted to know what the paper was for. "Notes of my own"; the
witness smiled. Oh, well, then, Mr. Murphy objected; he thought it
was an official record. The judge wondered if it helped him refresh
his recollection. "It certainly does," said the witness. Mr. Murphy
didn't like the look of it, and Mr. McLean sighed at the witness:
"Mr. Kellogg Smith, at my request, have you checked certain records

and verified dates?" He had. And could he say when Mrs. Hiss stopped taking that course? He inclined his head at the paper and said brightly: "The 26th of July." And when that was done, were Mr. and Mrs. Hiss at the camp thereafter every day of the first two weeks of August? That was right.

Mr. Murphy sauntered up to the witness stand. He would like to see that paper. Mr. Smith showed it to him.

"When did you prepare this paper, Mr. Smith, do you remember?"

"Last week from the records that I had from the hospital."

Would he tell the Court and jury what records he had about Mrs. Hiss's course in Baltimore? Well, said Mr. Smith brightly, it was "just memory." Mr. Murphy drove him to identify the "records" he examined which would confirm the date of Mrs. Hiss's return from her course.

"Pure memory," said Mr. Smith, right as rain.

"Fine," said Mr. Murphy, his arm akimbo again, "and when had you previously talked to any of the lawyers from Mr. Hiss?" Not before last Friday, he said, sucking his teeth. The little judge's face puckered; he couldn't mean *last* Friday (it was only Monday now). Yes he did, Mr. Smith said, "three days ago." But, he ambled on, he knew he was coming to New York a week ago.

"Now how did you know that?" Mr. Murphy wondered.

Slap back came the honest answer: "Mr. Hiss called me in Chestertown." I see, said Mr. Murphy. But we were clear that Mr. Hiss was at the camp all through July? "Through July and August both . . . they rented an apartment for two months." Mr. Smith went on pleasantly putting his foot in his mouth.

"Now, how do you know when Mr. Hiss's vacation began and ended?"

"Well, I was.—I got that from him because I asked him."

"How recently did you get it?"

Mr. Smith stretched. "About a week ago."

"And then you used those dates, did you, to help you?"

"Absolutely."

Mr. Murphy had the paper now and asked the witness if he could recollect when Hiss ended his vacation. Well, Mr. Smith thought it was for a month from the 15th or 16th of July on. How did he remember that? "I have a pretty good memory." Mr. Murphy began to read aloud from the paper its notes about the Hisses' comings and goings. He fed them to Mr. Smith as leading questions, and Mr. Smith firmly said "Yes" and "Oh yes" and "correct." Mr. Murphy put the paper in evidence as a Government exhibit. "Now that," he said, "I take it you got word for word from Mr. Hiss?" Yes, that was correct.

After this debacle the afternoon was devoted again to discrediting the Chambers story. A neighbor of the Hisses who had been on cordial, dropping-in terms with them said he had never seen the Chamberses at Thirtieth Street, either in the house or in the garden. He had seen the Hisses in the evenings, at week-ends, at the ends of afternoons; he had seen their friends, but he had never seen Chambers. What color was the outside of the Hiss house painted? It was a vivid yellow, and the shutters a bright blue. When the Hisses moved to Volta Place, he visited them for about five years. And was there at that house a brick or stone structure with an iron railing around the top in front of the front door? (Mrs. Chambers had said there was, and the 1949 photographs showed one.) In 1938, the witness replied, there was no such railing, and the only masonry he recalled was a wall into the garden. On the contrary, he seemed to recall some shrubbery, he wasn't sure it was a tree, now supplanted by the masonry. Mr. Murphy asked him if he ever saw "strange people" in the garden and he replied: "strange to me, yes sir," not to the Hisses. Mr. Stryker thereupon called a building contractor who swore that, starting in December 1946, his firm had torn down a tree at the Volta Place house and built the "stoned-in porch" the pictures showed. He also confirmed the neighbor's remembrance that at the time the Hisses were in the Thirtieth Street house, the walls were painted yellow and the shutters blue. Mr. Murphy could not budge this builder from his documented recollection and let him go.

A man from Pennsylvania came in to testify on Mrs. Chambers's story of the holiday in Pennsylvania, where Mrs. Hiss was supposed to have cared for the child while Mrs. Chambers painted. The man recalled renting a cottage at Smithtown, on the Delaware River, to a Mr. and Mrs. Breen (a confessed Chambers pseudonym) in the summer of 1935. He gave a plausible description of the Chamberses and said he saw them around at the time, often dropped in for a cup of coffee. But before "last night" he had never seen Mr. or Mrs. Hiss. Again, at Mr. Murphy's prodding, he admitted he left the Chamberses very much to themselves, that he took all his meals five miles away, and hadn't recognized the Chamberses' photographs when the F.B.I. showed them to him. But he stuck to his story that the only woman who cared for any baby was a woman "of olive complexion with very dark hair and high cheekbones."

The next day was yet another steaming, rancid day in a summer of interminable heat. But Mr. Stryker walked into the cool, wet air of the courtroom with a smart tread and a glinting eye that promised great events. He had no sooner read, with the judge's permission, a deposition from Mr. Adlai Stevenson, the Governor of Illinois, attesting to the reputation of Hiss, than he swung around, hooked his thumbs in his shirt, and announced: "I will call Mr. Justice Frankfurter."

The court looked up agape, conceivably listening for the Olympian swish of a black gown, and awaiting the gaunt cheeks and the mantled brow of the Hollywood stereotype of a Supreme Court justice. Instead a little summer suit and a bow tie were twinkling towards the witness stand. Mr. Justice Frankfurter was a tiny bird of a man, but as he perched in the middle of the witness chair, and Judge Kaufman rose to greet him with obvious pride, he managed to convey to the court that the rules of evidence and the proprieties of cross-examination were about to receive their acid test. This manner visibly affected the judge, who was later to sing out a vague and guilty appeal to "the rules, Mr. Murphy, the rules," without specifying which rules he had rather not mention. Mr. Stryker took up his most imperious stand at the end of the jury box and invited assent to a series of imposing questions that were no questions at all to anybody who can run and read. Was he a justice of the Supreme Court of the United States? He was. How long had he been a member of that Court? Since January 30, 1939. Was he formerly associated with the Harvard Law School? He was. Had he known Mr. Justice Holmes? He had. Would he tell the court how young men were chosen for the editorial board of the *Harvard Law Review*? Would he say that they were chosen "on the basis not only of integrity but for reason of character"?

Justice Frankfurter replied that "his Honor will keep me within bounds if I stray outside of them, but inasmuch as men are chosen by the students, which students made the choice by their own minds, and who I should think have a very direct and rather fair determination, as we all know, as their qualifications are passed upon by their fellow students—"

Mr. Stryker paused briefly for the sentence to end. But the "inasmuch" was simply a legal starter, and apparently the sentence was at an end. Well, did he have something to do over the years with selecting the "secretaries for the great Mr. Justice Holmes"?

"I think," the Justice nodded, "a year after I joined the faculty of the Law School Mr. Justice Holmes was good enough to ask me to designate for him—perhaps recommend would be the more accurate word, but it was in fact a designation because he did not know the man who was to be designated for what you call secretaries, but who are technically known as law clerks to the justices." In short, and after an account of character requirements which in this court sounded judicial but elsewhere might have been thought garrulous, Mr. Justice Frankfurter admitted that he knew Alger Hiss and had chosen him as the man who, of all the ones in his class, could be most confidently recommended to become the law clerk of Mr. Justice Holmes.

Mr. Stryker, with his eyes on Mr. Murphy, was feinting for an opening that would let the Justice come through and report, short of hearsay, what Mr. Justice Holmes had thought of Hiss. "I presume," Mr. Stryker said, "Mr. Murphy would object if I asked you what Mr. Justice Holmes said." Judge Kaufman thought he should object. And Mr. Murphy rose up sheepishly and murmured: "I think I should, too, your Honor. I am under an obligation here"—an obligation apparently to go on being a lawyer even in the presence of the Honorable Felix Frankfurter and his forbidding syntax. The judge obliged Mr. Stryker by thinking it would be enough to ask Mr. Justice Frankfurter whether he had occasion to discuss Mr. Hiss with Mr. Justice Holmes. At which the witness said at once: "The answer to that is yes." Mr. Stryker went no further than to ask if the Justice had met "many, many persons in Cambridge, the Harvard Law School, Washington and elsewhere" who knew Alger Hiss. He would say yes. And was his reputation for "loyalty to his Government, integrity and veracity . . . good or bad?" The Justice replied: "I never heard it called into question . . . it was excellent."

When Mr. Murphy came to cross-examine, he faced the Justice like a man again. Greatly daring, he began by taking up from Mr.

Stryker's question and asking: "Didn't you hear in 1944 that it wasn't too good? . . . did Judge Frank ever talk to you about him, Judge Jerome Frank?" (an old New Dealer with whom Hiss had quarreled during an administrative upheaval in the A.A.A.). The Justice allowed that Judge Frank had had "differences of opinion with Mr. Hiss . . . that did not bear on questions of loyalty or integrity."

"But you remember talking to Judge Frank about it?"

"No, I remember his talking to me."

Mr. Murphy touched his mustache. "Then I assume that you talked to him when he talked to you?"

"Well, let us not fence. All I meant to say was—"

"Well, you were the one that started fencing with me, weren't you, Judge?"

Justice Frankfurter looked tolerantly pained at this neophyte. He said: "I am trying to answer as carefully as I can with due regard to your responsibility and mine, and the jury's, and the responsibility of this case." He would "deny unequivocally" that any differences between Hiss and Judge Frank "affected loyalty to this country." He had no independent recollection of recommending Hiss for Government service, but if Judge Frank had come to him and asked for suggestions he "certainly would have recommended Mr. Hiss unqualifiedly."

Mr. Murphy asked if the Justice had ever testified in a federal court before "on the character of anybody at all." He was quite sure he never had. "And," drawled Mr. Murphy innocently, "has the Court adjourned for the summer, your Court?"

"It has not sir."

Mr. Murphy turned away and rolled a mischievous eye.

"But it is not in session today, Mr. Murphy."

Mr. Stryker stood up with his chest out. "Thank you very much, Mr. Justice Frankfurter."

One Supreme Court Judge was followed by another, giving rise to the first speculation among some people about the possible shrinkage in the qualified membership of the Supreme Court, if ever this case should be appealed there. This was Mr. Justice Reed, who had once had Hiss on his legal staff when he was Solicitor General. He was a big, impassive man with no disposition to exercise his prestige or be more than an obedient witness. Hiss was recommended to him by Judge Jerome Frank. He knew Hiss well. Before "these matters came up," he had never heard his reputation questioned. As far as he knew, Hiss's reputation was good. An old friend from the Harvard Law School, now the Chief Judge of the United States Court of Appeals for the First Circuit, said his reputation was excellent; "unequivocally excellent" was the testimony of another old lawyer friend.

We were now at a disturbing stage in the presentation of the defendant's case. Whenever there was documentary evidence—like the building contractor's—the Chambers story was plainly in question. But whenever the evidence was a witness's memory, it often seemed as dubiously pat as the original accusation. This mood may have been induced not by the weakness of the witnesses' recollection but by an unsuspected competence in Mr. Murphy's tactics in cross-examination. When he was facing his own witnesses, Mr. Murphy had been as phlegmatic as a respected master of foxhounds, but with the Hiss witnesses he began to reveal a devilish streak of bushbeater which had his quarry darting all over the countryside for shelter. Where Mr. Stryker had adopted an attitude of nauseated contempt for Chambers, Mrs. Chambers, and Wadleigh, Mr. Murphy conveyed the subtler imputation that the Hiss witnesses were sentimentally united in a rather snobbish plot to prove that the defendant was altogether too charming a type, too scholarly a lawyer, and too devoted a husband to be capable of associating with such low characters as the Chamberses and the Wadleighs of this world. "It goes without saying," they managed to imply, just so long as Mr. McLean fed them leading questions; but Mr. Murphy would then take over and show that to an unpretentious Government servant like himself, bent on doing his duty, nothing is too indelicate to doubt.

WHEN the next witness came on, a big comfortable colored woman peering through dark glasses, Mr. McLean was extraordinarily successful in encouraging the view of her as a simple, intelligent woman, a devoted servant and friend of the Hisses with a happy memory of her work with them and a grateful memory for many favors. She was Mrs. Claudie Catlett, usually known as Clidie.[1] She had worked for

---

[1] And at various times in the Trials as Clytie and Claudia.

the Hisses at P Street, all the time they were at Thirtieth Street, and for some time at Volta Place. She was a day-worker doing general housework and cooking and stayed till about eight in the evening. Did the F.B.I. people confront her with Chambers some time this spring? They did. Had she ever seen him before? Yes, at the P Street house. Did he ask her questions? Yes. What did he ask?

"He asked me about a table and some chairs in the dining room . . . he said it was on 30th Street, and I said No, because it didn't belong to them and they didn't move them, so it was not on 30th Street. It was a dining suite and some things in the dining room."

Chambers had mentioned some yellow rugs and she had told him: "No yellow rugs." He had also wanted to know "where Timmie slept" and where the kitchen was at Thirtieth Street, and how you got in there. Chambers had said he remembered her. He said: "You are the woman that can mash potatoes." And what had she said to him? She had said: "Anybody can mash potatoes." The F.B.I. also showed her pictures of Mrs. Chambers and her child, but Mrs. Catlett had never seen them before.

Now, said Mr. McLean, let's get back to his one appearance at P Street. Mrs. Catlett composed her big hands in her lap and told how one afternoon he had rung the doorbell, given his name as "Crosby," and she had let him in. Mrs. Hiss was home alone.

When the Hisses moved either from P Street to Thirtieth Street, or from Thirtieth Street to Volta Place, "did the Hisses give you and your family some things?"

"Yes, they did."

"What did they give you?"

"They gave me a chair, a victrola, one of them old kind victrolas, and some clothes, but I don't know now . . . some pictures and them little things."

"Anything else?"

"And they gave the children a typewriter."

"So that at the time the Hisses moved—"

Mr. Murphy unwound his great height, his patience exhausted. "I am going to insist now we have no more leading questions."

The judge told him to "take it easy" and said he didn't think they were leading questions. Mr. McLean went sunnily on. Mrs. Catlett thought the children got the typewriter when the Hisses moved to Thirtieth Street, but she wasn't sure which move it was. At Thirtieth Street did the Hisses have a portable typewriter? ("Leading question," growled Mr. Murphy.) She really didn't know.

"You don't remember what kind it was?"

"I don't remember no typewriters at all."

But how about the typewriter that went to the children (her sons Pat and Mike)? What kind was that? She didn't remember. Mr. McLean was careful to get in the fact that he had talked to her about the typewriter early in the year. Then he delivered her into the hands of Mr. Murphy. As soon as she faced his uncompromising hulk, her memory came out in handfuls and was left bald and ragged. When the F.B.I. first talked to her about the typewriter, "you didn't remember any typewriter at all, did you?"

"No, I did not."

"As a matter of fact," said Mr. Murphy leaning engagingly forward, "you don't remember now anything about getting that typewriter, do you?"

"No, I don't remember nothing about the typewriter."

"Nothing at all?" Mr. Murphy said in exultation.

"No, I don't remember what kind it was, or nothing."

"Well, even if you can't remember what kind it was, do you remember the Hisses giving it to your boys?"

"No, I didn't. At that time I didn't remember it."

But she certainly remembered that one half-hour visit of "Mr. Crosby." Tell us about that, Mr. Murphy suggested. How was this man dressed?

"He wasn't dressed too good."

"Pretty shabby, would you say?"

"That's right."

"And you fixed tea for him, is that right?"

"I did."

"But he was a pretty shabby fellow?"

"Well, he wasn't so bad."

And how long did he stay? Well, she wasn't interested "because I didn't have no business with him." Yet she remembered his name was Crosby? That was right. Did the Hisses have other callers, other friends? Naturally. Did she remember their names? No, she didn't . . . "some Washington people, I don't remember." And hadn't she

signed a paper for the F.B.I. only the previous February saying that
when they showed Mr. Chambers to her she had not recalled his
name, and couldn't then recall any name for him? That was right.

Did the Hisses have a rug in a closet? That was right; in a closet
at Thirtieth Street, and on the floor of Timmie's room at Volta
Place.

Mr. Murphy began to switch from topic to topic and suddenly
swooped down on the typewriter again. Did she remember the F.B.I.
asking about it the first time they questioned her? No, they did not;
if they did she didn't remember it. Mr. Murphy wanted to get it
"very, very clear": "they didn't mention the word, the name typewriter, the first time that you saw the F.B.I., is that right?" In exasperation Mrs. Catlett replied: "They put everything down that I
said, and you get the papers and read them." Supposing we do that,
Mr. Murphy breezily suggested. He took a yellow paper and read:
"I recall that Alger Hiss had a typewriter which I first saw on P
Street." [1]

Well, she remembered the typewriter being there, but didn't
think the F.B.I. had mentioned it then.

Mr. Murphy wouldn't let the typewriter go, until at last she
admitted she first remembered about the typewriter "this year sometime," 1949, after the F.B.I. interview; that one of her sons told her
they had had a typewriter from the Hisses. Then Mr. Murphy would
go back to the F.B.I. interview again and press another topic ("is it
Crosby, like Bing Crosby . . . or Crosley?"), till the now confused
Mrs. Catlett reflected sadly: "I don't know, it's on the paper when it
was," and "There were so many times they asked me so many
questions."

Mr. McLean took over with the gentle promise that he had not
many more questions for her. How often had the F.B.I. examined
her? It might be seven or eight times, sometimes at Winchester,
Virginia, where she now lived, sometimes in Washington. Did she
tell him (Mr. McLean) once about a toy she had bought for her
daughter Mary? Yes, it was a child's toy typewriter. Why did she
buy it? Well, Mary always wanted everything that Burnetta had,
and "I bought it to keep down the fuss." And what was it Burnetta
had? "She had the big typewriter that Pat gave her, the one Mr. Hiss

---

[1] Her own home there, that is.

gave him." And was there one F.B.I. report, on a conversation with her, which she had never seen and never signed? There was.

NOW came her son, a sprightly young Negro wearing a big green tie. He was Raymond Sylvester Catlett, usually known as Mike. From him, for the next three hours, we were to hear testimony that touched one extreme of human articulateness, as Mr. Justice Frankfurter in the morning had wallowed in the other. It would be hard to improve on this duet to demonstrate the wide range of human misgiving that exists about the game we solemnly worship as "due process of law." Justice Frankfurter's performance had been a legal charade put on for the benefit of the peasant laymen, but in the afternoon, watching the graveled and outraged Mike Catlett, it was the layman who felt as learned as the nine Supreme Court judges rolled into one.

He began well enough by agreeing enthusiastically with Mr. McLean that he was a handy man, twenty-seven years of age, who had washed the Hisses' car, cleaned up their yard, waxed their floors. He hadn't recognized any pictures of Chambers and he told the F.B.I so. Nor of Mrs. Chambers and the baby. When the Hisses moved, they gave him clothes, books, a typewriter. What kind of typewriter? A Woodstock, he flicked back without a second thought. What condition was it in when he got it? "It was broke." Tell us, coaxed Mr. McLean, "how it was broke." Mike Catlett rubbed his chin for a second; "Well, the keys would jam up on you and it wouldn't work good. You couldn't do any typing hardly with it." There was a knob off, and the wheel and the ribbon wouldn't work.

Mr. McLean bent down and pulled out a big box from under the defense table. There was a rumple of cardboard and he lifted up a big old-fashioned office typewriter and lugged it along the well of the court and plumped it down in front of Mike Catlett.

"I show you this typewriter and ask you if that is the one the Hisses gave you."

There was a long, aching pause. Mike Catlett lifted a dark index finger over the machine and poked at three keys. "This is it," he cried and sat importantly back in his chair.

When he first got the typewriter, what house did it go to first? It went to "our house" on P Street (the Catletts lived a couple of blocks away from the Hisses). He had kept it about a couple of years and then given it to his sister-in-law, and finally "my sister (Burnetta) got a hold of it." Well, let's take it step by step, said Mr. McLean. His sister-in-law was Pat's wife, right? And she got the typewriter before she married? That was right. Now, did he, Mike, have a talk with him, Mr. McLean, at Donald Hiss's house early this year? Yes, in February. And "did I ask you to help me in doing something?"

Mike Catlett bent forward. "Sir?" he asked.

"Did I ask you to help me in doing something?"

Mike Catlett frowned. "Help you in doing something?" He was meant to say "search for the typewriter," but for all he knew he was floundering at the throne on Judgment Day. Mr. Murphy got up and asked that the witness be told to tell the conversation. Mike Catlett glowered at Mr. Murphy; and Judge Kaufman, sensing a prickly exchange ahead, quietly leaned towards the witness to ask him if he remembered "everything that you said to Mr. McLean and everything that he said to you." This was eerier than being asked to help Mr. McLean do something. He glanced at Mr. Murphy, made an appealing gesture with his palms out wide, and burst out: "I'm sorry. I'm tryin' to get things clear, you know what I mean. I don't want to get this thing wrong and then this fellow over here"—indicating Mr. Murphy—"would talk back to me and say something else, you know—get me all crossed up. This is not the first time I've been in court, see?"

The judge reassured him that nobody was trying to cross him up. Just tell everything he had said to Mr. McLean and Mr. McLean had said to him. He started gamely, but got into reported conversations again, and as Mr. Murphy rose, the judge decided that "in view of the fact that this witness is not particularly articulate . . . I think that counsel is left free to ask" a leading question. Mr. Murphy righteously announced: "I submit that is not so, sir, I don't agree with it." The judge snapped that no one was asking him to agree with it, he didn't expect he would agree with it. And Mr. Murphy sulked back into his seat.

Mike Catlett went on, doing his baffled best to accommodate a simple story to the foolish taboos of the law. And he managed to tell how he had gone off in search of the typewriter, talked with many a neighbor, started "getting warm" with a Mr. Lockey, located it after a month; and how one Saturday morning Mr. McLean came again to see him. "Did I have something with me?" Mr. McLean asked. "You sure did," said Mike Catlett. It was the typewriter.

Mr. Murphy, up again, asked to have the time fixed. The time? Now what was this, Mike Catlett wondered. "Give us the month of the year as best you can," Mr. McLean put in. For Mike Catlett, due process of law had achieved a frightening absurdity. He spread a black hand toward the court reporter. "I mean," he protested, "I haven't got no papers, no secretary to copy all that stuff down."

Well, when he saw the typewriter that morning what did he do? He looked at it to see if it was the same typewriter. And it was.

Mike Catlett jostled in his seat as Mr. Murphy came in to cross-examine. "What was there," Mr. Murphy began, "about the typewriter?"

Fairly disgusted now at this ritual procedure, Mike Catlett cried: "I'll just tell you the same thing. You were sitting right there and listening to me." Poor Mike Catlett, unaware of the loving traps the law has fashioned for the statutory "protection" of such innocents as he. The judge asked him just to answer questions, not to argue. Mr. Murphy slowly, teasingly questioned him all over again about the mechanical defects of the typewriter, till it turned into a monster at his elbow and he protested: "*I* don't type."

"You *don't type* at *all?*" Mr. Murphy shrieked incredulously. He meant he was not a typist; he could "put my name down." What system did he use? Mike Catlett looked at Mr. Murphy blank as a wall. "What system? ! . . . you mean to—what, type with this?"

"Type," Mr. Murphy primly said.

"One finger," said Mike Catlett.

After fifteen minutes of resentful backchat Mike Catlett revealed that he didn't type, but that he kept the machine in a "den" to which he retreated, whenever he felt like it, to type his name out with one finger. He never typed anything but his name.

When did he get the typewriter from the Hisses? It was "in the moving." Which moving? He couldn't recall, it was so long ago. (This date was, of course, the nub of the Catletts' testimony. The defense wanted to prove that the Catletts had the typewriter before Mrs. Hiss was alleged to have used it for documents in the Volta Place home. The documents bore the dates January-March 1938. And the Hisses moved into Volta Place on the 29th of December 1937.

It would suit the defense perfectly if it could be established that the typewriter had gone to the Catletts just before the move to Volta Place.)

Mr. Murphy moved down the well. He would offer a truce. "May I call you Mike?" My name, said Mike, "is Raymond Sylvester Catlett." All right, Raymond Sylvester Catlett, then Mr. Murphy had no recollection of hearing the date of the typewriter's changing hands "when Mr. McLean was asking you. Do you have a different recollection?" Mike Catlett didn't understand—"explain this more." All right, did he remember Mr. McLean's putting him on the stand? He did. Did Mr. McLean ask him and did he tell us when it was he had received the typewriter?

Mike Catlett shrugged at the air and blurted out: "It's been so long ago, and you come right back and you ask me the same thing. I mean they're not my own thinking of what it was. I mean you're getting me all balled up here." Mr. Murphy stroked his walrus and looked down at his feet. Then, with a chin-up-tolerance-is-everything sigh said he hoped Mike Catlett believed him when he said he didn't want to confuse him? Mike Catlett shook his dark head. "There's a whole lot of things you believe and a whole lot of things you don't believe." And he'd been told, "when I was brought up young."

"What," begged Mr. Murphy, "were you told when you were brought up young?"

"To believe a whole lot of things like God, and about fellows like you, I mean."

The judge waved the quarrel down. And Mr. Murphy tried again for the date of this vague, long-ago "moving." Was it when the Hisses moved from P Street to Thirtieth, or from Thirtieth to Volta Place? Mike Catlett appealed to the judge. "Judge," he said, "it's kind of hard. I mean, that's a big problem before me." Well—Mr. Murphy barely concealed an interior groan—could he at least remember whether it was Mr. Hiss or Mrs. Hiss who gave him the typewriter? Mike Catlett objected to that: "When someone gives you something, they would leave it, I mean they would do it that way and then you wouldn't know who it was who gave it to you. I didn't ask who it was from, and I only do so when I would get it and I would say thank you." *He* couldn't recall who told him there was something for him. It might have been the maid. All he knew was he got the typewriter.

He clapped his hand to his mouth and shook his head and said aloud the glum thought: "I got it and they too have it, but I suppose they're going to go against me. I don't know. I don't know."

"Don't you worry," the judge comforted, "about anything being against you at all." But to the end, in answer to the simplest declarative question, he always shook his head. Mr. Murphy asked how much younger than him was his sister Burnetta (to whom the typewriter had gone at last). Mike Catlett marveled at the tangents of the law. "What are you worrying about how old she was?" Mr. Murphy cleared his throat and unwound the whole story, over and over again, taking it up strand by strand. Well, in the years Mike Catlett and his brother had it, did they ever take it out of the house? The Catlett chin shot up from the hand it was resting on. "What would I want to take it out of the house for?"

The hot afternoon staggered along and gave out. It was not until the next morning that Mr. Murphy began to get a few things admissible as facts. After the F.B.I. had first come to see Mike Catlett in May, did he go to Donald Hiss and tell him the F.B.I. had talked to him about a typewriter? He did, sir. But he didn't tell the F.B.I. agents about a typewriter, did he? No, he didn't. And he refused to sign a statement for the F.B.I.? Why, sure he did. All right, now when he had the typewriter at his house, it was in pretty good shape, wasn't it? Yes. And he never tried to get it fixed? No, he didn't. Then it went in time to his sister Burnetta? That was right. And she used it to do her school work on? That's what she wanted it for, he thought, but he didn't know because he wasn't living with her. She was living at a Dr. Easter's. Was she the girl that later got married and lived in Detroit? Yes, sir.

With obvious pride at last Mr. Murphy drew from him that Donald Hiss had given him about forty dollars to use in trying to track down the typewriter.

Mr. McLean came in to make sure that he had never paid anybody that money (now changed to fifty dollars)—for the obvious reason that he, McLean, had found the typewriter. No, sir, he never paid anybody. Mr. McLean had just one more question. Once the typewriter was found, did the F.B.I. interview him again? They did. How many men? Oh, about five men and a lady. "How long did they keep you down there?" Well, he got down about four thirty and "I didn't get out until about 9." Did they say what they thought the typewriter was worth? "The agent told me it was worth $200 or more, saying he would give me $200 or more if I got this typewriter for him."

Mr. Murphy's six feet five came up like a ramrod. "What agent told you that? . . . What was his name?" "Jones," said Mike Catlett, clasping his hands, his elbows straddled.

"And that is your oath here?" Mr. Murphy was shouting.

"That is what I said."

How long after he had had this talk with Jones did he tell "that" to Mr. McLean? It wasn't long. And when was he with the F.B.I.? He didn't pay any attention to the month.

Mr. Murphy was so hot and bothered that his voice rose from a deep rumble to a roar. Mr. McLean objected to "this screaming at the witness," and the judge said it was "perfectly apparent that he does not know the month. He has told us a dozen times." But on his oath he'd say that Mr. Jones said that? That was right.

The ordeal of Mike Catlett was over. He could wish good riddance of this mad maze, and the absurdity of questions the lawyers knew the answer to: How old was he? When did they give him the typewriter? How old was his sister twelve years ago? How long before something did something else happen? . . . White folks sure ask the darndest questions.

HIS brother was called, Perry Catlett, known as Pat. He was a gentle, attentive man who, as it happened, was deaf. So Mr. Murphy had to modulate his roar to sound loud but well-bred. First to Mr. McLean, Perry recounted, in a low, shy voice, with none of his brother's sauce, that he had worked for the Hisses at Volta Place, had never seen Chambers there (he called him "Cambridge"); that Mr. Hiss had come to his wedding, and that was the last time he'd seen him. He testified that the Hisses had indeed given the typewriter to him and Mike when they moved from one house to another. Moreover, he knew which move it was. It was from Thirtieth Street to Volta Place. The typewriter was in "pretty bad condition" and he therefore carried it to a shop on K Street and Connecticut Avenue to have it repaired. There had been a knob missing, the lever didn't work, the ribbon was out of order, and the keys stuck. The man at the shop said it wasn't worth repairing.

Mr. Murphy, much subdued at the thought of an amenable witness, got it quite clear at the start that Perry had had the typewriter first at his mother's house on P Street; that it had stayed there until it went to his sister, Burnetta; that she took it with her when she went to live at a Dr. Easter's house. Now, where was the repair shop that he took it to? It was positively on the ground floor of a place at Connecticut and K. And it was the nearest repair shop he could find. Had he not told the F.B.I. that the Hisses "could have lived on Volta Place for several months before they gave it to me"?—Mr. Murphy hardly needed to ask. He had a statement signed by Perry which he read aloud. Perry conceded: "They could have." Supposing, Mr. Murphy said, looking triumphantly down at the witness, it was proved that that shop was a Woodstock repair shop, and "supposing I tell you that the Woodstock repair shop at Connecticut and K did not come into existence until September of 1938, would that cause you to fix the time after September when you took it there?" Perry didn't know, he just took it there and he didn't know what time of year it was.

That was all, from Mr. Murphy. It was plenty. To be able to leave a strong doubt that the Catletts got the typewriter even as late as the spring of 1938 could be enough to shake the foundations of the defendant's case.

Another colored man was called, the man at the end of the trail— Ira Lockey, the man who had had the Woodstock typewriter right along. He was a night watchman with a construction company, and one could see him back in the winter nights yawning by a stove amid dank scaffolding, while a score of F.B.I. men knocked on doors, peered for serial numbers, clambered through junk shops, "shook down the City of Washington to a fare-thee-well." All the while Ira Lockey had the typewriter in his home. By simply being the F.B.I.'s undiscovered prize, he brought into court a comic sort of majesty.

"In April of this year," Mr. McLean began, "did you and I have a business transaction?" Yes, sir.

"And what was that transaction?"

"You came to see about a typewriter, sir, that was in my possession."

"And what happened?"

"You bought it."

Mr. McLean read a scrap of paper: "Sold to Edward C. McLean, one Woodstock typewriter, model 5–N, No. N230099, price $15. Received payment. (Signed)—Ira Lockey. April 16, 1949."

He had had it since 1945, when he got it "at a moving job." He had seen it in the back yard of a family called Marlow. His daughter was taking typing at school, "and during the war you couldn't buy those things." So he asked Mrs. Marlow if he could take the typewriter by way of payment for the moving job. After the daughter married, she had no more use for it, and it went to his son, who let his little daughter "peck on it some . . . but she never did much with it because the keys would stick on it."

A colored lawyer came up briefly to tell how he had helped Mr. McLean track it finally to Ira Lockey.

THE court was getting impatient for the appearance of Hiss. In the corridor outside, there were winking intimations given during the recesses that it would not be long now. But before he came on, Mr. Stryker called a surprise witness. This was the well-known literary critic, an editor of the Left-wing *New Republic*—Malcolm Cowley. It was difficult at first to see why he had been called, and as Mr. Stryker led him around to a conversation he had had with Chambers long ago, Mr. Murphy clearly saw the defense walking the high-wire of hearsay and did his best to embarrass this delicate tactic by objecting again and again to this sort of testimony. But the judge had made his decision to allow it in a previous argument in chambers, and Mr. Murphy at last sat down scowling.

Mr. Cowley was a gruff, affable man of the rumply literary kind who in churches, courts, or funeral parlors always seem to be missing their pipe. The reason for his being there was soon made plain. He kept a literary journal. He had been a writer all his life and consequently, Mr. Stryker wished to show, there was nothing odd in his having kept a record of a lunch-time conversation he had had with Chambers in December 1940. The luncheon was at Chambers's suggestion. He was apparently writing a piece for *Time* about the growing defection of the American Left from the Soviet bandwagon and he wanted to trace the histories of some who had "jumped off the Moscow Express" and meant to include in the article Waldo Frank, Granville Hicks, Lewis Mumford, and Mr. Cowley. Warned that he must try to recall the direct conversation, Mr. Cowley puffed at his invisible pipe and told how Chambers had sketched his own history in the Communist Party and talked about work in the underground. He had mentioned names of various alleged Communists in the Government, including one Cowley said he would not repeat. Mr. Stryker was then bound to ask him to repeat it, but made a solemn declaration to the Court that the defense completely repudiated "in the most emphatic way within my power" the suggestion that the man named had ever been disloyal to his Government. The name was none other than that of Mr. Francis B. Sayre, Hiss's old chief in the State Department, and now the United States representative on the Trusteeship Council of the United Nations. The judge reminded everybody that this conversation was being offered only to show "inconsistent statements" made by Chambers. Regretfully Mr. Stryker agreed that that was so. Well, Mr. Cowley went on, "that shocked me." Mr. Murphy didn't care whether it shocked him or not, and the witness was again urged to stay with the conversation and away from opinions. Chambers had said Sayre was "the head of a Communist apparatus in the State Department." So they passed on to other topics, and Cowley had said he was glad he himself had never joined the Communist Party because it seemed to him that "all former Communists had been warped by their experience, that they felt the loss of something and could be likened to unfrocked priests." Chambers, on the contrary, had said he was glad he did join because he thereby "learned their methods and I am going to use their methods against them."

This sentence was what Mr. Stryker had been waiting for. It might do with a few remembered words what he had failed to prove in hours of wrangling with Chambers on the stand: namely, prove that long after Chambers had "reformed and repented" he was still apt to use "lying and deceit and falsehood" for his own ends. Over Mr. Murphy's faintly disgusted protest, Mr. Cowley described Chambers's unkempt appearance and a habit of "glancing suspiciously around the restaurant." Why was that, Mr. Stryker wondered. Well, Chambers had said something to the effect that "we were surrounded by spies, traitors and conspiracies." Did he say when he had left the Party?—Yes, he had said "about 1937." Mr. Stryker was allowed to read into the record a page or two from Mr. Cowley's notes, which reported his opinion that Chambers unquestionably

knew a great deal about the tactics of Communist infiltration. Mr.
Murphy handled him with not much less distaste than Mr. Stryker
had handled Wadleigh, but Mr. Cowley's notions about his own
politics were quite precise. He admitted he had registered on the
Party line for voting in the elections of 1932 and 1936. And the "fact"
was undeniable that until 1939 he had been "sympathetic" to the
Communists, but after the Nazi-Soviet Pact he then wanted dearly
"to get out of the whole business."

There was a short recess, after which Mr. Stryker stood up and
called "Mr. Alger Hiss."

FOR four dragging weeks of summer heat Alger Hiss had sat with
folded arms in the well of the clammy courtroom. For four weeks
his handsome head had tilted at an attentive angle, while the Government's witnesses had built around him a prison of accusations, which
if the jury thought it had been truly built could isolate him from
American society and honor as surely as the walls of a leper colony.
To any normal man so arraigned, this courtroom must have seemed
an air-conditioned nightmare. But Hiss had not only shown no trace
of uneasiness or inner conflict; he had been as gay, as interested, as
affably detached as some promising young lawyer allowed to sit in
on a case whose human tragedy provided merely the academic raw
material for a study of trial tactics he was learning to master. If he
was innocent, this serenity could be only the deep well of security
in a character of great strength and purity. In a guilty man, certainly,
his detachment would be pathological in the extreme.

He walked over to the witness stand in the last hour of the day
with the same nimble grace and compact charm with which he sat in
the highest seat to preside over the plenary sessions of the young
United Nations in the San Francisco Opera House. He settled a
candid gaze on Mr. Stryker, and Mr. Stryker looked hard at him. Mr.
Stryker did not fumble for an opening, even when the witness was
a nonentity. With his own clients he sounded at once the theme of an
aggrieved, noble protest. He squared his shoulders and tore at scherzo
speed into this trumpet catechism:

"Mr. Hiss, are you now or have you ever been a member of the
Communist Party?"

Quietly Hiss responded: "I am not and never have been."

"Or a fellow traveler or a sympathizer?"

"No, Mr. Stryker, I never have."

"Mr. Hiss, I call your attention to Exhibits Baltimore 1 to 4, inclusive, in this case. I show you these and I ask you if they are in your handwriting?"

"Yes, Mr. Stryker, they all are."

"Mr. Hiss, did you in the months of February and March, 1938, or any other time in your life, ever furnish, transmit or deliver those exhibits to Whittaker Chambers?"

"I did not."

"I show you Exhibits Baltimore 5 to 47, inclusive—the Baltimore papers . . . did you ever furnish, transmit and deliver those documents, or any of them, to Mr. Chambers?"—a pause and then three times as loud: "Ever-in-your-life?"

"I did not, Mr. Stryker."

"Did you in your lifetime ever furnish, transmit and deliver to Whittaker Chambers or any other authorized person any restricted, secret or confidential documents of the State Department of any kind, character or description whatever?"

"I think," replied Hiss with a tentative smile, "you meant 'unauthorized.' "

"I did," Mr. Stryker threw in hastily, impatient at missing the beat.

"As amended, the answer is I did not."

"Have you read the questions and answers set forth in the first count of this indictment?"

"I have, Mr. Stryker."

"Were the answers that you gave to those questions true?"

"They were and they are."

"Have you read the questions and answers set forth in the second count of this indictment?"

"I have."

"Were the answers given to those questions true?"

"They were and they are."

Mr. Stryker raised his voice in a more soaring affirmation still: "Whether or not it was the State Department, the Nye Committee, or any other department of the Government with which you at any time were in any way concerned or connected, did you ever at any time procure, transfer and deliver to the man who calls himself

Chambers here, or anyone else, any unauthorized paper of any kind?"

"I did not, Mr. Stryker."

"Mr. Hiss," said Mr. Stryker in the same challenging tone, which he at once modulated into an easy conversational query, "where were you born?" And so into the andante. It was to be expected that Mr. Stryker would put on display all the honors and responsibilities in the long, and till lately happy, life of Alger Hiss. We leaned back for the necessary preliminaries of getting born, schooled, trained for a career, and married; and then the biography of the golden boy: Johns Hopkins, Phi Beta Kappa, Harvard Law School 1929—*cum laude, cum maxima laude* all the way; chosen secretary to Mr. Justice Holmes—a job calling for the most intimate trust and for a knowledge of Supreme Court confidences that he must not, and never did, disclose.

Reassured about this, Mr. Stryker asked him to tell in great detail his career as a lawyer and a Government servant. Through it all— from a distinguished Boston law firm to Yalta and San Francisco— Mr. Stryker never missed a chance of impressing the court with the fact that Hiss had moved almost monotonously into offices of the highest trust and had discharged them ably and honorably. This was the first of the two discernible lines of Mr. Stryker's defensive campaign, which he waged for two whole days. First, to show what manner of man Hiss was and is. A man who, as Secretary General of the United Nations San Francisco Conference, had guaranteed the personal safety and planned the daily co-operation of the statesmen of fifty nations. A man who had been thought fit to trust with securing "the safety and safekeeping of our President" in time of war. (Hiss had helped the military "in a very small way" with President Roosevelt's itinerary after the Yalta trip.) A man who had resigned from his presidency of the Carnegie Endowment on a point of honor when the endowment's trustees had refused his resignation and were willing to share the humiliation of his present ordeal. The second line of defense, it was to appear, was to persuade Hiss by implication to remind the jury as often as possible that his immediate and continuing concern, from the moment Chambers accused him before the House Committee, was for his honor: that he had searched for personal papers to turn over voluntarily to the Department of Justice; that he had scorned his constitutional privilege to refuse to testify before the House Committee, or to spurn the inquiries of the F.B.I., or the grand jury that indicted him; but that he had rather welcomed and assisted the fullest investigation of a story he knew was a calumny.

But while he was solidifying these battle lines, Mr. Stryker never failed to snipe away at the Chambers story. Did it come about, for instance, that Hiss argued a case before the Supreme Court of the United States? Yes, one and one only. And what was that? United States *v.* Knott. And when was that? March 1936. Well, if he argued it in March 1936, he was not arguing it in 1935? (Mrs. Chambers had said he joined the two wives once in 1935 after he had been arguing a case before the Supreme Court.)—No, sir.

Then Mr. Stryker got the most minute account of his job and duties in the State Department, especially his daily routine in assisting Mr. Sayre. "Mr. Sayre was a very busy man. One of my duties was to take the material which came to him primarily for his information and weed it out and send him only what seemed of the essence for him to know."

"And in the course of that, did you sometimes make handwritten memoranda to refresh your own recollection as you talked to him?"

"Yes, I did that in two different ways. For example, if there were a fairly lengthy paper, only a part of which seemed to me to be of interest to him, I might send that particular paper together with a little memorandum addressed to him, a handwritten memorandum, saying, 'Note page so-and-so, paragraph so-and-so.' On other occasions, I would take the papers into his office, describe them to him, and say, 'I don't think you need to read them or look at them. This is the gist of this one,' and then put it into his outgoing basket."

And what, in particular, was he doing in the years from the time he entered the State Department in the fall of 1936 through the year 1938? When he first went there, the Reciprocal Trade Agreements Act (passed in 1934) had only nine more months to run. So through "the fall of 1936 and the better part of the winter of 1937," his chief preoccupation was to prepare "the arguments on the constitutionality of the Act" and prepare arguments for its renewal to put before the committees of Congress. During 1937 Mr. Sayre's duties began to extend to the Philippines, of which he later became High Commissioner. The Philippines had already been promised their independence, and although they were at that time administered by the War Department, the whole commercial future of the relations between the two countries had to be gone into. The year 1938 was given over

almost exclusively to "very difficult, prolonged and complex negotiations" over the British trade agreement and a new Canadian agreement. During 1939 he felt that war was imminent. Mr. Sayre went
to the Philippines and Hiss moved over to the Far Eastern Division
to work with Dr. Hornbeck. During 1939 there was the question of
whether "shipments of scrap iron, of oil, and of other commodities
should be allowed to go to Japan without restrictions."

(These, we were left to reflect, were Hiss's "preoccupations and
responsibilities" during the years when Chambers put him with such
nonchalant audacity in an active Communist conspiracy.)

Mr. Stryker gave him his head to make a lucid and informative
talk on the work of the conferences at Dumbarton Oaks, Yalta, and
San Francisco. When he had described what Mr. Stryker saluted as
"this gargantuan order" of running the San Francisco Conference,
he was quietly asked: "And did that also involve security for the representatives of the fifty different nations?" It did; the number-two
man of the F.B.I. helped Hiss set up the arrangements for the personal
security of the foreign delegates.

Mr. Stryker was fascinated. "You say the F.B.I. was then col-
laborating with you?" Yes, said Hiss with a smiling nod.

"Well!" murmured Mr. Stryker.

During the whole of this long recital of the career of Alger Hiss,
and the wealth of diplomatic history it touched on, Mr. Murphy sat
mentally tapping his teeth. A defendant's day in court, when the
Government is the accuser, is an invitation to open and voluminous
confession. Only once towards the end of it did he rise. Mr. Stryker
had got out of Hiss his opposition to the public protest of two well-
known lawyers who maintained that American aid to Britain and
France, after the signing of the Nazi-Soviet Pact, would be an un-
neutral act. Hiss felt there were "political and spiritual reasons" for
feeling differently. Didn't the United States, pressed Mr. Stryker,
thereafter take a position, "though we were not at war, of aiding
those who subsequently became our allies?" Mr. Murphy chimed in:
"Your Honor, I submit that perhaps the Congress of the United
States did." Judge Kaufman thought it was useful background. And
Hiss went right on to say that "neutrality did not require us to fail
to help our friends."

But this was a useful storm signal to Mr. Stryker. Sensing, rather
late perhaps, that more people than Mr. Murphy might consider a

skillful political lecture a tribute to a man's intelligence but not necessarily to his honesty, Mr. Stryker looked thoughtfully at the jury and wound up the Hiss career with a pointed appeal to patriotism. During the time that Hiss was in the State Department, did he offer his services as a soldier? Hiss replied that he had tried to get into the Navy, but the State Department thought his work was equally as important ("corresponded in importance," was Hiss's phrase) as the job of the armed services.

Mr. Stryker posted himself again at the far end of the jury box, as if to invite firm clear answers and the manliest denial to the questions he was going to ask about the unavoidable calumnies of the man Chambers.

"Now tell his Honor, please, and these ladies and gentlemen when you first met the person who now calls himself Chambers." Hiss replied clearly and carefully that it was either in the latter part of December 1934 or early in January 1935, and said later he had never seen him again after early June 1936 (before the Hisses moved to the Thirtieth Street house).

A man calling himself George Crosley had called on him when he was counsel for the Nye munitions investigation because he said he was preparing some articles about munitions. He came again once or twice, and then in the spring they had lunch together, when Crosley said he wanted to move to Washington, to finish his series of articles. Hiss happened to be "in the process of acquiring a house on a rental basis in Georgetown" (the P Street house), so he offered to let Crosley rent the apartment "at cost" for the remainder of the lease. Crosley came to look at the apartment one night in April. The day Crosley was to move in, his furniture van failed to show up; and so the Hisses invited the Crosleys and their child to spend the night with them at P Street. They spent in all one or two more nights, and during this time Mrs. Crosley painted a portrait of Timmie Hobson, Mrs. Hiss's son and Hiss's stepson. The Crosleys never again had a party with the Hisses, or spent a night with them anywhere, either at P Street, or at a cottage in Pennsylvania, or up in New Hampshire. But they moved into the Twenty-eighth Street apartment and moved out a day or two before the lease was up. They never paid any rent. Hiss saw Crosley in the fall some time and mentioned the rent, and Crosley said he was about to market his articles and would pay up shortly. During the winter of 1935 the unpaid rent was brought up again, by one or the other. Several times earlier Crosley had asked for small loans—"$10 and $5 and $15, something like that." He asked for another loan, at the latest in June 1936. Hiss told him that he "had become convinced that he would not repay the sums he owed me; that I intended to forget all about the money that was owed me and that I thought any further contacts had best be discontinued." Hiss never gave a key to Chambers for any house and never saw him again anywhere until they were brought together at the Hotel Commodore in August 1948.

That was the independent story of Hiss's relations with Whittaker Chambers. Now Mr. Stryker turned to the Chambers chronicle and hurled the questions at Hiss for him to spew out with gentlemanly contempt. Again, did he at any time in 1938, or any other time, "furnish, transmit or deliver" those documents to Chambers at any time? He certainly did not. Were there at that time any restrictions in the State Department requiring visitors to give their name or have a badge? "At that time there were no restrictions as to visitors entering the building whatsoever." Had he ever come into his office and found a stranger there? Once he came in and found an elderly, pleasant-looking man standing in front of the fireplace; it turned out he wanted to stand again in his father's former office, which he had often visited as a boy. Did Wadleigh ever come into his office? Several times. Did Crosley ever give him a rug? He did, probably in the late spring of 1936; it was—according to Crosley—from "some wealthy patron" and he passed it on as a gift. Who first referred to this rug before the House Committee? "It was I," said Hiss. Did he ever drive Chambers up to New York in his car? That was correct. Did he ever go with Chambers on a train to New York? He did not. Was there a word of truth about his ever going "into some remote part of Brooklyn to a moving picture theatre house" to meet a man called Bykov or Bekov? "Insofar as it refers to me, Mr. Stryker, there is not a word of truth in it."

"Did you ever meet anyone by the name of Bekov or Bykov with Mr. Chambers in Brooklyn—or," shouted Mr. Stryker, "any other place in the world?" Never, "with Mr. Chambers or with anyone else." And did he ever make any arrangement to supply typewritten copies of State Department documents with Chambers or "with anyone else in the world"?

"Of course not," said Hiss, contemptuously calm. The responses

never varied all morning long. Either incapable of anger at such ab-
surdities, or disdaining to show it, Hiss sat with his fingers locked and
his elbows on the arms of the chair, and to each of Mr. Stryker's
roaring strophes gave out the terse antistrophe: "Of course not,"
"Certainly not," "There certainly is not."

There was the subtle and threatening matter of the four-hundred-
dollar withdrawal from the Hiss bank account four days before Chambers had shown that Mrs. Chambers paid rather more than that in
cash for a new car. How about that? Hiss could explain that. Mr.
Stryker advanced along the jury box with a brown bankbook. Did it
show a withdrawal of four hundred dollars on November 19, 1937?
It did. Mr. Stryker put the bankbook in evidence. And Hiss explained
it all: during the summer of 1937 he and Mrs. Hiss decided that the
Thirtieth Street house was too small. They looked around for a bigger
one and by about the 18th of November had "a commitment" from a
broker that he was confident they could get the Volta Place house for
the price they were prepared to pay. There were more rooms in the
new house and it needed more furniture and furnishings. With the
four hundred dollars they had bought extra chairs, a table, glassware,
prints, and such.

Mr. Chambers, Mr. Stryker said, testified that they had bought
some Hitchcock chairs for the moving to Volta Place; "you did have
Hitchcock chairs, didn't you?"

"We have had them," said Hiss, "ever since we were married."

And how about the mirror Chambers had testified to seeing? That
was a memento left to Hiss in 1935 from the estate of Mr. Justice
Holmes, a handsome Queen Anne mirror [1] which meant a great deal
to him, and which he hung prominently in every succeeding house
"because of the affection and regard I have had for Justice Holmes
and his memory."

Mr. Stryker then went into his finale, retracing not so much the
explosive events of the accusation and the House Committee hearings
as Hiss's prompt and honorable response to them: waiving his immunity, never looking up records or leases; his pleading with the
Committee for a confrontation; how at last he got it, but was never
properly made aware it was to be a hearing until he got to the hotel
room; the story of the confrontation; his challenging Chambers to re-

---

[1] It had no gilt eagle; that was another mirror.

peat his accusation in public; his making the challenge again at the last public hearing; how Chambers had accepted it; how Hiss's lawyer was in London, but how as soon as he returned, in the middle of September, he instructed him to sue Chambers for libel in the amount of $50,000; how Chambers, when he was served, made another derogatory remark and how Hiss amended the complaint for a further $25,000; how Chambers was asked for documentary evidence and produced the papers; how those papers were presented to the Department of Justice on Hiss's orders; how the F.B.I. shortly afterwards called him in the middle of the night, and he dressed and caught a train to Baltimore and freely answered the F.B.I.'s questions for a whole day —mentioning the typewriters he had owned, and promising to search for specimens of typing, and in fact producing some; how the Government returned some of the earlier specimens; how he had "straightforwardly" told the grand jury that he thought he might have had the office typewriter as late as Volta Place; how he had instructed his counsel to find the typewriter; how he had told Mr. Stryker, if it was found, to offer it to the Government for their inspection; how the Government also returned a paper typed on a portable Hiss had bought in the fall of 1937.

Again, a final fusillade of Chambers shrapnel: ever arrange an ambush at Volta Place? Not there or any other place. Any word of truth in the child's rolling-pin, the plea to break with the party? Never a word of truth.

Mr. Stryker encouraged Hiss to recall his grievances against the tactics and procedure of the House Committee. And he recited them all with a controlled but unmistakable disdain and bitterness. In his presence he had been congratulated for not having counsel present. On the 16th of August he'd been told he couldn't have anyone even if he so desired. On the 25th his counsel was told to keep quiet when he referred merely to the facts. No opportunity had been given him to consult records. Some of the most important records had already been subpoenaed by the Committee.

"Was there," asked Mr. Stryker, catching the infection of Hiss's loathing, "anyone there presiding, similar to a judge of a court, to hold the case to an issue and to see that order and fairness and decorum were enforced?" Mr. Murphy objected. The judge thought Mr. Stryker had gone too far. There was no issue before the Committee, "isn't that a correct statement, Mr. Murphy?" Mr. Murphy had "long since refused to concede a lot of things," so, he grumbled, dropping into his chair, he "just wouldn't concede."

Mr. Stryker gave a little impervious sniff. He would come to the issue.

"Mr. Hiss, you have entered your formal and solemn plea of not guilty to the charges here against you, have you not?"

"I have."

"And in truth and in fact you are not guilty?"

"I am not guilty."

"Your witness."

MR. MURPHY began with a courtesy that boded no good. Did "Mr. Witness" (he never called him "Mr. Hiss" until the Second Trial) want to amplify or change any of his testimony? . . . any explanations or distinctions he would like to make? Hiss knew of none. If there were any, Mr. Murphy said, he would allow Hiss to "do it now." There was nothing the witness was conscious of. Very well, Mr. Murphy walked across to the Government table and fetched a volume of evidence. Literalness was Mr. Murphy's favorite hunting ground, and patience his most dependable rack. He turned over hundreds of pages of testimony with the routine diligence of a printer setting up a railroad timetable. Did Mr. Hiss make it sixteen times he had testified to seeing and talking with Chambers? No, Hiss's recollection would be about ten or eleven. All right, supposing they go over them together one by one. Even by the time they fell to niggling about the number of lunches Hiss and Chambers had had together, Hiss was parrying Mr. Murphy's legal nicety with responses equally legal. For example: if he had previously testified to something as a fact, then it was a fact; or if Mr. Murphy had inferred a fact Hiss could not now testify to, then Mr. Murphy had misunderstood. The count of Hiss's and Chambers's meetings was ruefully abandoned by Mr. Murphy when Hiss replied to one question: "Well, I was not counting the separate motions in and out of a room, for example." The P Street visit, extending over two or three days was "all one." That, said Mr. Murphy, his pretty list upset, "is going to throw the tabulation off."

When, when did he first "demand" the rent from Chambers? Hiss was not going to be caught inventing hard dialogue for what had been a vague mood of distrust. So he said he didn't think he ever made a firm "demand." He might have put it up to Chambers or Chambers might have "volunteered" his inability to pay.

Did Hiss pay the gas and electricity and other utility bills for the Twenty-eighth Street apartment? He paid all the bills. Did he ever ask Chambers to pay them? No, they were included in the flat rental. So Hiss had to stand the cost of the gas and electricity the Chamberses used? Oh, yes. And the telephone too? Certainly. But if he'd had long-distance charges of any size, "you'd have ran after him for that?" Hiss said: "I would have run after him." Mr. Murphy froze the gesture he was moving through. Humbly he asked: "You didn't mean to correct me that way, did you?" No, he was merely giving his testimony. Was it merely Hiss's desire "to use whatever correct grammar came to your mind?" It was "merely that I was testifying in my normal speech."

Well, then, how about the car? Hiss said he had given Chambers "the use of" his old Ford when it was the only car he had, but it was while he was "shopping for another one." Chambers came to get the keys for the car and probably at that time also picked up from Hiss the registration card and the title certificate. He used the car for about two months and then brought the keys back. So that, Mr. Murphy profitably mused, if a policeman had stopped him, and Chambers exhibited the title certificate, "the policeman would have gotten the inference that he was Alger Hiss?"

Hiss was touched by Mr. Murphy's concern for a policeman's inference: "I imagine that would depend on how Mr. Crosley behaved himself in his talk to the policeman."

He thought he next saw him the following spring, of 1936, when he brought the rug. He simply came to the door of the P Street house one evening and rang the bell. He was carrying the rug. Was Hiss's impression now of Chambers merely standing at the door? Hiss was not even sure he went to answer the door.

"I thought you said he came to the door."

"That," said Hiss precisely, "is the way he entered the house."

The bursting response to this caused Mr. Murphy to wonder if his Honor would "ask some of the clowns to stop laughing." But his Honor thought there was no justification for such a remark. And Mr. Murphy went back to his pages considerably riled. So Chambers's appearance with the rug simply led Hiss to imply that he was bringing it in part payment of the rent? Hiss smiled with his characteristic tolerance of a mind a little less exact than his own: "I think he implied it. I inferred it." The rug didn't quite fit any room until they got to Volta Place, where it went in Timmie's room.

Hiss was not sure if Chambers came to pick up the car for keeps in that same spring. He was sure Chambers had not returned the title certificate when he brought the keys back in the fall. Over the winter, so far as Hiss knew, the car just sat around the streets of Georgetown near to his house, and Hiss had "no independent recollection" of signing over the title certificate to the Cherner Motor Company. Also, anything he had said about the car to the House Committee was his "best recollection" at the time. (The judge opined there was nothing inconsistent between the long passages of House testimony that Mr. Murphy read and Hiss's testimony in this court.) But when Chambers did come back for the car, he still owed Hiss money? That was right. And the gift of the rug did not "wipe out whatever debt he owed you?" Not in Hiss's mind. Some time, it might have been then or later, Hiss told him he had no confidence in Chambers's repaying him in the future. Had he repaid anything? Hiss thought possibly about five dollars on the small loans he had made. He agreed he hadn't mentioned any repayment in his direct examination by Mr. Stryker. Anyway, that was the last time he ever saw Crosley. He saw the same man again next at the Hotel Commodore in New York in August 1948.

When did he first hear the name of Chambers and in what connection? Some time in the winter of 1948 he heard that the man was calling him a Communist. Did anybody else ever tell him there were rumors he was a Communist? Mr. Justice Byrnes, when he was Secretary of State, told him in March 1946 that he understood two or three members of Congress were going to say on the floor that Hiss was one of "a lot" of Communists in the State Department. And what did he do about it? He went immediately to his office and put in a call to Mr. J. Edgar Hoover. A couple of days later he went to see the F.B.I. and offered to submit himself for "full interrogation and inquiry." He told the F.B.I. the various college clubs and associations he belonged to, "that seemed to me to be completely irrelevant to any such inquiry." He mentioned "an editorial group" he had written for in 1932-3 "known I think as the International Judicature Society," which specialized in putting out notes on current labor cases. He next saw the F.B.I. at his office in 1947. They went over a list of forty or fifty names and asked Hiss to say if he knew them and in what association.

Mr. Murphy's lot did not seem a happy one through the eight hours of cross-examination. Hiss was a superlative witness getting by very thriftily on the investment in legal precision he had made before the last public session of the House Committee. No matter how much he then enraged the Committee by preferring his "best recollection" to the quixotic denials the Committee liked to provoke, it was apparent when he faced Mr. Murphy that he was reaping dividends from that old intransigence.

The most promising discrepancies Mr. Murphy turned up were, perhaps inevitably, to do with the Woodstock typewriter.

"Did you type, Mr. Witness?" Mr. Murphy abruptly asked. Hiss thought he might have "banged out one or two pages in college," but he didn't think he had typed half a page since. Well, was it his testimony now that he "wrote" the letter or memorandum to the school describing the "personal characteristics of Timmie Hobson," his stepson? By "writing," queried Hiss, "you mean typing?"

As long, said Mr. Murphy breathing hard, as they were going to be exact, they might as well be quite exact: "I show you Government Exhibit 19-B and ask you whether the impressions on that paper are the result of you using an instrument known as a typewriter?" Hiss was confident they were not. "Do you know who did use such an instrument to cause the impressions on the paper?" He believed Mrs. Hiss did. Did he tell the grand jury he might have typed it? He had said he could physically have typed it, but he was confident he had not.

Had he told the F.B.I., on December 4, 1948, that Mrs. Hiss disposed of the typewriter, after 1938, to some second-hand or used typewriter place in Georgetown? That was his best impression at the time, though he thought he had said "sometime in 1938." That would be his present recollection. Mr. Murphy took up an F.B.I. report, signed by Hiss, saying "subsequent to 1938." What was his testimony based on at that time? On discussions with Mrs. Hiss and his own previous recollection of having seen the typewriter at Volta Place some time. Mrs. Hiss thought it had probably gone to the Salvation Army or a junkman or she might even have sold it.

Now, did Mrs. Hiss type? Yes, but she was an amateur, not a proficient typist.

Was there any doubt in Hiss's mind that the two Government exhibits—of specimen typing—the report to the Bryn Mawr alumnae, and the letter to an insurance company—were done on the Woodstock typewriter? Hiss "assumed" they were typed on that old machine; he had no doubt they were done "in my household." Had not his own lawyers' experts advised him that they were done on *the* Woodstock, and had he not so testified to the grand jury? He knew only he was told they were done on *a* Woodstock.

Mr. Murphy then tried to get from him an admission that he had changed his recollection about the disposal of the typewriter when he heard that the Chambers papers had been expertly proved to have been done on the same typewriter. He harked back to Hiss's statement before the F.B.I. on the 4th of December 1948 (only eleven days before he was indicted) that he had had the typewriter at Volta Place. "Isn't that your impression today?"

"It certainly is not, Mr. Murphy. . . . My *knowledge* today is that we gave the typewriter to the Catletts at the time when we moved from 30th Street to Volta Place in December, 1937. . . . I say I *know* from what the Catletts have told us."

"And it is knowledge that has been recalled or refreshed because of the testimony of the Catlett boys? . . . how was it recalled?"

"It was not recalled. It was established."

Did he have any "distinct recollection" of the machine's being in poor shape, of his wife complaining about it? No, not particularly.

So was it fair to say that he had today no independent recollection of the disposal of the typewriter? No, he had not.

So he did not know now, of his own knowledge, whether or not the typewriter was given to the Catletts or not, was that correct? Hiss nodded, but replied: "In the sense of my recollection it is correct. In the sense of my knowing an established fact it is not correct."

Well, "what part of the [Catlett] mother's testimony refreshed your recollection?"

Hiss frowned. He got handsomer when he frowned, a change that nauseated his detractors and charmed his admirers. He looked, according to your point of view, like a puzzled Mr. Deeds or an ingratiating Dr. Jekyll and said: "Mr. Murphy, I'm afraid we are misunderstanding each other. I have not spoken of a refreshing of my recollection with respect to the typewriter." Mr. Murphy blew out his round cheeks. He would lead him again through his recollection, or

absence of recollection, of Mrs. Hiss's possible "complaints" about the
mechanical defects of the machine. They got nowhere at all with it.
Did he tell the grand jury that he gave a typewriter to the Catletts?
No, he was sure he had not told them so, because "I thought Mrs.
Catlett was dead at the time." Mr. Murphy rattled the changes on all
the essential topics, coming back later to ask Hiss how often he'd
rented apartments. Three, he could recall. (Mr. Murphy jogged his
memory for a fourth.) Did he throw a car in with any of them? No.
Hadn't it been his experience that landlords usually asked for the rent
in advance? Not for any short period that Hiss had ever rented.

Then back to Mr. Byrnes and the list of names the F.B.I. had
asked about, and a pacing of Hiss through many of these old names
and relationships that were by now a witch's curse on the case. Then
back to the Catletts. Then to the handwritten memoranda; how
would such notes normally come to be written? Well, Mr. Sayre was a
busy man. At first Hiss would put tags on documents he ought to see.
But this was a heavy burden on Mr. Sayre. So then he put notes
directing his attention to particular pages. Still too laborious. Finally
Hiss would take in documents to which were clipped notes about
their content that were addressed "to myself rather than to him."
If Mr. Sayre wanted to see the document itself, Hiss would take the
memorandum and put it in his pocket. If the memorandum was
enough, it would go out with the rest of Mr. Sayre's outgoing mail.
. . . Any memoranda he put in his pocket he would later "toss . . .
in the wastebasket."

And how about the four-hundred-dollar withdrawal from the
savings account? Did Mrs. Hiss take out four hundred dollars "at one
clip?" That was correct and then the next month they borrowed three
hundred dollars from the bank and deposited it in their checking account. All during the month of December, purchases they bought
out of that four hundred dollars were either shipped or brought home
in the car to Thirtieth Street, and some he transported "on our own
hook into the Volta Place house."

The next day Mr. Murphy was back remorselessly beating every
bush that might hide a fledgling perjury, or some "then recollection"
impossible to reconcile with a "present recollection." He would spring
from the gift of the rug to the X-rays of a stepson's broken leg.
He looked for Red skeletons in the closet of every Hiss friendship. He
rustled Hiss's recollections again of his 1937 vacation in Maryland. He

would no sooner start reading a doctor's report about "a comminuted fracture" (of Timmie's leg) than he was discussing makes of type-writers again, or crawling once more over the Oriental rug. Old court hands confided that this was a technique known as "laying the ground-work." The implication was that Mr. Murphy would come in for the second day of cross-examination and start rounding up all the maverick memories of Alger Hiss and whip them into a stampede. But there was little agreement during the recesses in the corridor that Mr. Murphy was succeeding. The anti-Hiss faction applauded Mr. Murphy's sarcastic mastery of the evidence (he had been called in on the case fairly late) and remarked that Hiss was "a smooth article." The pro-Hiss faction saw in Hiss's shrewd calm his demonstrable innocence and in Mr. Murphy's sarcasm the exasperation, as one reporter put it, of "an amateur photographer in a darkroom, fishing up rolls of film here and there that never seemed to turn into printable negatives."

He began the second day by recalling the suicide of Chambers's brother and asked if Hiss had "had such experiences in your family." Mr. Stryker objected to it and was sustained. And when Mr. Murphy appealed again for an answer, the judge ruled it was "purely im-material" and did "not affect the credibility of this witness in the slightest."

Did Hiss remember saying that he had argued one case and one only in the Supreme Court, and that was in 1936? He did. Had he not also been in the Supreme Court in December 1935 for United States *v.* Butler, a case for which he had prepared the brief? That was right.

Mr. Murphy prodded Hiss about his vacation in Maryland in 1937, asked him about the house he stayed in, and about an accident to the landlady's son, and wondered if Hiss would take the landlady's word that the accident was in 1937. Hiss broke into the smile of a cat hearing the mousetrap snap in the night. He wouldn't doubt the land-lady's word, he said, but "I think I would check records if it became important."

Mr. Murphy now proceeded to examine for scratches the halo Mr. Stryker had put over the Hiss career. Had Hiss been willing "to share" with the Secret Service "whatever measures they took" to se-cure the safety of the President on the Yalta trip? Hiss simply replied he was not responsible in any such sense for the President's safety. Did he know that three other men had turned down the presidency of the

Carnegie Fund before he was offered it? That he did not know. Had he not had a conversation with Mr. John Foster Dulles about the appointment? On the telephone, yes. Did he not tell Mr. Dulles "that you had checked with Mr. Justice Byrnes specifically as to whether he thought the issue had been laid to rest, and Mr. Byrnes said it had"? That was a fair summary, Hiss replied, "I checked through Mr. Dean Acheson." Mr. Murphy saw a bull's-eye here. But Hiss would not let him make "I checked specifically" mean "I checked personally." Mr. Murphy had another trap ready. Was he not asked at a dinner of the Carnegie trustees in December 1948 "when and where did you personally see Secretary of State Byrnes, and particularly check with him . . . ?" Hiss could not recall the exact language and insisted on his own precise version, which had Hiss asking Mr. Acheson to check with Secretary Byrnes.

Did he ever meet a woman known as Hede Massing? He never did. Did there come a time last December when the F.B.I. had asked him to sit in a room with two or three people and say afterwards if he knew a particular woman there? That was correct. And he didn't recognize the woman? That was correct. And he never talked with her in the home of a Noel Field? No.[1]

When the F.B.I. first asked him for specimens of typewriting, on the 4th of December 1948, he knew then the Government was looking "to compare known standards with disputed documents"? He understood that. Now, did he not give to the Government specimens typed by his stepson on a portable machine he had? That was right. And weren't the others an original and a copy of a letter which in fact had not been sent? He thought they were both copies of letters he had sent.

Another time Mr. Murphy strained and strained to get Hiss to say he had testified before the House Committee that his wife was with him and Chambers on the drive to New York, whereas in this trial he was sure she had not been. Hiss would not yield. Whatever he had told the Committee was his best recollection at the time. Mr. Murphy read the House testimony: "Whether my wife was present or not I am not sure. I rather think she may have been." Mr. Stryker jumped up to protest that he had left off a sentence that "in common

---

[1] This was to be a great issue with the Government in the Second Trial. See page 291.

fairness" ought to be included. Mr. Stryker was allowed to read it for him and recited with heavy emphasis: "I would have to ask her and I haven't asked her."

All right, Mr. Murphy enlarged, "it was your recollection then at the time you testified that your wife accompanied you and Mr. Chambers, is that correct?"

"Mr. Murphy," Hiss replied with handsome patience, "you are characterizing what you have just read . . . why don't you just read it again."

All Mr. Murphy's frustration at the canny lawyer on the stand exploded into a regimental sergeant-major's scream: "Now, your Honor, would you instruct this character to refrain from making remarks to me?" Riding high over the ensuing tumult, Mr. Stryker's outraged civility could be heard thundering: "I consider it offensive and improper, and were it not for the fact that I do not want a mistrial I would move for it."

"The incident," panted the judge, once the court was calm again, "is closed for the moment."

Mr. Murphy in the last of the eight hours he had Hiss on the stand kept up a steady recital of House testimony, and grand jury testimony, always ending with the customary phrase: "Were you asked those questions and did you give those answers?" To which Hiss would invariably reply: "I was and I did," or "I may very well have, but I don't recall it now," or "I did."

Hiss was just as graceful and collected as he had been all along. It was Mr. Murphy who was husky. And he roused himself for a final jab. Some time before Mr. John Foster Dulles went to Europe to a United Nations General Assembly in the fall of 1948, some time during the House Committee hearings, didn't Mr. Dulles ask him "out of consideration for the Endowment" to resign voluntarily as its president? He did not. Did he say, "pursuant to any request from him," that he would resign after the Committee hearings were over? He couldn't answer that simply yes or no; would Mr. Murphy like to be told what happened? No, Mr. Murphy would not. Mr. Murphy would go on to ask him if he had not told Mr. Dulles that he wanted to put off any question of resignation while the Committee hearings were on? "I most assuredly did not." Well, when he was elected a trustee of the Endowment, as distinct from its president, was that

election for life? It was. He submitted his resignation as a trustee also,
but it was not accepted.

"No further questions," said Mr. Murphy.

BEFORE Mr. Stryker began his redirect examination, there was a
squabble about his right to read all of the days' grand jury testimony
that contained the parts Mr. Murphy had read. The judge was
adamant for Mr. Stryker's right. Mr. Murphy knew "no way to
turn" if his Honor so directed. But his Honor did so direct and said:
"I understand Mr. Murphy, I understand." It meant passing to Mr.
Stryker six whole days of Hiss's grand jury testimony and also an
F.B.I. report. Mr. Stryker's intention in reading them was to shift
the stress of their meaning reasonably to support the versions Hiss
had sworn to or conceded. He got him also to tell again at length his
conversation with Mr. Byrnes, during which Hiss added the point
that he had offered to resign from the State Department if the Secretary thought these charges might be an embarrassment; but Mr.
Byrnes had said: "Not at all. I wouldn't think of your resigning in the
middle of a fight." He had originally meant to resign and go back to
private practice as soon as the war was over, but the then Secretary of
State, Mr. Edward Stettinius, had persuaded him to wait a year;
then, just about the time he would have left, this rumor cropped up
and so he stayed through most of 1946.

Mr. Stryker ended by rereading Hiss's denials before the grand
jury of ever being a Communist and of ever having "furnished any
information to any person known to you or suspected by you to be a
member of the Communist Party." Were those questions asked and
did he give those answers? Those questions were asked and he *did*
give those answers.

Hiss bowed to the judge and went back to his seat and smiled at
his wife, who then was called.

SHE was a slender, meek little woman with graying hair on top of a
face wide-eyed as a Kewpie doll. She had sat by her husband's side
through all the days he was not on the stand. Being, as her husband
said, of "the Quaker persuasion," she "affirmed" rather than "swore"

to the oath. Mr. Stryker put to her the main events of her life, requiring from her no more than a series of assenting monosyllables, given in such a small voice that she was asked several times to try to keep it up. She was born in Evanston, Illinois, and her father's name was Fansler. At about the age of four or five she moved to Philadelphia and went to school there and so on to Bryn Mawr. She took a graduate course at Yale, and "there came a time when" she married a man by the name of Hobson. She was divorced and in 1929 married Alger Hiss. She had one child, Timmie, by her first marriage, and one by Hiss—Anthony. She confirmed her husband's story of the Crosleys, adding without hesitation that Mrs. Chambers was introduced to her as Mrs. Crosley, and that she never called this woman by any first name, nor ever by Lisa or Liza. How was Mrs. Hiss called by her husband? Usually as Pross or Prossy. Had Mrs. Chambers ever used that nickname? No. How did she call her husband? Hilly. Did Mr. Hiss ever call her Dilly, as Mrs. Chambers had testified? No.

Seeking to discredit Mrs. Chambers's memories of the Hiss homes, Mr. Stryker drew from Mrs. Hiss many a feminine detail about her furnishings, which he excused himself from grasping on the grounds of being "a mere man." With his own witnesses Mr. Stryker always suggested the relationship of two thoroughly intelligent people being sporting enough to straighten out for a third party a preposterous misunderstanding. When his own witness was a lady, Mr. Stryker seasoned this kinship with an apologetic chivalry that turned the witness into a confidante.

When the Hisses left the Twenty-eighth Street apartment and moved into the P Street house, she left "everything but linens, silver, pots and pans and Timmie's bed, and our clothes; and lamps, I think, we took too." Otherwise it remained, for the Crosleys' stay, a furnished apartment. She had had the Hitchcock chairs since 1927 and bought no others for the move to Volta Place. She left them incidentally at Twenty-eighth Street (where, presumably, the Chamberses could have got to know them). Yes, Mrs. Chambers did paint a portrait of Timmie while she stayed at P Street. Did she also paint a landscape for Mrs. Hiss when they were supposed to have gone up to the Delaware River? "Nothing of the kind ever happened." Nor had she ever visited Mrs. Chambers at any of her homes. She had never sat in any park with Mrs. Chambers "with or without her baby."

She never used the car to move any belongings of the Chamberses. Mr. Stryker would show her a picture of the Thirtieth Street house. What color was it painted? A bright yellow. Had Mrs. Chambers visited that house twice? No. What color was the living-room? (Mrs. Chambers had said pink.) It was green, both walls and woodwork. All right, now they move to Volta Place. Was there a large tree in front of the doorway? There was. And was "the structure that we have all become so familiar with . . . there when you lived there?" It was not. Did the Crosleys ever visit at Volta Place? They did not. "Specifically, did they ever come to any house-warming, New Year's Eve party, wedding anniversary, or any other kind of party at the Volta Place house?" No. Or did she attend any kind of party at any home of the Crosleys anywhere? She did not. Where were the dining-room and kitchen at Volta Place? (Mrs. Chambers had said in the rear.) They were in the front. Mr. Chambers had testified there was paneling in the dining-room; was that right? No, the wallpaper went straight down. Mr. Stryker put her through the paces he had prac-ticed on her husband and with the same brisk certainty that, however frail she looked, there was no hurdle she was too weak to take. Did she ever hand the handwritten notes and the typewritten notes to Mr. Chambers at any time? She "certainly did not." Did she ever agree in 1937 to make typewritten copies of State Department documents for the purpose of transmitting to Mr. Chambers? No, Mr. Stryker, she didn't. Did she ever hand the microfilmed documents to Mr. Cham-bers or ever see her husband do so? No, Mr. Stryker. Ever take a trip to Peterboro, stay at Bleak House, see *She Stoops to Conquer* there? Never. "By the way, Mrs. Hiss," Mr. Stryker threw in a picayune reminder, "do you like ice cream?" Yes, she liked it. Did she re-member "the rug." Yes, Chambers came and gave it as a present and they kept it, still had it in their home. Yes, she had been on the Eastern Shore of Maryland for the first two weeks of August 1937. And yes, she had taken a "course in chemistry for pre-med., and I think dental and pharmacy students." But had she ever taken a "nursing" course? She never had.

Mr. Stryker was racing along and Mrs. Hiss answered with little twinkling smiles as if he were stirring her nicest memories. He took off up the well at one point saying: "perhaps this question is unneces-sary, but I shall ask it unless his Honor thinks it isn't necessary. Perhaps I do myself." Well, Mr. Murphy reflected at his table, "isn't that enough right now?" The judge tremulously thought that if it was unnecessary, it shouldn't be asked. Well, Mr. Stryker declared, then "I won't ask it." Everybody relaxed.

There remained the crucial matters of the typewriter and the four-hundred-dollar "loan."

"Now, Mrs. Hiss, did there come a time fairly early in your married life when your father, Mr. Fansler, gave you a big office type-writer?" Yes. Did she use it herself, could she type? Certainly she could type. Could she identify "this typewriter here" (it had sat there formidably all the while), as that same typewriter? Yes, she was sure it was the same machine. Did she later obtain a portable type-writer? Yes, about the fall of 1937; they kept it until they moved out of Volta Place in 1943 and since then had another portable, which was still in their possession. And she told the grand jury that she had dis-posed of "the big typewriter" to either the Salvation Army or a junk-man? That was just what she had said, but she now thought that is what had happened to the first portable machine. The Catletts' testi-mony had "certainly" refreshed her recollection about the disposal of the big typewriter.

Now, did there come a time on or about the 18th of November 1937 when she withdrew four hundred dollars from the Hisses' joint savings account? Yes, she did. And had she been talking about going into the Volta Place house around that time? She had, Volta Place was a roomier house and would need more furnishing. Mr. Stryker asked her to tell how she disposed of that money, and he listened as charitably as a bridegroom while Mrs. Hiss guessed about the cost of a metal bed and a mattress, a pine bureau, a workbench for Timmie, a wing chair, a cotton rug, organdie curtains, many yards of pongee, lamps, candlesticks, and other oddments—including a dress for a White House reception—all of which she recalled buying with cash from the lump sum of the withdrawal. And all this took up the four hundred dollars or thereabouts? "I am afraid it did."

Mr. Stryker had a final "by the way," which was of course of the most tremendous relevance to the Hisses' contention that Chambers never had access to any house of theirs later than 1936.

"By the way, while you were at Volta Place, was there an oc-casion when you missed a pocketbook?"

"Yes, there was."

"And do you know whether there was a key of the house and the key of the car in that pocketbook?"

"There was."

"Did you hunt for the pocketbook?"

"I certainly did."

"Did you find it?"

"No."

"Did you then go and have a new key made, both for the car and for the house?"

"I did."

WHEN Mr. Murphy took over he was noticeably considerate and easygoing. This big lumbering man with the genial pale-blue eyes and walrus mustache, we said to ourselves, was that never-ending surprise, the giant with a gentle heart. It may well be so. Mr. Murphy may still recall the dreadful three hours that came to pass as a creditable exercise in self-restraint. If an opposition witness is vague, or won't admit a contradiction, and happens also to be a woman, perhaps the only available method is to tease her memory with a feather. This is what he appeared to do, patiently, relentlessly, with a politeness far more menacing than Mr. Stryker's indignations.

He came at once to the matter of the four-hundred-dollar loan. The items Mrs. Hiss had been listing were only the ones she bought with cash? That was right. Now, where did she have charge accounts at that time in Washington? Well, it was a little hard to remember, but she mentioned a couple of department stores, a book store, a flower shop, a grocery, a tailor. And as she bought each item she only used a part of the four hundred dollars? Oh, yes, that was right. It would be fair to say that she didn't constantly carry the four hundred dollars around in her purse? Yes, that would be fair. When was it exhausted? By the time they moved into Volta Place, a matter of about forty days. And the pongee curtain material, and the cost of some carpentering she'd mentioned, and the worktable, and everything else, all bought before she moved? That was right. Delivered to Thirtieth Street? No, to Volta Place. Un-huh, said Mr. Murphy, and looking down at a paper began to check with her all the items she had bought and the prices she had guessed at. But he did it knowingly, lovingly, where Mr. Stryker had paid merely respectful attention to a feminine mystery.

Then Mr. Murphy got straight on all the vital statistics, birth, marriages, divorce, children's birthdays, and asked her to define the periods she worked at a book store in Boston, the period she (too) worked for *Time*, the period she worked at the Library of Congress. Without any suggestion that Mrs. Hiss would have to watch her step Mr. Murphy was delicately making it plain that he knew a great deal about her. Once she had lived on Central Park West above Ninety-sixth Street, in New York, but was afraid she couldn't remember the street. "In the 300's you think?" Mr. Murphy casually threw in. And at that time was she a member of the Socialist Party? She didn't think so. Not? Well, Mr. Murphy would refresh her recollection. He showed her a page "from a rather large book that they use here in New York when you register to vote"; in fact, it was a registry of the Board of Elections for 1932. After Mrs. Hiss's signature was the party with which she was presumably enrolled: it said simply, "Soc." Yes, said Mrs. Hiss, she was sure that was an election registry page, and added: "you have to register before you vote"; and she had voted for Norman Thomas, the Socialist candidate that year. Mr. Murphy corrected her that this was the registry of names qualified to vote in which "you don't have to tell whom you are voting for. You have to register as to the party you want, you don't have to designate it." Mrs. Hiss insisted she had not been a member of the Socialist Party and thought she was indicating whom she meant to vote for.

"Mrs. Hiss," said Mr. Murphy quietly, "don't you know that the records of the Socialist Party, Morningside branch, list you as a member?" She certainly did not. In 1932? No. Mr. Murphy said no more but showed her the three typewritten pages describing the character of Timmie Hobson. She agreed it was a joint effort done by her and Hiss. How about "the physical typing of the document, whose effort was that?" She was sure it was hers, and that it "would have had to" be done on the big typewriter. The same went for the Bryn Mawr presidential report, and for the application for the summer course at the University of Maryland, and for the letter to the insurance company. Mr. Murphy now began his teasing probe of her typing ability.

"All right. What system do you use, the touch system?"

"I guess it's my own system."

"I mean do you look at the keyboard when you type?"

"I have to for a lot of the letters. I don't have to for all of them."

"Would you say as one who types that it's easier to work with a standard office machine or a portable?"

"I don't know the answer to that, Mr. Murphy."

"You don't know?"

"No."

"You don't know whether it's easier to use a large machine or a portable as far as comfort, feel and touch and so forth?"

"No, I don't."

"Really?"

"Is it?—excuse me."

"How long have you been typing?"

"I think I first started trying to type in 1926, the summer of 1926."

"Would it be fair to say that you are still trying?"

"I don't understand what you mean by that."

"Well, I mean, since that time would you say that you improved but you've not yet reached the state of perfection that some typists have?"

"Certainly that is so."

"Would you say you gradually improved?"

"Yes, definitely."

She had passed a test at Columbia, hadn't she? She didn't think she was ever given any test. Well, Mr. Murphy did have here an official college record from Columbia saying she had passed tests in English and typewriting. Would she be willing to take their word for it? Certainly she would.

Now, as of May 1937, did she have any trouble typing with that typewriter? Yes. But despite it she typed these exhibits, the letter to the University of Maryland for instance? Yes, she typed them. Mr. Murphy persisted in trying to get her to say if these mechanical defects lasted all through 1937, but she insisted she could not fix the time. Well, what were the defects? First, she remembered the ribbon: it "puckered like a fold of cloth" and it didn't wind automatically. Then, the keys didn't always fall down, they stayed up "like a hammer on a piano." And couldn't she say for sure that these imperfections happened when she typed these exhibits? She wouldn't be able to say that.

"Would you want to hazard a guess how long it took you to type that?" (showing her a single-page letter). She couldn't possibly guess.

"Can we say it took less than three hours?"

"Yes, we can certainly say that."

"Can we say it took less than two hours?"

"I think we can safely say that."

"Can you say you would rather do it . . . by typing than by writing in longhand?"

"No, I don't think we can say that at all." She had no idea of the comparative speed of her typing and her writing. The reason for typing the letter was certainly not speed. It was "because it was a formal letter."

"Is it your practice to write formal things with the typewriter?"

"Yes. I don't have occasion to write very many things like that."

Specifically, Mr. Murphy said in a heavy-lidded way, "did you have occasion to write the exhibits in evidence?"

"Which exhibits?" Mr. Stryker cried.

Mr. Murphy indicated the Baltimore typewritten documents: "Government's exhibits 5 to 47."

"Certainly not."

"You did not type those?"

"I have already said I did not type them, Mr. Murphy. I repeat I did not type them."

"But you would rather I wouldn't ask you any more about that?"

"No. You may ask me whatever you wish to ask me."

It is hard to convey in a snatch of transcript the effect of this sort of thing on the witness after an hour or so. Mrs. Hiss's face had lost all its color. Her eyes were dead as raisins in a circle of dough. Towards the end she fingered inside her bag and it seemed she must be about to break. But she didn't. Nevertheless, Mr. Murphy had demonstrated a ruthless skill superior to anything we had thought him capable of in the early days of the trial. Cross-examination is so familiar a game in our courts that, as with the Fourth of July or the Easter parade, the mind runs to honest clichés of reporting it rather than to noting the surprising variety of emotion it can contain. In this trial, for instance, Mr. Stryker's dramatic anger often appeared to have the opposite effect from the one he intended. In cross-examination it was frequently directed against an unlikely culprit; or it seemed to dissipate the issues on a frivolous plane and thereby throw into more effective contrast the menace of Mr. Murphy's offhandedness. Listening to Mr. Murphy with Mrs. Hiss, a foreigner who knew no English might have thought she was his witness. To a native it was made distressingly plain that patience too can be a whip.

Now he turned to the disposal of the typewriter and drew from Mrs. Hiss the admission, which he defined, redefined, patted, and lingered over, that: she knew now for certain where the typewriter had gone because Mr. McLean, Hiss's attorney of record, had told her before the trial about the Catlett children's recollection of coming to Thirtieth Street with a little express wagon and picking up an old Victrola, some clothes, and the typewriter; that recollection, repeated in turn among other things in this court, had roused memories of her own and assisted "my own recall." Which was now that she disposed of it in December 1937 before they moved to Volta Place.

That being established and accepted, Mr. Murphy suddenly raised his voice. "Did you know that they didn't move it to P Street until January 17th, 1938?" (It came out that there was a lease ostensibly to prove it.) But Mrs. Hiss thought that from her knowledge of Georgetown "and people like the Catletts," a lease would "in no way" affect their residence in the house.

"In other words," Mr. Murphy put in, back to a more familiar manner, "you think that perhaps they were squatters?" Oh, no, she would never call them that.

"It's a legal term, you know."

Still, Mrs. Hiss meant "that they were poor people, and there is a great deal of overcrowding, and I think they may have lived there much longer."

Hadn't she told the F.B.I. in Mr. McLean's presence in this building on the 7th of December 1948 that "I don't recall now how I disposed of it"? She thought that was probably what she'd said. "In other words," said Mr. Murphy, "you were not confused then about the disposition of the portable," there was no "conflict" in her mind then?

"I didn't know about this conflict until later, so I don't see that that enters in. I don't understand your question, Mr. Murphy."

"I think that," Mr. Murphy flatly commented, "is quite clear."

And she didn't remember, last December, the name of the old typewriter she'd had "from 1932 until you gave it to the Catlett boys"? That's right, it was always "just the typewriter" to her. But of course she realized "now looking at it that the name Woodstock is in pretty large letters across the face of the machine?" It certainly was in large letters, but it never registered. Well, she'd heard, of course, about the artists' colony in New York with that name? Yes, she knew of Woodstock, N.Y. Of course she did, didn't she? Yes, she certainly did, because she had been a guest there in 1948.

Then Mr. Murphy again resumed his feather treatment: what sort of a typist would she say she was, fair to middling? proficient? amateur? Did she type more now than in 1938? Did she get along better with the portable? He took up the line of questioning two F.B.I. agents might have taken with her when, as she acknowledged, they had called on her in June 1947. Had they said in substance that her husband, when he was in the Government service, had turned over to a third party information from Government files? She didn't remember their saying that. Mr. Stryker objected strongly to a line of attack "very far afield from the issues in this case." And the judge sustained him.

At the end of the day Mrs. Hiss was flushed and wide-eyed again, and when she was done she was given a warm smile of relief by her husband, who had sat there with his lips set and a wet forehead. By that time Mr. Murphy had done the most painstaking exegesis on the testimony of Priscilla Hiss *v*. Esther Chambers. In particular he had dared Mrs. Hiss to deny, as she calmly did, ever having taken a course at the University of Maryland in nursing. That is what Mrs. Chambers had called it—"Mrs. Hiss was enrolled at Mercy Hospital to learn nursing." But Mrs. Hiss's letter of the 25th of May 1937 to the University of Maryland did refer to necessary credits for "Mercy Hospital's training course in medical technology" (which could be, of course, a different thing). Mr. Murphy had also managed to expose one major discrepancy and a puzzling bit of forgetfulness between Mrs. Hiss's testimony before the grand jury and her testimony in this Trial. She had said in the trial that the first time she saw Chambers was when he came alone to look over the Twenty-eighth Street apartment with a view to taking it. To the grand jury she had said it was "her strongest recollection" that both Chambers and his wife came to look at the apartment, and that she "must have seen him two or three times before that."

Just as soon as the jury had gone for the day, Mr. Stryker stalked over to the seats inside the well of the court in great agitation and, pointing to a small bald-headed man wearing thick glasses and a high collar, asked that his Honor direct him to remain in court. The judge so directed and Mr. Stryker made a formal complaint that this man, William Marshall Bullitt, a Louisville attorney, had told a newspaper that Hiss had not resigned from the Carnegie presidency when Mr. Dulles had suggested he ought to. Mr. Stryker further complained that this man sat in the press section, conferred with the F.B.I., and had written and passed to various people a brochure purporting to analyze "the testimony only before the House Committee" without his having had access to the Baltimore testimony or any other. Mr. Stryker submitted that "upon those facts there is a question before you as to whether or not contempt of court has been committed." Judge Kaufman replied that any application for contempt would have to wait until the trial was over. But he deplored "such comment about a trial in progress," felt bad about the open commentaries on the case of various columnists, and regretfully concluded that "if we are going to get into trials by publicity, the function of courts will end."

Next morning, Mr. Murphy was back for a final joust with Mrs. Hiss. Mrs. Hiss was quite sure she had been in Chestertown, Maryland, without interruption through the first two weeks of August 1937? She was. Never taken her boy to a doctor, any doctor, in Washington, for instance? No. He read to her long passages from her testimony to the grand jury on the 10th of December. This was evidently what Mr. Murphy had been waiting for: for at that time, only six months before this Trial started, she had said she could not visualize the old typewriter at Thirtieth Street, but thought she remembered it at Volta Place; that she could recall no defects like broken letters or keys that jammed; that she didn't know when the portable typewriter was bought, and had "no idea" when she got rid of the old one. Was she asked those questions and did she give those answers? "Exactly as you read it," Mrs. Hiss replied, sitting up neat as a pin, her eyes bright and wide again.

Mr. Stryker kept her for a few minute longer to identify her typewritten specimens (which Mr. Murphy always identified as "Government exhibits") as "the papers that you asked Mr. McLean to turn over to the Government"; and to erase any suspicions Mr. Murphy may have left about her political wholesomeness. "You were asked about your voting record I think in 1932, and you told us that you voted for Norman Thomas?" Whom did she vote for in 1928?

"I voted for Al Smith."

"Al Smith?!" Mr. Stryker cried in delighted surprise. And whom had she voted for in the last election? "For President Truman."

MR. Stryker sat down after calling Admiral Hepburn, a character witness previously mentioned, and then stood up again blithe as a bullet and turned, as he invariably did when a dramatic surprise was in the offing, and stared at the windows. He proclaimed the name we had hoped for, forgotten about, and hoped for again: "Dr. Carl Binger!" Dr. Binger had not appeared since Chambers had left the stand. He now strode up to the witness chair, a big, spectacled, genial man of impressive bone structure. There was a rising hiss and whisper, among the newspapermen in the know, about an imminent "hypothetical question." But before he put it, Mr. Stryker drew from Dr. Binger the modest admission of a brilliant career—as a medical student, the recipient of high honors from General Pershing for his work in the First World War on influenza and meningitis, a notable research worker in heart disease and pneumonia, and his later translation into a distinguished psychiatrist. Mr. Murphy was as tense as a platoon commander eying his watch for zero hour, and the moment Mr. Stryker asked if Dr. Binger had received or been promised or expected "any compensation for the time—" Mr. Murphy jabbed in with a "That is below the belt, your Honor." Judge Kaufman thought it proper foundation and Dr. Binger replied in a resonant voice: "I have not received compensation, and I have not been promised compensation, and I will not accept compensation in this case."

Mr. Stryker strode firmly towards the witness chair. Had the doctor been present in the courtroom during the entire sessions that Whittaker Chambers was on the stand? He had. And did he during that time observe Whittaker Chambers? Of course.

Mr. Murphy seethed quietly at his table, as Mr. Stryker marched back to the bar, took breath, and began: "Now, Doctor, assume that the following facts are true:" . . . There followed a roll-call of conjunctive clauses, lining up like a battalion of deserters, each pointing a shabby finger at the life and character of Whittaker Chambers. Mr.

Stryker incorporated at once as putative facts the testimony of an old school-friend of Chambers he had called the day before: that Chambers as a boy was a shabby dresser; that he was more often than not in need of a haircut; that he delivered at school a class prophecy the principal had forbidden; that he would walk home from school through a brook with his shoes and stockings on, saying that he did this to cool his feet. Then Mr. Stryker summoned up again a forgotten legion of all the disreputable things he had imputed to Chambers, or made him admit, at the beginning of the trial: "that he . . . ran away from home . . . . went to New Orleans" and lived among drunkards and prostitutes, that at times he expressed "atheistic sentiments," that he used many aliases. . . .

Mr. Murphy was up and demanding that they "come to the hypothetical question without all of this," or asking that the jury be discharged for the rest of it. Judge Kaufman shook his head, saying the defendant had the right "to make this record."

Mr. Stryker's measured lamentation roared on: "that he wrote and published . . . a highly offensive treatment of Christ"; that he lied to his dean; that he was charged with stealing books; that as a result of his brother's suicide, "Whittaker Chambers found it very hard physically to move for a couple of months"; that he became a Communist; that he lived with a woman not his wife; that he believed the world outside the Communist Party was incapable of saving itself; that he once bought an automobile and moved to Maryland and sold the car to himself; that he broke with the Party and watched through the night with a gun or revolver; and so on through the dreadful history of the dumb-waiter shaft in Brooklyn, the pumpkin, the feared assassination, the wooden rolling-pin, the typewriter left on a streetcar deliberately to forget the past; on and on until Mr. Stryker's "question" had become—as Mr. Murphy indignantly noted—a highly selective, forty-five minute summation of the most damaging parts of Chambers's testimony and the odder aspects of Chambers's behavior.

At last the moment came, and Mr. Stryker declaimed: "now, Dr. Binger, assuming the facts as stated in the question to be true, and taking into account your observations of Chambers on the witness stand, and your knowledge of his writings and translations, have you as a psychiatrist an opinion within the bounds of reasonable certainty as to the mental condition of Whittaker Chambers?"

Mr. Murphy charged in like the Light Brigade. He objected to the question and he begged to be heard. He was heard. He had asked before it began that Mr. Stryker make an offer of proof in the absence of the jury. He thought his Honor had indicated to the counsel that he would not permit the doctor to testify. The question, which was now in the jury's mind, was really a summation given "before the time of summations," and the opportunity given to deliver it was "a grave injustice to the Government and one on which we have no right of appeal." The question was "not a complete summary of the witness's testimony here by a long shot": it left out his marriage to his "only wife," his present Quaker religion, his other writings, especially the child's book *Bambi,* and "innumerable things." But the damage was done; and would his Honor now tell the jury that Mr. Stryker's summary was no part of the record and then pass on the question of law?

While Mr. Stryker stood back in the well, anxious as a terrier, Judge Kaufman leaned far forward over the bench and gave his ruling. When the briefs were submitted, he said, he had meant to admit the doctor's testimony "because the tendency of the law is" to do so. However, both the defendant and the Government were agreed that "the question of the credibility of Mr. Chambers is one of the crucial elements in this case." Yet in spite of the trend of judicial decisions, he had decided to exclude Dr. Binger's testimony, "because I think that the record is sufficiently clear for the jury, using its experience in life, to appraise the testimony of all the witnesses who have appeared in this courtroom." If the question that had been put did not conform to the jury's recollection, "your recollection will control." Mr. Murphy protested that if the question was not answered, the jury ought to disregard it. The judge nodded and told the jury to disregard it. He waved Mr. Stryker down and excused Dr. Binger, who walked out, taking with him forever, we then thought, the secret of his professional opinion.

Mr. Stryker came back after lunch that day, reconciled to Dr. Binger's silence and visibly well pleased at the miserable cartoon of Whittaker Chambers he had been allowed to draw for the jury. He rose at once and announced: "The defendant rests."

On some people this tactic might have had quite the wrong effect. For by isolating only those characteristics which went to make up the plotter and the cheat, it presented a picture so complete and terrifying that the spectator was thrown back in even deeper doubt on the contrasting picture of the intelligent, placid man we had seen. If such a contrast between the public and the private life of a man could be made real to the jury, it almost forced them to accept a rigid and dangerous alternative and choose once for all between an imbecile lout or a man telling the whole truth. If a juryman reflected that Chambers was something far more amiable than the picture Mr. Stryker had drawn, the danger from the defendant's point of view would be not that the jury might simply dismiss the picture as a fake; but that the mind had already been drugged into looking for no alternative less violent than the one the hypothetical question suggested. And then the juryman, with the memory of Chambers on the stand before him, might go on to think that if Hiss was not the smiling gentleman he seemed in court, perhaps it was he who was, after all, the indicated alternative: a Mr. Hyde.

THE REBUTTALS

❀

IT is one of the penalties of the comparatively loose rules of evidence in American courts that they allow counsel to elaborate an issue almost into oblivion; so that instead of deepening in the jury's minds the main impression you want to leave, there is a good chance that at the end of the trial the jury may be thrashing in so many cross-currents, none of which seems to lead upstream to the source of the trouble, or downstream into the broad ocean of truth, that the jury will seize at the end on any floating log that might bring them safely to shore. I think this is proved by the enormous length of time it takes American juries to make up their minds. And veteran jurymen often say that the first few hours in the juryroom are spent sloughing off the welter of counsel's rhetoric, the strangling flotsam and jetsam of introduced "evidence."

This Trial was now in its fifth week, and the jury had taken on that look of bewildered and ghastly neutrality which might have come from what the judge had called their "experience of life" or from the dyspepsia of chronic indecision. The parade of rebuttal witnesses is the last chance for the counsel to rescue the "issues" from the riot of speculation, rhetoric, documentary detail, and hearsay that the American system encourages. And Mr. Murphy was quick to seize it. For his purpose seemed to be to damage three main parts of the disputed testimony of Mr. and Mrs. Hiss: the condition and disposal of the typewriter; Hiss's relations with the Carnegie Endowment; and his whereabouts during his 1937 summer vacation.

The Government's first witness was one that many spectators must have longed to hear from: Burnetta Catlett, the sister to whom in the end the typewriter had gone.

She now lived in Detroit, a married woman with four children, a status that emphasized how unreal a mystery this whole affair must have been; for the part she played in it was "in another place and long ago": in Washington when she was a little girl. She was in high school, living with Dr. Easter, when she got the old typewriter. And she had used it, she said, to type up her homework in biology, hygiene, and chemistry.

"And did you have it fixed before you used it?"

"No."

When she had finished her schooling, she put the typewriter "in the attic of the house where I was living," and then she got married and moved to Detroit. Mr. Murphy asked her if before the trial one of the defense lawyers had come out to Detroit to see her. She said he had. And had he asked about the typewriter? Yes, he had. And did he say she would be called as a witness? He said she might be called.

"And were you called by anybody other than the Government?"

"No, I was not."

"You may examine," said Mr. Murphy.

There was very little to examine. Mr. McLean put in the inference that somebody else might have used the typewriter by asking her if a "Vernon Marlow" had lived in the Easter house part of the time she was there. She said he had. Mr. McLean managed to get from her that when this man married, he merely moved across the street and was there as late as 1945, when Dr. Easter died.

The next witness was the daughter of Ira Lockey, the night watchman from whom Mr. McLean had eventually rescued the typewriter. She verified that it was a standard machine, a Woodstock, she had used for typing lessons when she, too, was going to high school in Washington. Mr. Murphy put his teaser:

"Did you have it fixed?"

"No."

"How long did you use it . . . approximately, or the best you can?"

"Well, approximately two years or two and a half years."

And when she moved to New York? Yes. And when was that? In October 1948.

"Would it be safe to say you used the typewriter up to the time you moved to New York?"

"Yes."

"And you said you never had it fixed?"

"No." Of course, she changed the ribbon and cleaned it with kerosene and a toothbrush. But yes, she could type on it. The keys sometimes stuck, in fact frequently. But she would "just pull the key back" and go on typing.

This last remark was handsome enough for the defense, and Mr. McLean had no questions. Her husband came in briefly to confirm the make of typewriter, to say he had used it himself, and that it was the only one they had in their home.

Then appeared a Mr. Henry, a real-estate man responsible for renting offices in the building on the corner of Connecticut Avenue and K Street, where Perry Catlett said he had taken the typewriter, to a ground-floor shop, for repairs. Mr. Henry's records showed that the Woodstock Typewriter Company rented an upstairs office there on September 15, 1938 for the two succeeding years, and that there were no other typewriter shops on Connecticut Avenue. Since September was at least nine months later than the time the Hisses said the typewriter was positively in the Catletts' hands, it was all Mr. Murphy wanted the real-estate man to say. Mr. McLean came in to try to discredit the rental record by showing that although the lease was signed for occupancy on the 15th of September 1938, on the line marked "date of occupancy" there was no entry. But Mr. Henry said he was "very clear" on the fact that the company couldn't have moved in before that date. Then Mr. McLean threw a small bombshell at Mr. Henry; he told him what he did not know, that the previous location of the same company was on K Street only a block and a half away from the building in question.

Although this may possibly have jarred Mr. Murphy at the time, he was quite recovered two days later when he called the real-estate man who had rented out these previous premises on K Street. Did his people enter into a lease with the Woodstock Typewriter Company? They did.

"What was the term of the lease?"

"The term of the lease was two years."

"To commence when?"

"To commence on May 1st, 1938."

But, Mr. Murphy extracted from him, the lease was subject to a ninety-day cancellation clause, and on June 18th the real-estate agent did in fact take advantage of the clause. So the typewriter company presumably left by the middle of September. It seemed to fit perfectly the Government's strong implication that the Hisses had not got rid of the typewriter until after Chambers broke with the Party; that is, some time after April 1938. But Mr. Murphy had another implication to add:

"Were you subpoenaed by the defense, weren't you?"

"Yes."

"And were you in this building on Thursday?"

"Yes, I was."

"And you did not testify?"

"No, I did not . . . I was excused."

THAT was the end of the testimony about the typewriter. Before he moved on to Hiss's presidency of the Carnegie Endowment, and his 1937 vacation, Mr. Murphy put in a witness who would deny the unfortunate recollection of Mike Catlett that the F.B.I. had offered him two hundred dollars if he found the typewriter. It was meant to be a brief and summary dismissal, but Mr. Stryker converted it into a major attack on the F.B.I., which upset Mr. Murphy's rebuttal routine. The witness was a thin, dark young man, attentive in every wrinkle of a thin handsome face. He was Courtland Jones, a young Virginian with an equable manner and a painstaking Southern accent. Surprisingly he turned out to be an F.B.I. man, in fact the special agent in charge of the great typewriter mystery. He was the man who had first interrogated Mike Catlett about it. And he was "the big fellow" who Mike Catlett said had made the arrant offer of two hundred dollars. At Mr. Murphy's request, he admitted, he had made a list of every typewriter store and repair shop existing in Washington in 1937 and 1938. He had then stuck pins in a map to mark these locations. With the help of a score or more F.B.I. agents he had then presumably "shaken down the City of Washington to a fare-thee-well." One of his ports of call had been the Catlett home.

"Now, Mr. Jones, did you on May 13th, 1949 speak with Mike Catlett?"

Mr. Murphy raised his voice to invite the lie direct to the next question:

"And did you at that time mention anything about money in any way, shape, form or manner?"

"The only thing mentioned concerning money was the fact that he told me that he had received $40 from Donald Hiss to assist him in locating the Woodstock typewriter."

It was a better answer than Mr. Murphy could have wished for, and he didn't deign to look at the defense table as he sat down and said: "You may examine."

This was one witness that the defense was not going to excuse. Not only the question of money was in doubt. There was a question, which the Government naturally had never mooted, of the possible intimidation by the F.B.I. of the whole Catlett family. Young Mr. Jones appeared to be an unlikely prototype of a tough special agent; but he offered the defense its last chance to insinuate the sort of terrorism that would throw an illiterate colored family into more kinds of confusion than a forgetfulness about dates. It was a job for Mr. Stryker. And in the next forty minutes he gave a bravura performance of cross-examination that probably few modern lawyers could rival, in this the age of the bureaucrat and the corporation lawyer sticking prosily to his brief. Considering that Mr. Jones was wildly miscast for a Stryker victim, looking as he did like James Stewart trying to play Richard Widmark, the defense might have given pause to consider the ways of boomerangs. But Mr. Stryker only scowled at the attentive Mr. Jones and lit into him at once with an ack-ack crackle of insinuation that had the court reporter's good right hand shuttling like a piston.

Where did he first meet Mike Catlett? In the office of the Federal Bureau of Investigation, at Washington, D.C. (This was after the typewriter was found.)

"Did you ask him to come there?"

"Yes, sir, an agent was sent out and—"

"What?"

"An agent went out to his home and brought him into the office."

"Oh, you mean you arrested him?"

"No, sir."

How far was the Catlett home from the F.B.I. office? About two miles. Did they notify him they were coming? There was no way, he didn't have a phone. They didn't telegraph him? No, sir. How many agents went out? Two.

"Wouldn't one have sufficed for this request?"

"They wanted—we also interviewed Mike's other brothers."

"No, just answer the question. Wouldn't one agent have sufficed to make this request to come down to the office?"

"Possibly."

"But two went?"

"Yes, sir."

"Armed?"

"I don't know, sir."

"Well, you always are armed, aren't you?"

"No, sir."

"Well, you have a badge 'F.B.I., we are from the F.B.I.,' isn't that right?"

"We have badges."

Wasn't it a custom to notify people at their homes? Not necessarily. If they wanted to go down and see a prominent white person, would they go down to him and say "Well, just come right along with us in the car"?

Mr. Murphy objected to the form as "sarcastic and argumentative." The judge overruled him. Mr. Jones explained, "if your Honor please," that there were numerous children at the Catlett home and it was much more convenient for them to interview him in their office "if he has no objection."

Mr. Stryker was taking short angry steps across the well of the court.

"Did you think it was convenient for him or just you?"

"Well, I didn't ask him."

"Your agents didn't give much consideration to that?"

Mr. Jones didn't know, he wasn't there. But he was there when Mike and his brother Perry were brought in. Mr. Stryker tore through the rising snickers to infer that little consideration would be given to a colored man who, no discredit to him, was "not too well educated." How long did the interview take? Forty-five minutes with Mike. And how long with the other one? About fifteen minutes. Wasn't that long enough to determine they were only ignorant colored boys? Yes, sir. "You found that out, didn't you?" Yes, sir. And how many agents were in the office? Mr. Stryker made him count them till they reached three agents and a stenographer. They were, said Mr. Jones, "in the room."

"In the room, what do you mean? There was someone else listening outside?"

"No, sir."

"Well, did you have some qualification to that when you said 'in the room'?"

"No, sir."

"All right. Now what did you do? Ask him questions?" Yes, they had asked a great many questions, "all about the Woodstock typewriter." Nothing derogatory to Mr. Hiss? No, sir.

"Did you finally, when you got through, put that in a statement?"

"No, sir."

"Did you hand him a transcript of what your questions were or your answers?"

"No, sir."

"Isn't that what you do when you take a citizen of the United States and question him, give him a chance to see what you have done to him?"

Mr. Murphy protested that there was no testimony showing "anything was done to Mike Catlett and Mr. Stryker knows it." The judge sustained him. But Mr. Stryker whirled without pause into a clever reframing:

"Isn't it your custom when you have a citizen, an intelligent citizen who knows his rights, and when you interrogate him and ask him questions, to give him a transcript of what the questions were and the answers?"

"We don't do that when a man is intelligent or not intelligent, sir."

"You don't do that?"

"No, sir."

"D'you do it if it's requested?"

"On occasions."

"Who makes that decision?"

"The Bureau does."

"In other words, you sit there and you determine whether a citizen who has been interviewed shall see what you have asked him or not, is that it?"

An unfair repetition, cried Mr. Murphy. Overruled, said the judge.

"Is that right?" Mr. Stryker bellowed.

"I understood that the question was overruled."

"You want to help with the ruling? The *objection* was overruled."

"I beg your pardon."

"Now the question has been put and I would like an answer."

"If you want to put it that way, yes, sir."

It was just the way Mr. Stryker went on putting it, squeezing every simple answer for some diabolical F.B.I. intent. And by the way, didn't they bring Mrs. Catlett in that day? Yes, they "went out and took and brought" her over to the Catlett house. Was that from Winchester, Virginia? Yes. How far was that? About seventy miles.

How long did she stay in the F.B.I. office? About an hour. And was *she* given a copy of any statements that she made? No, sir.

"And she is a lovely colored woman but not too educated either, isn't she?"

"Yes, sir."

How long was Mike Catlett kept at the F.B.I. office? He waited to be interviewed from about three forty-five to five p.m., and his interview was over at six forty-five. Then he was "taken to his home, sent to his home."

"During that period was he given anything to eat, or a glass of water?"

"He probably had some water. He didn't have any food."

"Are you sure you even gave him a glass of water?"

"I don't recall it."

Mr. Stryker was beside himself.

"You don't recall giving him a glass of water?!"

"He could have had it if he had asked for it."

Well, Mr. Stryker marched off along the jury box, his right eye reflecting terrible things. This was all during the period, he assumed, when they were "moving heaven and earth" to find the typewriter? They were doing everything they could. How many agents? About thirty-five. And when they found that "Mr. McLean, who is not a detective at all, but just a lawyer, went down and got it by using a little intelligence, I suppose you were quite angry about it, weren't you?"

"No, sir."

And when they got Mike down again, did they keep a stenographic report of the interview? No, but he made handwritten notes.

And where were they? Destroyed. Destroyed? Yes, he made a report from them. Did they know what they were trying to get? They were trying to learn why he hadn't told them about the typewriter and how he helped in locating it. And they were also, weren't they, trying to "place the location of the typewriter during the months when Whittaker Chambers says that he got these documents from Mr. Hiss, you know that was the point, didn't you?" Yes, sir. And they wanted some evidence "to put the typewriter right there in the Hiss house during that period?" Yes, sir.

"Now tell me, wasn't your real purpose to try to destroy them as witnesses for the defense?"

"No, sir."

And yet Pat Catlett had clearly said (Mr. Stryker showed Mr. Jones his own notes, borrowed from Mr. Murphy) that he got the typewriter "during the period that Alger Hiss moved from 30th Street to Volta Place"? He had, but Mr. Jones insisted, through many more rapid challenges, he didn't know whether he got it before or after the move. Mr. Stryker hammered away at the locations of the typewriter repair shops to try to prove that Perry Catlett's memory had been assisted by the F.B.I. towards a recollection in the Government's favor. But he confused Mr. Jones rather more than he proved a plot. And he threw this limp young man back to Mr. Murphy. Mr. Murphy was strikingly matter-of-fact. Who first suggested that the repair shop was located at Connecticut and K? Perry Catlett. And that's why the F.B.I. went to look at that place? Yes. And when he, Mr. Jones, prepared this report or statement, didn't he let Perry Catlett read it and sign it in his own hand? Yes, he did. And when he first mentioned the address, they didn't know there was a repair shop there? That was right. And there was a reason why two F.B.I. agents, not one, always went out on an interview, wasn't there? Yes, sir.

Mr. Stryker had one more F.B.I. performance to expose: the search for specimens of the Hisses' typing. Had Mr. Jones interviewed or written to "six hundred members of Mr. Hiss's law class at Harvard Law School"? He had not; he knew they had interviewed a great many. Did he know they had interviewed people in Chicago? Probably. San Francisco? Yes, sir. Denver? No, sir. Cleveland? No, sir.

"Thank you, Mr. Jones, that is all," said Mr. Stryker.

Now Mr. Murphy was able to turn back to his themes. The word had got out the night before that the Government had under subpoena Mr. John Foster Dulles, the man who had missed being Secretary of State by the hair's breadth of a Truman victory. The line outside the courtroom grew like a tapeworm, and the press section was again loaded with heavily tanned golfers, pretty women, and other forgetful working pressmen. Now Mr. Murphy called him. He ignored a formal check on the witness's career. It was enough for his purpose to identify him as an attorney and chairman of the board of the Carnegie Endowment for International Peace, of which Alger Hiss had been the elected, salaried president until a few weeks before this Trial began.

Yes, he had been the first to broach to Hiss, in 1946, the prospect of leaving the State Department for the Carnegie job. Just before Hiss took up the appointment in January of 1947, Mr. Dulles had telephoned him and asked him about the rumors that he at one time had Communist affiliations. Hiss reassured him by saying he had gone to the F.B.I. and he "thought he put those rumors to rest or had satisfied the F.B.I., or some such language." In March 1948, however, Mr. Dulles heard "more responsible" rumors and asked him to come down to his office. It was the day, as it happened, that Hiss was testifying before the grand jury. Hiss told him that the grand jury had asked him if he were acquainted with various persons and—

Mr. Stryker jumped up to object on the grounds that the Government was trying to rebut "on a collateral matter" (presumably on alleged Communism, which the judge had tried throughout to exclude from the testimony). The judge agreed with Mr. Stryker, but let Mr. Murphy go on "to see where he will get to."

Well, Mr. Dulles went on, Hiss had said that he was unacquainted with most of the people named, and that there was only one association, with Lee Pressman, whom he had known as a lawyer, that might possibly have led to these rumors. Mr. Murphy soon came to the meeting about which the recollections of Mr. Dulles and Hiss were expected to clash. It was a meeting between them on the 18th of August 1948, in the middle of the House Committee hearings. Mr. Murphy asked Mr. Dulles to recall the substance of their conversation. Mr. Dulles had told Hiss that the testimony brought out in the House Committee Hearings had "created a rather serious and somewhat embarrassing problem for the trustees and doubtless also for him." He said that "as far as the trustees were concerned, I felt their course of duty was perfectly clear"; that in a free democratic society the individual has primary rights, and in a Communist society very few; "and I said I hoped and believed that the trustees would live up to the best American traditions and do everything possible to prevent any wrong being done to the individual concerned through seeming to prejudge his case by being actuated by the passions or prejudices of the moment . . . that was the duty of the trustees." He said also he "had no doubt that he [Hiss] was considering what his duty was as President of the Carnegie Endowment and that it might very well be that he would have to come to the conclusion that his ability to discharge the duties of President had been somewhat impaired by the publicity . . . irrespective of the truth or falsehood of the charges made and denied." Hiss replied that "he was conscious of that duty . . . and had given it a good deal of thought and he was disposed to agree with my suggestion . . . but that he had in mind a resignation at a fairly early date." But they finally agreed "it would not be wise for him to resign while the hearings were still going on" before the House Committee. He said "he would contemplate resigning from the Endowment probably sometime in September."

And did he resign or offer to in September? Mr. Dulles had no personal knowledge of that, because he went abroad, but when he got back in January he learned that Hiss's resignation had been considered at the December meeting.

Mr. Stryker rose to say he failed to see any conflict between the testimony of Mr. Dulles and Mr. Hiss and he would like to have it pointed out to him. "That," remarked the judge, "is your job." So Mr. Stryker got up again for the cross-examination with a cordial hint that he was sorry to embarrass such a distinguished man who had done such "fine work for the United States and the United Nations." Mr. Dulles would agree, would he not, that he would need to have "an indelible memory" to remember every word Alger Hiss had spoken in three talks two years apart? Mr. Dulles agreed. He wouldn't even be sure who had first mentioned the question of his possible resignation. Had not Mr. Hiss expressed the desire to do what would be most helpful to "this great institution"? Yes. And Mr. Dulles wouldn't state that Mr. Hiss had made "a definite, flat, binding promise that he would resign in September, would that be right?" That was correct. Mr. Dulles, too, was one of the members of the committee that had made "careful inquiries" about Mr. Hiss before choosing him? Correct. And the reports received by "this committee of distinguished men regarding Mr. Hiss were all good?" That was correct. And on the basis of that report "he was then elected, I think we have it, as the first paid president of the Endowment, is that right?" That was correct.

Mr. Murphy was quickly in with a written memorandum Mr. Dulles had put before the trustees for their February 1949 meeting. From it Mr. Murphy put the question: "then did you record that you went to see Mr. Hiss and told him that while you were confident that the trustees would not themselves want to take action" that might be prejudicial, "you thought that Mr. Hiss, out of consideration for the Endowment, should voluntarily resign and relieve the Endowment of embarrassment . . . did you say that, Mr. Dulles?"

The difference between "it might very well be that he would have to come to the conclusion" to resign, and "you thought he should voluntarily resign" was delicate but, one might have thought, indisputable. But Mr. Dulles drew no attention to it and simply answered: "If it is in the memorandum, I said it, but I doubt very much that it is in the memorandum that I said I went to see Mr. Hiss." Out of this testimony two wire services and a distinguished American daily drew the certain conclusion that Mr. Dulles had asked Hiss to resign and Hiss had not taken the hint, and that their testimony therefore was seriously in conflict. There were others in the courtroom who were equally sure that Mr. Stryker had turned up in Mr. Dulles an unexpected, if unsuspecting, character witness for Alger Hiss. This, however, was not the opinion the country picked up from its newspapers.

Mr. Murphy stood up stroking his mustache and put his arms akimbo. "Your Honor," he announced, "I have one more witness. I am sure there is going to be a fight about it. Let's have it and get it over with." The judge admonished Mr. Murphy with the thought that "we are not fighting here at all, Mr. Murphy." And Mr. Murphy allowed he meant it only "in a spirit of jest." It was the end of the day, and Mr. Murphy's jest set the corridors buzzing again and provoked some newspapers into flaring headlines over feature articles promising that the Government would call the ex-wife of Gerhardt Eisler to add the only other human corroboration to the word of Chambers by saying that Hiss had indeed been in a Communist apparatus and tried in her presence to squabble over a new recruit.

This rumor would not be fit to mention here if it had not been at the time the most flagrant of the many supplementary stories the newspapers ran along with the trial reports. There is no legal impediment in the American system to publishing comment, conclusive assumptions, or even running slander on the principals of a trial while the case is still under judgment; with the result that the newspapers tend, according to their editorial sympathy, to publish an extended case for the prosecution or the defense and thereby pass on to the people a view of the proceedings the whole system of trial by jury is created to debar.

Late the next morning, when countless thousands of newspaper readers already had a rough notion of what the former Mrs. Eisler was likely to say, Judge Kaufman came into court and announced to the jury: "Ladies and gentlemen, there has been a long discussion about the testimony of one Mrs. Hede Massing. The Court has ruled that her testimony is not admissible. She will not be called as a witness." Mr. Stryker had protested in chambers that she was an inadmissible witness, being offered in rebuttal on a collateral matter. His own understanding of the rule was that "even a matter that might be relevant to the issue will be excluded if its real tendency is to cause prejudice rather than to prove or render probable some fact in the case." Mr. Murphy asserted on the contrary that the defendant was "a party to the action and his credibility is always an issue," and that he ought at least to be allowed to call the witness and then have her testimony excluded. Judge Kaufman thought that even this concession might be "inflammatory and prejudicial" and might land him with a reversible error, if this case ever came to appeal. He thought he had better get advice on the point. He apparently got it, as his announcement to the jury showed. Then Judge Kaufman said: "the next witness, Mr. Murphy," and leaned back and rocked.

Mr. Murphy had a typewriter dealer confirm that he had rented a Woodstock typewriter (not *the* Woodstock) to the defendant's lawyers for three months at the beginning of the year—1949. After a discussion at the bench Mr. Murphy walked back to his place and announced he meant to call "an officer of the Cherner Motor Company, to prove the purchase and sale of a Ford automobile." The judge ruled it was not proper rebuttal evidence and excluded it.

After these legal excursions the trial got under way again and Mr. Murphy took up his third and last rebuttal theme by calling a man

who said that in the first two weeks of August 1937 he had lived in
the same apartment house in Chestertown, Maryland, where the
Hisses lived during their vacation. He testified that it was a small house
and that he had never seen or heard of Mr. and Mrs. Hiss. Put briefly
under the lash of Mr. Stryker, he admitted he could not swear to
having been there every day, that his mother was an invalid and he
normally took his meals with her in their rooms, and that he very
often didn't go downstairs at all. Did he know the landlady, Mrs.
Wickes? He did. Did he know her handwriting? Reasonably well.
Mr. Stryker handed him a letter that was not in evidence and asked
him if it refreshed his recollection. He took it obediently and began
in a loud, clear voice: "My Dear Alger—" He got no further, for a
howl of pain went up from Mr. Murphy. "No, no," the judge came
in, "read it to yourself." Mr. Stryker judicially concealed a magnificent grin and Alger Hiss collapsed in laughter into cupped hands.
The witness came to and replied it didn't refresh his recollection,
but—at Mr. Stryker's insistence—he said that, yes, Mrs. Wickes was
a very honorable lady and he had a high regard for her truth.

The Government had only a few more witnesses left: an F.B.I.
man who had talked to Hiss in 1946, at—Mr. Stryker was alert to
point out—Hiss's request; and the William Rosen whom the Government would say had bought the Ford car Hiss had turned over to the
Cherner Motor Company. He was not on hand; in fact, the Government had searched for him without any luck, but Mr. Murphy asked
to call him just the same. And the judge promptly said that the same
ruling would apply to him as to the Cherner Motor Company and
Mrs. Hede Massing. Mr. Murphy thereupon called his last witness,
a Washington real-estate man whose testimony has been reported,
and when he had done, the Government's case was completed.

NOW the end was in sight. Mr. McLean rose to call the defendant's first witness in sur-rebuttal. She was the medical record librarian
at a hospital in Wilmington, Delaware, where Mrs. Hiss had a sick
relative in the summer of 1937. The hospital records listed the address
of Alger Hiss as "care of Mrs. Wickes, Chestertown, Maryland."
Mr. Murphy laconically noted that the entry showed no date. Next
came the lady who had testified earlier, the assistant registrar of the
University of Maryland. Her records were introduced to clinch once

for all a definition of the course Mrs. Hiss had taken in Baltimore the same summer. The official name was "inorganic chemistry." The report of Mrs. Hiss's grade had been sent to her on the 5th of August at Chestertown, Maryland. Mr. Murphy was up for a moment to get her to say that that address was the one the student had given as a mailing address.

The last defense witness to appear was a gangling young man who had been a counselor at the Chestertown summer camp to which the Hiss stepson had gone that summer. He knew the Hisses very well, said they were there during the disputed period, and said that Alger Hiss went to call on his stepson so often that his visits amounted to "part of the camp activities." He had, in fact, come to take "Alger's" visits for granted. But in Mr. Murphy's hands he admitted he couldn't be sure of seeing Hiss every day, but knew that Mrs. Hiss was "around town," at least he "assumed" she was around. Which was a pity for the defense, because it left him at this interval with a friendly sense of Hiss's presence but no sure memory of any particular day when Hiss was there or away, no independent certainty that Hiss was there on the day that *She Stoops to Conquer* was playing, nearly five hundred miles away in New Hampshire.

The defendant's final piece of testimony was offered on the morning of the 6th of July 1949. It was a deposition from the Chestertown landlady, Mrs. Wickes. She was forbidden to leave her bed, and Mr. McLean and Mr. Murphy had together taken what Judge Kaufman tactfully hoped had been a "pleasant ride" down to the Eastern Shore of Maryland. The deposition stated that the Hisses had been tenants in her house in 1936 and 1937, specifically as the sublessee of an apartment. Mr. Hiss had been there in July and part of August. She had a check from Mr. Hiss dated later in the year for what she presumed was "a forgotten telephone call." Mr. Murphy's bedside manner elicited that fifteen days before, she had not been able to "specify the time" until she recalled her son had broken his back. And then what did she find out? She decided that fixed the time at 1936. She agreed now she was wrong by a year. She also agreed that there was another man on the same floor as the Hisses, and that he was the man the Government had called who had never heard of the Hisses. As for the Hisses' being in Chestertown every single day, she had "no way to swear it" but she would say they had been, because "they had no other place to go."

The judge allowed the defense to read in evidence some of Mrs. Chambers's Baltimore testimony about her meetings with Mrs. Hiss. At which stage Judge Kaufman raised his eyebrows and put the blessed question: "Defendant rests?" The defendant rested. "Government rests?" The Government rested. "Motions?" asked the judge. Mr. Stryker renewed the motions he had made in chambers at the end of the Government's case. The judge denied them and said the case would go to the jury. He called a short recess, after which the marshal cried: "All in," the jury entered, there was a scramble for every available seat, the audience composed itself, the court rose, the judge came in, nodded toward the defense table, and Mr. Stryker walked slowly over to the jury box and put both hands on the rail. At last he could legally look the jury in the eye.

THE SUMMATIONS

HE thanked them for their considerate attention in performing "the most noteworthy service that a citizen can perform to aid in the administration of justice." Here they had sat "in a dignified and beautiful courtroom where order has been preserved, dignity and decorum has been followed, presided over by a distinguished and able jurist whose conduct of this case I think may well serve as an example to every judge in the United States."

Having dispensed the compliments in his own incomparable way, Mr. Stryker asked the clerk for the indictment, read it aloud, and noted that "count two is telescoped into count one, and the bill of particulars makes it perfectly clear that the times when Mr. Hiss is supposed to have seen Mr. Chambers after January 1st, 1937 were the times when the documents are alleged to have been delivered." Mr. Stryker confided in an undertone that he didn't really know why the second count was in there at all: "certainly it is not a crime to see Mr. Chambers." However, what they were here to decide was the truth of three verbs: "furnish, transmit, deliver." It was the burden of the prosecution to establish "beyond a reasonable doubt" that Mr. Hiss had "furnished, transmitted, delivered those papers to Chambers." A reasonable doubt was no more than "a doubt based upon reason." That, at least, was his view of it, and if he was wrong his Honor would correct him.

Mr. Stryker left the jury box and marched thoughtfully over to
his table. He thought that Mr. Murphy, in his opening address, had
stated the issue "very potently. . . . I could not have stated it
better, perhaps not as well." Mr. Stryker put his glasses on and
gestured to his staff for "page twenty-four." He picked up the court
transcript. Yes, here it was, Mr. Murphy talking: " '. . . if you don't
believe Chambers then we have no case under the federal perjury
rule, as Judge Kaufman will tell you, where you need one witness
plus corroboration, and if one of the props goes, out goes the case.' "
Well, Mr. Stryker was "afraid" (so, very likely, was Mr. Murphy)
the jury would hear those words from him "again and again."

Mr. Stryker stopped in a stroll that followed, and reached for
a metaphor:

"In a good orchestration . . . there is always a theme, sometimes
a very simple theme. I have heard Toscanini and so have you, leading
some of the great orchestras of the world, playing perhaps Beethoven's
Fifth Symphony . . . a simple thing really, just about four notes
. . . a child could play it with one finger on the piano. And then
after you've heard him strike his baton, and they begin, perhaps the
first violins lightly with that theme . . . then maybe the bassoons
and the oboes . . . and then the boys up in the rear with the trom-
bones and the French horns." Mr. Stryker's arm went high for the
fortissimo and he crashed roaring down on the words: "and then as
though the whole orchestra had gone mad, with the kettledrums and
the cymbals sounding, the whole stage of Carnegie Hall is alive with
that one simple theme . . . and the audience is erect with applause
from the emotion."

The jury looked as if there were practically nothing they could
take with more aplomb than a Toscanini fortissimo. And Mr. Stryker
diminuendoed into a sort of apology: "Now I am not going to appeal
to your emotion. I am going to try to restrain myself . . . but I
would pray that I could stand here in the presence of this orchestra
of justice and take the theme"—his arms flailed up and out like a
semaphore signaler and he crashed his fists down in a measured beat
on the rail as he turned purple and thundered: "if—you—don't—
believe—Chambers—we—have—no—case!"

Now, "who is it that is to believe or disbelieve Chambers? Me?
I—to use the proper grammar I guess—or Mr. Murphy?" Well, he
thought the jury knew what *he* believed, but it was up to the jury,

"the sole and exclusive judges of the facts." And that was not a light obligation. The courtroom was "a holy place to me, second only to a church." This was not "the mob scene of a Congressional Committee hearing . . . no judge, no order, no rules of evidence, no counsel to hold the case to an issue"—a scene "not unlike the French Revolutionary tribunal in 1793, where they would haul in a suspect from the streets and somebody in the audience would yell at him, somebody else would walk up and spit in his face, somebody else would say that he heard somebody else say that he heard somebody else say something or other, and the tribunal would read back 'Guilty!' and he would back into the tumbril and that would be that."

He wished that the F.B.I. might put their platform (easel) up again and get a good portrait-painter; he was sure they had one—"I see they have most everything else." And he wished they would put up two canvases, two portraits, one of the accused and one of his accuser. And maybe the F.B.I. would also put up a big five-foot sign saying: "If you don't believe Chambers, the Government has no case." And then they would instruct the painter. Mr. Stryker figuratively turned to the portrait of the accuser.

Now, he said, sobering into a meditative trot, "let us take it quietly and calmly and let us see what this man Chambers is." He began life with trickery and deceit . . . "writing some essay or other for his school and there was something offensive in it to the teachers and they said, 'Well, we don't want that,' and then he said, 'All right,' and then, breaking his word, he did just what they had asked him not to do.". . . Then we find the pattern of an unusual personality. . . . He goes down to Washington and gets a job with the railroad company, and he starts then using false names. He used the name Charles Adams. Why?—because he wanted to be something like the son of John Quincy Adams. Well, he starts his long masquerade of deception . . . we find him going down and living in a dive in New Orleans . . . one of his co-occupants a prostitute. . . . He gets a job in the public library and he is dismissed for stealing. "Apparently, apparently, he said he did not steal the library books, he just stole the books from Columbia University." He goes to college, writes a blasphemous play, and cloaks his conduct under the name of John Kelly. Then he is dismissed from Columbia. And how did he get back? By writing a letter to the dean in which "I simply lied." Then he decided life was not worth living, or our system was not worthwhile, so he joined the Communist Party, among whose tenets were "lying, stealing . . . street fighting . . . and to destroy the United States by any and all means." His wife testified she knew he was part of a criminal conspiracy.

Mr. Stryker withdrew a few steps from the rail and looked hard at the jury. "I will tell you, ladies and gentlemen . . . if I didn't know anything else about a man but just that . . . I would not believe him if the F.B.I. erected a stack of Bibles as high as the building!"

The man admitted he hadn't believed in God, in the sanctity of an oath, in the holy state of matrimony. But this was the man "on whose sole word they are asking you to destroy Alger Hiss." This man brought a woman not his wife to live in his mother's home. "I should think of him," said Mr. Stryker cocking a wily eye at Dr. Carl Binger, who was in court, "as a psychopathic—and I use these words as just laymen's words, that's all I have—sadism, enjoyment in the creation of suffering by a filthy act."

Now, let's see "what we have established for our artist here: a man that for twelve years or so was an enemy of the Republic that we love, a blasphemer of Christ, a disbeliever in God, with no respect either for matrimony or motherhood"; a man who had told the House Committee three times that he left the Communist Party and repudiated "Stalin's tactics" in 1937 . . . "Remember that date." A man who yet in 1940 told Malcom Cowley that he intended to use the methods of conspiracy he had learned with the Communists.

Now, in 1948 Chambers was earning good money on *Time*, "and here was a great Presidential campaign, and we all know . . . what the Gallup polls were saying, and he chose what he thought was the stronger side . . . so he comes down there to Washington with an idea of doing sort of a fast sideswipe on Alger Hiss." And he said Mr. Hiss was a member of some "apparatus—it sounds Russian, and it sounds ominous and it sounds something very bad." And then in the same statement he couples that with the reminder that it was Mr. Hiss "who organized the Yalta Conference, Dumbarton Oaks and San Francisco. . . . Well, those who didn't like the New Deal . . . well, it was great stuff for a political campaign." Chambers thought he could pull this fast one and nothing else would happen. "But he guessed wrong on that . . . because Alger Hiss is the kind of man, gentle and kindly as he looks, with steel in his frame, and he didn't

take that lying down. . . . What did he do? Leave the country or
go into hiding? No, he telegraphs right away, 'I want to be heard.' "

And he was heard. He went to Washington, not wanting perhaps
to injure "a George Crosley . . . [who] might not be the man." But
"the Committee forced him to state it." Then the Committee
"badgered" him and showed him the picture: "Well, here . . .
don't you know him?" Well, finally, "the Committee permitted
some of the propagandists to use the Committee's *ex parte* work for
all it was worth in the middle of a campaign . . . and of course
Whittaker Chambers here was quite a figure, Whittaker Chambers,
unimpeached . . . so in typical Stripling-Parnell Thomas style they
asked Mr. Hiss to come to the hotel without saying what it was for,
and there was this fellow Chambers. And when Mr. Hiss says, 'Are
you George Crosley?' And the answer is, 'Not to my knowledge,' well,
that's something, isn't it? Are you Lloyd Stryker . . . is your name
Gyp the Blood?—'Not as far as I know.' "

So then they bring Chambers in and "it turns out he has gained
30 pounds or more, seemed to have prospered since he left the hard-
tack of Communism . . . and he had put on quite a girth under our
much-abused competitive system." Also, he'd had time to get his
teeth fixed.

Well, at that hearing Mr. Hiss says: "Say that outside, where you
haven't the protection of the Committee." Now Chambers was in a
good deal deeper than he thought. Mr. Hiss sued him for libel. "Do
you think that if there was established a scintilla of truth in the story
Chambers has told that Mr. Hiss would have asked his lawyers to
have Chambers produce any papers that he had . . . ?" They asked
Chambers that on the 4th of November. "Ten days come and go;
where Chambers spent that time, who he saw, what of his former
rogues whom he clandestinely met, the record doesn't disclose."
Then the bathroom incident in Brooklyn . . . "and the undisputed
facts in this case are that Chambers had about five minutes alone with
this envelope in the kitchen." Then on the 17th of November he
turned over the papers he *said* he had found in that envelope. And
he explained that he wanted "to do no more injury than necessary to
the individuals involved in the operation." Now, there was much to
be said for a penitent, but "I see very little to be said for a person who
claims that he is a penitent but is still a rogue." So on top of everything "we now have not only a traitor, a thief, a liar, a perjurer, an

enemy of his country, but a hypocrite." He didn't want to do his friends much injury, "no, not much, except to say under oath: 'Mr. Hiss represents the concealed enemy against which we are all fighting and I am fighting.' " Could they, the jury, think of anything worse than calling a man a concealed enemy of his country?—"it reminds me of the lady who picked up a shotgun and let her husband have both barrels in the head, you know, taking right off the top of his head. She was asked about it afterwards and she said, 'Well, I pulled the trigger sort of soft because I'd been very fond of him.' "

When Chambers had the papers, what did he do? Did he send them to the Attorney General, the F.B.I.? No, he was in his own words "incapable of deciding." Then his counsel "very strongly urged me, in the nature of the case." And on the stand he, Mr. Stryker, had asked him if he referred to the libel suit and he said: "That is right." All we knew was that "a lifelong espionage agent, trained in every form of Russian depravity and traitorous conduct, is alone with an envelope for five minutes . . . what he did, I don't know." His only motive in producing these papers was to bolster his own libel suit. But if he produced them he would have to admit sooner or later that he had kept the knowledge of espionage back from the Committee. He faced the alternative of having nothing to show in the libel suit or having to admit perjury. That had been his boasted "turmoil," not his concern for the reputation of Alger Hiss. Chambers had (in Baltimore) "honorable and fine counsel whom he should have trusted." But he didn't tell them about the two strips of microfilm. And he offered no explanation for holding them back. Was it because he didn't get the microfilm from the envelope, "that he got them later from one of the rogues whom he had collaborated with"? What did he do with them?—"the fantastic story" of the pumpkin. Was that the act of a rational man? "And, remember, if you don't believe Chambers, the Government has no case." He did not disclose espionage to Mr. Berle, or to the F.B.I., or the State Department, or the House Committee, or the grand jury. And yet he says that when he went to Washington in 1939 to tell Mr. Berle "all I knew," he was "like a soldier going forth to battle." "Big stuff. I hope we don't have any soldiers like that if we want to keep that flag flying."

Mr. Stryker turned to the "preposterous" story of Chambers's friendship with Hiss. The proper frame of reference, he implied, was the "behavior of a criminal . . . Wadleigh and the other criminal, Chambers." Mrs. Chambers had never seen Wadleigh. *They* never met or went around "because they were the real thing," who acted as true conspirators do act. Whereas, "what is the story here about Mr. Hiss?" He had let a fellow who said he was a writer have his apartment, "and then, like a perfect rash, we have the story of Mr. and Mrs. Chambers of this intense, this really intense friendship and association." (Mr. Stryker belittled the fuss over "this great Ford car" as something that came out of Hiss's being forced to testify without records.) Then, according to the Chamberses, they were everywhere together—"just couldn't do enough to incriminate themselves." And then "this famous trip to Peterboro . . . they motor four hundred miles . . . so they can sit in the car while Whittaker Chambers goes down and talks to a dead man" (Harry Dexter White) who can't refute the story. Chambers had told this to the F.B.I., but they found out that the lady who "always required everybody to register" had no knowledge or record of them. So the Government had to prove the Hisses were not in Chestertown either. Mr. Stryker absolved Mr. Murphy of this "terrible thing in this case"—he blamed the F.B.I. for it. One thing he didn't like was that "the F.B.I. have been all over this thing." But why did the F.B.I. have to bring in the man who had been in Mrs. Wickes's apartment house and never seen the Hisses? Simply because Chambers said he had taken "that fantastic automobile ride." They had to build up association, "very public association . . . visits in Baltimore, restaurants. . . . It's as though Benedict Arnold had gone around with André all over the place, gone to New York cocktail parties, and came back and forth and said, 'Here we are together.'" It was absurd. If Hiss had been in this thing, would he not have acted as Wadleigh acted?

And while Chambers was supposed to be in hiding, fearing for his life, he put his name in the Baltimore telephone book, and Mrs. Chambers got a driver's license. And he got "right on the payroll of the Federal Government, and he was all over the place as Whittaker Chambers." He had sworn "in as many ways as I can think of" that he left (the party) in 1937. If that were true, then of course there could have been no conspiracy in February or March 1938. Now, the Government has to ask you to believe these stories, "otherwise Mr. Murphy would stand up and ask for the dismissal of this case, as the

Attorney General sometimes does. . . . In England in 1793 . . . there was a great lawyer, and I wish he were here instead of me— Thomas Erskine, who was not afraid to stand up against the Government and observe the absurdity of the hysteria." If Chambers left the party in 1937, wasn't it completely clear and didn't it "additionally explain the turmoil" of Chambers when his lawyer told him the necessities of the libel case demanded the production of these papers?"

They had heard Clydie Catlett, "a lovely Christian character," whose testimony was "at least as credible as a man who spent twelve years of his life trying to tear down his country, and who had perjured himself ten times since he said he was reformed." In the F.B.I. office "we have a complete story . . . with Chambers trying to add verisimilitude" by finding out how the furniture was arranged, and so on.

Now for the documents in this case. The first four exhibits were in the acknowledged handwriting of Alger Hiss. Miss Lincoln was "quite correct" in saying that some of them were on an official pad with the tops apparently torn off. "The innuendo is that Alger Hiss tore that off lest it convey information about the Secretary of State's office." If they were incriminating, Hiss's handwriting would have been enough. But if somebody else had picked them up out of a wastebasket, he would not want to be found with the legend of an office to which he did not belong. And consider the content of the notes themselves. . . . Consider the second one: "About March 2, U.S. Embassy in Paris called that although France was permitting shipment of military supplies to China via Indo-China only to fill existing orders, it was understood that this restriction was being liberally construed. For instance, the Military Attaché had learned that China had recently placed an order in France for 30 Potez-63 planes, one of the latest types, a light bomber pursuit." Just remember "from the cables in evidence that all the Governments were supplying China with planes." Now, the underlying document to this note was one in which the French Ambassador in Tokyo had reported he had the feeling that the Japanese might be preparing for a move against the Russian maritime provinces. That information was not in the handwritten note, and the implication had to be that "a brilliant member of the State Department was prostituting his soul . . . trying to help

the Russians and would give this little pad note, which would be of
no help to the Russians, and would fail to include information that
Japan was about to strike at Russia."

As for the microfilm documents, Chambers had testified in Baltimore "time and again, time and again under oath" that he didn't
know who had given him these documents. And three of them, it
was not disputed, did not go to the Sayre or Hiss office.

Now, on the question of "this now famous typewriter." It was the
defense that found it, and offered it to the F.B.I. to examine. "But
they never accepted our invitation ever." Instead, they brought in
their "expert" with elaborate charts and graphs who purported to
show that the questioned documents "were done on the same typewriter, period." Well, Mr. Stryker had listened to his testimony and
was not convinced by any of it. Had the F.B.I. expert or anybody else
excluded "any characteristics on those questioned documents that
would be the characteristics of Whittaker Chambers"? Did they mark
any of Chambers's typewriting for identification? Did anyone say
there were characteristics that were "the characteristics of the *person*"
who typed the documents? Did any Government expert say that the
little bits of handwriting put in between the lines of several documents
"were not written by Chambers"? The Government could prove
nothing about the interlineations, so they forgot about that part of
the case altogether. "Where is Mr. Feehan on that?"

Mr. Stryker thought the evidence proved that the typewriter left
the Hisses' home on the move to Volta Place. The F.B.I. had written off to a great many cities in search of a standard from the machine,
a specimen written by either Mr. Hiss or Mrs. Hiss. "And the last,
the last paper that the F.B.I. could find anywhere," was one dated
May 25, 1937 (the letter to the University of Maryland). The Government, by the way, had said nothing about the fact that the defendant had furnished all the standards he could get.

The jury had also heard the testimony of Pat and Mike Catlett,
"undoubtedly very ignorant colored boys but honest. . . . Now I
say to you, ladies and gentlemen, that the corroboration is perfect
and complete." He also was bound to say that in respect of the Catlett
family the conduct of the F.B.I. had been "close to oppression." Did
not the May 25th letter prove that the typewriter was not in use by
the Hisses any more? That letter was "the finest possible corroboration of the Catlett testimony."

Mr. Stryker had another word to say on the general significance of typewriters. The jury surely remembered Chambers's testimony that there came a time when he disposed of a typewriter because, he had said, "he did not wish to be reminded of the past. In other words, there was something about a typewriter that evinced consciousness of guilt on the part of Chambers . . . I am talking to you about his unusual personality and mentality: I think I have proved to you that he has no regard for an oath at all, but whether he is a psychopathic liar or just a plain liar does not matter much now, and I think I can understand the rationale of his Honor's decision in excluding Dr. Binger's testimony; namely, that this is a matter that twelve intelligent members of this community can pass upon." Recall also the story of Chambers about his visit to Volta Place in December 1938. He said he went fearing an ambush, by which he said he meant "that he might be kidnapped or killed by Alger Hiss, and then when he got there he sat down and had supper with him." That was the testimony of "the only witness in the world who says that these documents were transmitted." He couldn't see how any fair-minded man or woman in the world could fail to have a reasonable doubt about the veracity and credibility of Whittaker Chambers.

Mr. Stryker would leave it to the ladies to judge the truth of Mrs. Chambers's story, because "we mere men, I think, are not able to judge women as well as ladies can." But there were two things in her testimony that were not only "perjury clear, simple and mathematical, but evidently it suborned perjury" (with no reflections, Mr. Stryker hastened to say, on the opposing lawyers). One was her interjection that Mr. Hiss was pleading a case in the Supreme Court. The record stood undisputed that that happened a year later. But Chambers "or one of his confederates found the undoubted fact that there was a time when Mr. Hiss did plead a case in the Supreme Court. That circumstance was given to Mrs. Chambers. She took it and added it to her narrative and put it in." And when she had been caught out on that, she said she "assumed" he was arguing a case in some other court; whereas Hiss was too busy at that time to be arguing any case in any court.

The other thing was an example of how "things get by" in the "avalanche of proof" the jury had been offered. Mr. Stryker read from Mrs. Chambers's testimony in Baltimore where she was attesting to her acquaintance with Mrs. Hiss in 1935 and 1936. Now, in the

Government's rereading of her testimony, the letter of May 25, 1937 somehow got in, and "the impression was sought to be conveyed that the time when that was done was not in 1935 or 1936 but in May 1937." In other words, "somehow, from some source" Mrs. Chambers learned about Mrs. Hiss's having taken a course of some sort, and she had learned about the phrase "Mercy Hospital." From "that learning she wove the perjurious statement that Mrs. Hiss was taking a nursing course in 1935 and 1936" and that those were the times Mrs. Hiss had come over to sit in the park with her. "She wanted to multiply and amplify and exaggerate and lie about the association which they never had."

The judge warned Mr. Stryker that he had a very little time left. And Mr. Stryker moved up to the jury box and to his close. Mr. Murphy, he said, had called Alger Hiss "this character." It was not meant in a friendly way. But he would take it in that way, for "If there was ever a man in the world who has established a finer character than Alger Hiss, I don't know where that happened." Alger Hiss was "good enough" for Admiral Hepburn, not for Whittaker Chambers; good enough for John W. Davis, for Supreme Court judges. "You heard him. You watched him through his long, long bitter ordeal. He did not have to take the stand. He could have sat silent. . . . This case comes down to this: Who is telling the truth? Alger Hiss or Chambers? . . . it is the Government's burden to establish . . . and beyond a reasonable doubt, that it is Chambers that is telling the truth." He doubted there was "any jury in the world that could sleep with their consciences and say that they believed beyond a reasonable doubt that Chambers is the truthful man." Everywhere Alger Hiss had been and gone "and everything he has done and every trail he has left behind is pure, wholesome, sound, clean, decent, fine." Had Alger Hiss prostituted that career for a rug? For the non-payment of rent, or the little loans? For the privilege of lending Chambers four hundred dollars?

Mr. Stryker took a step back and shouted: "This is not a case. It is an outrage. This is the long culmination of the job that was done by the Un-American Activities Committee, an un-American committee, the way they handled the job." He wanted to say he had "nothing but personal goodwill for Mr. Murphy," but, he said turning and looking towards the Government table, "I hope that when you have had your talks, in the preparation of this case, with Mr.

Chambers—you have had good witnesses present and have left none of *your* handwriting around the table."

There was a titter from the mass of the courtroom. "That," Mr. Stryker said quickly, "is not so funny either, because I've defended district attorneys and assistant district attorneys and sometimes the rascals they deal with turn on them."

He was back at the rail again with his small hands on it. "Ladies and gentlemen . . . with all my faults, if I have done anything that you don't like, if I have offended any one of you in any way, hold it against me, not against Alger Hiss. . . . Ladies and gentlemen, the case will be in your hands. I beg you, I pray you to search your consciences, and I have no fear, 'Yea, though I have walked through the valley of the shadow of death.' " He turned round again and stood erect, looking with red eyes at Hiss. "Alger Hiss, this long nightmare is drawing to a close. Rest well. Your case, your life, your liberty are in good hands. Thank you, ladies and gentlemen."

Without any swagger or semblance of poise, Mr. Stryker pattered back to his chair.

THE court assembled again and for the first time we caught something more than glimpses of Mr. Murphy's face. His habit throughout the trial had been to stand, often at a lectern, at the end of the box and remain looking at the witness. The spectators had seen only the back of his smooth head of hair, two powerful shoulders, and the alarming investment of cloth required to drape his vast back. Most of the time, he moved only to ease the burden of his two hundred and thirty pounds from one leg to the other, when the sweeping creases of his coat and trousers would go into reverse. Now he was free to face the jury and even, after Mr. Stryker's infectious example, to stroll up and down the well. But we still had to gauge his facial expression from the inflections of his voice, for his eyes were small and his mouth was almost invisible under the sleeping walrus of his mustache.

He, too, put his hands on the rail and thanked the jury for their patience and for their "exhibition of courage" in deciding not to have their pictures taken. It made him feel very proud and he thought to himself: "This is a real jury."

Now, this case was in its essence rather simple. The facts were very, very narrowly confined. He thought Mr. Stryker was—he hesitated for the proper nuance of criticism—"a little bit confused when he said it was the doubt of reasonable men. The law presumes that we are all reasonable men. The doubt in a criminal case is the doubt that exists in your minds *after* you have applied reason." In other words, you couldn't say: "I don't like the way he combs his hair—I wouldn't believe that guy on a stack of Bibles." Under their oath, they simply had to have a reason. That's what "reasonable doubt" meant.

Now, "let us see if we can analyze the facts by applying reason and not emotion." There were three solid witnesses to this charge: the typewriter, the original State Department documents, and the documents Chambers had in his possession. There was no contradiction of the fact that Chambers had undoubted copies, sometimes verbatim copies, of "original, secret, confidential State Department documents." They were all dated in the first three months of 1938. All the typewritten ones, except one, done on the Hiss typewriter. That was uncontradicted, and that was what they had to start with. The only inference they could draw, he submitted, was that "that smart, intelligent American-born man gave them to Chambers."

The judge would tell them that in federal perjury trials you had to have two witnesses, or one witness and corroborating evidence. Well, they had Mr. Chambers and the corroboration was the documents and the typewriter they were done on. As a homely example of corroboration, he asked them to consider a child caught in the kitchen with jam on his face. "You asked him whether he was in the pantry and had some jam and he said, 'No.'" Well, everyday intelligence would tell you he was lying, although there was no proof he put it in his mouth. We are only mortals and "we don't have to take a stomach pump" to prove it.

Being mortals, we might also succumb, he implied, to the emotional factors in the case. What were they?

One was "a clean-cut, handsome, intelligent, American-born male of some 44 years." Another was the fact that "Mr. Chambers is short and fat and he had bad teeth. . . . Mrs. Chambers is plain and demure. Mrs. Hiss is demure and attractive, intelligent to boot. Very intelligent."

But those were emotional factors. When they got in the jury-room, they had under their oath to decide the *facts* "on reasons."

Mr. Murphy took three routine steps, enough to get him from one end of the box to the other. He touched his thumb and knuckle to the ends of his mustache. He was very leisurely. "Mr. Stryker . . . said he was going to call as a witness for this defendant the shade of Oliver Wendell Holmes." Well, Mr. Murphy had said to himself when he heard that, "there are a couple of shades that I'd like to call here." One was Judas Iscariot and the other Major General Benedict Arnold. Mr. Stryker didn't call the shade. But he called, he thought, fifteen character witnesses. Of course, he guessed they'd want to think for themselves "whether two judges from the United States Supreme Court could with propriety come into this courtroom." They didn't know the facts, they could only testify about a reputation.

"Now, just how important is a person's reputation in this Year of Our Lord, 1949? . . . I daresay Judas Iscariot had a fairly good reputation. He was one of the Twelve. He was next to God, one of the Twelve, and we know what he did. Brutus, Caesar's friend, I daresay he had a good reputation. He got so close to his boss that he stabbed him. And then Major General Benedict Arnold. He came from a fine family . . . captured at Fort Ticonderoga . . . made a colonel . . . led the siege against Quebec, wounded . . . made a brigadier general." Then some money found its way into his pocket and he swore to the court martial he was innocent, when "at that very time he'd been dealing eight months with the British. . . . And what happened? He is made Major General and he sold out West Point. . . . He wasn't caught." But if he had been caught, didn't they think "he could have called George Washington as a reputation witness"? And did they know who the Devil was? "Lucifer himself, one of the fallen angels. He traveled within the sight of God; now, he had a reputation I daresay, and what happened to him?"

He would say: "Ladies and gentlemen . . . just forget" the character witnesses. It was window dressing. Mr. Murphy turned and pointed to the typewriter and the pile of documents on the Government table. "Those are the facts."

Mr. Stryker had made much of his relief at being away from the Klieg lights and being here in a court of law, "with the rules all printed and defined and known." So he told them first thing that Chambers was "a moral leper, a thief, an income tax evader." Of course, the mere pittance Chambers earned as a Communist didn't require him to file a return. But that's what Mr. Stryker said—an income-tax evader. But if Mr. Stryker called Chambers a moral leper, what was "his bosom pal"? What "is the name of an employee of this Government who takes Government papers and gives them to a Communist espionage agent? . . . Very simple—Alger Hiss was a traitor."

Happily, Mr. Murphy reflected, the courtroom was a great leveler. Here they could try anybody. "It doesn't make any difference whether they went to Harvard or P.S. 36. . . . Roses that fester stink worse than weeds. And a brilliant man like this man who betrays his trust stinks." Mr. Murphy bared his mouth on the last word and went on: "Inside of that smiling face, that heart is black and cancerous."

This sort of thing sounded more like Mr. Stryker's vein, but Mr. Murphy said it with an easy rumbling contempt, and his face was never redder than his fine protective tan.

Did they recall how Mr. Stryker had asked Chambers: "Were you living with a prostitute [in New Orleans] named One-Eyed Annie?" Where did Mr. Stryker get his knowledge from? He got it from one place only, from thirteen hundred pages of Mr. Chambers's pre-trial testimony in Baltimore. "How many lawyers would love" the opportunity of unrestricted cross-examination before trial? And the fact implied in that question wasn't true, "but he gave you an overtone. . . . Ladies and Gentlemen, he is glad to be right here, away from all those dramatics." What did Mrs. Chambers think of her husband, a man Mr. Stryker said "had no respect for womankind"? She said: "He is a great man."

"To build it up a little more," Mr. Stryker had him stealing books ("how many college men do you think you could hit if you threw a stone out this window," and how many who had a few books from college?); then stealing news from the *New York Times*.

Not once, Mr. Murphy confessed, had he discovered what the defendant thought was Chambers's motive. What was the motive of a senior editor of *Time* in throwing up a $30,000-a-year job to come forward with these papers? At one point Mr. Murphy had thought it might be because Chambers hadn't paid back about $135 in debts. "And I wondered—good God, that can't be the motive." Then Mr. Stryker had talked about the political campaign of 1948. So, what was Chambers going to get out of it? "Judge Kaufman gets $15,000. D'you know what members of the Cabinet get? . . . Nothing like $30,000." So what was there in it for Chambers? And the defense put in that motive on the basis of two sentences read at the confrontation from "the opposition magazine."

No motive had been proved. Confronted with the story of Colonel Bykov, all Mr. Stryker could do was stumble over the name, say "Bykov-Bekov." Well, "that kind of bumpkin stuff is old, old." That was all part of the window dressing.

Mr. Murphy went to the table again and patted the documents—"Those are the *facts*." And for how long had Mr. Stryker talked about the documents? "By actual timing," he had talked about them for eleven minutes, in a four-hour summation.

When the defense came into court they had "everything": they had thirteen hundred pages of testimony from the Chamberses in Baltimore, they had the House Committee testimony, they had copies of the Hisses' statements to the grand jury, they had the documents, "they even had the typewriter." The only thing they hadn't heard before was about "the $400 loan." And what did they do with it? "They fumbled, they dropped the ball on that one."

The only way "to determine the credibility" was to put the testimony of the Hisses and the Chamberses side by side. Just consider the Chamberses' description of Volta Place, the detail of Mrs. Chambers's knowledge. "Now it seems to me she was either there or she is psychic." What was Mrs. Hiss's contradiction? It took about ten minutes to find out which was the front of the house, and "in effect the testimony was contradicted by what was front and what was rear. There was no dispute that the dining room and living room were on the ground floor. Nothing was said about upstairs." Was it humanly possible for two people to describe two houses in such detail without having been there?

And then the confrontation, "the opportunity that Mr. Hiss was crying for." When Hiss heard that Mr. Chambers had given some details of Hiss's private life, Hiss "started to think who could that person be . . . and he wrote the name George Crosley . . . a freelance writer he knew back in '34–'35," the man who "sublet his apartment . . . he also remembers that in order to clinch the deal . . . he threw in a Ford, just sort of threw it in. That must be the fellow, George Crosley," a man Hiss said he had barely known—"drove him to New York, he once borrowed a couple of bucks, didn't bother much with him," except he stayed once at the house on P Street. Then the jury would remember what happened at the confrontation:

Hiss asked him to talk, open his mouth. He examined his teeth, wanted to know the name of the dentist. Then he asked about the sublease, and how did he reconcile the apparent contradiction of saying he had not subleased an apartment but nevertheless had occupied it? Then Chambers says: "You and I, Alger, were Communists together." And then Hiss says: "I now recognize him from what he has just said. I am convinced that this is George Crosley." Not from his teeth, pitch of voice, hair, jewels, stature. The subleasing was what did it. That's what happened, not what Hiss said on the stand: "I recognized him without hesitation."

Now about the car. Assume that Hiss did not honestly remember what year it was that he gave the car away. He first testified he gave it "to clinch the rental agreement"—and to "a guy that he didn't know where he came from." No written lease, nothing like that. "Can you imagine being 44 before meeting that type of character—a landlord who was not concerned with wanting the rent in advance?" Later on he said he gave him "the use of the Ford . . . the use." That was Mr. Hiss's forte: "he is able to distinguish, to combine truth with half-truth, a little bit to color it, a little bit more to testify, and then—if placed in a corner—to rely upon the truthful part. . . . You have to be pretty good to do that, and he *is* pretty good." Finally, on the stand Hiss said he had given him the car "in 1936, because he promised to give it to him in April of the year before." He had made a promise, and although "the guy gypped him a little bit in between," when the man said: "Where is the car?" . . . "Here it is." But what did the assignment of title say? That Hiss had "assigned, transferred and sold that car to the Cherner Motor Company, and Judge Kaufman would not let me prove what happened after that."

Then the rug. They had put in evidence the bill of sale, Professor Schapiro, the rug dealer, "and here"—Mr. Murphy held out a slip of paper—"is the check of Dr. Schapiro." And to this Hiss said he did get a rug, still had it, "but he has no idea why he gave it to him."

Now the typewriter. First bear in mind that Mr. Hiss's firm of lawyers rented a Woodstock typewriter for three months from February to May 1949. Now, on the 17th of November, Chambers produced the typewritten documents. Hiss had said that "they frantically tried to get hold of the Attorney General; they wanted to be the first ones to bring this matter to the attention of the head of the Department of Justice." Did that "plan of attack seem familiar"?

Hiss surely didn't expect that Mr. Chambers's lawyer "was going to dig a hole and hide it"? No, but Hiss and his lawyers thought "if they got there first, that would prove they were innocent. They wanted to be the first to yell 'Cop!' Who yells 'Cop' first? Our Communist friends outside this building [1] . . . get in there first and therefore you are innocent." What else could Hiss do if he didn't deny it immediately?—"he could get on a train and that's the last we'd hear of him." And the same with the specimens: "Here are some, I found these. Are these any good?" Then "to help the F.B.I. find the typewriter," he said they only had one, but he gave it away, or his wife did, sold it to a second-hand dealer in Georgetown *after* 1938. "They thereby eliminated all the other cities in the United States . . . that was the only thing he wanted to do in December, was to help the F.B.I." Mrs. Hiss told the grand jury that Claudie Catlett was dead . . . "that would help . . . just eliminate her from the list of people to see." The F.B.I. agents saw the Catletts at the end of January 1949. And the Catletts denied knowing anything about a Hiss typewriter; "but what did they tell the Hisses?" The little Catlett boy had gone to Donald Hiss, the day after the F.B.I. had been around, and told him the F.B.I. were looking for a typewriter. "And then, ladies and gentlemen, things started to buzz. . . . We find Mr. Rosenwald, a fellow classmate, out in Detroit the end of January."

"Now I suggest to you that this is what happened:" the Hisses knew the typewriter was a link between the Chamberses and them. They knew that from May or June 1937 until April 1938 "that typewriter was going all the time." If there was ever going to be a charge against the Hisses, the typewriter would be "the immutable witness forever against them." So they didn't sell it—there would have been a record of that—they gave it to the Catletts in the belief it would fall into disuse "and disintegrate . . . and end up in some ash can." Until he was indicted, Mr. Murphy believed, Hiss "never once mentioned it to his lawyers." He had not told the F.B.I., but he did tell one of the Catlett boys. He went to him and said: "If the F.B.I. ever come looking for a typewriter, don't telephone me but tell my brother Donald." In other words, "if the agents didn't find the Catletts, all well and good." But *when* did the Catletts get it? The mother knew nothing about it. Perry Catlett said in May 1949 he didn't know whether he

---

[1] There were parades going on in Foley Square in support of the eleven Communists, who were on trial in the same building.

got it before, after, or during "some moving." What he did remember was that he took it to the northwest corner of Connecticut Avenue and K Street. "And that is true, I think. . . . He did take it to some place . . . in 1939." Unfortunately for the defense, the Woodstock people didn't come to that address until September 1938. But suppose the boy was in error about the address, suppose—"as the defense intimated"—it was the other Woodstock shop down the block on K Street. "Well we checked that, and you heard the witness say that the shop didn't come into existence until May 1938." The jury could take its choice of shop. It made no difference to the Government.

Now, when Mike Catlett was being interviewed by the F.B.I., he called his real-estate agent and found out that the Catletts moved into their home on P Street on January 17, 1938. But supposing all this was not in evidence. Let's assume that they got the typewriter about January 1, 1938. "Who typed those documents?" . . . Are we supposed to visualize Chambers coming around to the Catlett house at night and typing those documents himself?"

He submitted that the Hisses had the typewriter until at least Mr. Chambers left the Party, and the Catletts had it some time after that.

When Mr. Stryker was confronted with the repair-shop testimony, "What did he do? Well, he started on the F.B.I. You know, there's an old saying, when you haven't the facts on your side then you knock the District Attorney's head off. That's changed now. It's the open season on the F.B.I. . . . it's the smart thing to do. It's the liberal approach." Well, he, Mr. Murphy, was going to make the jury "a firm offer: . . . if one juror thinks the F.B.I. was unfair" in its treatment of the Catletts, "acquit this man." This was just another of Mr. Stryker's "overtones . . . it adds to the symphony [he] was writing for you. It's all background—the muted brass way off there— the F.B.I. open season."

Now let them look at another piece of corroboration. If Mr. Chambers was the cunning liar Mr. Stryker would have them believe, why would he mention the day he went to Peterboro, the hotel, the owner's name? That was leading with his chin. But he said it because it was true.

And what did Chambers do about the error on "Dent Place"? Did he say "Dent" and "Volta" sounded alike and maybe the stenographer got them mixed? "By God, he did not."

"Now, let us see how Chestertown comes into the Peterboro

picture. There is no doubt the Hisses were in Chestertown. But that's not what they said." They said they were there every day, and all the Government did was to "prove" they were not there every day.

Now, another item—"the $400 loan." They knew Chambers's story. If it was a true story and there was an exact four-hundred-dollar withdrawal, "he too is psychic." What did Mrs. Hiss say to this? She said she bought all the items for Volta Place. "I am going to ask the ladies on the jury. Is that the way you do it when you have a checking account and a charge account, and you've not moved in? Do you take the $400 out in one lump? Do you go around and buy items for the house to be delivered later and pay for them in cash? . . . Is that $400 explanation reasonable to you or is it just another lie, another peg upon which you can tell which side credibility lies?"

He wouldn't even talk about Mrs. Hiss's statement to the grand jury that "she could not type, how she was a longhander. A long-hander—the girl with all of these degrees . . . the girl who passed this typewriting test at Columbia." The typewritten documents were "a pretty good job. Take a look at them."

True, the last specimen anyone had found was dated May 25, 1937.

Mr. Murphy hit the rail and braced himself for his big line. Then he came in with a voice rising to a bellow: "I suggest to you the reason why there are no other specimens around is because that typewriter was otherwise occupied. . . . It was humming. SMOKE was coming from that typewriter. . . . It was really burning." And for how long?—"for nine months from June of 1937 until April of 1938." That's why there were no specimens around because—and Mr. Murphy threw a careless hand towards the documents—"these and others like it were being made."

Government's exhibit number 17 was "the one that hurt, the one in which Mrs. Hiss said she was going to the University in order she might take courses at Mercy Hospital." Mrs. Chambers knew about that too and "if she was not psychic, she was chumming with Mrs. Hiss, and I submit that's how she knew it."

That brought them to 1938, an important date, "because when Chambers testified first, 1937 was the date he spoke." He had a subpoena two days before he testified, but in the same hearing he said 1938. Thereafter he said 1938. "Wrong by a year the first time. What significance in that?"

"But let me speak about the lawsuit." Hiss *had* to bring the lawsuit. If he hadn't, "he would have been laughed at from here to Borneo . . . in self-defense he had to bring the suit." The Hiss lawyers spent an awful lot of time examining Mr. Chambers. But did Mr. Chambers examine Mr. Hiss? Mrs. Hiss? No. Because he had a defense. The defense was truth, which "is always a defense to a libel suit."

Similarly, Mr. Stryker hadn't known what to do with Wadleigh, "because Wadleigh told the truth." Mr. Stryker "handed in his cards when Mr. Wadleigh was on the stand." He said: "Well, you are an Oxford man, I can't handle you." Mr. Stryker quit. Why? Because Wadleigh was one of Chambers's men in the State Department, "the same as that traitor Alger Hiss there." And they didn't even ask Chambers what he had said to Cowley. Then they brought in the old schoolmate who said Chambers didn't get his hair cut as a boy. "Just imagine some day in the future your child being confronted with a man" like that saying: "You don't get your hair cut."

And then John Foster Dulles. Mr. Stryker could see no contradiction. Well, it was right there. Mr. Dulles "put the lie in this man's mouth on three separate occasions." Hiss was asked if he hadn't said he "personally checked with Justice Byrnes," and then it came out that Mr. Acheson did it. "I personally checked," he said.

Now the documents. Look at the first one (a handwritten note). "May 28. Moscow 28. . . . This was a summary in order to tell his boss of important matters like trade agreements—Telegram from Mary Martin, widow of Hugh Martin, formerly employed for special work by legation at Riga. Remember well Rubens while working for Hugh, be strict if needed, write Library Congress, Law Division."

One thing more. Notice the way it was creased. Did it look like a paper that was "finished with, thrown in a wastebasket? With those creases?"

Mr. Murphy ran his finger delicately across its smooth top. "And look at the phrasing there: '30 Potez-63, latest French type, a light bomber-pursuit.' . . . And then to make it clear for the photographer, it is all written out."

They could forget about the typewriter and just confine themselves to the handwritten documents. Those were the things Hiss couldn't explain. "That is the jam on his face." Mr. Murphy laid a tiny scrap of paper on the rail, like a derisive petal on a traitor's grave.

He folded it neatly in the middle and slipped it thoughtfully into his breast pocket. That, he implied, was the way the memoranda got out of the State Department. "Wastebasket?" Mr. Murphy picked up a blank piece of paper, a calculated waif from the incriminating file. He crumpled it quickly and tossed it at the jury's feet. "There," he said, "is the way you do that."

Mr. Stryker had said he did not cross-examine the F.B.I. expert. Why? Mr. Stryker knew the documents were typed on that machine.

And finally, "how would you . . . feel on that chair and have some psychiatrist look at you for seven days? Did you see any change in Mr. Chambers? Any? He was telling the truth, and that's why he didn't fear him, or any other of the settings and props that have been going around in this case."

This was the second jury to hear this case. The grand jury heard the same story. And that grand jury indicted Hiss.

Mr. Murphy pulled his coat down. "You gave your oaths when you were sworn on May 31st that you would decide this case on the evidence here. . . . Today is the day. I ask you as a representative of the United States Government to come back and put the lie in that man's face. Thank you."

JUDGE KAUFMAN'S CHARGE

❧

WHEN the summations are over is the time that the marshal comes into his own. He sits for weeks listening to testimony he cannot use or pass on. He sits in a chair near the door and dozes fitfully with one eye, the other eye crawling around the heavy coughers, the knowing ones, the ladies in mink trying to look like the press. Often he goes out into the corridor for a snack of lifelike dialogue with the cop on duty and strolls back in from time to time, like a jaded movie usherette, to see if "the exciting part" has come on yet. But just before the judge gives his charge, the marshal straightens up and stretches his caged ego. He has a key in his hand. He times the last quick cigarettes before the judge's bailiff flashes the signal for the judge's entry. Then the word is given, and he bawls: "Everybody in, nobody allowed out during the charge, everybody in!" Everybody pours in. The marshal locks the door.

Judge Kaufman darted in, flushed and lively-eyed. He was a small neat man with a sort of Disney apprehensiveness. His big black bow tie came over the top of the bench and he squatted like a meditative black rabbit. The jury sat up as straight as they had done when they were sworn.

This was a "comparatively long and comparatively simple but most unusual case." It had attracted much public attention. Numerous accounts of it, "including editorials, and feature stories . . . [on] the radio and television" had appeared, and they would be more than human if they had managed to avoid all contact with some of these reports. But he wished to stress that they must now exert every human effort to disregard everything except "the evidence received

266

in this case from the witnesses, the exhibits and instructions that I am about to give you."

They were to be concerned only with the charge against the defendant. They could have a copy of it in the juryroom. Stripping that charge of all its legal verbiage, the defendant was charged with having "falsely testified" before the grand jury "that he did not turn any confidential documents of the State Department or copies of confidential documents over to Whittaker Chambers or to any other unauthorized person"; that in truth he did do so to Chambers "in or about the months of February and March, 1938." In other words, the charge said that in denying this the defendant had committed perjury. The second count had been amplified by a bill of particulars "furnished by the Government upon an order of this Court," which asserted that the times when the defendant saw Chambers after the 1st of January 1937 were the very times he was charged with having turned over the documents. And the place "is said to have been the defendant's Volta Place residence."

Both counts charged that by so testifying the defendant had broken a section of the United States code, the pertinent portion of which ran as follows:

Whoever, having taken an oath before a competent tribunal . . . in which a law of the United States authorizes an oath to be administered, that he will testify, declare, depose or certify truly, . . . wilfully and contrary to such oath states or subscribes any material matter which he does not believe to be true, is guilty of perjury. . . .

As a matter of law, he instructed them that "there is no excuse or justification for perjury." He also charged them as a matter of law that the statements referred to in the indictment were material to the espionage investigation being conducted by the grand jury.

If they found the defendant guilty of having furnished, transmitted, and delivered the documents, "then you may find him guilty of . . . perjury" on the first count. And since the Government's bill of particulars fixed the time of the meetings referred to as "the occasions, and the only occasions" on which the documents were supposed to have been passed, "it follows that if you find the defendant did not meet with Chambers then, you must also find he did not testify falsely" on the second count. It was up to the Government to prove these two contentions "beyond a reasonable doubt." He charged them therefore "that if you find the defendant not guilty on the first count, you must find him not guilty on the second count. If, however, you find him guilty on the first count, you may find him guilty on the second count."

He said all the usual, proper things that judges are bound to say to all juries: an indictment is an accusation merely; a defendant need not take the stand, and is presumed innocent until he is found guilty; the judge alone passes on matters of law, and any errors he makes may be reviewed by an appellate court; the jury alone are the judges of the facts, including someone's credibility; in spite of what he or the counsel might imply, their recollection was alone the controlling factor; the Government was not privileged, it was like any other party. And a reasonable doubt was "a doubt based upon reason." *Beyond* such a doubt did not mean "beyond all doubt." To find the defendant guilty they must be "abidingly convinced" of his guilt. And if they found their minds in "a state of suspense," then "such a state of mind goes to the benefit of the defendant." But they must not "arbitrarily and capriciously" seize on the phrase "reasonable doubt" to avoid "a disagreeable duty."

These were general principles. Now they came to apply them to this case. They must carefully weigh the testimony of Mr. Chambers. He was the only person who testified that the witness turned over the documents. "The testimony of Mr. Chambers is not to be taken like that of a disinterested witness . . . it would be only natural" for him to try to sustain his original assertion. Because of the pending libel suit, Mr. Chambers was an interested witness. They should also bear in mind he had admitted making, sometimes under oath and other times not, statements "inconsistent with and contrary to" what he had said in this trial. They must remember he did not disclose the documents during the years he said he had them, although he was under a duty to do so. He didn't disclose them until he had been examined twice in the Baltimore libel suit. "It is for you to determine whether his prior statements were false and his testimony here was true, or whether his prior statements were true and his testimony here was false." They should consider also that Chambers had been a Communist and that he had previously said he left the Party in 1937. This was important in considering the validity of his testimony. They must take into account all the evidence about "his life, his Communist activities, his code of ethics, his demeanor on the witness stand, his apparent success when he joined *Time* magazine in early 1940, the plausibility, the logic, and the effect of all of his testimony."

He stressed this because "the credibility and veracity of Mr. Chambers . . . are crucial to this case." If in the light of all his testimony they did not believe Mr. Chambers beyond a reasonable doubt, "then I direct you to find a verdict of not guilty in favor of the defendant on each count of the indictment." If they did believe him, "then you must also consider all of the evidence adduced at this trial, and the instructions which I have given and am about to give you." Mr. Murphy, in his opening statement, had stated that if they did not believe Chambers, the Government had no case against the defendant. "My direction to you to find the defendant not guilty" if they did not believe Mr. Chambers was made because "Mr. Murphy's statement crystallized in great brevity the law in perjury cases," which he would now explain.

Under the law, no person could be convicted of perjury unless the falsity was testified to by two independent witnesses, or by one witness and corroborating facts and circumstances. Unless that was done, they must acquit the defendant. Corroboration had to substantiate the evidence of the single witness; and also it had to be trustworthy evidence. To be sufficient in this case, corroborative evidence would have to confirm that part of Mr. Chambers's testimony about the turning over of the documents.

Ordinarily witnesses were allowed to testify only to facts and not to matters of opinion. Mr. Feehan (the F.B.I. typewriter expert) was an exception, the exception of a man who had become an expert in an art, science, or profession. They must weigh his expert opinion, but they were not bound by it. If the reasons given for it appeared unsound to them, they might reject it.

The production of the documents was what is called circumstantial evidence. In this case such evidence "must not be merely consistent with the guilt of the defendant; it must be inconsistent with any reasonable hypothesis of innocence and susceptible of no reasonable hypothesis other than that of guilt."

Then they must consider the testimony offered in the defendant's behalf. They must consider too the defendant's life, his education, his "standing in the community . . . the conduct of the defendant at the time" he was first publicly charged before the House Committee; his conduct thereafter; the repetition of the charges; the libel suit; the defendant's explanation about the typewriter and the documents. He charged them as a matter of law that the defendant was an interested witness. If they believed his testimony against that of Chambers, then of course "your verdict must be not guilty." If they believed Chambers beyond a reasonable doubt, then of course "you may find a verdict of guilty." The evidence of good character brought by witnesses "may engender and bring about a reasonable doubt where otherwise there would not be one." But, "as each one of us knows, a man may commit a crime even though he was theretofore a person of good character."

Both wives were interested witnesses.

Upon all the evidence, it was for the jury to say "whether the government had established the allegations of the indictment beyond a reasonable doubt." If it had, "you may find the defendant guilty on both counts." If they believed the defendant or if they found the government had not made out its case beyond a reasonable doubt, "then your verdict must be not guilty."

Finally, let him say that the verdict of the jury should represent "the opinion of each individual juror." But that did not mean that opinions could not be "changed or exchanged." In fact, the object of the jury system was "to secure unanimity" by such an interchange. Therefore, they must go into the juryroom and listen patiently to their colleagues. A verdict must be the verdict of all twelve. It must be reached in "the solemn obligation to decide the issues solely upon the evidence" and they must do this, to the best of their ability, "free from all bias, prejudice or partiality. I am confident that each of you will exert every effort to come to a just conclusion."

THERE were no requests from the counsel. The judge explained to the two alternates, as genially as it is ever possible to do, that only twelve could go in the juryroom, so that the alternates were free to go their ways. The two martyrs meekly retired with the thanks of the court. The foreman asked if all the exhibits would be available to them. He was told they would be. And at twenty minutes after four in the afternoon of the 7th of July 1949 the jury retired.

THE VERDICT

❁

ONCE the jury was out, the courtroom was transformed. Formality was gone with the judge and the marshals, and anybody could wander in and out. The clerk of the court doodled and swiveled in his chair. The lawyers would come in, pass a kidding word with their opponents, go out again. A newspaper was no longer a sinful thing to carry in, to tear apart and leave on a bench. The newspapermen stalked around the forbidden pasture of the well or sat in the jury box and mimicked their favorite juryman.

Outside, the flanking corridors were taking on the exhilaration —and among old trial hands the pretended boredom—of a siege. Trials touch the deepest springs of human behavior, and the jury's retirement excites a very primitive suspense; but it is thought childish to admit this, and consequently the watchers either adopt the cover-up of fatigue or vent their anxiety in rapid bursts of dogmatism or driblets of facetiae. Just as an amateur onlooker at a chess tournament is shocked to notice the professional's addiction to something which his solicitous friends might very well have persuaded him to adopt in preference to opium, so the stranger off the streets who has been fetched by the newspaper reports of a trial goes up to see the verdict and is at once struck by the disguised hysteria of the groups milling around the courtroom.

This change of emotional tone was only just getting under way when a note came from the juryroom and we docked cigarette stubs and shuffled hastily back in. The bailiff appeared, then the judge, and the counsel. Judge Kaufman said the jury had requested the indict-

271

ment and its bill of particulars, all the Baltimore exhibits, and all the typewriting specimens (or "standards") used by the prosecution.

We were out in the corridors again. The press room belched musty smoke every time a man with frantic copy threw the door open. A raddled messenger, leaning at an angle to catch up with himself, shuttled between the corridor and a restaurant outside and came whipping in with sandwiches and coffee.

Five hours later, the judge summoned Mr. Murphy and Mr. Stryker again to agree to call the jury back at ten thirty and see if they wanted to be locked up for the night. The jury filed in at that time and saw no prospect of a verdict, and the clerk said he would have to swear the marshal. Which he did, charging him "to keep the jurors empanelled and sworn in this cause together in some private and convenient place without meat and drink except water." This formidable oath is only another brave relic of the English trial system and was not binding on the marshal at meal times. And before we saw them again, they had had breakfast.

They had been in the juryroom two hours the next morning when they sent out to ask the judge to restate the part of his charge "relating to corroborative and circumstantial evidence." They accordingly filed in at noon again and the judge read it over. Hiss sat as gracefully as ever by his wife's side, but he was never again to fold his arms. He patted the lapels of his coat in a gentle effort to keep up the self-possession that for six weeks had seemed so effortless.

In mid-afternoon came the first break in the growing tension, which for the newspapermen and the roaming hangers-on was an irritation merely, and for the Hisses, dawdling over magazines and crossword puzzles in a private room, must have felt like the very rack of time. The jury sent a note to the judge asking to come in and they walked down the aisle pretty glumly. Judge Kaufman read their note: "The jury feels that it cannot arrive at a verdict." All the lawyers, who had been peering humbly at the grain of the wooden tables, looked up to see what the judge would do. Hiss did not move a muscle. The judge asked for his charge and turned its end pages. Then he looked nervously at them and fingered their note. He wanted to remind them that a jury was a composite body. He did not wish to imply that anyone should give up his conviction. But at the same time "the jury system will not function if every juror goes into the juryroom determined that his and his view alone must prevail, and that he is the only one that has seen the light." He would ask them to go back and deliberate again, to make one further effort to reach a verdict. "Let me know as soon as you can about the situation, whether it be ten minutes, one hour or three hours. We are at your disposal, and I will take you at your word. If you tell me after you make another try that you cannot agree, come back and tell me."

On the way out, the foreman asked for a copy of the judge's complete charge. The judge was not sure whether the rules would let him give it to them and they retired without it. Nearly an hour later he brought them in again to tell them it was available. The foreman stood, a slim, delicate-featured man with prematurely silver hair. He hesitated and then said he did not believe now that the charge would materially help them. "Then," said Judge Kaufman, "the jury may go back." Again we jostled out, and again the Hisses had to fall back on whatever reserves they had left.

Only twenty minutes later the jury asked to come in again. Before they were called, the judge read another note. The note said what it had said before. They could not reach a verdict. Mr. Murphy looked at his thumbs, the press had its pencils ready, Mrs. Hiss was as white and forlorn as a discarded doll. What suggestions, the judge wondered, had Mr. Murphy? Mr. Murphy whispered with a new figure in the courtroom, his superior—Mr. John McGohey, United States Attorney for the Southern District of New York. Mr. Murphy did not know whether the burden to discharge the jury should be put on him; if it were, he feared there might be some question of double jeopardy. Mr. Stryker, too, preferred to leave it to the judge. "Bring in the jury," said Judge Kaufman.

The moment their door opened, Hiss turned his head and his deep eyes scanned every one of the twelve faces—a castaway looking for a sail. When they were in their places, Hiss was still looking grayly at them. His head still traced the proud outline of a good bronze, his fine bone was set in a mold of emotion impossible to fathom. And his mouth was still firm. But his affability was a lost memory, a faded picture in a family scrapbook of a drowned favorite son.

Judge Kaufman was plainly reluctant to take them at their word. If they would not agree, he said, it might mean the case would have to be tried over again at further, "very, very great" expense to the Government and the defendant. He would ask them to make another effort in the interests of the Government and the defendant. Did they think it was possible? The foreman glanced uncertainly at his colleagues. He thought it was possible to make another effort.

It was five o'clock now. An hour and a half later the judge brought them back to see if they wanted to go to dinner. Several of them coughed and mumbled at this invitation, and the foreman hastily turned it down. Judge Kaufman looked for help to the counsel, but this time they were looking down their noses. He put the unavoidable question: "Is the jury deadlocked?"

"Yes, sir, it is," said the foreman.

Several jurymen moved their haunches and exchanged black glances, as if the foreman had muffed his cue. Apparently he had, for he saw what had happened and said that one juror wanted additional time. He added quickly that they would prefer not to go to dinner. All right, then, the jury would retire again.

We had no certainty then that this was to be the final agony. We relapsed at last into real fatigue and sprawled around the courtroom to wrestle tiredly with some of the plot dilemmas, the political implications, the bizarre unsolved friendship of the families, the tremendous consequences for the country of such an event as the Hisses' serving supper to the Chamberses one night long ago in 1935 in a house on P Street in Washington, D.C. Whatever happened now, one happy delusion of the New Deal's pure in heart would have to be abandoned for an unpredictable length of time. It was the belief that in the previous summer, at the Progressive Party's convention in Philadelphia, Henry Wallace had hammered into a doctrine: the belief that American Communists somehow had a natural prior allegiance to their own Government, that Communism could not possibly ripen in the soil of Iowa or Pennsylvania or New York, where you can plant such excellent hybrid corn. Alas, it was one more to add to Koestler's generous "fallacies of the Left": the grass-roots fallacy.

We took only timid or ribald glances into the deep pit of human character, whose mysteries a court of law must for its self-respect replace with two circumstantial puppets as grossly opposed as boxers. We preferred to stay with the uncomfortable new knowledge that in our society, at least, a Communist—whatever his idealism—is first and last a conspirator. For heartless light relief, we turned again to unravel the unwritten Erle Stanley Gardner epic—the Case of the Missing Typist.

FROM these puzzles and private thoughts, and from nothing more complicated than hunger, we were aroused just before nine in the evening. Another hot sun had gone down like a sweating orange. The beaches would be empty. The night ball games had their great lights on, spotting the flying legs as thousands cheered, far from this tragedy. It was the prospect of release into a normal life that brought on these summer thoughts again. They were banished by another note from the jury. The counsel came briskly in and the Hisses glided in like phantoms, Hiss gray again, Mrs. Hiss with her permanent doll-like blush. The jury came in, some of them drawn and disgruntled, others obviously angry. They found the word, and used it: "Impossible," the foreman said, to reach a verdict. The judge wondered aloud if there would be any point in sending them again to a hotel. The foreman said there would be none. "Well," sighed the little judge, "that leaves me no alternative but to discharge the jury . . . you are discharged with the thanks of the Court."

The jury was excused. And, as all tragedies must, this one put upon its officers, if not on the principals, the task of struggling back to the norm of life, to dinner, and good sense, and tidying up the stage.

Mr. Murphy made a motion to impound the typewriter. Mr. Stryker said it would not be necessary, he would be very glad to turn it over to the Court. The judge, anyway, had it impounded. Nobody was sure where it was. Mr. Stryker thought he had put it away somewhere.

THE JUDGE: You will see that one of your men turns it over to the clerk at this time.

THE CLERK: The jury had it, your Honor.

MR. STRYKER: Oh, the jury has it. I'm glad to have it kept here. Good night, sir.

THE JUDGE: Good night.

THE newspapermen bounded for the door and surged out, leaving for a moment two figures motionless in the well of the court. Alger Hiss sat quite rigid, with a keen dizzy look about his eyes, like a man steeling himself against the first undeniable symptom of an internal hemorrhage. A woman journalist sailed, with miserable enterprise, up to him. He dropped his head and shook it wide. "Please," he said. The woman turned away, and Hiss put out an arm for his wife and they walked quickly away to their privacy.

Now we were down in the press room, where, to the naïve astonishment of the softer European breed, three or four of the jury were sounding off as freely as a revival meeting. One thin man, his eyes on fire, was cursing the "idiots" who would not believe Whittaker Chambers. There was a tremendous clatter of typewriters and hectic phone-calls, and weary newsreel photographers packing up the equipment they would not need just yet for a triumphant interview with Hiss. But after a time it was possible to talk with four members of the jury and check, against the outpourings of a couple of holy rollers among them, what had happened in the juryroom. Since the judge had not given a last and specific instruction to go home and keep their thoughts to themselves, some of them were only too delighted to enlarge on their solemn performance of good citizenship. And since, again, there is apparently no rule against advertising the holy secrets of the juryroom, they can be put down in this chronicle.

When the jury first retired, one man—they said—had wanted to take an immediate vote and acquit Hiss right away. Three others, it appeared, resented very much this truculence and stood against it by letting their vote be marked as "undecided." By the time they went to a hotel for the night, the vote was eight for conviction and four for acquittal. It never wavered through all of Friday, the last day. After they had heard part of the charge read over, the eight were all the more convinced that the documents and the samples of Mrs. Hiss's typing amply corroborated the main charge. The rebellious four stood firm on the grounds of Chambers's doubtful credibility. So all day long the convinced eight went to work on the stubborn four. When they retired for the last time, the jury decided to do something that the Government had not offered to do. They took all the typewritten exhibits and tried to see, not whether they had been done on the same typewriter, but whether they could have been typed by the same person. This involved a presumption of expert knowledge that neither the Government nor the defendant had dared to assert. Although it was, of course, the test we had all hungered for, evidently neither side had found an expert who would be willing to testify that it could be done. Thus the jury accepted as the crux of the case an experiment that had not been hinted at in evidence or charged by the judge. It was very enterprising of them but suggests that juries do not, in matters that absorb them, bother very much about their "solemn obligation to decide the issues solely upon the evidence"; or mark the reverential distinction that judges and lawyers make between law and fact, which for better or worse is the best defense of the jury system.

However, it was done. They looked for personal characteristics of mis-typing and over-typing. Some of them believed they had found a few that showed up in both sets of papers. It was enough to clinch the conviction of the eight. The still resisting four were begged to go off into an inner room and make their own scrutiny of the papers by this test. They joined the majority forty minutes later and announced that what they had found was not enough to persuade them to accept the word of Chambers. They clung to Mr. Stryker's admonition, picked up from the enthusiastic lips of Mr. Murphy himself—"If you don't believe Chambers, the Government has no case." The division between them was now irreconcilable. And their tempers were fretted to the point where another dinner together would have invited bloodshed.

This, then, was the end not of Alger Hiss's nightmare, but merely of the first of his Trials.

PART FIVE

THE SECOND TRIAL

The United States District Court Southern District of New York

UNITED STATES OF AMERICA
v.
ALGER HISS, Defendant

Judge:—

Hon. Henry W. Goddard, District Judge
and a Jury

New York City, Thursday, November 17, 1949
at 10.30 o'clock a.m.

Appearances:—

For the Government—

Irving H. Saypol, Esq., United States Attorney
By Thomas F. Murphy, Esq., Assistant United States Attorney
Clarke S. Ryan, Esq., Assistant United States Attorney
Thomas J. Donegan, Esq., Special Assistant to the Attorney
General

For the Defendant—

Debevoise, Plimpton & McLean, Esqs., Attorneys for the Defendant
Claude B. Cross, Esq.
Edward C. McLean, Esq.
Harold Rosenwald, Esq.
Robert von Mehren, Esq. of Counsel

JUDGE, JURY, AND COUNSEL

❀

THE new judge was the second senior judge of this circuit, Henry W.
Goddard, a magnificent old American bald eagle with two white nests
of hair sprouting from long ears, curving quizzical eyes, an imperial
hook of nose, and a huge clapper of a mouth. He was a leisurely
veteran of the federal courts, obviously able to handle the whipper-
snapper impatience of any of the young legalists at the counsel tables;
and it was made evident the first morning that the judge's temperament alone, quite aside from any ampler view he took of the rules of
evidence, would discourage by indifference or urbanity the guerrilla
warfare of "objections" that Mr. Murphy and Mr. Stryker had conducted whenever one of them was on his feet and the other at his
table. At the beginning of the day Mr. Murphy drew up his impressive
six feet five to protest against a defense request to look at a ship's
passenger list belonging to the Department of Immigration (something unspecified to do with the transatlantic comings and goings of
Whittaker Chambers). Judge Goddard wondered indulgently what
was odd about the request. "Of course, if your Honor so directs . . ."
sighed Mr. Murphy. But Judge Goddard was in his seventy-fourth
year and not the sort of man who wastes his dignity on directing
anybody when he can mildly say: "I think it is the simplest thing to
do, Mr. Murphy." Most often afterwards, for the nine weeks ahead,
Judge Goddard sat back with his eyes almost closed. And when there
was a fuss or challenge between counsel, he would ignore it or open
his eyes and say in a clear, mild voice: "I think not, Mr. Cross," or "I
have no doubt you're right, Mr. Murphy, but I think I shall let it
stand." The effect of this mellow acceptance of the human animal at

281

play was to weaken the professional impulse towards rhetoric and cutting a figure for the jury's sake. When you lunge into a riposte it is almost as satisfying to have the referee rush in as to have him signal a hit. But when the referee goes on rocking in a deck chair, even the most brilliant fencing looks like exhibitionism. So the counsel soon learned to save their rhetoric for the summations. There was a sharp warning when Mr. Cross, the new defense counsel, was cross-examining Chambers. Mr. Cross, as it will appear, was a diffident sober man, a million light-years away from Mr. Stryker's fireworks. But in a Puckish moment he asked Chambers how he had disposed of the child's rolling-pin Hiss supposedly had given him: "You didn't hide it in any pumpkins, did you?" Chambers coughed comfortably and said nothing. There was an awkward pause. Judge Goddard asked if Mr. Cross had meant it as a serious question. Mr. Cross gasped out a flustered syllable or two. And Judge Goddard said he didn't think lawyers should ask foolish questions just because a witness's answer might be inappropriate: "This case will take long enough as it is." Mr. Cross apologized and Mr. Murphy filtered a chuckle through his mustache. This rebuke promised a quicker, uninterrupted trial.

But the same quality in the new judge's temperament also canceled out this promise. For it was soon evident that he would rather err on the side of letting things in than keeping them out. And he had none of Judge Kaufman's fear that by allowing testimony on a collateral matter (Chambers's implied accusation of Hiss as a loyal, disciplined Communist) he might be judged guilty of a reversible error by the courts of appeal. He allowed the debarred testimony (about the old Ford car) of the Cherner Motor Company and William Rosen and yielded to the Government's pressing wish to call the ex-wife of Gerhart Eisler. As these witnesses appeared, to bolster the Government's case, the question of the judge's impartiality came up around the courtroom. It was easily answered. For everybody was waiting to see whether the defense would try again to impeach the credibility of Chambers with the expert testimony of a psychiatrist. Once Judge Goddard decided to let it in, there was no doubt to the layman that the judge's impartiality embraced the widest definition of "evidence." It may have been simply that the judge, like everybody else, wanted to try and get to the bottom of a story that had hung one jury and might hang another. Whichever it was, the judge's liberality towards the counsel's view of their rights helped to make the Second Trial go on three weeks longer than the first.

The new judge had a more decided view about the limited rights of the counsel outside the courtroom. At the end of the first day he called them to the bench. He wanted them, he said, to look up the code of ethics of the Bar Association of New York "with regard to lawyers talking to newspapermen during the conduct of a trial. Read it and respect it . . . we don't want this case to be tried by the newspapers." [1]

THE jury was chosen faster the second time. The first tentative dozen to take their places in the jury box appeared for a while to be almost as spotless as the final choice in the First Trial. But when the number-one juror admitted to knowing a former defense lawyer, he was excused. Seven other number ones were called and excused after a pause for reflection. Altogether thirty-one were excused. As the morning wore along, more and more of the substitutions who stayed on unbiased and unchallenged were seen to be females; till in the end the jury was complete—eight women in a wild menagerie of autumn hats, and four men already declining into a slightly henpecked look. It was very noticeable that far more men than women doubted their own lack of bias, an issue in the ancient war between men and women that has not previously been noticed as a turning-point in our judicial system. There was another interesting difference from the summer in

---

[1] In the First Trial, the newspapers had printed attacks on the fitness and presumed political sympathies of the judge, series of feature articles on the character of the principles, free speculation among editorial writers, and a wealth of invective from the columnists; all this, while the Trial was on, made up a fairly obscene travesty of our boasted freedom of the press. It was a little better in the Second Trial, partly because Judge Goddard's warning made the lawyers less disposed to hint at alarming testimony to come; but in the main because city editors severely cut the space they assigned to a topic they guessed, often incorrectly, was no longer of public interest. All in all, though, the indignities some newspapers forced on the judicial system seemed to strengthen the argument for the adoption sometime soon of the English rule, whereby all comment, dramatization, and editorial opinion of any kind, may not be printed while a case is under judgment; and whereby, because of the risk of defamation, the reporting of trials falls to newspapermen at least half as competent as the court stenographers in taking down verbatim testimony. This hard rule is nothing that adults might not get to accept with a good grace, and is not, I believe, inconsistent with any decent definition of a free press.

the prevailing vogue of prejudice. Droves of prospective jurors had been excused in the First Trial when they allowed they very likely harbored prejudice against any witness who had been a Communist. By the autumn of 1949 the reformed Communist was in some places the most trustworthy of American patriots. In a courtroom evidently he had lost his threat for the common man. Only one of the whole sixty talesmen asked to be excused on this stated ground. Most of the others—many grave and palpably modest men who might at a guess have seemed like fine jury material—declined to be thought incorruptible and accordingly left it to the brash, the insecure, or the truly serene; from whom were recruited the twelve who eventually withstood all aspersions on their imperviousness to the political climate of our time.

After nearly two hours the apostles were chosen:

> Seven housewives,
> A company treasurer,
> A lawyer's mortgage expert,
> An optician,
> An electrical company's manager,
> A retired manufacturer of plastics.

The demands of "color reporting" incited some newspapermen to notice, while the jury was being picked, that Alger Hiss looked older and grayer. But so did we all. It was more a characteristic of winter than of Hiss. Mr. Murphy, who was again the Government prosecutor, looked grayer than most, but only because his complexion had faded over the months into that look of near-jaundice which is the autumnal penalty of all men who sport in summer such roaring suntans as he did. The counsel looked grayer, the newspapermen looked grayer, the seersucker suits had gone with the hot days. Mr. Lloyd Paul Stryker had faded away altogether, and any room is the grayer for his absence. The courtroom was just across the hall from the one we had sat in last time. Its layout was identical, but everything was in reverse. And here again, as counsel took their places and the jury was sworn, it looked like the same old trial seen in a glass grayly.

Freed from the gadfly competition of Mr. Stryker, Mr. Murphy was at once more confident and off on a cannier tack. The willingness of four members of the jury in the First Trial to accept his sporting offer on a question of credibility had taught him bitterly not to repeat his bargain: "If you don't believe Whittaker Chambers, the Government has no case . . ." (though it had been such a godsend to the defense that Mr. Cross said it for him). This time Mr. Murphy took two very different lines: one was to admit in full the early sins of Chambers's now shriven soul; and the other was to keep the jury focusing on what he maintained was the real, unblinkable issue: the "immutable" evidence of the typewriter and the documents. The defense, he said, would try to make "great capital" out of Chambers's innumerable lies. But the jury must try to throw themselves back to the prewar years; if they didn't they wouldn't "quite grasp" the behavior of such intellectuals as Chambers, who saw in Fascism a perilous threat, who believed that only the Russians could stop it, and who therefore became "involved with . . . these foreign philosophies." Chambers was apt for it, because he had had a miserable childhood and no religious training. Yet he was not without courage. He had in all sincerity become a Communist agent and adopted a dangerous profession. But once he saw that the Communist philosophy was false, he quit. And being the man he was, he then "had to get back into the stream of life . . . he had to again be a man." This he did by laborious hard work, which in the end broke his health. He had bought a farm, and that's what he now was—a farmer. He would have been willing to let bygones be bygones if "on one day's notice" he had not been subpoenaed by the House Committee and asked to say what he knew. He said it, told all about his own disreputable past, but deliberately held back the documents that were to damn Hiss. He held back until Hiss denied all Communist connections and forced a libel suit on him. Then, reluctantly, he came forward with the documents. And why did he hold back so long? Mr. Murphy would tell them: "He just couldn't bring himself to go that far with his former friend."

Mr. Claude Cross, the new defense counsel, was a small, plodding, gray-haired man, so undemonstrative as almost to appear apologetic for taking the floor and the jury's undivided time. He followed at an earthbound interval Mr. Stryker's appeal to "look here upon this picture and on this": Hiss, a "normal," gentle, scholarly boy rising from one position of trust to another; and Chambers, rootless and unreliable, insensitive enough (this was a new item) to apply for a passport by offering the birth certificate of a dead child, tricky enough to acquire—from the evidence of the House Committee and the questions put in Baltimore—an intimate acquaintance with the furnishings of houses that the Hisses had lived in. Mr. Cross had one new line, but if he could follow it up, it would certainly shake a whole deck of aces down on Chambers. The defense would prove, he said, that while some of the documents never went to Hiss's office, every one of the typewritten documents went either to the Far Eastern Division, or the Trade Agreements Section, or an adjoining office, of the State Department. That, he implied, was the place to look for the thief, for Chambers's "pipeline" out of the Department. He would show that it was this missing thief, aided and abetted by Julian Wadleigh, who had passed to Chambers the papers falsely wished on Alger Hiss.

THE CONSPIRACY

❊

THE Second Trial got under way inevitably with the reappearance
of Chambers. Up against the city slickers with their faded tans, the
farmer now looked ruddier than he had in the summer. With no
Stryker to plague him, he was spruce and confident. He crossed his
short legs and with great good humor was painlessly encouraged by
Mr. Murphy to assist the Government's first tactic: which was to
confirm the alleged conspiracy with new evidence, and to make it
vivid by having Chambers recall enough additional anecdotes to
suggest that if he cared to he could reconstruct the whole human
chronicle of his life with Alger Hiss. He insisted now that Hiss was
such a trained and obedient party member as far back as 1935 that
he had asked permission of the higher-ups to take his job with the
Department of Justice. Chambers went meticulously over the layouts
of the Hisses' houses and said he particularly recalled the third floor
of the P Street house because he had himself done "some photographic
work" there. Mr. Murphy got him to tell about a small farm he had
bought in 1937 in Maryland (not far from his present farm) and declare calmly that it was the same farm he and Hiss had driven up to
look over a couple of years earlier. In fact, said Chambers, Hiss had
put a down payment on it and then withdrawn from "the deal."
There were, remarkably, letters from Hiss to an agent introduced in
evidence. And though Hiss denied ever going to see the place with
Chambers, or knowing until lately that Chambers had bought it, he
plainly had to admit the coincidence; which Mr. Murphy seized on
in his summation to wonder: "Just how psychic do you have to get?"
Chambers occasionally threw his eyes up to the ceiling to capture

287

some elusive memory he had overlooked in the First Trial. Whatever it was, it was never anything to alarm him. The defense, for instance, had managed to learn about a forged passport of Chambers's made out in the name of David Breen, a dead child. Mr. Murphy was well aware of this new tidbit and casually asked Chambers, before the defense could get in, if it had belonged to him and how he got it. Chambers smiled. Yes, it was his, and the way of getting such things was ridiculously easy for a Communist insider. They simply consulted the public records of births and deaths and chose a name. J. Peters had got it for him in 1935, when he was meant to go to England and link up with the Communist underground there under cover of being a visiting church worker. His wife and child, he added, were meant to stay with the Hisses, and incidentally the Hisses could have known him by that name. But he didn't go to Europe and never used the passport. It showed him with a mustache, for the simple reason that he had a mustache at that time and the Hisses knew him with it. (He had never said so before.) When Mr. Cross came in determined to goad him about this deception and asked: "Did you know David Breen?" Chambers asked back, with a nonchalant gaze: "Did I *know* David Breen? I *am* David Breen." He admitted the routine perjury of a false application, false oath, and the rest of it; and Mr. Cross could not embarrass him at all with the suspicion that he had used a false mustache.

"Did you have a *grown* mustache," Mr. Cross pressed him, "in contradistinction to a *false* mustache?"

Back came the solemn answer: "I never wore a false mustache except at Hallowe'en."

How about the car he had had in New York under the name of Breen before he switched the registration and resold it to himself? How much did he pay himself? Mr. Cross taunted. "I can't recall just now," said Chambers grandly. He was equally ribald about the nice question of how he got into the Hisses' Volta Place home at nights? Chambers's recollection had been that at all the Hiss homes he either let himself in with a key he had from Hiss or rang the bell. Now he thought it might have been a knocker at Volta Place, a concession Mr. Cross insinuated came from his knowledge of the proved new fact that there never was a doorbell at that house. Chambers said: "I do not recall whether I knocked on a door ten years ago."

Chambers had plainly overcome his reluctance to do Alger Hiss an "ultimate damage." He enlarged on an interview he had had (with the State Department's security officer) to explain that the New Deal offered a "favorable climate" for Communist infiltration and that the party had decided that Hiss's job, once he was acclimated to his role as a detached agent working inside the Government, was "to mess up policy." Mr. Murphy coaxed him to recall some other meetings and memories with Hiss. And from this random harvest, he mentioned sitting in a restaurant once with Hiss and being greeted by a woman named Plum Fountain. The defense brought Mrs. Olivia Fountain Tesone into court to say that she had lived in Georgetown and known the Hisses, that her nickname was "Plum," but that she had never known or seen Chambers. She swore that Hiss's reputation was "beyond reproach." But this didn't throw Mr. Murphy off the heavy sarcastic stride of his summation. "Plum Fountain!" he goggled. "Who could think of a name like that?"

Chambers brightly recalled several new automobile trips with Hiss, one to a place called Erwinna, Pennsylvania, in what must have been 1935. He didn't know why they had gone there, but he distinctly remembered it, and it must have been around Easter time, "because at a red light in Norristown we passed a policeman carrying an Easter lily. And that," said Chambers, "pleased Mr. Hiss." Hiss, sitting far back in the well, gave a rueful, head-shaking grin.

Chambers now said that from the envelope in the dumb-waiter shaft in Brooklyn he had also rescued a sheaf of yellow papers in the handwriting of Harry Dexter White. At the defense's insistence, the notes that Mr. Adolf Berle had made on Chambers's interview with him in September 1939 were put in evidence by the Government. They added many more names, including Wadleigh's, to those of the original "apparatus" Chambers had given to the House Committee, though Perlo was missing; they named both Hiss brothers as party members and carried under the name Alger Hiss the notation: "Ass't to Sayre—CP-1937—Member of the Underground Com.-Active Baltimore boys; Wife—Priscilla Hiss—Socialist—Early days of New Deal." The paper bore the heading: "Underground Espionage Agent," which probably referred to the first entry, but in Mr. Murphy's reading it was made to suggest that Chambers had testified to espionage at least nine years before he decided to retrieve the documents to pin on Alger Hiss. Hiss mentioned that he had been a guest at the Berle home two months after Chambers's visit and Mr. Berle had not mentioned any such accusation.

On the mystery that had dogged Hiss ever since the House Committee subpoenaed documents from the Motor Vehicle Bureau—the question of the *old Ford car*—Chambers was this time allowed to put in his explanation that Hiss had wanted to pass the car on to a poor Communist organizer; that J. Peters had been very much against it but finally agreed to it; that the car was accordingly transferred, the day it went to the motor company, to William Rosen. The vice-president of the Cherner Motor Company took the stand and said that although his file of invoices for that year showed no missing numbers, there was no record of the transaction. But he identified the bill of sale and his own signature, which proved that Hiss had turned the car over to his firm; on the same day the agency reassigned the title to Rosen. The Government had found Rosen in California since the First Trial and put him on the stand. He said he never knew J. Peters or Alger Hiss. But more than that he would not say. To every question Mr. Murphy put to him trying to link him with the car or the Communists, he chanted in a rapid and wheezy whisper: "I respectfully decline to answer this question on the grounds that any answer I may give may tend to incriminate me." He was not of much exploitable use to either side, and when he stepped down Judge Goddard warned the jury not to draw any unfavorable inferences from his legitimate refusal to testify. Mike Catlett was not much help to the defense either. He was suddenly positive the Hisses had the car when they left P Street (July 1, 1936), by which time Hiss himself agreed he had turned it over to Chambers. Mr. Murphy wanted to have the pleasure of getting Hiss to admit a discrepancy and asked him if he would not now concede that his testimony before the House Committee was "false" and "different." Hiss would not say false—nor could he see that it was "different." Well, didn't he say to the House Committee he had had two automobiles at the time he thought of giving Chambers the use of the Ford? No, he didn't: "I thought I said it was at *about* that time." He had "actually acquired physical control" of the new car in August. Mr. Murphy wryly wondered if he had "some other kind of control of it prior to August." The answer was a flat No, sir.

Mr. Stryker's vein of righteous indignation did not come easily to

Mr. Cross, who seemed rather uncomfortable when he was merely trying to look shocked at Chambers's barefaced lies in the past. Mr. Cross's taste and skill ran towards a painstaking brief and he scored impressively with a piece of detective work he had done on Chambers's physical routine of picking up and photographing the documents. At the time when the conspiracy was supposedly most productive, Chambers was living in Baltimore and working on a Government job in Washington. By laboriously totting up Chambers's own memories of the time he spent in getting from one place to another, Mr. Cross put it up to Chambers that his daily routine would entail: getting from his office to the Hiss house by about five in the evening, waiting for Hiss, picking up the papers, going to the station, taking the train for forty minutes to Baltimore, going to the photographer, waiting for the laboratory work to be done, getting back to Washington on a later train, returning the documents to Hiss some time between midnight and two in the morning, getting back to the station, up again to Baltimore and into bed, then up and on the train again to be at work in Washington by nine in the morning.

Challenged to defend this athleticism, Chambers simply admitted it was probably true and calmly left the courtroom with a hint of the rat races a "dedicated" Communist can get himself into.

THE Government's most prized new item, on the theme of conspiracy, was the testimony of Mrs. Hede Massing, Gerhardt Eisler's ex-wife. She was the only person they had found who swore she could corroborate Chambers's accusation that Hiss was a member in good standing in a Washington Communist underground. At the very end of the Government's case she was allowed to appear. She first made it abundantly clear that she had been an active worker for the Communists, most recently as a member of an apparatus and working between New York and Washington. She said she met Alger Hiss, in Washington, in the late summer or early fall of 1935, in the home of one Noel Field. She reported now (after much legal pressure to make her stick to the memory of an actual conversation) that at this meeting she had said to Hiss: " 'I understand that you are trying to get Noel Field away from my organization into yours.' And he said, 'So you are this famous girl that is trying to get Noel Field away from me.' And I said: 'Yes.' And he said, as far as I remember: 'Well, we will see who is going to win.' At which point I said: '. . . Well, you realize that you are competing with a woman.' At which either he or I said—the gist of the sentence was—'Whoever is going to win, we are working for the same boss.' "

Now, asked Mr. Murphy, did there come a time when she saw Mr. Hiss in this building? There did. In December 1948, the F.B.I. had brought them together in a room in the courthouse. Hiss appeared with his lawyers. She tried then to make him recall the Washington meeting. She told him her own story to help him identify her. He was friendly, but he said he did not remember her.

Mr. Murphy wondered if she had changed much in her physical appearance. Mrs. Massing looked to be in her early fifties but she held her head high and managed an air of challenging chic. Yes, she thought she had changed considerably. "The color of your hair?" Mr. Murphy hinted with heroic tact. No, she had put on weight. Any operations on her face at all? No, said the former Viennese actress.

Mr. Cross tried to ruin her credibility by suggesting that in a hearing supporting her husband's application for citizenship she had sworn a false oath and said many things inconsistent with the story of her personal life she had just told. It was evident that there were discrepancies. The dates of marriages and divorce were different. She admitted the possibility that one relationship (she had been married three times) might have ignored the legal knot for a time, since in Germany at that time marriage was "a technicality which liberals did not observe." Mrs. Massing was visibly flustered by Mr. Cross but very decided about her relations with Hiss. Hiss, when his turn came, denied the whole story, said he had never been at Field's home without Mrs. Hiss, and denied ever knowing or seeing Mrs. Massing, except in the F.B.I. office, when, he said, she had never used the word "communism" but talked always about "world socialism" and "anti-Fascism."

Mr. Murphy asked Hiss if he had ever recommended possible markets to aspiring authors. For a moment this sounded like an academic digression, until Hiss grinned shrewdly, having correctly guessed that the Government had turned up a letter he had written in May 1948 to this same Noel Field who was then in eastern Europe and wanting to place articles in the United States. All the incrimination Mr. Murphy could squeeze out of it was that Hiss had started the letter "Dear Noel" and had suggested possible outlets in the *Nation*, the *New Republic*, and *Harper's Magazine*. Considered as an explosive piece of evidence it was a damp squib. But Mr. Murphy was content to let the name of Field register again, for the whereabouts of Field and his wife had become by now something of an international mystery. They had disappeared in Bratislava in May 1949 and had not been heard of since.

MR. CROSS in his summation dismissed the alleged conspiracy as just another emanation from Chambers's "bad" and "dishonest" motives. Why, Mr. Cross, wanted to know, would Chambers accuse Francis Sayre to Malcolm Cowley in 1940 and never mention Hiss? "You can't rationalize Chambers's actions," Mr. Cross warned. And why didn't he accuse Hiss of espionage before the grand jury, when he appeared in October, right after the defamation suit was filed? Because, Mr. Cross was sure, Chambers thought the suit was "a bluff and Mr. Hiss was not going to follow through. When he found that Mr. Hiss intended a vigorous prosecution of the suit, he went out and dug up a file he had prepared for Hiss, for Sayre, and very likely for somebody in the Far Eastern Division" of the State Department.

This was to be Mr. Cross's theme to the end: that Chambers had kept through the years a protective file of private lives, and incriminating documents, so that he could throw suspicion on other people if the day ever came when it was turned on him. Another careful bit of Mr. Cross's research had turned up a letter to a publisher written in July 1938 in which Chambers mentioned "a project" he had just finished in Washington. Mr. Cross had no doubts about that project: "he was in Florida in May . . . that [June] project was . . . making a file against Alger Hiss." Wadleigh had been amazed that Chambers knew so much about Darlington (the former assistant chief of the Trade Agreements Section who had been a character witness in the First Trial). And Chambers had said: "I make it my business to know all I can about people."

There was another doubt about the conspiracy that Mr. Murphy faced serenely enough but that the defense oddly failed to play up in its summation. This was the blanket misgiving frankly planted by Mrs. Chambers herself that her husband was her lord and master and she would follow his word and plans without question and without guilt. It was pointless for Mr. Cross to advertise his horror at Mrs. Chambers's never having known about the passport application made out in the name of a dead child. "It would not have mattered either way," she remarked. She was in "entire sympathy with my husband's work" at all times. She confessed no shame at all the aliases. Was she ever falsely known as Edna Rogers Breen? If that was the time her husband was David Breen, she retorted, then that was the name she bore.

Mr. Murphy reduced this line of quizzing to absurdity when he put to her the pawky proposition: "If he (your husband) said to you: 'Tomorrow we are going to Ypsilanti and your name is Hogan' . . . ?" Then, Mrs. Chambers replied with the ready smile of a child playing a spelling-out game, "We should go to Ypsilanti and our name would be Hogan."

THE FRIENDSHIP

❀

WHEN Mrs. Chambers came to tell again her story of the friendship, she too profited greatly from the absence of Mr. Stryker and the presence of an old indulgent judge. Moreover, like most other witnesses in the Second Trial, she had learned by now that the difference between "present" and "then" recollection is not only human but legal. As Mr. Cross ticked off the dates of visits and meetings she had previously sworn to, she saw the way his suspicions were headed and said: "Mr. Cross, these were not the only times I saw Priscilla and Alger Hiss. These are the times that stand out in my memory. The Hisses were family to us; they were friends." And when Mr. Cross brandished the transcript of her Baltimore pre-trial testimony, as he did countless times to try to show her inconsistency, she was no longer distressed by the tricks of her memory. "This," she said, "is the product of fourteen years of trying not to remember any of this." She was altogether more animated and astute than we had seen her, and one became aware for the first time of something that her defensive fright had hidden: she was a very handsome woman. Her get-up again did not seem quite real, as if it were a costume department's guess at a female Communist turned farmer's wife. But if the jury cared in their mind's eye to take off the floppy blue-black hat and sweep the black hair high from her olive face, the revelation of fine feature and warmth in the eyes would have presented them with quite another character to fathom. She held tight to her old memory that the Hisses never knew the Chamberses' last name, calling them simply "Carl" and "Lisa"—the oddest aberration in a very odd friendship. She appeared untroubled by the fact Mr. Cross brought out that she had never seemed to know any of her neighbors. She had, for instance, lived nine months in a house in Baltimore and couldn't remember the name of the woman on the second floor to whom she paid the rent. If, as she thought, there was a name-plate under her bell on the front porch, surely there must have been a name on it? She had a night to think this over and when she came back, and Mr. Cross showed her a recent photograph of the place with three bells and name-plates, she undauntedly decided that when she was there, there was only an outside, old-fashioned bell that you pulled "that set up a terrific clang through the house."

She went through the Hisses' furnishings again, and to corroborate her the Government brought in a Mrs. Gladys Tally, whose family had rented the Volta Place house to the Hisses. This woman repeated a couple of details of the Chambers story. She thought her mother had left "drapes in the living room" dyed a plum color. About the wallpaper she knew that "the background was a pale gray or off white and it had a sort of mulberry design in it."

Mrs. Hiss denied it all in her meek, equable voice. She denied she and her husband had ever visited any Chambers house, or done any baby-sitting for them, or been on parties together, or gone on any trips anywhere. The only visit between the families was that of the Chamberses to P Street. Mr. Cross brought in William Marbury, Hiss's lawyer in the Baltimore libel suit, and asked him if Mrs. Chambers had ever in her Baltimore testimony made any mention of visiting Thirtieth Street. Mr. Marbury said she had not, but Mr. Murphy roared in with a three-hundred-page volume of Baltimore transcript defying Mr. Marbury to show that he had ever asked her the question. He had not, Mr. Marbury agreed after looking through the testimony overnight. But in reading some of it to the jury, the defense managed to get in that in Baltimore she had not been able to remember a single time that the Hisses came to the Chambers home at Mt. Royal Terrace in Baltimore. Mr. Murphy directly challenged Mrs. Hiss on her letter to the University of Maryland inquiring about the "inorganic chemistry" class that was a preparation for the Mercy Hospital training course she never took. Mrs. Hiss's course at the university, it will be recalled, was in the summer of 1937, and her letter about it was written that spring, when—according to Mrs. Chambers—they had talked about it at lunch together at Hutzler's. Mr. Murphy airily asked Mrs. Hiss: "You hadn't told Mrs. Chambers about your plan, had you?" To which Mrs. Hiss (who maintained she hadn't seen the Chamberses since 1935) of course replied: "I certainly hadn't."

The man who rented the cottage to the Chamberses on the Delaware River and his sister said they had never seen the Hisses there or anywhere else. And Mr. Cross came forward with new and important evidence to refute Chambers's story about *the Peterboro trip* to see *She Stoops to Conquer*, and Mrs. Chambers's revised and positive testimony that they had been with the Hisses at a *New Year's Eve party* at Thirtieth Street on the 31st of December 1936.

Mr. Cross read a solicitous letter written by Hiss from Washington, and postmarked December 30, addressed to his wife in Chappaqua, N.Y. Hiss said they had spent Christmas in New York with his brother-in-law and then gone to stay with relatives in Chappaqua. He came back to Washington and Mrs. Hiss was meant to follow with Timmie. But Timmie got chicken pox; and Hiss's letter was a tender assurance that she should stay till Timmie was well, that he would manage all right, and that he would go alone to some "shindig" on the night of January 2nd. Since in the normal course of the U.S. Post Office's couriers Mrs. Hiss could not possibly have had this letter before New Year's Eve, the Chambers tale of the party seemed finally refuted. But Mr. Murphy confounded the old confusion by bringing in a Washington pediatrician, a Dr. Margaret Nicholson, who produced her records to show that Mrs. Hiss and Timmie had visited her Washington office on the 2nd of January. Timmie may well have recovered in time to rob this date of any aspersion on the Hisses' testimony. And Hiss, while mentioning one party in his letter, had said nothing about a planned New Year's Eve party. But the question was left unanswered whether Timmie's recovery had been rapid enough to bring him and his mother back to Washington before midnight of the old year.

Hiss's *summer vacation in Chestertown*, Maryland, in the first two weeks of August, 1937, was important to both sides because it involved the only occasion on which Chambers had specified the date of a trip or meeting. The defense was agog with new evidence. Mr. Cross put in evidence an advertisement from the *New York Times* of the stock company's performance at Peterboro—to suggest the source from which Chambers might have been able to extract a solid date. Thomas Fansler, Mrs. Hiss's brother, said he was with Hiss over the disputed week-end and on the morning of the 9th of August (when Chambers said he met Hiss in Washington). The Hisses drove him north to Wilmington to put him on a New York train. The local bank records showed that Hiss had deposited one hundred dollars in a Chestertown bank on the 10th of August, the date when he was supposed to be in New Hampshire; though it couldn't be proved whether he had made the deposit in person or through the mails. The wife of the camp director, Mrs. Kellogg Smith, swore Hiss was in Chestertown on the 9th, 10th, and 11th of August. And even Chambers himself admitted, under some more of Mr. Cross's damaging arithmetic, that by his own word he would have had to get up in Baltimore, take the train to Washington, hop into the Hisses' car, and then drive back north again on the way to New Hampshire—an implied waste of intelligence in an intelligent man or an excess of accommodating zeal. The Peterboro trip was just about blown into thin air when Mr. Murphy asked the same Dr. Nicholson to consult her records and see if Mrs. Hiss had ever visited her Washington office in the summer of 1937. Dr. Nicholson consulted and found that Mrs. Hiss had come to Washington with Timmie on the 15th of August. In both Trials the main defense against the Chamberses' Peterboro story was that Hiss had never left Chestertown during his vacation, and Mrs. Hiss had been nowhere but Baltimore. His vacation had ended on the 15th. Again, another Chambers story had been practically discredited, only to have one plausible doubt keep it alive.

There was the teasing business of *the $400 "loan."* A bankbook and a bill of sale together proved what was not denied: that on the 19th of November 1937 Mrs. Hiss withdrew $400 in cash, and that four days later Chambers bought a car. *Post hoc, propter hoc* was the Government's deduction. Chambers placidly said he bought the car with the $400 "loan" from Hiss; and just as placidly said to Mr. Cross that he had never paid it back and never made any effort to. The Hisses entered a calm and unchanging denial: the $400 had gone to buy furnishings for their new house. Now Mrs. Claudie Catlett was called back to say there were indeed many new furnishings at Volta Place. The defense could not show any cash receipts for these things. But it did show in new detail that the state of the Hisses' finances was such as to make a $400 loan to anybody just then a wild extravagance. Hiss proved from records that in September of that year he had bought a new automobile on the installment plan. The purchase price was $785 and he traded in his old car for $410. The balance he paid off in monthly installments of $36.12 (plus interest charges) and could not legally call the car his own until September 1938. The implication the defense left with the jury was a powerful one: would Hiss, or anybody else, lend $400 to a man to buy a car and leave only $14.69 in his own account, so that he had to borrow $300 from the bank from which to pay off, among other things, the monthly installments on his own car? As a detective problem considered quite aside from this case, it would pose to any normally shrewd reader the simple question: why was he being blackmailed? Mr. Murphy did not attempt to dispute the Hisses' financial straits (though he pointed out that on December 1 Hiss's salary check boosted his balance to $248.02). In rebuttal, he merely doubted the Hiss story of having furnishings delivered to Volta Place between the time of the cash withdrawal and the 5th of December. For he quoted records to show the Volta Place house was not advertised until the 5th. And there was the testimony of Mrs. Tally that the house was quite empty then. It was a rather small suspicion to work on, and Hiss confidently kept to his story that he had a "commitment" with a real-estate broker before that and that if the Tally family, the landlords, said different, they were confused. Anyway, there was the fact that the lease he signed was dated December 2.

There was one more witness whose tale could, like so many others, be interpreted according to the spectator's prejudice. She was a lively colored woman, Mrs. Edith Murray. In the Government's view, she meant as much to the friendship as Mrs. Massing had meant to the conspiracy; and they brought her in to offer the most plausible human corroboration of the Hiss-Chambers friendship that the Government could put its hands on. She had worked in two Baltimore homes of the Chamberses. Without turning a hair she remembered having seen Mrs. Hiss at least four times and Alger Hiss once. She gladly identified them sitting in court. Once Mrs. Hiss had come up from Washington to stay overnight while Mrs. Chambers went to a doctor in New York. How, Mr. Cross marveled, could she so readily identify Hiss when she had seen him only once, and then when she left almost at once without serving dinner? Hiss had come to the door and she remembered his smile: "of course I could see the difference of the two couples . . . and when I see him, I seen the difference in the two of them, and naturally I noticed." She chuckled, but didn't enlarge further on this happy memory except to remark that the Chamberses "never had no company at all, only those two." She recounted how the F.B.I. had lately located her, shown her a miniature of her portrait done by Mrs. Chambers, and taken her next day to the Chambers farm in Westminster, Maryland. There she was delighted to see the people she had known as the Cantwells ("they were very nice people to work for") and she had recognized some of the furniture from Baltimore. Mr. Cross could hardly keep down his withering contempt for the Government's prize witness. It came out that on the first day of the Second Trial the F.B.I. had had her mingle with the crowd in the corridor outside the courtroom and tell them when she recognized Hiss. She had been shown a photograph of Hiss; and when he and Mrs. Hiss came out of the elevator—"right away I knew them." But Mr. Cross also got from her the disarming admission that when the F.B.I. had first shown her a photograph of Mrs. Hiss she had thought "it looks like someone that I know. It looked like—I thought maybe it was an actress or something." Chambers, said Mr. Cross feelingly in his summation, "put ideas into her head that were never there."

THE CHARACTERS OF HISS
AND CHAMBERS

❧

THERE was little to add in the Second Trial to the overwhelming impression of the First that wherever Hiss had been, and whatever he had done, he had left an enviable reputation for "integrity, loyalty, veracity." Most of the character witnesses came again and several new ones though the defense decided not to call the two Supreme Court justices. Since the new judge had allowed evidence that bandied around the names of the rest of Chambers's accused apparatus, Mr. Cross was quick to have Hiss elaborate on his friendships with some of these men and show that they were innocent. A Joseph C. Green, executive director of the board of examiners for the State Department's foreign service, gave his word in a deposition that Hiss never took documents from the State Department during his time with the Nye investigation. Judge Wyzanski actually told how Hiss had opposed recommending Lee Pressman to a job in the Department of Labor which Judge Wyzanski was vacating. Hiss's Baltimore lawyer, William Marbury, gave a full account of Hiss's unfaltering decision to turn over at once to the Department of Justice the typewritten documents Chambers had produced in Baltimore; how Hiss had the day afterwards telephoned the Attorney General and failed to reach him, but the next morning had asked an Assistant Attorney General to take the incriminating papers. Mr. Francis B. Sayre was very forthright in implying his trust in Hiss and itched to put in his own view of Hiss's reputation as being "of the best"; but he was held to the strict form of the challenge and could only confess that he found "people falling into two groups . . . some who believe absolutely in his integrity—there are others who do not."

Mr. Murphy's tack was to sail head on into Hiss's reputation through the character witnesses; he went at them with a boisterous indifference to their own good name that perceptibly shook some and infuriated others. Dr. Stanley Hornbeck, for instance, said he could "see no good reason for bringing in" the name of a man who had gossiped, possibly as far away as 1939, that Hiss was a fellow traveler. But Mr. Murphy was immune to such scruples and made him say it. It was William C. Bullitt, former Ambassador to Paris and Moscow, who also—Dr. Hornbeck admitted in suppressed anger—had called Hiss a Communist eight years later. Even Mr. Marbury, Hiss's lawyer, was forced by the new Murphy truculence into repeating a rumor picked up from Robert Patterson, when Secretary of War,—a rumor they had both dismissed as "ridiculous." Mr. Cross put in evidence a document excluded from the First Trial which demonstrated that one month after the Nazi-Soviet Pact, Hiss was urging American aid to the Allies over the objection of Dr. Philip Jessup. (In summation, Mr. Murphy ridiculed this stand. Once Chambers had broken with the party, Mr. Murphy explained, "Hiss became the hottest thing in Washington . . . [he] *had* then to take the opposite position.") Mr. Murphy put up to Hiss his attitude to the lie-detector test the House Committee had proposed; and while Hiss agreed he had not insisted on it, it was the House Committee, he said, that had dropped the idea. Without any discoverable nuance, Mr. Murphy got clearly into the record two facts against the mention of which Mr. Stryker had reeled in protest: the suicides of Hiss's father and sister. Hiss calmly thought they were both due to financial trouble; and Mr. Murphy took him at his word. From John Foster Dulles came another guarded denial of Hiss's story of his resignation from the Carnegie Endowment and a politic rephrasing of what in the First Trial had amounted to a character reference. This time Mr. Dulles said precisely that Hiss's reputation was "very high . . . up to that date [his election to the endowment] you mention." Dr. Philip Jessup appeared in person this time. Without expression, and without yielding any helpful reservations, he stood by his view of Hiss's reputation. Mr. Murphy tried to hint at Dr. Jessup's dark affinity for various liberal causes, but Mr. Cross promptly deflated this attack by having Dr. Jessup list some old colleagues on one suspect organization—the Institute of Pacific

Relations: they were such unlikely subversives as Newton Baker, Henry Luce, and the president of General Electric.

AS the accuser, and the cause of all Hiss's present misery, Chambers was necessarily exposed in both Trials to a massive attack on his character and by inference his credibility in this incredible story. Mr. Murphy took up the canny attitude, the Second time, of conceding at the start the trickeries of Chambers's party life and indulgently allowing the perjuries that the defense last time had hailed as strikes of purest gold. Mr. Murphy was even conscientious enough to put in evidence Chambers's "blasphemous" play, which had got him into trouble at Columbia; and so there should be no doubt about its impieties, Mr. Murphy read it aloud. Outside the courtroom it might have been identified as an ironic passage from Anatole France's *Procurator of Judea* but the defense had shouted it was an atheistic horror. This time, Mr. Murphy implied, he was only too willing to take the same view. This almost sacerdotal partnership between Mr. Murphy and the accuser lent to Chambers the calm of a man who has gone through purgatory and who now, like the emerging Dante, sees the clear vault of heaven above with the wonder of a child and the purity of a saint. It was a very useful protection against the cross-examination. For Chambers now had a stagger-proof stance, which implied that while he was a Communist there was no honor in him, but since he had become a God-fearing man his memory was as human as anybody else's. Accordingly he could feint and tumble with Mr. Cross in a spirit of good clean fun and stay cheerful as a pixie when he was confronted for many hours on end with his old disreputable life, his life in the underground, his discrepancies of testimony. For two days the blithe responses came back at the dogged Mr. Cross: "that is correct," "that is also correct," "I don't recall," "it may well have been," "it may well be you're right." Mr. Cross showed him a letter to a Columbia teacher to prove that Chambers had been a year out all along in his recollection of when he became a Communist (it was 1925 not 1924). He appeared almost grateful to Mr. Cross for setting him right. He was then challenged to deny Wadleigh's memory [1] of the shadowy Colonel Bykov as a one-armed man. Chambers

---

[1] In a series of newspaper articles, quoted in the Second Trial, which Wadleigh had written and published before he took the stand.

found this interesting but unimpressive; he remembered two arms. Mr. Cross dared him to say that Wadleigh had not been reproved for turning over useless documents. Chambers granted that he had. And had not Colonel Bykov then said: "We want something hot"? Chambers pursed his lips, implying that Wadleigh had a right to his colorful memoirs. "Very prettily phrased," he commented, and looked at the ceiling as steadily as Sydney Carton. Before he left the stand, Mr. Murphy wanted to be quite clear what was his defense to the libel suit. That was very simple. "It's true," said Chambers.

The defense managed to bear with this insouciance because there was always at the back of their minds the invigorating promise of the psychiatric testimony, which Judge Goddard eventually allowed in on January 5, 1950 and thereby set a precedent in the federal courts, which had not before permitted psychiatric testimony to discredit the credibility of a witness.[1] Mr. Murphy asked, without much hope, for a reversal of the judge's decision on the grounds that "it is for the jury and the jury alone to determine where the truth lies, and that duty, under our system of law, cannot be usurped by a medical expert." Before Dr. Carl Binger was called, Judge Goddard said that up to now the federal courts had followed the ruling that a psychiatrist should be allowed to testify only to reputation and not be allowed to give an expert opinion. But this, said the judge, was a ruling made in a case in 1921, "before the value of psychiatry had been recognized." It was apparent to him that "the outcome of this trial is dependent to a great extent upon the testimony of one man—Whittaker Chambers. . . . Evidence of insanity is not merely for the judge on the preliminary question of competency but goes to the jury to affect credibility." He thought that the foundation had been laid for evidence which he regarded as relevant and material. And he would therefore allow it.

Dr. Binger, a big genial, leather-lunged man, was in the witness chair in no time. And after seventy minutes, and the long bugbear of the hypothetical question again, Mr. Cross put the great challenge: what was the doctor's opinion "within the bounds of reasonable certainty" of the mental condition of Whittaker Chambers? Dr. Binger gave the measured answer: "Mr. Chambers is suffering from a condition known as a psychopathic personality, a disorder of character the

---

[1] Such testimony, the judge remarked, has been allowed in the state courts of Georgia, Michigan, New Jersey, New York, and Texas.

distinguishing features of which are amoral and asocial behavior." Such people, he went on, did not take into account the ordinary conventions of morality, had "no regard for the good of society and of individuals," and were therefore frequently destructive of both. Some of the symptoms of this condition were "chronic, persistent, and repetitive lying; acts of deception and misrepresentation; alcoholism and drug addiction; abnormal sexuality; vagabondage, panhandling, inability to form stable attachments, and a tendency to make false accusations." The most outstanding characteristic was "what we call a defect in the formation of conscience."

Mr. Cross was alert to the false inferences that are readily drawn by laymen from psychiatric language and got the doctor to say that an understanding of this sort of personality "has nothing to do with the conventional judgment of sanity"; that a psychopath stood "on a kind of middle ground between the psychotic and the neurotic." It was an old and well-established diagnosis, but the statistics on the incidence of this condition were unreliable because such people were "usually unaware of the nature of their disturbance and therefore do not seek psychiatric help" and were often recognized only when they ran afoul of the law. On the surface they might live normal lives while in fact they were living out the roles their imagination suggested and "on the basis of such imaginations they will claim friendships where none exist, just as they will make accusations which had no basis in fact." Because they were always playing a part which was true for them, they were "amazingly isolated and egocentric." In the late war about seventeen per cent of the nearly two million men rejected for psychiatric disabilities were of this sort. For a whole day Dr. Binger drew telling analogies between these symptoms and Chambers's known behavior and writings.

At the end of this notable day some people thought they heard the courtroom begin to croak and snuffle with hacking coughs, a psychosomatic protest that did not pass unnoticed by the learned and caused many a knowing aside when next day one of the jurors broke out in a fever and a heavy cold and caused the Trial to be postponed for a day and a half. When it resumed, there was a big crowd on hand to watch Mr. Murphy make what amounted to a first public trial run of the common man's resistance to psychiatry. In this joust Mr. Murphy asked no title more glorious than that of representing the humble layman. And he stood for the ordeal like Hamlet's Horatio, the time-honored *punctum indifferens*, more commonly recognized in this country as the gruff, genial, no-nonsense, all-American regular fellow.

First Mr. Murphy wanted to be honestly clear about the good doctor's qualifications. He guilelessly revealed that although Dr. Binger had graduated from medical school thirty-five years ago, he had been certified as a practicing psychiatrist only three years before. Mr. Murphy would not let Dr. Binger explain the complex of technical requirements which would dispose of this apparent anomaly (and which, to be truthful, would technically disqualify half the most celebrated psychiatrists in Europe). Mr. Murphy just wanted plain answers to plain questions—about the most alarming assignment anyone could wish on a psychiatrist. He asked Dr. Binger if he himself had ever been psychoanalyzed, to which the doctor alertly replied: "Certainly, nobody can do psycho-analysis without having been psycho-analyzed." Mr. Murphy dropped a friendly head: "Would you try, doctor, just to say 'yes' and 'no' and we will go much faster?"

It seemed we might go very fast indeed when Mr. Murphy, having laid out in laboratory array every Chambers episode that had led the doctor to his opinion, provoked the doctor into the warning: "I have to consider the totality of the picture. I can't isolate my judgment according to specific parcels of information." Time and again Dr. Binger refused to say whether an act, a statement, or a mannerism was in itself a conclusive symptom of a psychopathic personality. Well, wouldn't the doctor agree you couldn't "form a complete opinion on a person's personality by merely observing him" on a witness stand? The doctor reluctantly agreed, but pointed out he had the evidence of the man's writing. (Mr. Murphy showed that though the doctor had read assiduously in the works of Chambers he was unfamiliar with his more celebrated "cover pieces" done for *Time* magazine.) And the doctor couldn't know, could he, what was and what was not true in the assumptions of the hypothetical question? Of course not. And, without being disrespectful, wasn't it fair to say that the term "psychopathic personality" itself was rather vague, hardly a recognized clinical entity, rather a "wastebasket classification of a lot of symptoms"? Yes, the doctor thought it was a fair statement.

They came back to the validity of the relation between certain acts of Chambers and the pigeon holes Dr. Binger had put them into. Surely, honest Mr. Murphy seemed to say, there must be some act, some flagrant lie, that would stand alone as a symptom. How about a man's telling a lie to his wife to avoid an unpleasant argument? "Pretty normal," Dr. Binger thought. Telling children over a period of years there was a Santa Claus? No symptom, said the doctor, just an accepted part of folk mythology. Well, would he say that "telling the children for many years that the stork brings the baby—would that indicate that the parent *perhaps* was manifesting a symptom of psychopathic personality?" If the parents believed it, "I would think it might," said the doctor; a dead-pan sally that convulsed the court and the reporters and had Judge Goddard grinning with the rest. "If the parent believed it," Mr. Murphy twinklingly suggested, would it be only a symptom of psychopathic personality? No, indeed, it would be a symptom of much else. "You said it," remarked Mr. Murphy.

In his direct examination Dr. Binger had said that the first symptom he diagnosed in Chambers was "based on a series of repetitive and continuous lies covering approximately twenty-four years of this person's life." It was Mr. Murphy's set course to pare them down to many less, a procedure Dr. Binger thought "futile," because he certainly didn't base his diagnosis on "a statistical count of lies." But Mr. Murphy hacked away, patiently shaving "malign" intent from most of Dr. Binger's total of falsehoods and arriving at the creditable count of "about ten lies over a period" of thirty-three years. "Doctor," Mr. Murphy threw himself sportingly on Dr. Binger's charity, "what's par [for the course] for a normal person?" Dr. Binger thought Mr. Murphy had had more experience than himself, a remark that hurt Mr. Murphy, until Judge Goddard smilingly explained that the doctor was referring to Mr. Murphy's experience as a prosecutor, which indeed he was. Then Mr. Murphy ranged through all the suspect behavior of Chambers and made Dr. Binger grudgingly excuse one symptom after another. "Panhandling," for instance—had there been any tittle of evidence that Chambers cadged money on the public streets? "You win," Dr. Binger smiled. Mr. Murphy tried to damage the method Dr. Binger had used in forming an opinion of Chambers from his writings. He tried to get him to guess how psychopathic, for example, Thomas Merton, the newly converted Trappist, might be; or "a great many sinners and saints." Dr. Binger declined on the grounds that you would need to know the whole life pattern of these people, and "I don't know the life pattern of a great many

saints and sinners." He had to admit, though, that he knew nothing
at all about the first sixteen years of Chambers's life.

Dr. Binger was able to get into the cross-examination a sketch of
the plot of Franz Werfel's *Class Reunion*,[1] which the defense strongly
suggested had provided Chambers with a morbid cue for his attack on
Hiss. The story, said Dr. Binger, had impressed him with "extraordinary analogies": "there are two principal characters in the book.
One is Sebastian and the other is Adler. The name Adler is very close
to the name Alger. . . . [He] is described . . . as a man of great
sincerity and sweetness, the closest friend of the other character
Sebastian, later became the enemy whom he is trying to destroy. . . .
[Sebastian] is describing how he himself committed a forgery and he
signed a paper that the other man had done the thing and not he. . . .
How he had proposed a suicide pact with him by the use of illuminating gas, which is, as you recall, the way Chambers' brother committed
suicide . . . and Sebastian ducked out and let the other man almost
die. . . . Adler is described as having gray eyes, as having a ludicrous
walk when seen from behind" (Chambers had said that Hiss had "a
mincing gait when seen from behind"). ". . . Adler's father is said
to have committed suicide when he was a small child. That is, Hiss's
father committed suicide when he was a small child. Adler's mother
is said to be a domineering woman; that Hiss's mother was described
in some such terms. . . . Sebastian describes himself at the age of 43
as too fat, as smoking too much, as drinking too much, as working
too hard, as fearing a heart attack. He says that his father died of a
heart attack. And whether I'm allowed to tell this or not, I have seen
the medical record of Mr. Chambers with the same facts in it, and I
can't dismiss that from my mind. . . . The crime which was actually
committed in the book is one of falsification of documents by a man
who says of himself: 'I would lie. I would—I have no conscience. I
would stop at nothing to gain my end.' The crime was then pinned
on to the character Adler; and Sebastian signed a document saying,
'I did not do this, I didn't falsify the records, I wasn't the forger;
Adler was.' And then to get out of the mess there is this suicide pact.
. . . [Sebastian] plagiarized a poem and was admitted into the inner
circle of the intelligentsia at school. And Adler made fun of him and
because he said something slighting to him, at that moment he sealed

---

[1] Translated by Chambers in 1929 when he was temporarily out of the Communist Party, and shortly after his father died.

his own doom; and then started a process in Sebastian which was not completed until he came very near destroying this other man. Those are the analogies which might be pointed out." Dr. Binger agreed he had found no analogies in the child's book *Bambi*, which Chambers had also translated.

"Doctor," said Mr. Murphy, again inviting from Dr. Binger a confession meant to clear away oppressive masses of pseudo-science and incidentally to leave the prosecution in command of the field, "would you say that other psychiatrists, let us say as qualified as yourself, might perhaps have a different opinion based upon the facts you have?" Dr. Binger said he would be very surprised if they did; he had talked to a great many.

"Apart from your surprise would a difference of opinion be possible?"

"Naturally it would be."

"Doctors have been known to disagree frequently on diagnosis?"

"Frequently."

"Have you ever been wrong, doctor?"

"Certainly."

THERE was at least one other doctor, however, whom the defense had on hand to support Dr. Binger's opinion. He was a gaunt, engaging man from Harvard, Dr. Henry Murray, former director of the Harvard psychological clinic and the inventor of the thematic apperception test. Mr. Murphy suggested to the judge that to let in a psychologist who was not a psychiatrist would make "a burlesque of a court of law," but Judge Goddard nevertheless took the risk and Dr. Murray was called. He was a tougher nut for Mr. Murphy's crackers. His specialty, he said, had been the analysis of psychopathic personalities through the evidence of their writings. He had looked into the work of Whittaker Chambers and found there "a higher proportion of images of disintegration and destruction, filth and dirt, decay and decomposition and death than in any writings I have ever examined." He completely concurred with Dr. Binger's opinion that Chambers was a psychopathic personality given to the lying, false accusation, grandiosity, and egocentricity of the type.

Mr. Murphy tried to ensnare him in an ingenious trap he had set for Dr. Binger. He prodded the doctor into discounting Chambers's deceptions while he was a Communist on Chambers's conscious admission that he had been a dedicated and loyal "soldier" in a cause. During the war, Mr. Murphy casually brought in, didn't thousands of loyal citizens and normal men enlist in the service of the Office of Strategic Services—the famous cloak-and-dagger men—and had they not as a regular thing to take out false passports, swear falsely, and generally conduct themselves like slippery characters? Dr. Binger said they had, but he thought the analogy was false. Mr. Murphy put the same teaser to Dr. Murray: surely the O.S.S. men were not psychopaths? On the contrary, Dr. Murray replied, the ranks of its applicants were full of them, and he himself had had the job of weeding them out. "The whole nature of the functions of the O.S.S.," he explained "were particularly inviting to psychopathic characters; it involved sensation, intrigue, the idea of being a mysterious man with secret knowledge."

The general opinion of the onlookers that Dr. Murray was an ingratiating and able man, and that he was a secondary witness, made it conclusive that Dr. Binger's testimony was what Mr. Murphy had to shake. And it was Dr. Binger who had to bear the long-suffering and unenviable role of a profession which, if not attempting to be holier than thou, is at least dedicated to the proposition that it knows better than Everyman why he behaves the way he does. This is a perilous stand to take before a jury, and Mr. Murphy, by playing on it with an artful air of being no more than an interested layman, exposed the central risk of bringing psychiatrists to testify in cases where the suspect character is in obvious control of his senses, and— if he is Whittaker Chambers—of his intelligence and his wit. The common man will probably rise for generations against the seeming pretentiousness of a psychiatrist in a courtroom under the misguided assumption that such an expert robs him of his self-respect, whereas the expert doubtless means only to free him from self-deception. Under Mr. Murphy's casually delivered, but exquisitely prepared, inquiry Dr. Binger was made to speculate about personal motives in matters like religion, friendship, marriage, penitence—which for most men are thought to be the conspicuous badges of their better nature. And since it is the job of psychiatry to think most clearly about what is unthinkable, Dr. Binger, however gently he probed into these sacrosanct relationships, was tickling the nerve-ends of human pride and got the protesting sigh, the giggle, and the smarting postoperative sarcasm that all such superior surgeons must expect for a long time to come.

It might be that Mr. Murphy's most effective passage, from the jury's point of view, was one in which he attempted with a deliberately stupefied sincerity to follow some of the diagnostic abstractions of what another great American debunker has called "the head-feelers." Let us see now, Mr. Murphy seemed to say, letting his eyes roam over Dr. Binger's display of symptoms—now here, for instance, the good doctor says personal untidiness and bad teeth are suspect. But, doctor, how about dear old Will Rogers, and Owen D. Young, and Bing Crosby: no fashion plates, they; were they psychopathic? Not on that evidence, Dr. Binger allowed. And how about Chambers's leaving a typewriter on a streetcar?—Don't thousands of wives throw away their wedding rings in Reno, "to forget the past"? And hiding the documents in a pumpkin—is that so bad, doctor? How about putting the Connecticut charter in the Hartford oak?—were the early colonials psychopathic? Dr. Binger had the sense to imply they certainly were not. Well, Mr. Murphy countered, you say normal people hide things in banks; didn't the mother of Moses hide him in the bulrushes? "She could scarcely have put him in a safe-deposit box," Dr. Binger reflected.

But by now Dr. Binger seemed a little weary of the desperate task of bucking the ca'canny and four-square common sense of the prosecutor. Moreover, Mr Murphy rightly saw that Dr. Binger and the defense counsel had spread their suspicious net much too wide in presuming to see pathological symptoms in many things they would very likely on second thoughts have preferred to forget. For instance, Dr. Binger had noticed that Chambers on the stand seemed to establish no contact with his questioner and constantly looked up at the ceiling. Well, Mr. Murphy had kept a check of Dr. Binger's ceiling-gazing. He had done it fifty-nine times in twenty minutes. Psychopathic, doctor? Not by that token alone, Dr. Binger decided.

And then Dr. Binger had been very struck by the way Chambers rarely answered questions by stating the fact but said mostly "it must have been," "it would have been," or "it should have been." This did not tally with the memory of the reporters who had sat through both Trials, and Mr. Murphy came in after a week-end's loving scrutiny and announced that in 770 pages of the official transcript,

Chambers had used one or other of those expressions only ten times. But would the doctor like to know how often Alger Hiss had used them? The doctor clearly would have preferred not to. But Mr. Murphy would tell him? 158 times in 550 pages of testimony.

At the end of his long ordeal Dr. Binger stuck adamantly to his diagnosis. Mr. Murphy would offer him one more big-hearted chance to be saved. "Can you still say, doctor, that this man is psychopathic?" The doctor could and did—most certainly. The doctor had done noble work for a suspect cause. But Mr. Murphy, for all his feigned archness and voluntary astonishment, had put just the questions that a jury would want to ask. Any layman might have called in question two or three of Dr. Binger's symptoms ("inability to form stable attachments," for instance, applied to a man married for eighteen years). But Mr. Murphy recruited dozens of them into a war of attrition that not only reduced Dr. Binger at the end to a weary acquiescence but left him rather like a magician who has pulled out wonderful and frightening objects but failed to perform the final trick of making the typewriter and the documents disappear. How unerringly Mr. Murphy gauged the mood of the jury's curiosity and interest in all this may be gathered from some questions the grand jury had put to Hiss on the morning he was indicted. Mr. Murphy had found an excuse to read the relevant passage of the grand jury's minutes earlier in the Trial.

It seems that Hiss had asked the grand jury, on the morning of the 15th of December 1948, to hear Dr. Binger. They declined the offer after this exchange:

Q. Mr. Hiss, is your psychiatrist in any position to offer (any in-formation . . . with reference to explaining to this grand jury) how it came about that the documents, the Baltimore documents of November 17 . . . was written on the same typewriter?
A. No, he is not. He can only talk from the point of view of motive which has come up . . .
Q. . . . motive on whose part?
A. Mr. Chambers.
Q. Has he examined Mr. Chambers?
A. No, he has examined his writings, letters, testimony and every-thing that we have been able to find out about him—his whole career.

Q. Has he had any personal contact with Chambers that you know of?

A. No, he has not been able to.

Q. . . . have you any further thoughts that you want to express to the grand jury with reference to (the fact that neither you nor your wife have explained in any way how that machine could possibly come into the possession of Chambers)?

A. No, I don't think so. I was asked if we had ever lost anything from our house and I testified that I did not recall anything. My wife reminded me of a theft from that very house [Volta Place] or disappearance, let's say, of a not very sizeable sum of money, about thirty dollars, from a pocketbook. . . .

Q. Was that reported to the police?

A. No, it was not. Nor was the loss of a diamond wristwatch. . . .

Q. In 1938 were you conscious of the loss of the typewriter, of the Woodstock?

A. I have never been conscious of the loss of it in terms of thinking that someone had taken it. I do not recall the disposition of it.

This passage ran at once into the questions that were the basis of the indictment. It seemed to one reporter, when the psychiatric testimony was over, that what Mr. Murphy had done, with deceptive calm, was to demonstrate that when a psychiatrist is in the offing hell hath no fury like a layman scorned; and that the common man in the mid-twentieth century, ninety-four years after the birth of Freud, would still rather steer clear of the mysteries of emotional health, and that when they are invoked he is inclined to retreat into a down-to-earth protest, as Westbrook Pegler did at the solemn analyses of the mysteries of love in books of marriage counsel: "We all, baby-havin', 'tater-hoein', homespun folks of the great American majority —well, stranger, we don't regard sex as any fittin' topic for a book."

THE TYPEWRITER AND
THE DOCUMENTS

❦

IN the First Trial both sides had seemed to be spoiled for a choice of weapons: one never knew, and suspected that the counsel didn't, whether the general credibility of Chambers was the thing to establish or impeach or whether it could only be upheld by the corroborating force of the typewriter and the documents. Mr. Murphy's blunder, in asking the jury to throw out the case if they didn't believe Chambers, was manna to the defense and fed Mr. Stryker's prearranged campaign to show that Chambers was nothing but a chronic liar and conspirator whose word was worthless on anything. But it also encouraged Mr. Stryker to belittle what literary critics call the "internal evidence" of the State Department documents. What gave to the Second Trial its superior seriousness was the tacit agreement of both sides that the defense of Hiss would stand or fall on the circumstantial weight of the typewriter and the documents. Instead of Mr. Stryker's eleven minutes' dismissal of the documents in a four-hour summation, Mr. Cross gave the best of his laborious but considerable skill to these matters. Most of his summation was devoted to proving that while Hiss had probably never seen some of the documents, all of them (including Baltimore No. 10, the only one not done on the Hiss typewriter) went through a physical unit of the State Department comprising the Far Eastern Division, the Trade Agreement Section, and an adjoining office. In his meticulous examination of the State Department's stamping, routing, and filing systems, and his plea to the jury at the end to think carefully about these things, there was always the exciting invitation to the jury to decide once for all either that Mr. Cross had released doubts that were not beyond reason or that he was giving his manful best to a lost cause.

First, the defense had to solidify its conviction that *the Woodstock typewriter* was positively out of the Hisses' hands by the 29th of December 1937, when they had moved from Thirtieth Street to Volta Place. In the Second Trial this attempt had rough treatment at the hands not only of Mr. Murphy but of the defense's own witnesses. Hiss himself had hardly ever come into this. He said now that he didn't type and he had no idea how the typewriter had been disposed of. Mrs. Catlett offered some help with her thought that she had moved into her house in P Street in 1937. But Mike Catlett was now so inured to the terrors of due process of law that he grew expansive in the Second Trial and obviously thought he was doing the defense a good turn by his honest, new decision that the Catlett family had moved into P Street in 1936 and that the typewriter had come to him and his brother when the Hisses moved from P Street to Thirtieth Street. This would have put it at the latest at the 1st of July 1936, an obviously impossible date for the defense's comfort and a joyous confusion for the Government. For Mrs. Hiss admittedly used the typewriter as late as the 25th of May 1937 (the University of Maryland letter). Over the plainly agonized pleadings of the defense Mike Catlett stuck to this wild recollection. The Government's record of the Catletts' renting agent showed that the family had moved into their P Street house on January 17, 1938, not late enough for all of the documents to have been typed in the Hiss house but still too late. Mike Catlett did support Mrs. Hiss's suspicion that colored families moved in and out of houses a little more haphazardly than the records would show and that the Catletts could have been in their new home for a time on someone else's lease. He bravely opined to Mr. Murphy that he still thought somebody was "making some money" in putting the Catletts' possession of their P Street house as late as 1938. His memory of the early days in P Street was movingly reinforced by his recollection of kerosene lamps the family had had to use "for a good while" before they could afford to have electricity at P Street. Mr. Murphy smothered this pathos with a routine reading of utility records, which showed that the electricity had no sooner been turned off at the Catletts' old house than it was turned on when they went into P Street. The Government also brought all the way from the Aleutians a Sergeant Roulhac, who had signed the P Street renting agreement according to the custom the Catletts had explained in the First Trial that house agents are reluctant to do legal business with a colored woman. Sergeant Roulhac said they had used candles for lighting for one night before the electricity was turned on; he incidentally testified that he couldn't remember seeing the typewriter in the Catletts' P Street house until about three months after they had moved in. It was "out in the hallway." Mike Catlett also responded, perhaps one trial too late, to Mr. Stryker's promising innuendo that the F.B.I. had bullied the Catletts into their present confusion. He told of a drive around Georgetown during which two F.B.I. agents bought a case of beer and kept "punching" each other to give him another beer and get him drunk. Mike said "they didn't give me a chance" to tell this at the First Trial. He admitted that he had told the F.B.I. when they called in 1949 that he knew nothing about a typewriter at the Hisses' home. He agreed he had then gone off to see Donald Hiss and had offered to help in finding it. He was not to be budged from his story of the F.B.I. offer of two hundred dollars. If Mr. Murphy meant to intimidate him into retracting it by bringing the F.B.I.'s Mr. Jones into court, he did not succeed. "Mr. Jones," said Mr. Murphy over his shoulder: "Will you stand up so there will be no mistake." The thin Virginian, Mr. Stryker's victim, stood up at the back of the courtroom. Mike Catlett stared at him: "Yes, sir, that's the man right there. That's Mr. Jones. He's the one that offered me the $200 too . . . and if he's a man he'll tell you."

He now thought that the typewriter had been brought by Mrs. Hiss driving her own car to the Catletts'. Mrs. Hiss could not go along with this. She, on the contrary, was sure that the Catlett boys had appeared at Thirtieth Street with a little express wagon, on which they had piled an old phonograph, some of Hiss's old shirts, and the typewriter. Perry Catlett wasn't sure how it got to them, but he was sure they had it "during the period" when the Hisses moved from Thirtieth Street to Volta Place; and he meant "before" and not "after" they moved.

Mr. Murphy handled Mike Catlett this time with condescending ease. "Is the story," he asked, "about the beer just as truthful . . . as

the story about the kerosene lamps and no electricity?" Yes, sir, said
Mike. That was all.

To rebut the defense's story that the typewriter was in poor
shape, Mr. Murphy brought in an F.B.I. typist, who sat in the courtroom and banged out a copy of one of the documents in two or three
apparently effortless minutes. Mr. Murphy stood by in triumphant
boredom while this old typewriter, with its unreliable roller, its missing knob, the keys that jammed, was expertly played by the F.B.I.
The performance was dramatically pat. But it did not disprove the
well-known fact that broken typewriters can be mended.

MR. MURPHY again put in evidence all the documents. Again he
read them aloud, reciting eighty-seven documents line by line, making every word sound like a casual tolling bell. There was a new one,
kept out of the First Trial at the request of the State Department.
It was now safe for all to see. It was a section of a cable sent from Paris
on January 25, 1938 by the then Ambassador William C. Bullitt. It
went as follows:

> Delbos [then the French Foreign Minister] said that he was con-
> vinced that Germany desired genuinely to come to terms with France at
> the present time. He then related to me a conversation which he had had a
> few days ago with the Soviet Ambassador in Paris. The Soviet Ambassador
> complained that the French Government seemed to be working for a rec-
> onciliation with Germany and intimated strongly that if France should
> begin serious negotiations with Germany the Soviet Union would come to
> terms with Germany at once.
>
> Delbos said that he had replied that he was quite certain that
> Germany would prefer to come to terms with France rather than with the
> Soviet Union and any such attempt on the part of the Soviets would be
> anticipated by France. He added that he felt a true statement of the situ-
> ation was that the Soviet Union could not sell its friendship to anyone at
> the moment because there were no buyers for that commodity.
>
> In the course of the discussion on the general situation M. Delbos
> said that, while he was aware that Great Britain was flirting constantly with
> Germany and Italy, he did not believe that so long as Mr. Eden was
> Minister for Foreign Affairs England would recognise the King of Italy as
> Emperor of Ethiopia. He knew that throughout history the French had
> often been surprised by Britain's actions; but he was very positive of one
> thing: that Eden hated Mussolini more than any living human being.

(Professor Namier says about it: [1] "I know of no other which deals with the point so directly at that time. But it was inherent in the situation all along. The Bolsheviks were throughout obsessed by the fear of a coalition of 'Imperialist capitalist Powers' settling their differences at Russia's expense; they were therefore determined to guard against it by getting in with one side or the other, and by keeping them apart; and any danger of a Four Power Pact would make them try and forestall and outbid the Western Powers with the Germans. And for that they had the means then, as they have now. Delbos's tour of Eastern Europe with Moscow omitted, and his talk with Neurath at the railway station on December 3rd, 1937, were bound to disturb and annoy them.")

Hiss was perfectly unruffled in his insistence that *the handwritten memoranda* were what he had always said they were: summaries of documents not worth his chief's while to read at length; or notes written to remind him or his chief of contents he wanted to explain. He thought they could easily have been picked off his desk, which was usually scattered with papers. Francis B. Sayre, however, was called (by the defense) and had to admit he had no recollection of any of them: they were "not comments on memoranda nor personal advice in any way. They are rather digests or copies of incoming cables." But he thought a couple clearly referred to the body of the documents they might have accompanied. Miss Lincoln, the Sayre-Hiss secretary, said she had not seen anything "similar" in all her years in the Department. Dr. Hornbeck thought three of them were unlike Hiss's usual memoranda and said interdepartmental notes were not usually written in pencil. But Hiss explained that he had had on his desk blue pencils, lead pencils, and pens and simply took whichever came to hand. He was also asked to explain one of the handwritten memoranda about an American secret agent called Rubens who had been arrested by the Russians in 1938. Hiss's office had had an information copy of the telegram from Moscow about this affair, though Mr. Sayre said he had never seen it. Hiss said that when the United States had started diplomatic relations with the Soviet Union there was a firm understanding that Americans should not be arrested and held incommunicado. That is just what had happened to Rubens, and the State Department, Hiss said, was very exercised about it as a test case. Hiss's explanation was so straightforward and knowledgeable

---

[1] In a private letter of April 16, 1950. See also page 163.

that Mr. Murphy apparently gave up the hope of loading this note with any more sinister undertones.

Of all the lawyers at the two tables, Mr. Cross might have been thought the least likely candidate for the profession of hard-bitten private detective. He was slow and mannerly and deferential to the judge. He seemed like a portly corporation lawyer of the old school. But in fact he had labored prodigiously on the implications of every mark and stamp on *the typewritten documents* and *the microfilm documents* and rendered to Hiss probably the most convincing analytic service that could be done. Wheeling his heavy shoulders and bull-neck around at the display easels, he nibbled away at every blade of grass in the dreary pasture of the documents. One day he almost got from Chambers a confession, hastily amended the next, that Julian Wadleigh "could possibly" have passed one of the papers. Checking the stamping and distribution markings, he spat out two other documents and worked all through one afternoon to try to get Mr. Walter Anderson, the State Department's chief of records, to concede that neither of them went to the Hiss office. These two will serve as an example of Mr. Cross's tenacious laboratory style. There were four papers involved, two memoranda and two reports, a short one and a long one from a Dr. Boyce, then consular officer in Yokohama. After Mr. Cross had got Mr. Anderson to agree that master documents usually had their accompanying memoranda stapled together in the record room, he proved that there was no indication anywhere that the short Boyce report was ever distributed to the Hiss office. Therefore, Mr. Cross tried to show, the memorandum that referred to it did not go there either, and consequently Alger Hiss never had access to either document. Mr. Cross then worked over an aide-memoire that had gone to Germany. The distribution list showed that this had gone to many offices either in the form of its German original or in English translation or both. Again, Mr. Anderson granted there was nothing to show Hiss had received the German text, which was among the Chambers papers, whereas he did receive the English translation, which was not.

This lucid digest of an appalling half-day could only be deduced from a persistent quizzing of defense counsel when the Court had recessed. It was not available, of course, to the jury and it is possible they were just as stupefied as the rest of us by the actual court exchanges, in which Mr. Cross exploded dates like firecrackers and Mr.

Anderson put in many well-tempered distinctions between dispatches, reports, aide-memoires, letters of transmittal, and other diplomatic mysteries. It was a pity for the defendant that the most impressive part of his defense was bound to be on display in this subtle and un-dramatic chore. At the end of it Mr. Anderson deferred to neither Mr. Cross nor Mr. Murphy and his "that is correct" or "not neces-sarily" left Mr. Cross unable to prove absolutely that Hiss could not possibly have seen these disputed documents and Mr. Murphy un-able to prove that he certainly did. But Miss Lincoln made the dam-aging remark that her office frequently got papers she did not stamp, since she was obliged to stamp only those documents that bore on the distribution sheet a routing through her office. And for Mr. Murphy there was the heavy consolation that even if Mr. Cross had thrown doubt on four or five or even seven documents, the remaining forty still abided our question.

Mr. Cross clung in heroic hope to the one Baltimore (typewritten) document that the Government allowed was done on a different type-writer (and which Chambers said he might have had from Harry Dexter White). Mr. Feehan, the F.B.I. expert, said it was typed on a 1936 Royal. Mr. Cross wondered what sort of machines the Trade Agreements Section and the Far Eastern Division were using in 1938, but the Government didn't offer to let him impound any. Wasn't this exceptional paper the only one to show a Government water-mark? It was. Wasn't it a strange quality of paper? Mr. Feehan thought it was a very ordinary paper. Wouldn't a chemical analysis show it was a Japanese tissue? Mr. Feehan thought Mr. Cross meant "a fibre analysis" and said that if the paper had been called Japanese tissue it was an erroneous description.

All the defense's hopes rested with Wadleigh, who Mr. Cross had been bold enough to say was one of the two missing thieves. The de-fense's aim was to show that Wadleigh had long ago [1] taken all *the microfilm documents*. Mr. Cross got Chambers to agree that they had all been reproduced in "a single photographic run." In other words, said Mr. Cross, "if you knew who gave you one . . . you would know who the lot came from?" No question about it, said Chambers.

---

[1] Eastman Kodak and Du Pont laboratory experts had testified that a section of the microfilm had been manufactured in 1937 and another section could have been made in either 1937 or 1944.

And hadn't he told the House Committee that he "could possibly" have had some of them from Wadleigh? He had. And would he not now admit that it was physically possible? Chambers replied without emotion: "It was physically possible but contrary to the fact." Mr. Cross had to retreat into the satisfactions of Chambers's perjury by seizing the House Committee testimony, reading it, and putting a final challenge: "You either lied to the House Committee or you lied to his Honor and this jury?" That, said Chambers, was correct. Mr. Cross's challenging formula was an improvement on Mr. Stryker's repeated inference that Chambers was telling the truth for the first time in the courtroom, but it did not remove the microfilm documents from Alger Hiss's doorstep. Everything would now depend on the nerve of Wadleigh.

Mr. Cross handled him with what the defense evidently took to be the required contempt. But there was in Mr. Cross's manner a new vigilance that conveyed how priceless to the defendant's cause would be a breakdown or even a momentary slip. Mr. Cross made him go over the papers one by one. But no, he shook his gawky head and remarked that he might have handled some of the originals and even passed them to David Carpenter or Chambers—but "never these copies." Besides, Mr. Murphy hinted soothingly on cross-examination, he had gone, had he not, on a mission to Turkey on the 10th of March 1938, and that "would put you somewhere out on the ocean" when some of the documents were being passed? That was right. Mr. Cross decided to see how green was Wadleigh's memory for the four hundred-odd papers he admitted having passed, or "stolen," as Mr. Cross put it. Wadleigh knitted his shaggy brows and would not allow the word "steal." "I take it you mean the procedures that I described. . . ." When he stole papers, Mr. Cross insisted, did he not know he was a traitor to the United States? Wadleigh's mildly bloodshot eyes steadied on Mr. Cross and he replied very levelly: "No."

"You knew these papers were to be turned over to the Communist Party?"

"Yes."

"You think you were performing a patriotic service to the United States?"

". . . I thought I was doing the right thing according to my principles at that time."

Mr. Cross put to him the most sacred challenge of our day, and Wadleigh's answer to it flared up, like Marley's ghost, from the embers of the brave old days of the evangelical thirties.

"Did you believe in the American way of life?"

Wadleigh put his index finger to his cheekbone and thought deeply for a moment. Mr. Cross took a pace forward, waiting to hear the trap spring.

"Substantially I did."

Mr. Cross would not give up. He challenged Wadleigh to show "a distinct recollection of one single document" out of the hundreds he admitted passing (Mr. Cross now used "passing"). After a time Wadleigh remembered one, a telegram from Bullitt in Moscow, for no sensational reason at all. Seemingly despairing of provoking Wadleigh into breaking down or having a precious second thought, Mr. Cross at the day's end tried to wring his withers by making vivid the anxiety of the years his crime had gone undetected. But by now Wadleigh's tolerance of a balked and ageing lawyer was all-embracing.

"During all that time, you were on pins and needles, weren't you?"

Wadleigh ran his hands through his shock of hair. "During all those ten years? . . ." He looked kindly at the agitated Mr. Cross. Come now, he seemed to say, let's be mature about this whole thing.

"Oh, no. Maybe for a year or two, but after a while I pretty much stopped worrying."

Mr. Cross had not pinned the microfilm documents on Wadleigh. And the "thief" in the Far Eastern Division was unidentified and was to remain so. In his summation Mr. Cross could only reiterate his conviction that the documents were part of an incriminating file Chambers had stored up; that when Hiss pressed his libel suit, Chambers decided to "look up the Alger Hiss file"; and that "the documents themselves prove there was a thief in the Far Eastern Division. I don't know who it was, but it was the person who stole these documents and gave them to Chambers." As for the typing, he hinted, the typing might have been done by a stooge or by Chambers himself having easy access to the hospitable open house the Catletts ran. Mr. Murphy took this very serious suggestion of the defense and had ruthless fun with it in his summation: "What probably happened, Mr. Cross testified, is that somebody, not Chambers—he's too smart, but one of his conspirators, one of his confederates (those are good

names . . .)—he went up to the Volta Place house and asked innocent Clidi Catlett: 'I'm the repair man. Where's the machine?' I can
just see it now. It's terrific. You can have this guy coming with a
Woodstock hat on,—'Woodstock Repair' . . . saying: 'I'm the repair man to fix the typewriter.' Then Clidi says: 'Well, which one do
you want? The Remington, the Royal, the L. C. Smith . . . ?' 'No,
we want the Woodstock.' 'Oh, that's over in my boy's house, over at
P Street.'

"And then the next scene; it is in the middle of one of these dances.
And you see Chambers sneaking in at night, mingling with the danc-
ers, and then typing, typing the stuff, holding the State Department
document in one hand." Mr. Murphy puffed his jolly cheeks and
blew through his walrus: "Oh, Mr. Cross, you got better than that."

Mr. Cross might have retorted that Mr. Murphy had caricatured
the defendant's contention that some time, somehow Chambers or a
willing stooge had typed the documents. Substantially the defense
asserted just that, but was unable to say how or when the job had
been done. But Mr. Murphy too was unable to prove that no one but
Mrs. Hiss had done the typing. And to the very end of the Trials,
neither the Government nor the defendant had cared, or been able,
to produce a typewriter expert who could identify personal characteristics of the typist (of mis-typing, over-typing and so on) or
otherwise to offer scientific proof that the documents had or had not
been typed by Mrs. Hiss. Whether this can ever be done, whether
such subtleties are within the skilled knowledge of experts, was left
for the jury to deduce from the "mute" but damning corroboration
of the typewriter and the documents themselves.

JUDGE GODDARD'S CHARGE

❁

THE clerk told the marshals to lock the door. Judge Goddard flapped his elbows out to ease the gown around his shoulders, and for one brief moment looked like the original American eagle. Then he proceeded to read the charge quietly, with few stresses or pauses and only the punctuation of an occasional cough. It might have been— for the first ten minutes or so—the standard charge in all perjury trials.

He summarized the two counts and read, as Judge Kaufman had done, the pertinent provisions of the United States Code that the defendant was charged with having violated. He told the jury there was no excuse in law for perjury. He advised them that Hiss's "testimony was material in the investigation being conducted by the Grand Jury." It was not for Hiss to prove how or from whom Chambers received the documents; it was up to the Government to prove that Hiss or his wife did deliver them. The Government was not required to prove this "beyond all possible doubt. For if that were the rule, very few people would ever be convicted." It must be done "beyond a reasonable doubt," which he—coming after Mr. Stryker, Mr. Murphy, Judge Kaufman, and Mr. Cross—was the fifth man to redefine. To Judge Goddard it did not mean "a doubt arbitrarily or capriciously asserted" to avoid an unpleasant task, nor "a possible doubt or a fanciful doubt," nor a doubt "arising from the natural sympathy which we all have for others." It was "a doubt which a reasonable person has after carefully weighing all the testimony." They should be governed by "the convincing force of the testimony."

They should disregard legal arguments addressed by the counsel to the Court, and the Court's ruling on them. The Court decided questions of law, the jury questions of fact. They should not infer the comparative weight of any evidence from the Court's calling attention to it. Their own recollection was the only recollection to follow. The Government's witnesses should be given neither "more nor less weight or credence" than the witnesses called by the defendant. The jury must simply consider the demeanor of all witnesses, their candor or lack of it, and make up their own minds "solely upon the evidence presented in the court, uninfluenced by anything read in the newspapers or heard on the radio or in private conversation." To reconcile all the testimony was impossible, and they should accept or reject any part of it they chose. They should consider that if a witness had an interest in the case, he would be strongly tempted to color his testimony and possibly "to withhold facts." He charged them that "the defendant Hiss has a great interest in the case" and "Mr. Chambers also has a deep interest in the result." They ought not to draw any inference from a witness's refusal to answer questions on the ground that he might incriminate himself in answering. It was "as if the questions had never been asked."

Now, there had been testimony about the previous good character of the defendant. This they should consider, as well as all the other facts and all the other evidence, in determining his guilt or innocence. "Evidence of good character may, in itself, create a reasonable doubt where, without such evidence, no reasonable doubt would exist." But if they were satisfied beyond a reasonable doubt of the defendant's guilt, "a showing that the defendant previously enjoyed a reputation of good character does not justify or excuse the offence," and he should not be acquitted on that account. "It may be that those with whom he had come in contact previously have been misled and that he did not reveal to them his real character or acts." The testimony of a character witness should not be taken as the witness's "personal opinion of the defendant's character." If after considering carefully all the testimony and the exhibits, they were convinced of the defendant's guilt in a way they would rely on and act on "in the more important matters of your own life," then they could be said to have no reasonable doubt.

The defense had called a psychiatrist and a psychologist. "As is the case with all expert testimony, these opinions are purely advisory." They could be rejected entirely if the jury thought the hypothetical question had been "incomplete or incorrect," or if the reasons of the experts seemed "unsound or not convincing." The expert "testifies that in his opinion," assuming the facts in the hypothetical question to be true, "the witness is suffering from a mental disorder which would tend to reduce his credibility in general." They had seen and heard Mr. Chambers for several days. It was for them to say "how much weight, if any," they would give to the testimony of the experts—and of Mr. Chambers. They had to answer the questions: did Mr. Hiss commit perjury when he said neither he nor Mrs. Hiss in his presence had passed the documents to Chambers in and around February and March 1938; and that he did not think he had seen Mr. Chambers after January 1, 1937. Was Mr. Chambers telling the truth when he testified he did see Mr. Hiss after that date and had the documents from him?

Even though they might accept the experts' opinions about Mr. Chambers's mental condition, "you may still find that Mr. Chambers was telling the truth when he testified regarding those particular matters."

They would "draw reasonable inferences and conclusions" from direct statements of fact or from circumstances. Circumstantial evidence was that which tended to prove or disprove a disputed fact "by proof of other facts which have a legitimate tendency to lead the mind to a logical conclusion as to the existence or non-existence of the disputed fact." The law made no distinction between "direct evidence of a fact and evidence of circumstances from which the existence of the fact may be reasonably deduced."

They had seen in evidence the papers the Government alleged Mr. Hiss had passed to Mr. Chambers. They had seen the Woodstock typewriter, and letters admittedly typed on it by Mrs. Hiss. They had heard an F.B.I. typewriting expert testify that in his opinion all these papers and letters were typed on the same machine. They might "weigh his reasons, if any, and give his testimony such weight" as they felt it deserved. They might reject it entirely.

Now, the law said that no person might be convicted of perjury unless the alleged falsity was established "by the testimony of two independent witnesses or by one witness and corroborating facts and circumstances. In the absence of such proof, the defendant must be acquitted." The Supreme Court had held that the evidence, if true, must substantiate the testimony of a single witness; and that the corroborative testimony must be trustworthy. It followed in this case that to find the defendant guilty on Count I, they must believe the word of Mr. Chambers about passing the documents and find other trustworthy evidence to substantiate his word. To find the defendant guilty on Count II, they must believe Mr. Chambers's word that he met Mr. Hiss after January 1, 1937; find trustworthy corroboration of his testimony about their meeting, either in other evidence of a meeting or meetings or in Mrs. Chambers's testimony about "that particular meeting of Mr. Hiss and Mr. Chambers after January 1, 1937."

If they believed Chambers, and found corroboration, on Count I, then "you may find the defendant guilty on Count I even though you have a reasonable doubt on some other" parts of Mr. Chambers's testimony.

Similarly, if they believed Chambers, and found corroboration (either by other evidence or by Mrs. Chambers's testimony on this point), "you may find the defendant guilty on Count II, even though you may have a reasonable doubt on some other portions of Mr. and Mrs. Chambers' testimony."

To reach either or both of these verdicts, they must "believe beyond a reasonable doubt that the corroborative testimony is inconsistent with the innocence of the defendant."

The Government had said the affair was "carried on with great secrecy so as to escape possible detection, and that no one else was present when the alleged acts took place. The Government, however, urges that facts and circumstances have been proved which, it says, fully substantiate the testimony of Mr. Chambers. This is an issue to be determined by you."

If they didn't believe Chambers, or did believe him and did not find corroboration, they "must return a verdict of not guilty on that count."

They might find the defendant guilty on both counts or might find him not guilty on both counts. If they found that neither the defendant nor Mrs. Hiss passed the documents, "then he may not be found guilty" on Count I. If they found that the defendant did not see Mr. Chambers after January 1, 1937, "he may not be found guilty" on Count II.

If they found Mr. Hiss did not pass the documents to Mr. Chambers and was therefore not guilty on Count I, "you may still find him guilty on Count II," if they thought he had committed perjury when he said "he thought he had not seen Mr. Chambers" after that date.

If they found that Mr. Hiss did not see Mr. Chambers after that date, as charged in Count II, it followed "necessarily" that they "must also find him not guilty on Count I."

If they found Mr. Hiss guilty on Count I, they "should also find [him] guilty on Count II."

Their verdict must be unanimous and "must represent the decision of each individual juror." This verdict should be reached "through an exchange of views, reasons and arguments among the several jurors."

If they found the evidence was "as consistent with innocence as with guilt, the defendant should be acquitted. If you find that the law has not been violated you should not hesitate for any reason to render a verdict of acquittal. But, on the other hand, if you find that the law has been violated as charged, you should not hesitate because of sympathy or for any other reason to render a verdict of guilt, as a clear warning to all that a crime such as charged here may not be committed with impunity. The American public is entitled to be assured of this."

JUDGE Goddard smiled benevolently at the jury. Mr. Cross was on his feet to ask to meet the judge and the Government at once. The judge called counsel to the bench, where the defense formally took exception to three parts of the charge: that in which the judge charged as a matter of law that the defendant's testimony before the grand jury was material to the grand jury's investigation; that in which he charged that the jury might find the defendant guilty on Count II, even though they acquitted him on Count I; and that "which related to the testimony of Mrs. Chambers with respect to the allegation of Count II." It was the second of these objections that struck everybody who had been at the First Trial as a puzzling variation on Judge Kaufman's charge. Judge Goddard had either ignored or reinterpreted the bill of particulars which, at the Court's request, the Government had attached to the original indictment. This bill agreed to specify that the meetings implied in the second count were the particular meetings at which the first count accused Hiss of passing the documents. Judge Kaufman had acknowledged this bill and therefore told the jury that Hiss was to be found innocent or guilty on both counts or neither of them.

At ten minutes after three, in the afternoon of Friday the 20th of January the jury retired.

THE VERDICT

❊

WE stretched for the long wait; and the lawyers—who had kept
themselves with proper archness from the press, after the judge's
admonition on the first day—began to unbend, stroke the backs of
their legs, and talk wryly with friends come in for the end. The jury
was back within two hours, stepping in smilingly from the juryroom
and facing a judge and counsel hard at work trying to decipher a note
the jury had sent in. It was a difficult scribble, but even when its
words were legible the counsel keeled over at their meaning. The
jury wanted the Baltimore documents and wanted to hear again all
the testimony of Mrs. Hiss, the Catletts, Julian Wadleigh, and Chambers on the Peterboro trip; and all testimony about the date of the
move to Volta Place. The judge brought them in and charitably
explained that if he took them at their word they would all be listening
to the stenographer for about five days on end. The forewoman
agreed that was quite a request they had there. After a little embarrassed whispering they retired, at the judge's suggestion, to reframe
their question. A half-hour later they had edited their note to request
all the typewritten documents and a reading of the Catletts' testimony
on when they got the typewriter, and Mrs. Hiss on when she disposed of it. They were already down to Mr. Murphy's "immutable
evidence." Their request could not be granted out of hand. The two
teams of lawyers would have to agree on what testimony it was fair
to isolate. So while the jury was led away to dinner, and the judge
dined in his chambers, the lawyers stayed in court and groaned over
testimony. It was straightened out in the end, and at a quarter past
eight in the evening the jury was called in and for an hour everybody

coughed and dozed and glared while the court reporter whined out a dreary evensong of repeated dialogue. Then the jury went off again and at half past ten were ordered to a hotel for the night.

Shortly after they met the next morning, they sent another note asking the judge to reread the part of his charge about reasonable doubt and the part relating circumstantial to acceptable corroborative evidence. He did so and the jury marched out again. But they had no sooner gone than the defense lawyers bridled at two notable omissions.[1] The judge had left out, the second time, a sentence in the middle of a paragraph which said: "Evidence of good character may, in itself, create a reasonable doubt where, without such evidence, no reasonable doubt would exist." And in explaining corroboration again he repeated the Government's contention that the affair had been carried on in great secrecy so as to avoid detection, and then he ended on the sentence: "The Government, however, urges, that facts and circumstances have been proved which, it says, fully substantiate the testimony of Mr. Chambers." In the judge's copy of his charge, the last sentence of that paragraph, which he did not read again, went: "This is an issue to be determined by you." The defense lawyers fumed in chambers, but the judge was convinced he had covered the points properly.

THE courtroom and the corridors were starting to resound again with the boisterous humor that, as these affairs drag on, seems to have no rhyme or reason. Everybody told his favorite psychiatry joke. The only ones who maintained a vigil apart from the general ribaldry were that solemn breed of renegades, the reconstituted patriots who survived their Russian baptism of the twenties and thirties and are now keen for anything that someone will dignify by calling the American Way. To these all jokes are suspect, honest doubts a weakness, and a liberal is a Communist on plain-clothes duty. These men, and their gleaming women, reconnoitered the fringes of the gossiping crowd and frowned at snatches of free speech that was not the same as theirs. They were—if what Mr. Churchill would call "this true account" is to be maintained—as nauseating a crew of relapsed heretics as it would be possible to find at large outside a Moscow Uni-

---

[1] They did not bring it up in the jury's presence because, they complained, they did not have a copy of the charge.

versity economics course. They, of course, propounded one of the
two simple, downright solutions which the faithful on both sides
held to, doggedly or hectically, to the end: either that Chambers
was wholly honest in his confessional and his accusation and Hiss was
"the concealed enemy" and a scoundrel; or that Hiss was the totally
innocent victim of a fabrication as subtle and malevolent as the
famous Papist plot of Titus Oates. In between these extremes were
others whose suspicions can be reduced to a number of popular
theories, which I think are now worth summarizing in their sharpest
form. By having them listed the reader may be helped to choose or at
least to appreciate the thickets he should plow through on the way to
his own broader, calmer view. I do not propose to evaluate them, for
we are in the realm of more things than speculation: of political
prejudice, of wishful feeling, of self-justification, of being too near
the event. I shall start with the extremes just mentioned and work
through their variations without any pretense of grading them into
a logical scale. Others who try to do this will soon discover that logic
is the last test to apply to theories of guilt and innocence. We have
only to look back to any historical character we personally admire to
rediscover the hard truth that the social acceptance of any strong-
minded character depends a great deal on their being born at the
right time. And in one's own time, everybody comes sooner or later
to realize that the central fascination of friendship is the flux of
private criticism and sympathy that goes on inside it. For its own
composure, the mind must daily come to compromises between
intuition and good sense which flout logic in the wildest way. And
what is galling about jury duty is that you are compelled to reach a
final judgment through a method that most people stay healthy by
sometimes ignoring and sometimes indulging.

  1. That Hiss was exactly what he said he was, the greatly
wronged victim of a brilliant psychopathic personality.

  2. That Chambers was exactly what he said he was, a disillusioned Communist so much in revulsion against his apprenticeship
in a conspiracy now turned into a threatening tyranny that he felt
it to be a patriotic duty, and a step towards his own salvation, to
expose the stuff that totalitarianism is made of. That Hiss had coolly
lied from the start and depended on his public reputation to discredit
the fantastic tale of an old friend and conspirator who was, in fact,
reluctantly telling nothing but the truth.

3. That Hiss was a dedicated underground Communist and still is and has gone down the line as a Communist martyr.

4. That in the 1930's Hiss was a Communist, or a fellow traveler, and is no more; that he has always done what he believed in; that in passing documents he, like Wadleigh, saw no conflict between his loyalty to the United States and his loyalty to an ideal; that he now sees no fundamental betrayal of himself or his ideals in denying an association and a deed that to admit to, in the political climate of our day, would have ruined the fine career he has made and the good work he is doing.

5. That in the 1930's Hiss was a fellow traveler or a Roosevelt liberal sympathetic to the Left, married to a wife who was either a more ardent fellow traveler or a Communist; that with or without his consent or knowledge she typed the documents and gave them, and the handwritten notes, to Chambers; that Hiss was obviously deeply devoted to her and had protected her by sacrificing himself.

6. That Chambers is still a Communist, an old and reliable campaigner detailed in 1948 to make a warning example of old party members or fellow travelers who now publicly renege on the Left and who are responsible in part for the present discomfort of the party.

7. That Hiss was a counter-spy: a theory that might account for his extraordinary composure through the Trials as the expression of a patriotic stoicism, but which also would make the Government's behavior through the whole affair odd, not to say sadistic, in the extreme.

8. That Chambers is still a Communist, under orders from the Kremlin or the American Communist Party to follow a shrewd propaganda line of softening up the American enemy: namely, to panic and confuse the United States by first making a public show of renouncing Communism, then to join some religious sect (preferably the Catholics or the Quakers) and from inside these sanctified forts to revile the Soviet Union and attribute infiltration and plots inside the Government; so as to provoke public anxiety and wasted statesmanship at home and wide distrust of the United States among her North Atlantic and Far Eastern allies. In this theory Hiss would be a rewarding victim, because he seemed to be the fine flower of the American tradition; by "exposing" him Americans would lose confidence in the best of America; and the embittered Common Man, believing his idols to be corrupt, would grow ripe for revolution.

9. That Hiss was a Leftist liberal or a mild fellow traveler
who got in with Chambers deeper than he meant to; that he passed no
papers; that he confidently lied about his association with Chambers
to the House Committee, and answered with legal precision, in the
certainty that he was fortifying a legal case and thereby making it
impossible ever to bring this charge into the courts; that he resolved
to do this when he saw what he thought was all Chambers had to
offer (that is, an accusation unsupported by documentary proof).

10. That Chambers met Hiss, under much the same circumstances Hiss testified to, and took a strong liking to him; that the
close friendship he sought from Hiss was at some point abruptly
rejected; that in later years this rebuff festered in Chambers, who
was neurotic enough to build on it a vendetta and take his revenge
out in a lovingly contrived plot.

To different people these speculations will seem varyingly fantastic or common-sensical. (It is worth reflecting, though, that once
the truth is known about any puzzling relationship, an earlier com-
mon-sense explanation often appears highly sophisticated.) There are
one or two other theories that went the rounds of Washington and
New York which, however, so mercilessly intrude into other people's
lives that the incompleteness of this report appears a small price to
pay for giving everybody so slandered the benefit of a large doubt.
The reader who is most prurient to know about such theories will
be the one most apt to hit on them.

HOW far the jury might be lost in such tortuous explorations we
shall happily never know. For the judge had warned them, as he
first warned the counsel, not to talk to the "very likeable and fair
newspaper representatives" present. Once their service was over, the
jury was to say no more to anybody and go home unsolicited and
unprobed. Which is what, in the end, they did.

But now, on the last afternoon, they were back from lunch. And
they had hardly gone into the juryroom before they sent out a note
to the judge, who thereupon asked the clerk to call the court to order.
We all went in again and took places anywhere, up against the anxious
faction of the Hiss friends, the glowing partisans of Mr. Murphy, the
dawdlers, the old patient ladies (one of them symbolically knitting),
and a smatter of genteel vultures ready for the kill. The doors closed,

the judge tugged at his gown, and a very different jury passed in. Alger Hiss again peered hungrily for a glance, a token of hope. It never came. Mrs. Hiss looked nowhere but ahead. And the clerk rose up. He read off the roll and the forewoman, a widow from the Bronx, came after several nervous false starts to her feet. The clerk turned towards her.

"Madam Foreman, have you and the members of the jury agreed on a verdict?"

The forewoman's little, rapid voice replied: "I have."

"And how say you—?" he had hardly started when the forewoman quickly said:

"Guilty on the first count and guilty on the second."

In the rustling silence the shortest gasp of surprise, a sort of whistling sigh, broke somewhere at the back of the courtroom.

"Guilty on both counts?"

"Yes."

"Madam Forewoman and members of the jury," said the clerk again, "kindly listen to your verdict as it now stands recorded. You find a verdict of guilty on Count one and guilty on Count two, is that your verdict?"

"I do," said the forewoman.

"And so say all of you?"

"We do," from the forewoman, as several of the jury nodded. They all looked straight ahead.

Hiss's head was high and immovable. He swallowed very slightly, flexing no muscles. He put one hand over the hands of his wife, a flushed and now ageless little gnome.

Mr. Cross tremulously asked if the jury might be polled. They were challenged in turn and either said "I do" or "It is." The judge thanked them for "making an earnest effort to render, and have rendered, a just verdict." They were discharged. When they had gone, Mr. Murphy rose and, looking hard at the table, moved in a blurred, heavy voice that Hiss be committed to jail, or at least have his bail increased "as all convicted defendants ought." Judge Goddard looked benevolently down at the prosecutor's black hair. "I think not, Mr. Murphy," he said.

THE END OF IT

❖

*Irony . . . as a generous scepticism, which can believe at once that
people are and are not guilty, is a very normal and essential method
. . . people, often, cannot have done both of two things, but they
must have been in some way prepared to have done either; whichever
they did, they will have still lingering in their minds the way they
would have preserved their self-respect if they had acted differently;
they are only to be understood by bearing both possibilities in mind.*

—WILLIAM EMPSON

ON the morning of the following Wednesday, the 25th of January,
Judge Goddard, the counsel, the defendant, and his wife came for a
last melancholy twenty minutes to a court filled to the last seat. The
newspapermen were crowded into the jury box.

The judge nodded towards the defense table, and Mr. Cross stood
and moved from one foot to the other and put his spectacles on and
off in a useless attempt to find a point of rest. He moved for a new
trial for eleven reasons and his motion was denied. But he had another
motion to arrest judgment. In this most important and unusual case,
he said, which had attracted more international attention than any
trial in decades, Alger Hiss had suffered "the worst punishment, that
of mind and heart, that he could undergo." He had suffered ever since
the August day that Chambers had accused him. As to what he had
done "since the Stalin-Hitler pact in 1939," his work for the United
States and international friendship, were matters beyond dispute.
"What little savings he has had were gone long before the conclusion
of the First Trial. He has borrowed heavily on notes still unpaid.

337

And the Second Trial has been financed by loyal friends and loyal Americans who believed and still believe in his innocence."

Against the wishes of his client, Mr. Cross said, with his head down and his hands trembling, he felt it was his duty to say he too still believed in the innocence of Alger Hiss. "There are only two or three people who know the real facts. The jury believed him guilty or they would not have returned a verdict. They don't know, I don't know, and until the true and complete facts come out there will always be the lingering doubt, which was manifested by a hung jury at the First Trial" and by the Second jury's request for a second reading of the judge's charge on reasonable doubt. "With this history, and with the uncertainty of circumstantial evidence, and with what the defendant has gone through already," Mr. Cross begged the Court to waive "any further punishment." He thought that "commitment to jail is not necessary and would not serve the best interests of society."

Judge Goddard sat imposingly through this plea and gently said that the jury's long deliberation had indicated to him "a very full consideration and conscientious effort to arrive at the right verdict" and that they had not reached it by "any snap judgment." Now, did Mr. Murphy wish to be heard?

Mr. Murphy took a very subdued stand. He just wanted to say that this was not a fitting time for "a prosecutor to be prolix." The defendant had had two opportunities to bring out all the facts and "to add now some air of mystery I think is not quite fair." The judge responded that this was not a case, he thought, where sentence should be suspended: "there should be a warning to all that a crime of this character may not be committed with impunity. The defendant will stand up."

Alger Hiss stood as Mr. Cross came up again with his hand in the air, asking if Hiss might say a word before he was sentenced. "Certainly," the judge allowed and like a great bird alertly watched Hiss as he came down the right side of the well. He was erect as always, but at a distance you could see how a strong emotion inside him could give an almost violent, jagged definition to his fine bone. He bowed to the judge and firmly said: "I would like to thank your Honor for the opportunity again to deny the charges that have been made against me. I want only to add that in the future the full facts of how Whittaker Chambers was able to carry out forgery by typewriter will be disclosed. Thank you, sir."

He stood still and the judge sentenced him to five years on the first count and five years on the second count. In accordance with the practice in perjury cases, the two terms would run concurrently. There was the merest token demand from Mr. Murphy for $25,000 bail, but the judge thought $10,000 would be as high as they should go. He imposed it and paroled Hiss in the custody of his counsel.

IN the moment of sentencing, it is impossible for the onlooker to say what he is feeling. But it is a moment when all the great swirling moral abstractions are blacked out in a crisis of the flesh. The principles we try to live by—honor, fidelity, tolerance, thrift, humility—considered not as maxims but as what most men have come to learn, dissolve into a formal ceremony in which none of the principals seems to be playing a known part. The defendant stands alone, the lawyers look through a glaze at their papers, the judge says: ". . . to run concurrently." And from this normal ritual there wells up a sense that compassion or hatred are not sharp single feelings at all but only the focal center at which monstrous opposites—of contempt and sympathy, pride and despair—are intensely reconciled. As we left the courtroom and Hiss swept a long, broken face through the rush of newspapermen, one middle-aged reporter who had waited for this moment, a man with a tic to his breathing, squared his shoulders and said: "Well, justice has been done." It would have sounded then, even if Crippen or Mr. Hyde had been the prisoners, an almost evil banality. For the man's eyes were a-gleam with triumph. He was the only such man I saw. People who had craved the confirmation of Hiss's guilt sighed and looked palely miserable. Mr. Murphy, rising after the verdict to ask for commitment, had been suddenly overcome with a rheumy blur of speech that could have come from the onset of a cold but most likely did not.

I had had this feeling before and, perhaps because of the association of Mr. Stryker in both cases, recalled the face of Jimmy Hines, although my only remembrance of his guilt had faded by now into the vaguest catalogue of graft. Mr. Stryker's view of Hines was tolerable to me only at the moment of sentencing. But in that moment neither the crime nor the personality condemned is clear. You do not respond as you might expect to the case resolved or the victim labeled, or the fox run to ground. The defendant becomes a symbol of the alternative fates possible to all our characters. Such a moment is close to the great occasions that strip men naked of their personality at the edge of the ocean of common experience: waiting for a child to be born, being in a fire, discovering infidelity, seeing a coffin lowered. No matter who the defendant, there is a yearning to see mercy and charity come in, like the sheriff, in the nick of time. The man about to be sentenced is suddenly at the center of the human situation; and because he is totally disarmed he takes on the helpless dignity of the lowest common demoninator.

Outside on the streets we were caught again in the political reverberations that lapped out like waves from this stony center of punishment. If he was indeed innocent, it might never be proved; he had ahead of him only the long trail to the Supreme Court, that grievous distance from the wound to the hospital which makes judicial review so cruel a kindness. If he was guilty, as twenty of the twenty-four "ordinary men looking on" had judged him, then what he owed to the United States and the people who had stood by him was a dreadful debt of honor. For his conviction clinched the popular fear that those who were contriving a "clear and present danger" to the United States were determined it should never be clear and were publicly devoted to showing it was always far from present. The verdict galvanized the country into a bitter realization of the native American types who might well be dedicated to betrayal from within. It gave to ambitious politicians a license to use vigilance as a political weapon merely. It brought back into favor the odious trade of the public informer. It gave the F.B.I. an unparalleled power of inquiry into private lives that in the hands of a less scrupulous man than its present chief could open up for generations of mischief-makers an official wholesale house of blackmail. It tended to make conformity sheepish and to limit by intimidation what no Western society worth the name can safely limit: the curiosity and idealism of its young. It helped therefore to usher in a period when a high premium would be put on the chameleon and the politically neutral slob.

All this and much more flowed from the verdict of the second jury. And its suspicions were shatteringly confirmed by the confession in England of a studious, gentle traitor, one Klaus Fuchs, a physicist working in the closed circle of Anglo-American atomic secrets, who admitted to passing on the best of his knowledge to the Soviet Union. After that, no sensible man could any longer maintain that there was no threat to his country. The problem now, for a nation built on a few ideas about liberty shared with triumphant innocence by one generation in the 1780's, was how to protect the innocent citizen from getting pinched between the reality of the threat and the epidemic fear of it. The knowledge rumbled like thunder through our senses that in other countries men might be being sentenced for *not* having stolen State papers when they had the chance. For the principals in this case were idealists at a time when idealism, and the nature of loyalty, were undergoing an historic test. If Hiss had said he had done all this, that he had passed papers proudly to confound the Nazis, to quicken the day of deliverance of enslaved populations, he could have been a greater Wadleigh. But because he had not stolen them, or could not or would not say he had, the defense had to argue from the impossible position that such gentle, trusted types are incapable of disloyalty. After Fuchs, we knew better. And what we were left with was not the tragic hero of a whole generation that had misjudged the endurance of national pride or the resilience of the Western tradition. What we were left with was a tragedy *manqué*.

Yet below the satisfaction of popular fears and desires, and the usefulness of arguments we happen to have at hand, lies a deeper region of the mind which holds in uncertain equilibrium the springs of self-love and self-hate; where seas of spite are able to rise and flood the low gauge of self-respect and the surrounding plains of neighborliness and patriotism. Here the real wound would fester: whether it was the false accusation, or the social betrayal of which this unhappy man had now become the public image; and somewhere in this dark region was tragedy enough, for all those who have had ideals and desires beyond, they dare to think, the understanding of their neighbors.

CHRONOLOGY

August 3, 1948	Whittaker Chambers accused Alger Hiss before House Committee on Un-American Activities in public session.
August 5	Alger Hiss denied the accusation before House Committee in public session.
August 7	Chambers before House Committee in private session.
August 16	Hiss before House Committee in private session.
August 17	Hiss and Chambers confronted before special subcommittee of House Committee in private session, in room 1400, Hotel Commodore, New York City. Hiss dared Chambers to accuse him in public, outside Congressional immunity.
August 25	Hiss and Chambers before House Committee in public session.
August 27	Chambers repeated his accusation on national radio program, *Meet the Press*.
September 27	Hiss sued Chambers for defamation in federal court at Baltimore.
November 17	Chambers produced copies of State Department documents before Hiss's lawyers during pre-trial examination in Baltimore suit.
December 2	Chambers surrendered under subpoena five rolls of microfilm, hidden on his Maryland farm, to House Committee investigators.
December 6	Department of Justice reconvened federal grand jury investigating espionage.
December 6–15	Hiss, Chambers, Donald Hiss, Mrs. Hiss, and Julian Wadleigh before grand jury.
December 7–10	Sumner Welles, Julian Wadleigh, and Nathan Levine before House Committee in public sessions.
December 10	Chambers resigned as senior editor of *Time*.
December 13	Hiss resigned as president of Carnegie Endowment for International Peace.
December 15	Hiss indicted for perjury by federal grand jury in New York City.
May 31, 1949– July 8	The First Trial of Alger Hiss: jury hung and discharged.
November 17, 1949– January 21, 1950	The Second Trial of Alger Hiss: verdict guilty.
January 25, 1950	Hiss sentenced to five years in prison and released on $10,000 bail pending appeal.

INDEX

i

A NOTE ON THE TYPE

This book is set on the Monotype in GRANJON, a type named in compliment to ROBERT GRANJON, but neither a copy of a classic face nor an entirely original creation. The design is based upon the type used by CLAUDE GARAMOND (1510–61) in his beautiful French books, and more closely resembles Garamond's own than do any of the various types that bear his name.

Robert Granjon began his career as type-cutter in 1523. The boldest and most original designer of his time, he was one of the first to practise the trade of type-founder apart from that of printer. Between 1557 and 1562 Granjon printed about twenty books in types designed by himself, following, after the fashion of the day, the cursive handwriting of the time. These types, usually known as "caractères de civilité," he himself called "lettres françaises," as especially appropriate to his own country.

This book was composed, printed, and bound by KINGSPORT PRESS, INC., Kingsport, Tenn.